VOLUME FIVE

SACRED PLACES

IOWA AND NEBRASKA

A Comprehensive Guide to Early LDS Historical Sites

Series Titles

New England and Eastern Canada

New York and Pennsylvania

Ohio and Illinois

Missouri

Iowa and Nebraska

Other Titles Planned for the Series

Wyoming and Utah

VOLUME FIVE

SACRED PLACES

IOWA AND NEBRASKA

A Comprehensive Guide to Early LDS Historical Sites

LaMar C. Berrett

General Editor

William G. Hartley

A. Gary Anderson

DESERET BOOK

SALT LAKE CITY, UTAH

All photographs, unless otherwise indicated, by LaMar C. Berrett.

Library of Congress Catalog Card Number 99-72525

ISBN-10 1-59038-197-1
ISBN-13 978-1-59038-197-7

Printed in the United States of America
Worzalla Publishing Co., Stevens Point, WI

10 9 8 7 6 5 4 3 2 1

Contents

List of Maps ix
Preface xi
Acknowledgments xiii
Information Contained in *Sacred Places* xv
IOWA 1
MORMON TRAIL AUTO ROUTE 5
MAIN SITES ALONG THE MORMON TRAIL 6
INTRODUCTION TO IOWA 9
Latter-day Saints in Iowa 10
Following the Trails 12
Southeastern Iowa 12
Mormon Emigration Routes in 1853 from Keokuk to Council Bluffs 18
Three 1846 Exoduses from Nauvoo: Winter, Spring, and Fall 23
IOWA HISTORIC ROUTE 1 27
Mormon Pioneer National Historic Trail and Variant Routes across Southern Iowa 27
Crossing the River on the Ice 29
Spring Exodus from Nauvoo—Ferry Crossings 30
The Miracle of the Quail 32
Nine Births in One Night? 37
Disputed Territory 58
Writing of "Come, Come, Ye Saints" 64
Official Mormon Trail Highways 82
Mt. Pisgah Encampment 86
Mormon Battalion Recruitment 86
Mormon Trail Variant Routes and Sites to Garden Grove and Mt. Pisgah 91
Mormon Trail Variant A: Drakesville to Garden Grove 92
Mormon Trail Variant B: Drakesville to Mt. Pisgah 93
Mormon Trail Variant in Monroe County 95
Resuming the Trail of Brigham Young's Camp of Israel 96
New Macedonia 112

The Mormon Battalion Enlistments 119
Miller's Hollow and Kanesville (Early Council Bluffs) 121
Downtown Council Bluffs 131
Southern Council Bluffs Area 134
Northern Council Bluffs Area 149
Southwest Iowa 151
North of Council Bluffs 155
Emmett Company's Return 161
Iowa Historic Route 2 163
Across Central Iowa along I-80 163
Eastern Edge: Davenport to Iowa City 163
The 1856 and 1857 Handcart Companies 168
The 1856–57 Handcart Route, Iowa City to Des Moines 172
The 1856–57 Handcart Route, Des Moines to Council Bluffs 179
Nebraska 183
Mormon Trail Auto Route 189
Main Sites along the Mormon Trail 191
Introduction to Nebraska 195
Latter-day Saints in Nebraska 197
The Missouri River and Mormon Emigration 198
The Platte River and the "Great Platte River Road" 199
The Historic Nebraska Mormon Trail 201
LDS Handcart Companies in Nebraska 202
From Prairie to Great Plains 203
Winter Quarters Area 207
Sites in Winter Quarters 208
Sites near Winter Quarters 216
Historic and Other Sites North of Winter Quarters 221
Historic and Other Sites in and around Omaha 224
Historic and Other Sites South of Omaha 231
The Ox-Bow Trail/Old Ft. Kearny Road/Nebraska City Road 239
The 1846 Ponca Encampment 245
The Trek of the 1847 Mormon Pioneers 250
Assembly Grounds at the Elkhorn River 250
Route, Landmarks, and Campsites 251
LDS Handcart Companies in Nebraska 336
The 1856 Handcart Companies 337

The James G. Willie Handcart Company, Aug. 16–Sept. 28, 1856 339
The Edward Martin Handcart Company Aug. 25–Oct. 6/7, 1856 343
THE TRANSCONTINENTAL RAILROAD 347
Construction of the Railroad 347
Mormon Railroad Travel across Nebraska 349
About the General Editor 351
About the Authors 353
Abbreviations Used in Photo Captions 355
Bibliography 355
Index 371

Maps

Iowa

Nauvoo to Centerville	2
Centerville to Creston	3
Creston to Council Bluffs	4
Locust Creek	60
Garden Grove, 1846–1851	73
Mt. Pisgah	84
Miller's Hollow, Kanesville, Council Bluffs, 1846–1852	125
Council Bluffs	133

Nebraska

Omaha to Grand Island	184
Grand Island to North Platte	185
North Platte to Bridgeport	186
Bridgeport to Henry	187
Winter Quarters	207
Old Wyoming	233
Liberty Pole Camp	254
Grand Island Camp	274
Ft. Kearny Camp	283
Junction-Odometer Camp	300
Courthouse Rock	318
Chimney Rock	321
Scottsbluff	324

Preface

When Moses came to the mountain of God and the burning bush, the Lord said to him, "Put off thy shoes from off thy feet, for the place whereon thou standest is holy ground" (Exodus 3:5).

Through the ages, the locations at which sacred historical events occurred have traditionally become holy. How holy or sacred a site is depends on the understanding of those beholding it. Elizabeth Barrett Browning wrote:

> Earth's crammed with heaven,
> And every common bush afire with God;
> But only he who sees, takes off his shoes—
> The rest sit round it and pluck blackberries.
> (*Aurora Leigh,* Book 7, 820–23)

The Church of Jesus Christ of Latter-day Saints has a long tradition of recognizing and recording sacred places and events. In 1838 the Lord said to Joseph Smith, "Let the city, Far West, be a holy and consecrated land unto me; and it shall be called most holy, for the ground upon which thou standest is holy" (D&C 115:7). Even earlier, when the Church was organized on Apr. 6, 1830, the Prophet was told that "there shall be a record kept among you" (D&C 21:1). Since those early times, places and events central to the Church's struggles and successes have been sanctified and recorded. *Sacred Places* was written to bring the history and geography of the early period of the Church to life.

Following the history and movement of the Saints from their early days in New York to their settlement in the valley of the Great Salt Lake, this series will function as a valuable resource for academic historians and amateur Church history enthusiasts alike. *Sacred Places* provides detailed maps, interesting narratives, and numerous photographs in its effort to document the many places made sacred by the faith and testimonies of past generations of Saints or are otherwise linked to Church history. The comprehensive nature of this series encourages readers to follow in the footsteps of Joseph Smith, Brigham Young, and other Church leaders, or to seek out the paths of their own ancestors. The series also enables armchair tourists to vicariously visit the many magnificent places relevant to Church history.

Sacred Places is the culmination of more than 25 years of research and study. Its authors, all university professors, have devoted much of their lives to this work of preserving and documenting the legacy of our literal and spiritual ancestors. By purchasing and preserving many of these sacred sites, the Church has encouraged member and nonmember alike to visit locations important to our history. Visiting sites such as the Sacred Grove, the Hill Cumorah, Adam-ondi-Ahman, or Carthage Jail enables us to understand the history of the Church in terms of the real places and real people who witnessed the very real and sacred events of the Restoration.

ACKNOWLEDGMENTS

Brigham Young University's College of Religious Education, Department of Church History and Doctrine, and Religious Studies Center have been instrumental in the realization of *Sacred Places.* Through various means—time, student assistants, secretarial help, research grants, and various other forms of financial aid—these organizations and the people associated with them have been indispensable.

Gratitude is expressed to past and present General Authorities of The Church of Jesus Christ of Latter-day Saints who have ensured that significant Church history sites have been purchased and preserved for the edification and enjoyment of future generations. LaMar C. Berrett, general editor, is particularly grateful to President Spencer W. Kimball, who told him that "we need to know and tell the truth about our Church history sites." President Kimball also related a fable concerning the Joseph Smith home in Palmyra, N.Y. "Some used to say that when the angel Moroni appeared to Joseph Smith the first time, it occurred in the Joseph Smith frame home, but we know that this is not true." This statement has impressed upon the editor the great responsibility he has in providing correct information regarding our tremendous heritage and its relation to these sacred sites. *Sacred Places* has been significantly affected by President Kimball's interest and encouragement. Special thanks are also given to those writers, researchers, journal keepers, Church historians, and others who laid the groundwork upon which *Sacred Places* has been constructed.

We are grateful to the staffs and administrators of the many repositories who have been so helpful in our research. The staffs of the Brigham Young University Harold B. Lee Library and the LDS Church Archives were especially gracious. We are also grateful for the efforts of archaeologists Dale Berge, Ray T. Matheny, and Virginia Harrington in conducting archaeological digs at various Church history sites.

We are grateful for authors of journals, especially Stanley B. Kimball, who edited and published *The Latter-Day Saints' Emigrants' Guide,* by William Clayton (EmG).

No one can study Mormon Trail matters without relying on many studies and maps generated by the late Dr. Stanley B. Kimball. Likewise, local site experts and historians have been invaluable, particularly Paul and Karla Gunzenhauser, Elbert Pidcock, and Floyd Pearce in Iowa, Gail Holmes in the Omaha–Council Bluffs region, and Carl Jones, Val Rasmussen, and Ronnie O'Brien in Nebraska. Don Smith of Pullman, Washington, provided vital expertise regarding handcart history and routes. The Iowa State Historial Society in Des Moines and Iowa City and the Nebraska State Historical Society in Lincoln have been gold mines of source material. We have drawn much information from the National Park Service's National History Trails System Inter-mountain Region Office in Salt Lake City relating to maps and interpretive panels—Jere Krakow and Kay Threlkeld have been particularly helpful. And what an asset the Internet has proved to be, particularly in providing up-to-date maps and street names, state and local facts and explanations, and promotional literature for many sites mentioned herein.

The authors also acknowledge and thank Thomas S. Child for illustrating the maps.

We are grateful to the personnel at Deseret Book Company who have helped bring this series to publication. We especially acknowledge Cory H. Maxwell, Richard Erickson, Laurie Cook, Suzanne Brady, and Patricia Stokes for their efforts in editing, designing, typesetting, and publishing this important information.

Finally, we thank our wives and children for their patience and support over the past 25 years as we have labored to bring about this monumental work.

So many other individuals have contributed to the completion of *Sacred Places* that it is impractical, even impossible, to give personal credit to all those who deserve it. A blanket "thank you" is given to all who have helped in any way.

INFORMATION CONTAINED IN *SACRED PLACES*

Several symbols have been employed in *Sacred Places.* Small black squares (■), both in text and on maps, indicate sites with direct ties to LDS Church history. Small black circles (●) indicate important sites not directly related to LDS Church history. Dollar signs ($) indicate sites that cost money to see.

Because of the voluminous nature of the bibliographical sources used by the authors, abbreviations were used in the text to identify those sources. Along with noting the sources used in preparing the book, the authors have also included many references for the reader who is interested in learning more about a particular event or Church history site. A complete bibliography with an alphabetical listing of abbreviations is included in the back of the volume. A list of abbreviations identifies sources of photographs and other illustrations. Names of persons and places in **bold** may be mentioned briefly in one place and more fully in another; a thorough index has been provided to help readers locate such material.

Many maps and illustrations, including photographs, have been included in an effort to help the reader to locate, visualize, and more fully appreciate the numerous sites identified in *Sacred Places.*

This volume is a joint effort of William G. Hartley, A. Gary Anderson, and LaMar C. Berrett. William G. Hartley did the lion's share of the writing of both the Iowa and Nebraska sections. Unfortunately, Dr. Anderson died before the Nebraska text was finished. LaMar C. Berrett and William G. Hartley worked together to produce the maps.

Iowa

William G. Hartley

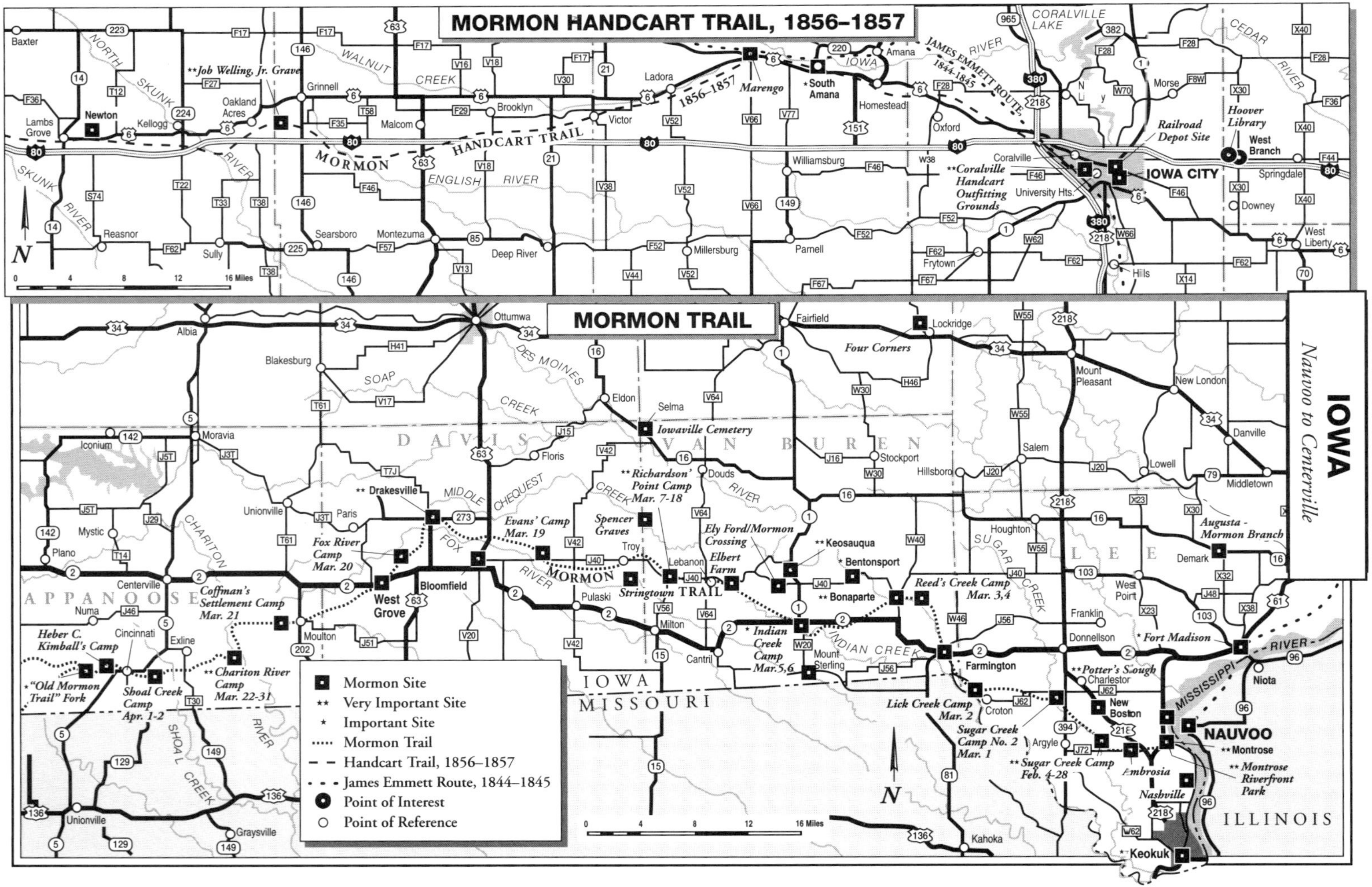

MORMON HANDCART TRAIL, 1856–1857
MORMON TRAIL
IOWA
Nauvoo to Centerville
Newton
Job Welling, Jr. Grave
Marengo
South Amana
Iowa City
Coralville Handcart Outfitting Grounds
Railroad Depot Site
Hoover Library
West Branch
JAMES EMMETT ROUTE, 1844-1845
MORMON HANDCART TRAIL 1856–1857
Nauvoo
Montrose
Montrose Riverfront Park
Nashville
Ambrosia
Keokuk
Sugar Creek Camp Feb. 4-28
Sugar Creek Camp No. 2 Mar. 1
Lick Creek Camp Mar. 2
Potter's Slough
Fort Madison
Augusta - Mormon Branch
Reed's Creek Camp Mar. 3,4
Bentonsport
Bonaparte
Keosauqua
Indian Creek Camp Mar. 5,6
Ely Ford/Mormon Crossing
Elbert Farm
Stringtown
Richardson' Point Camp Mar. 7-18
Spencer Graves
Iowaville Cemetery
Four Corners
Evans' Camp Mar. 19
Drakesville
Fox River Camp Mar. 20
West Grove
Bloomfield
Coffman's Settlement Camp Mar. 21
Chariton River Camp Mar. 22-31
Shoal Creek Camp Apr. 1-2
Heber C. Kimball's Camp
"Old Mormon Trail" Fork
MORMON TRAIL
Mormon Site
Very Important Site
Important Site
Mormon Trail
Handcart Trail, 1856–1857
James Emmett Route, 1844–1845
Point of Interest
Point of Reference
0 4 8 12 16 Miles
N
ILLINOIS
MISSOURI
IOWA

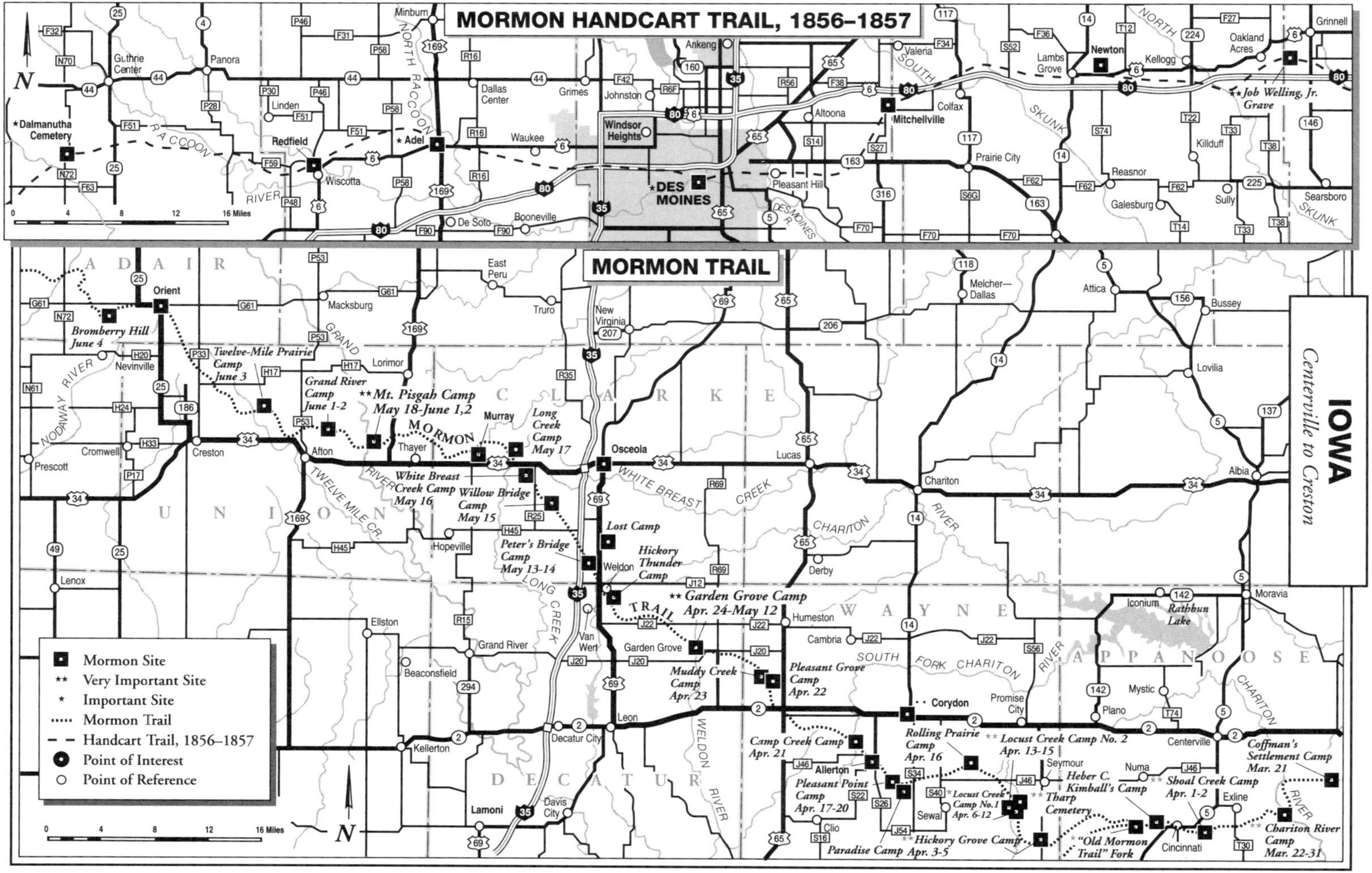
IOWA
Centerville to Creston
MORMON HANDCART TRAIL, 1856–1857
MORMON TRAIL
Mormon Site
Very Important Site
Important Site
Mormon Trail
Handcart Trail, 1856–1857
Point of Interest
Point of Reference
0 4 8 12 16 Miles
N
Dalmanutha Cemetery
Guthrie Center
Panora
Linden
Redfield
Wiscotta
Adel
Minburn
Dallas Center
Waukee
Grimes
Johnston
Windsor Heights
Ankeng
DES MOINES
De Soto
Booneville
Pleasant Hill
Altoona
Mitchellville
Valeria
Colfax
Prairie City
Lambs Grove
Newton
Kellogg
Reasnor
Galesburg
Killduff
Sully
Oakland Acres
Grinnell
Searsboro
Job Welling, Jr. Grave
Orient
Bromberry Hill June 4
Nevinville
Cromwell
Prescott
Creston
Lenox
Twelve-Mile Prairie Camp June 3
Grand River Camp June 1-2
Mt. Pisgah Camp May 18-June 1,2
Macksburg
Lorimor
Afton
Thayer
Murray
Long Creek Camp May 17
White Breast Creek Camp May 16
Willow Bridge Camp May 15
Peter's Bridge Camp May 13-14
Hopeville
East Peru
Truro
New Virginia
Osceola
Lost Camp
Hickory Thunder Camp
Weldon
Van Wert
Garden Grove Camp Apr. 24-May 12
Garden Grove
Muddy Creek Camp Apr. 23
Pleasant Grove Camp Apr. 22
Humeston
Cambria
Ellston
Grand River
Beaconsfield
Kellerton
Decatur City
Leon
Lamoni
Davis City
Camp Creek Camp Apr. 21
Allerton
Pleasant Point Camp Apr. 17-20
Paradise Camp Apr. 3-5
Clio
Rolling Prairie Camp Apr. 16
Corydon
Locust Creek Camp No. 2 Apr. 13-15
Locust Creek Camp No. 1 Apr. 6-12
Hickory Grove Camp
Sewal
Seymour
Heber C. Kimball's Camp
Tharp Cemetery
"Old Mormon Trail" Fork
Numa
Shoal Creek Camp Apr. 1-2
Cincinnati
Exline
Centerville
Coffman's Settlement Camp Mar. 21
Chariton River Camp Mar. 22-31
Promise City
Plano
Mystic
Iconium
Rathbun Lake
Moravia
Derby
Lucas
Chariton
Melcher–Dallas
Attica
Bussey
Lovilia
Albia
ADAIR
UNION
CLARKE
DECATUR
WAYNE
APPANOOSE

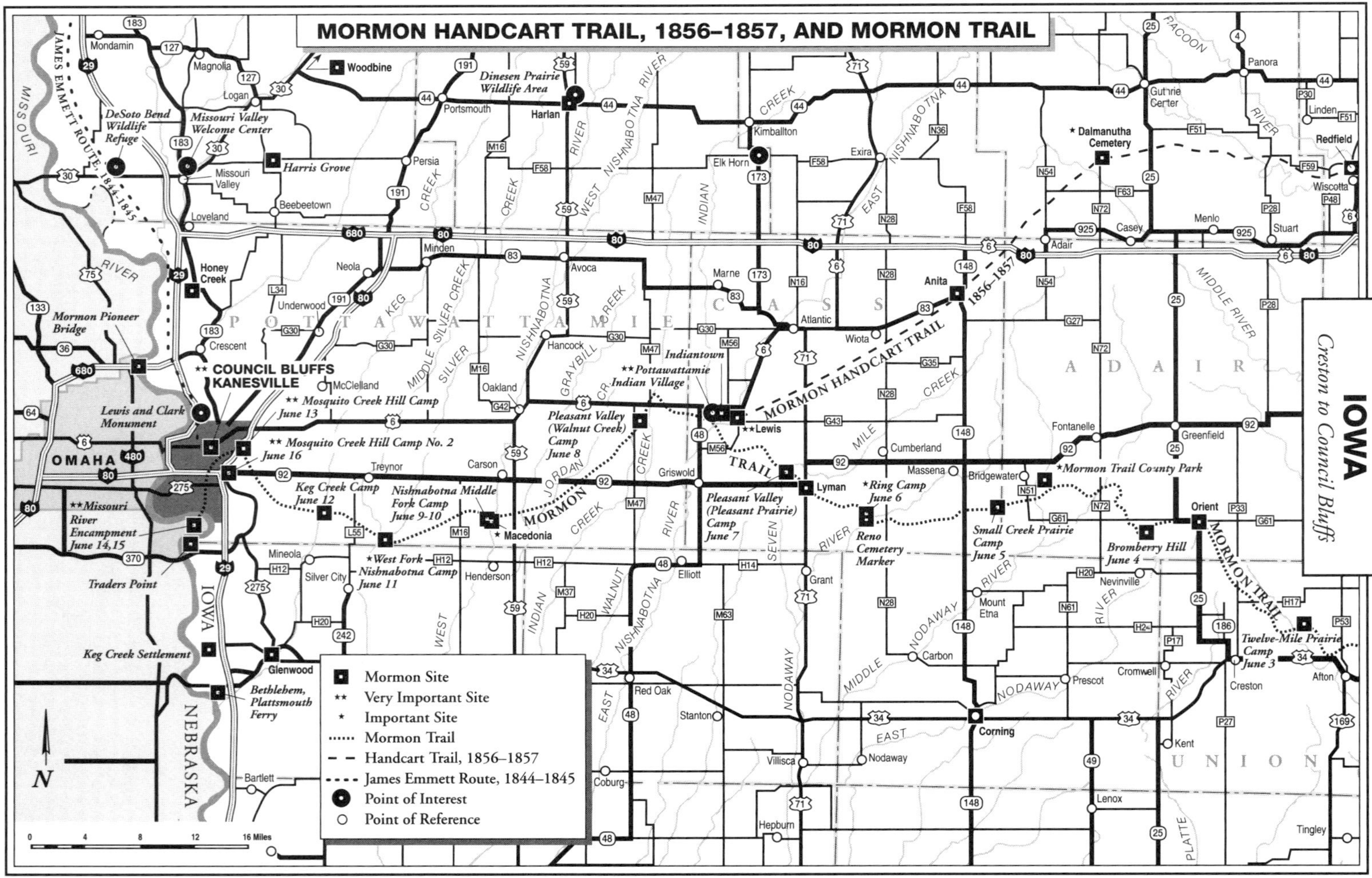
MORMON HANDCART TRAIL, 1856–1857, AND MORMON TRAIL
IOWA
Creston to Council Bluffs
Mormon Site
Very Important Site
Important Site
Mormon Trail
Handcart Trail, 1856–1857
James Emmett Route, 1844–1845
Point of Interest
Point of Reference
** COUNCIL BLUFFS
KANESVILLE
** Mosquito Creek Hill Camp
June 13
** Mosquito Creek Hill Camp No. 2
June 16
** Missouri River Encampment
June 14,15
Keg Creek Camp
June 12
Nishnabotna Middle Fork Camp
June 9-10
* West Fork Nishnabotna Camp
June 11
* Macedonia
Pleasant Valley (Walnut Creek) Camp
June 8
** Pottawattamie Indian Village
Indiantown
** Lewis
Pleasant Valley (Pleasant Prairie) Camp
June 7
* Ring Camp
June 6
Reno Cemetery Marker
Small Creek Prairie Camp
June 5
* Mormon Trail County Park
Bromberry Hill
June 4
Twelve-Mile Prairie Camp
June 3
* Dalmanutha Cemetery
MORMON HANDCART TRAIL
1856–1857
MORMON TRAIL
JAMES EMMETT ROUTE, 1844–1845
DeSoto Bend Wildlife Refuge
Missouri Valley Welcome Center
Harris Grove
Dinesen Prairie Wildlife Area
Woodbine
Mormon Pioneer Bridge
Lewis and Clark Monument
Traders Point
Keg Creek Settlement
Bethlehem, Plattsmouth Ferry
OMAHA
IOWA
NEBRASKA
POTTAWATTAMIE
CASS
ADAIR
UNION
N
0 4 8 12 16 Miles

Mormon Trail Auto Route

In 1978 President Jimmy Carter signed into law a bill designating the **Mormon Trail** as the United States' first National Historic Trail. The **Mormon Pioneer National Historic Trail** extends more than 1,300 miles from Nauvoo, Illinois, to Salt Lake City, Utah. Much of the 300 miles of the trail in Iowa, taken by Brigham Young's Camp of Israel companies during the **Winter Exodus** of 1846, is paralleled, followed, or intersected by federal, state, and county roads, many of which are well-marked with official brown and white Mormon Trail signs. President Young's company took 131 days to cross Iowa (HSM 21–38; maps of Iowa: Nauvoo to Centerville, Centerville to Creston, and Creston to Council Bluffs, pages 2–4). All mileages are approximate.

Montrose to Decatur City (143 miles)

Beginning at Montrose, take County Road J-22 west to U.S. 61 (1)

U.S. 61 south to U.S. 218 (1)

U.S. 218 northwest to State 2 at Donnellson (21)

State 2 west to I-35 at Decatur City (120)

Decatur to Creston (51 miles)

I-35 north to U.S. 34 at Osceola (20)

U.S. 34 west to State 25 at Creston (31)

Creston to Council Bluffs (105 miles)

State 25 north to State 92 at Greenfield (21)

State 92 west to state line at Council Bluffs (84)

Total miles: 299

Main Sites along the Mormon Trail

The main sites along the Mormon Trail are listed from east to west, in the order in which the Saints encountered or established them. In the site identifications and narratives that follow, LDS sites of particular importance historically are marked * and those considered very important are marked **. Be certain to obtain permission from the landowner before visiting any sites that are privately owned.

**Montrose Riverview Park
**Potter's Slough—Poor Saints Camp
**Sugar Creek Camp, Brigham Young, Feb. 4–28, 1846
Sugar Creek Camp No. 2, Brigham Young, Mar. 1
Charleston, Spring Exodus
Lick Creek Camp, Brigham Young, Mar. 2
*Farmington
Reed's Creek Camp, Brigham Young, Mar. 3–4
**Bonaparte
*Bentonsport
**Keosauqua
Iowaville Cemetery, Fall Exodus
Eldon
Ely Ford/Mormon Crossing, Spring Exodus
*Indian Creek Camp, Brigham Young, Mar. 5–6
Dr. John D. Elbert Farm, Mar. 6
**Richardson's Pt. Camp, Brigham Young, Mar. 7–18
Spencer Graves
Stringtown
Evans' Camp, Brigham Young, Mar. 19
Bloomfield
**Drakesville
Fox River Camp, Brigham Young, Mar. 20

*The "Old Mormon Trail"
West Grove
Coffman's Settlement Camp, Brigham Young, Mar. 21
**Chariton River Camp and Ford, Brigham Young, Mar. 22–31
**Shoal Creek Camp, Brigham Young, Apr. 1–2
Heber C. Kimball's Camp, Apr. 2
* "Old Mormon Trail" Fork
**Hickory Grove Camp, Brigham Young, Apr. 3–5
*Locust Creek Camp No. 1, Brigham Young, Apr. 6–12
**Locust Creek Camp No. 2, Brigham Young, Apr. 13–15
**Tharp Cemetery
Rolling Prairie Camp, Brigham Young, Apr. 16
**Corydon
Orson Pratt's Paradise Camp, Apr. 16
Pleasant Pt. Camp, Brigham Young, Apr. 17–20
Allerton
Camp Creek Camp, Brigham Young, Apr. 21
Pleasant Grove Camp, Brigham Young, Apr. 22
Muddy Creek Camp, Brigham Young, Apr. 23
**Garden Grove Camp, Brigham Young, Apr. 24–May 12
**Garden Grove Settlement, 1846–52
Lamoni
Hickory Thunder Camp, Brigham Young, May 13
Peter's Bridge Camp, Brigham Young, May 14
Lost Camp
Willow Bridge Camp, Brigham Young, May 15
Osceola
White Breast Creek Camp, Brigham Young, May 16
Long Creek Camp, Brigham Young, May 17
Murray and SevenMile Creek Camp, Ruts
**Mt. Pisgah Camp, Brigham Young, May 18–June 1
**Mt. Pisgah Settlement, 1846–52
Mt. Moriah Settlement
Winterset
Grand River Camp, Brigham Young, June 1–2
Twelve-Mile Prairie Camp, Brigham Young, June 3
Orient
Bromberry Hill Camp, Brigham Young, June 4
Greenfield
Mormon Trail County Park and Lake

Small Creek Prairie Camp, Brigham Young, June 5
*Ring (Circled Wagons) Camp, Brigham Young, June 6
Nodaway River—Hosea Stout Encampment, June 23–29
Burial site of Stout and Smith children
Lyman
Pleasant Valley (Pleasant Prairie) Camp, Brigham Young, June 7
**Lewis/Mormon Trail and Handcart Route
**Pottawattamie Indian Village
Indiantown
Pleasant Valley (Walnut Creek) Camp, Brigham Young, June 8
Nishnabotna Middle Fork Camp, Brigham Young, June 9–10
*Macedonia
*West Fork Nishnabotna (Silver Creek) Camp, Brigham Young, June 11
Keg Creek Camp, Brigham Young, June 12
**Mosquito Creek Hill Camp, Brigham Young, June 13
**Missouri River Camp, Brigham Young, June 14–15
**Mosquito Creek Hill Camp No. 2, Brigham Young, June 16
**Miller's Hollow/Kanesville/Council Bluffs, 1846–1852

Introduction to Iowa

French-Canadian fur trader Louis Joliet and Jesuit missionary Jacques Marquette provided the first descriptions of Iowa by Europeans in 1673. Iowa's first settlement by whites was by French-Canadian Julien Dubuque in 1788. In 1803 explorers Lewis and Clark passed along the western edges of Iowa, which was part of the Louisiana Purchase, as they journeyed up the Missouri River. In 1820 Iowa became a free territory under the Missouri Compromise Act but did not function formally as a territory until 1838. Settlement by whites started in 1833, with **Dubuque, Davenport, Burlington,** and **Ft. Madison** being among the area's first villages. Between 1824 and 1842 the Sac and Fox, Pottawattamie, Winnebago, and Sioux Indians were forced to give up their holdings, and whites quickly settled the vacated areas.

Iowa became the 29th state on Dec. 28, 1846. **Burlington** was the territory's first capital, followed by **Iowa City,** from 1841 until statehood in 1846. **Des Moines** replaced **Iowa City** as the state capital in 1857.

During the first decade of Mormon contact with Iowa, 1838–48, the eastern half of the state was just beginning to be settled by whites. In 1846 westbound Mormon refugees from Nauvoo first passed through several small counties but then faced unorganized territory across the rest of present-day Iowa.

Iowa has two great "coastlines," being bordered by the Mississippi River on the east and the Missouri and Big Sioux Rivers on the west. It is a prairie state, more hilly than flat. Iowa spans roughly 300 miles from east to west and 200 miles north to south. It is bisected from east to west by Interstate 80, which connects **Davenport** on the east with **Council Bluffs** on the west. A grid of county roads crisscrosses much of the land, outlining square-mile sections. Because more than 90 percent of the state is cultivated, the state has but few preserves of native prairie grasses. Iowa is America's top producer of soybeans, corn, eggs, and hogs, and a leading producer of livestock, manufacturer of farm equipment, and center for insurance companies. Northwestern Iowa is a lake region.

Iowa's population in 2000 was 2,926,324, spread through 99 counties, half a dozen large cities, and more than 900 small towns. Although Iowa is a premier agricultural state, six of seven Iowans live in urban areas. Ethnic communities are numerous: Dutch, Danish, Swedish, Norwegian, Czech, Mesquakie Indians, the Amana Colonies, and Amish groups. Famous Iowa natives include frontiersman **Buffalo Bill Cody,** actor-singer **Lillian Russell,** actor **John Wayne,** orchestra leader **Glenn Miller,** baseball pitcher **Bob Feller,** painter **Grant Wood, President Herbert Hoover,** President Dwight Eisenhower's wife, **Mamie Doud Eisenhower,** author **Wallace Stegner,** labor leader **John L. Lewis,** singer **Andy Williams,** actress **Donna Reed,** composer **Meredith Wilson,** columnists **Ann Landers** and **Abigail Van Buren,** pollster **George H. Gallup,** and TV commentator **Harry Reasoner.**

Iowa, with much for tourists to see and enjoy, effectively promotes tourism. Its **welcome centers** near Interstate entry points are attractive and well stocked with quality maps, brochures, and guides. The state's calendar year is packed with annual events and festivals, such as Tulip Days, Steamboat Days, the National Hobo Convention, Czech festivals, covered bridge festivals, and a frontier rendezvous.

Latter-day Saints in Iowa

Iowa is important to Latter-day history because of 13 major developments, all but two of them occurring before 1860:

1. After the "Mormon War" in Missouri, some Mormon militiamen fled north into the Iowa Territory in late 1838 and early 1839.

2. Early in 1839 LDS exiles from Missouri settled across from Nauvoo in and around Montrose in what became known as the Zarahemla Stake.

3. In 1844–45 the **James Emmett Expedition** of more than 150 Saints moved up the west shore of the Mississippi and then followed the Iowa River into central Iowa and, after some disaffections, on to present-day South Dakota.

4. Saints involved in the 1846 mass exodus from Illinois crossed Iowa, heading west. This included the initial vanguard of about 2,500 pioneers led by Brigham Young, who left Nauvoo in February (**Winter Exodus**), the larger wave of departures of about 12,000 from April to June (**Spring Exodus**), and the final group of about 700 "Poor Saints," whom mobs drove from Nauvoo in September (**Fall Exodus**).

5. The enlistment and departure of the Mormon Battalion from the Council Bluffs area.

6. The Mormon temporary settlements of Garden Grove and Mt. Pisgah.

7. Mormons in the Illinois exodus worked temporarily in southeastern Iowa.

8. The development of Kanesville (Council Bluffs) as a Mormon city between 1848 and 1852, having an estimated 90 LDS satellite settlements and clusters within 40 miles of its center.

9. Keokuk was the 1853 LDS outfitting camp for 2,500 Saints in 10 wagon trains.

10. Seven handcart and nine wagon companies trekked from Iowa City to Council Bluffs, 1856–58.

11. Mormons who didn't go west became early Iowa settlers.

12. Branches of The Church of Jesus Christ of Latter-day Saints were established in the later nineteenth century and wards and stakes in the twentieth century. A branch at Keokuk was in existence in 1875, and one in Council Bluffs by 1878. By 1878 Iowa was a missionary conference in the Northern States Mission (EnH 366–67). The Cedar Rapids Stake (1974) was the first stake organized in Iowa since the 1840s, and five more have been formed since then—Des Moines (1970), Davenport (1978), Ames (1995), Sioux City (1996), and Council Bluffs (1999). A separate mission for Iowa was created in 1976, the Iowa Des Moines Mission.

13. The Reorganized Church of Jesus Christ of Latter Day Saints (now known as the Community of Christ) in the 1880s made its headquarters in Lamoni, Iowa, where its prophet, Joseph Smith III, lived and where the church established Graceland College in 1895.

Following the Trails

To cross Iowa and follow both of the two important LDS routes across Iowa—the 1846 pioneers' route and the 1856–57 handcart route—during the same drive is not possible, as both routes cross Iowa east to west and arc essentially parallel and some distance apart. It is recommended that visitors follow one route crossing Iowa in one direction and then trace the other route during a return crossing—thereby seeing one route in reverse.

We present here the two Iowa routes separately. We start with the historical sites along the southern route, or **Iowa Historic Route 1**—the Iowa Mormon Trail route of the 1846 pioneers and its variants, accessed mainly by Iowa highways (going from east to west) State 2, U.S. 69, U.S. 34, and State 92. Then, we explain the other route, the central route or **Iowa Historic Route 2**—the historic sites relating to or reachable from the 1856–57 handcart and wagon companies—which is accessible most readily from I-80.[1]

Southeastern Iowa

■ **MONTROSE

Montrose (Lee County) is on the west bank of the Mississippi River, southwest across the river from Nauvoo. It is 10 miles south of **Ft. Madison** on U.S. 61 and then 1 mile east on State 404.

The Montrose town site was laid out in 1837 and named for wild roses on a bluff nearby. Early in 1839 the LDS Church bought land in Montrose, where leaders established a stake.

Riverview Park is at the northeast terminus of Main Street, near the river. Saints evacuating Nauvoo in February 1846 landed near here and then moved west 7 miles to organize for the trek west (see **Mormon Pioneer National Historic Trail**).

At the north end of Riverview Park, near Mormon Trail panels is a **history panel,** "Mormon Sojourn in Lee County, 1839– 1846." It provides a brief overview of the Mormon settlements in Lee County and the Latter-day Saint departure to the West in 1846.

---

1. Much of the discussion that follows owes great debt and much credit to the scholarship and meticulous map work of Mormon Trail expert Dr. Stanley B. Kimball, whose publications about Iowa historic routes and sites are voluminous, and to local site work by members of the Iowa Mormon Trails Association.

Crossing the Mississippi River on ferries, from Nauvoo, IL, to Montrose, IA. (Courtesy of Vernon Murdock, artist, 1973)

The Old Ft. Des Moines site, at the southwest end of Riverview Park, next to the railroad tracks, is identified by a **bronze plaque** (1923) at the old fort's well site. **A history panel,** "Fort Des Moines, 1834–1847," describes the early history of the Montrose area, the establishment of Ft. Des Moines by the U.S. Army, and the use of the fort by Mormons when they first arrived there in 1839. In early 1839 some 40 LDS families fleeing Missouri occupied the fort's deserted **army barracks,** including the families of **Brigham Young, John Taylor,** and **Wilford Woodruff.** That spring the Church bought land at **Montrose** for its settlers.

The **army barracks** are where a day of **miraculous healings** took place on July 22, 1839. **Joseph Smith** arose from his sickbed and administered to the sick in Nauvoo. He then crossed the Mississippi River with five of the apostles. He went to Brigham Young's quarters and commanded him to arise and be made whole. Elder Young was healed and then assisted the elders in blessing others. He visited Elijah Fordham, who was so close to death that burial clothes were being prepared for him. In a loud voice heard by neighbors, Joseph Smith called out: "Brother Fordham, in the name of Jesus Christ, arise and walk." Then, as witness Parley P. Pratt tells,

Mississippi River, looking west from Nauvoo, IL, to Riverview Park at Montrose, IA. (1985)

> Brother Fordham leaped from his dying bed in an instant, shook the poultices and bandages from his feet, put on his clothes so quick that none got a chance to assist him, and taking a cup of tea and a little refreshment, he walked with us from house to house visiting other sick beds. (APPP 254)

Joseph Bates Noble, who was also "nigh unto death," said that President Smith "commanded me, in the name of Jesus Christ, to arise and walk." He arose but passed out while dressing. Joseph asked him why he doubted and "again commanded me to arise," and "while he was speaking I felt the healing virtue flowing through every part of my system. I immediately arose and walked, rejoicing and praising the Lord. . . . I was made whole" (JI 15 [May 1880]: 112). Many were healed during that remarkable day (HC 4:4; WW 104–7; HCKM 252–54).

Brigham Young, with others, left Montrose for his mission to England in September 1839 (HC 4:9).

According to Anson Call, **Joseph Smith** pronounced a prophecy about the **Rocky Mountains** in Montrose Aug. 6, 1842:

> I prophesied that the Saints would continue to suffer much affliction and would be driven to the Rocky Mountains, many would apostatize, others would be put to death by our persecutors or lose their lives in consequence of exposure or disease, and some of you will live to go and assist in making settlements and build cities and see the Saints become a mighty people in the midst of the Rocky Mountains. (HC 5:85)

On June 23, 1844, **Joseph Smith** fled by boat to **Montrose,** hoping to **escape to the West.** But he returned, at the urging of his wife and others, and went to Carthage Jail, where he was martyred (HC 6:548–49).

■ ZARAHEMLA

The **Zarahemla townsite,** selected by LDS leaders in 1839, is 1 mile west of the Mississippi River, at Montrose's west side. Joseph Smith also chose a **temple site** on the bluffs—the precise location is unknown. At its peak, Zarahemla as a settlement had 30 houses (BYUS, Winter 1978, 139).

Late in 1839 the **Iowa Stake** was created at Zarahemla. In

March 1841 a revelation called on the Saints to build up **Zarahemla** as a gathering place opposite Nauvoo (D&C 125:3–4). When the name was changed to the **Zarahemla Stake** in 1841, it included eight branches and nearly 700 members. **John Smith,** uncle of Joseph Smith, was stake president; **Reynolds Cahoon** and **Lyman Wight** were counselors, and **Alanson Ripley** was bishop. For a brief time, the Zarahemla Stake was the second most important stake and community of Saints in the United States, Nauvoo being the first (HAM 58).

■ AMBROSIA

The **Ambrosia branch** spread from a point about 3 miles west of Montrose on present-day County Road J72 (known today as Ambrosia Lane) for another 4 miles west to Sugar Creek. Ambrosia was part of the Zarahemla Stake and at one time had 109 members (EnH 19, 139, 971; OPH 6:245–46; MHI).

Saints who settled there by the summer of 1839 first called it **Hawley's Settlement. Abraham O. Smoot** lived there by 1839—on Aug. 6 Wilford Woodruff "rode on horseback 4 miles [from Montrose] . . . to see our babe Sarah E at Brother Smoots" (Wilford Woodruff in AOS 106–7). Smoot entered title to 30 acres there in 1841 (10 acres in R6W T66N and 20 acres in R5W T66N).

When **Brigham Young** and the first wave of Saints evacuated from Nauvoo in February 1846, their massive **Sugar Creek encampment** was located in the Ambrosia settlement area within a mile of some of the Smoot property.

■ NASHVILLE

Nashville, an LDS town site, was located 3–4 miles south of Montrose. The site is reached by exiting Montrose's south side on 1st Street and following River Road along the Mississippi riverbank for 3.5 miles.

In 1839 the LDS Church bought some 20,000 acres south of present-day Montrose to establish Nashville (HC 3:378; T&S 1:174). Nashville became a branch, had a large stone building used for public worship, and provided a steamboat landing on the river. During the spring of 1846, many Saints evacuating from Nauvoo ferried across the river to Nashville.

At 3.5 miles south of Montrose on the east side of River Road is a replica of **Isaac Galland's 1830 log schoolhouse.** It stands in the area where Nashville once was.

**KEOKUK

Keokuk, a Mississippi River city first settled in 1828, is located at Iowa's southeastern tip. The county seat for Lee County, its population is about 11,500. U.S. 136 and State 61/218 intersect in Keokuk. The city is 10 miles south of Montrose and 15 miles south and west of Nauvoo, Illinois. In 1839 some Saints fleeing Missouri settled here and organized a branch. Bishop Vinson Knight bought land here for the Church (T&S 1:24).

Chief Keokuk's burial site is in **Rand Park,** north of the Mississippi River Bridge. From Main Street the site is northeast on 5th Street to Grand Avenue and then north up Grand Avenue 1 mile. Keokuk tourism literature labels Grand Avenue "the most beautiful residential street in Iowa." From Rand Park's commanding overlook, visitors can see almost 10 miles up the majestic Mississippi River. Near this overlook is a heroic-sized statue (1913) honoring **Chief Keokuk** and marking his burial site. At the base of the Chief Keokuk Statue in Rand Park is a **Mormon Trail plaque** placed there by the Daughters of the American Revolution (DAR).

Keokuk was a Sac Indian chief who visited Joseph Smith in 1841. About 100 chiefs and braves and their families were involved. Joseph Smith, with Nauvoo Legion members and band, met them at the river landing in Nauvoo and conducted them to **the Grove.**

Mormon pioneer emigrants' outfitting camp at Keokuk, IA. (Steel engraving by Frederick Piercy, 1853)

There he, through an interpreter, instructed them concerning their fathers and the promises made to them in the Book of Mormon. Keokuk replied that he had a Book of Mormon that had been given to him by Joseph Smith years before. The Prophet instructed them to keep peace with other tribes and the whites. Keokuk said he would "follow the good talk" Joseph had given them. The Saints provided the Indians with a feast of good food, dainties, and melons. In turn, the Indians gave a demonstration of their war dance to entertain the Saints (HC 4:401–2; CHC 2:88–89).

Keokuk served as the **LDS 1853 outfitting camp** for Mormon wagon trains. Within 1 mile south of present-day **Rand Park** some 2,500 Saints, mostly European immigrants, assembled into 10 wagon trains (WGH 43–77). These wagon companies included the **John Forsgren company,** the first large Scandinavian company to emigrate to Utah. LDS journalist Frederick Piercy described the Keokuk camps and illustrated the 1853 Mormon Trail trek in his book, *Route from Liverpool to the Great Salt Lake City Valley,* published in England in 1853. Keokuk histories praise the 1853 Mormons who, while waiting to head west, performed vital work for the city—they leveled Main Street and built Plank Road (HMEK 11–14).

Triangle Park, located where 5th Street ends at Grand Avenue, contains a historic marker panel, "Mormon Immigrants' Camp, 1853." It provides a detailed description of the 1853 Mormon encampment, very close to the encampment site.

An important historic building is the **Samuel F. Miller home** (1857), located at 318 5th Street, a few blocks west of **Triangle Park.** Miller became an associate justice on the U.S. Supreme Court in 1862, the first from west of the Mississippi, and served for 28 years. He issued 783 opinions and helped judge more than 5,000 cases, including constitutional cases about LDS plural marriage.

The **George M. Verity Riverboat Museum** is on Mississippi Drive, one block south of where Main Street (U.S. 218/61) meets the bridge spanning the Mississippi River. The boat, one of the last Mississippi River sternwheelers, was in service between 1927 and 1960. It is now a museum for Keokuk river history.

The **Keokuk Dam and Power Plant** was opened in 1913. At Keokuk the Des Moines River enters the Mississippi River, and above that confluence the Des Moines Rapids made river navigation by large boats impossible. During the mid-19th century, including the years when Saints were in Nauvoo, Keokuk served as a port where goods were transferred to and from smaller craft that could pass over the rapids. The dam created a lake that backs up beyond Montrose, which eliminated the rapids. For the Mississippi River this complex is considered **Lock and Dam No. 19.** The dam has the largest locks on the Mississippi, which let enormous riverboats and barges move up and down the river. The dam is .8 miles long and contains 119 spillways. Its turbines generate hydroelectricity, serving as a major power source for the region. The locks and powerhouse are open to tourists during the summer. Today the lake is called Cooper's Lake.

Mormon Emigration Routes in 1853 from Keokuk to Council Bluffs

In 1853 Keokuk served as the Latter-day Saints' main outfitting grounds for 10 wagon trains going to Utah. LDS emigrants arrived there overland or by Mississippi riverboats. Most had just crossed the Atlantic from the British Isles and had come upriver from New Orleans and St. Louis. In Keokuk, between late March and early July, emigration agent Isaac C. Haight and his assistants blended 2,598 Saints, 360 wagons, 1,440 oxen, and 720 milk cows into 10 wagon trains that rolled successfully some 1,400 miles overland to Utah by mid-October (WGH 43–76).

In 1835, while Iowa was being explored by the U.S. government, the 1st U.S. Dragoons under Col. Stephen W. Kearny blazed a route called the **Dragoon Trail,** which on today's map runs northwest roughly from Montrose to Des Moines and beyond. It followed the high ground between the Des Moines and Skunk Rivers, passing through the locations of present-day Libertyville, Ottumwa, Eddyville, Oskaloosa, Pella, and Monroe. The DAR erected half a dozen markers along that route (HSM 45–48).

Saints during the 1846 **Spring Exodus from Nauvoo** used that route before crossing the Des Moines at Iowaville or Eddyville or other ferry places (IMT 68–69). Two or more LDS wagon companies in 1853 left Keokuk and followed that route. Segments of the established road ranged from good to very poor (WGH 67–68).

The 1853 wagon trains followed two well-established routes

from Keokuk across Iowa, each one averaging 4 weeks to reach **Council Bluffs** (WGH 67–68).

The **Jacob Gates, John Forsgren, Daniel Spencer, Appleton Harmon,** and probably the **Moses Clawson companies** took the roads used or blazed by Saints during the **1846 Nauvoo exoduses.** From **Keokuk,** a first campground for the Forsgren company and others was at **New Boston,** which is 6 miles northwest of **Montrose.** These companies crossed the Des Moines River at Farmington and then joined the Brigham Young route near **Richardson's Pt.,** detoured slightly to pass through **Stringtown,** followed the old route to **Drakesville,** then followed the **Mormon Trail variant** that passed through **Unionville** and **Chariton** to **Mt. Pisgah.** From there they again joined **the 1846 main route** into **Council Bluffs** (JJFC).

A better but longer route was the one that followed the **Dragoon Trail,** which by then was termed the **Keokuk-to-Des Moines Road.** The **Joseph W. Young company** and probably the **Cyrus Wheelock company** went that way. They passed through **New Boston, Charleston, Winchester, Libertyville, Ottumwa, Eddyville, Oskaloosa, Pella,** and **Mitchell** to reach **Ft. Des Moines** (present-day Des Moines). There they crossed the Des Moines River and went west-southwest on the **Des Moines-to-Council Bluffs Road** that passed through **Winterset** and connected with the **1846 Mormon Trail** at the Middle Nishnabotna River, which they followed past **Indiantown** and into **Council Bluffs** (JWYCJ).

■ New Boston

New Boston is 5.5 miles directly northwest of Montrose and 9 miles southwest of the center of Ft. Madison. It is 6.5 miles south of Donnellson on U.S. 218.

In 1853 the **Joseph W. Young wagon train** moved here from Keokuk on May 20. For nearly three weeks, 420 souls, with 56 wagons, camped here while waiting for cattle to arrive from Keokuk. **Christiana Reeves,** age 35, died at the camping ground. On June 1 part of the camp moved west to Sugar Creek (JWYCJ).

Eddyville

Eddyville is 44 miles south of I-80, Exit 191, on U.S. 63, and 10 miles south of Oskaloosa on that same highway. It is located on the east bank of the Des Moines River.

Many LDS emigrants in the **1846 Spring Exodus from Nauvoo** crossed the Des Moines River at the Eddyville ferry. On June 14, 1853, the **Joseph W. Young company** "rested for the night on a good prairie about four miles east of Eddyville" and the next day "passed through Eddyville and encamped at 1 P.M. four miles west of that city" (JWYCJ).

In Eddyville, the ferry site was near the city park at the west end of Walnut Street (the city's main street), which overlooks the Des Moines River.

Oskaloosa

Oskaloosa is 31 miles south of I-80, Exit 182 (Grinell Exit), on State 146. On June 17, 1853, the **Joseph W. Young company** "passed through Oskaloosa, and entered upon the 35 mile prairie for the Dutch town Pella" (JWYCJ). The **Cyrus Wheelock company** apparently did so, too. The *Weekly Oskaloosa Herald* of June 17, 1853, reported that about 750 Mormons, principally from England and Wales, had passed through Oskaloosa.

The **Nelson Pioneer Farm and Museum** is located 3.18 miles northeast of Oskaloosa on County Road T65, at 2294 Oxford Avenue. The Nelson family homestead includes the Nelson brick home built in 1853, the year LDS emigrants passed through Oskaloosa. The home and a barn built in 1856 (the year of the **Mormon handcart migration**) and other buildings and implements demonstrate what farm life was like in mid-19th-century Iowa.

Pella

Pella is 44 miles southeast of Des Moines via State 163 and 14 miles northwest of Oskaloosa on State 163. From I-80, Pella is reached from Exits 164 and 173.

Pella was founded in 1847 by Reverend Hendrick Pieter Scholte as a colony for about 800 Dutch Separatists. Some Mormons in the **1846 Spring Exodus** passed through the area where Pella would be located the next year (PITH 38). On June 18, 1853, the **Joseph W. Young company** "passed through Pella and proceeded across the prairie towards Mitchell" (JWYCJ). Apparently the **Wheelock company** did as well.

Emigrants passing through Pella in 1853 probably saw the **Scholte House,** built by the city's founder 1847–48, which is now a tourist site. To this day, Pella's Dutch heritage makes it distinct from other Iowa cities. Downtown storefronts resemble typical Dutch buildings, tall and narrow. Near the town square, **The Klokkenspel** at the Franklin Place Arch features eight four-foot figurines that perform five times daily to music from a 147-bell carillon. The courtyard has scenes of Holland reproduced with Delft Dutch tiles. Pella's tulip gardens are the center of the Tulip Festival held each May. The **Pella Historical Village** of more than 20 buildings includes a gristmill, blacksmith shop, Dutch bakery, pioneer cabin, and the boyhood home of western lawman Wyatt Earp. The focal point of the village is the **Vermeer Windmill,** an authentic working grain mill patterned after an 1850s mill in Holland. Pella windows and doors products are recognized nationally for their quality.

■ *FT. MADISON

Ft. Madison is 6 miles northwest of Nauvoo, where State 2 starts west from the Mississippi River. At this city, which existed during the Nauvoo period, **Saints ferried the river,** traded, and traveled roads leading west and north.

Saints in the **James Emmett Expedition** passed through Ft. Madison in August and September 1844.

Many **Nauvoo refugees** passed through Ft. Madison in April, May, and June 1846 and headed in a westerly or northwesterly direction to cross Iowa.

Riverview Park is six blocks west of the Mississippi River bridge on State 2/61. It contains a **replica of historic Ft. Madison.** The fort (1808–13), named for President James Madison, was the first U.S. military post on the upper Mississippi River. Besieged by Indians during the War of 1812, the fort was abandoned and burned. The town of Ft. Madison was settled in 1833. The replica of the fort was built in the 1980s by prisoners from Iowa State Penitentiary, which is located in Ft. Madison.

State Highway 2, starting west at Ft. Madison, is a designated **Mormon Trail Highway,** even though the original 1846 pioneers began their trek 9 miles south at **Montrose.**

■ AUGUSTA—MORMON BRANCH

Augusta is 11 miles northeast of Ft. Madison and 16 miles northwest of Nauvoo. In 1840 several LDS families settled there (EnH 25). **Lyman Wight,** who became an apostle in 1841, was among them. The **Augusta branch** was part of the Zarahemla Stake. **Frederick Kesler,** later a prominent Utah pioneer bishop and millwright, joined the LDS Church here. While Joseph Smith attended a meeting in Augusta in January 1841, someone cut off the tails, manes, and an ear from two of his horses (HiR 8:944).

During a Church conference in Augusta Apr. 1, 1843, James Brown became the presiding elder of the branch, which had 84 members (HC 5:318).

■ BURLINGTON

Burlington is 24 miles directly northeast of Nauvoo on the west shore of the Mississippi River. It is 18 miles upriver from Ft. Madison on U.S. 61.

Burlington was **Iowa Territory's first capital,** from 1838 to 1840, and was Iowa's chief city at the time the Latter-day Saints founded Nauvoo. Joseph Smith visited Burlington Sept. 18–19, 1839 (HC 4:9–10).

By the mid-1840s Nauvoo and Burlington were the largest cities on the Mississippi above Quincy. A good deal of trade and riverboat pleasure excursions took place between the two cities. Burlington attorney **James W. Woods** served as one of Joseph Smith's legal advisers (HC 6:525). The *Burlington Hawkeye,* Iowa's leading newspaper in the 1840s, often reported about events at Nauvoo.

During the 1846 exodus, Burlington, population 3,000, provided housing and jobs for scores fleeing Nauvoo. "Every Steamboat that has visited our landing within the past week has been loaded with Mormons," the *Hawkeye* reported on September 17. Among them were **Enoch and Roxanna Tripp,** who "took a little bedding & clothing & fsened up the hause with the ballance of our things in it & took a Stem Boat in the evenign for Burlington Iowa" (EBTJ). The Mormons were received with reservation but were not molested. That winter, a **Burlington Branch** of 15 or 16 families was organized with **Alfred Cordon** as president (JH July 2, 1848). Most of those Saints went west by 1852 (RHG 104). In May 1848 in Burlington, the Cordons buried a five-month-old son, born there the previous December. Probably other Mormons are buried there, but no location for any LDS grave has been identified.

In the mid-1850s some **LDS handcart emigrants** who stopped at Iowa City to find work went to Burlington and found jobs. In 1856 about 150 Mormons went there. Elder **Christian Christiansen,** sent from Utah to assist Scandinavian Saints in the Midwest, helped them find employment in and near Burlington. "For the young men and women I also secured places as servants, and in Burlington alone I found places for 50 of them." He organized the emigrants under his care into several small branches (RHG 106). By 1858 the Mormon emigration route bypassed Iowa City in favor of railroad trains that crossed Missouri from Hannibal to St. Joseph.

A vacant **Burlington and Missouri River Railroad passenger station,** located at 237 South 4th Street, dates from the 1870s. In the 1870s and 1880s LDS emigrants again passed through Burlington when the Church booked them on the new Burlington and Missouri River Railroad (RHG 107–8).

Snake Alley is located between Washington and Columbia Streets on Sixth Street. *Ripley's Believe It or Not* judges it the "Crookedest Street in the World." Bordering the curved alley are several historic buildings that were standing when Mormon emigrants were in Burlington, including the **William Fordney House** (1845), the **Winter-Rand House** (1850s), and the **Garrett-Phelps House** (1851), now a Victorian house museum.

■ Four Corners

Four Corners, in Jefferson County, is about midway between Mt. Pleasant and Fairfield, 3.5 miles north of U.S. 34 on County Road H23, exactly 2 miles north and 1 mile west of the main intersection of the town of Lockridge. Four Corners is in the center of Lockridge Township Section 22 (T72N R8W).

In 1838 an LDS family group headed by **George Washington and Sarah Bradford Conyer** moved from Missouri to Jefferson County and settled at Four Corners, living there for nearly eight years. In the 1840 census, the group included Washington's brother John Conyer and Commodore Clayton, who was married to Rebecca Conyer, sister of Washington and John Conyer. When the Saints left Nauvoo, the Conyer group started west to meet them but stopped and established **Lost Camp** near present-day Osceola.

Three 1846 Exoduses from Nauvoo: Winter, Spring, and Fall

The dramatic, west-flowing story of some 15,000 Latter-day Saints vacating the Nauvoo area in 1846 involves three distinct movements. The initial movement is the well-known trek of

Brigham Young. (Steel engraving by Frederick Piercy, 1853)

Brigham Young's **Camp of Israel.** This hurried **Winter Exodus** took place during February 1846, ahead of the planned schedule to leave in the spring, because of fears that federal troops planned to block the Saints' move west and arrest Church leaders. During February hundreds of Saints crossed the Mississippi River, almost all by ferryboat but a few on a natural ice bridge when the river froze. They assembled at **Sugar Creek Camp,** 7 miles into Iowa Territory. The Twelve, with Brigham Young in charge, led this initial migration of some 500 wagons and 2,500 people, including apostles Heber C. Kimball, Willard Richards, and Orson and Parley P. Pratt; general bishops Newel K. Whitney and George Miller; and excellent diarists William Clayton, Eliza R. Snow, Willard Richards, Hosea Stout, and John D. Lee. The entire group, subdivided into companies of 100 wagons each, is usually termed the "Camp of Israel." They departed from the bitterly cold Sugar Creek encampment on Feb. 28 and Mar. 1, beginning a 3.5 month trek to the Missouri River, 300 miles away (IMT xiii-xxxii).

History books concentrate on the experiences of the Camp of Israel, the **Winter Exodus** group, rather than the groups in the much larger **Spring Exodus** because (1) it was the first wave of people who left Nauvoo en masse and who pioneered routes and travel methods; (2) it included most of the Twelve and other top leaders in the Church; (3) it was an organized (much of the time) caravan that shared a collective, common history; and (4) its experiences were well recorded. The pioneers' historic route through Iowa is now part

Winter evacuation from Nauvoo, IL, to Montrose, IA, Feb. 1846. (old print)

of what the U.S. government officially designated in the 1970s as the 1,300-mile-long **Mormon Pioneer National Historic Trail.**

A pioneer wagon train on the trail.

The numbers who left in the **Spring Exodus** dwarf the numbers in the Camp of Israel. Most of the Saints living in and near Nauvoo left according to the original plan—in the spring.

On May 1, Elder Orson Hyde and other leaders publicly dedicated the Nauvoo Temple, a ceremony thousands of Saints attended before leaving. Approximately 12,000 people, including families of Elder Hyde, Elder Wilford Woodruff, Newel and Lydia Knight, and Mary Fielding Smith left Nauvoo individually in groups of two or 12 or 20 during April, May, and June, heading for Brigham Young's encampments by the Missouri River. "We could look forward for miles and behold the prairie spotted with wagons, cattle, horses and sheep, men, women and children," Newel Knight wrote on May 10 (JNK 157; spelling and punctuation standardized). Amos Fielding, approaching Nauvoo on June 1, said that in three days of travel he counted 902 westbound Mormon wagons (JDL 87). The spring groups followed several better roads and routes than did the Camp of Israel, so they were able to cross Iowa in only a month, despite inconveniences caused by rain, mud, and sicknesses related to standing water and mosquitoes (IMT 61–83).

The final departures from Nauvoo were the **Fall Exodus,** which happened in September 1846 when armed anti-Mormons during and after the Battle of Nauvoo drove out the last few hundred Saints, most of whom were sick or otherwise ill-equipped

The Mormons are forced to leave Nauvoo, September1846. (Old print)

for the trek. At their Poor Saints camps on the Mississippi's west shore, they miraculously received unexpected food when flocks of exhausted quail flopped into their campground and tents. In Mormon history this is termed the **miracle of the quail.** LDS rescue teams from western Iowa retrieved many of these forlorn people. The others departed on their own.

Of those who left the Nauvoo area in 1846 in the winter, spring, and fall exoduses, between 2,000 and 3,000 stopped along the way in southern Iowa or in northern Missouri. Many of them lacked food, funds, good wagons and teams, or decent health, so they found temporary housing and jobs and did not reach the LDS camps at the Missouri River for months or even years.

Iowa Historic Route 1

Mormon Pioneer National Historic Trail and Variant Routes across Southern Iowa

The Mormon Trail, or the **Mormon Pioneer National Historic Trail,** in Iowa begins in **Montrose.** From this point westward, most LDS historical sites across southern Iowa relate to the **1846 pioneers'** 300-mile journey from Nauvoo to present-day **Council Bluffs** (see Iowa maps: Nauvoo to Centerville, Centerville to Creston, and Creston to Council Bluffs, pages 2–4). Campsites below are those of Brigham Young unless otherwise noted. The **name** of each campsite is followed, in most entries, by the **date** of the camp, **miles** the companies traveled during the day, and the closest **town** or **city** today. Mileages listed in different old accounts vary because (1) camps were spread out for miles, and (2) they had no way to accurately measure the mileage.[2]

In 1996, for the sesquicentennial of the state of Iowa and for the sesquicentennial of the Mormon Trail in Iowa, the National Park Service, the Iowa Mormon Trails Association, and local Iowa groups erected an impressive series of more than 30 **Mormon Trail interpretive panels,** wayside panels featuring maps, text, illustrations, and diary excerpts. At least one panel was placed in each

---

2. A fundamental source for information and maps about LDS trails and sites in Iowa is Stanley B. Kimball, *Historic Sites and Markers along the Mormon and Other Great Western Trails* (Urbana and Chicago: University of Illinois Press, 1988). Dr. Kimball is the recognized authority on the Mormon Trail. He also wrote the extremely useful reference tool *Historic Resource Study: Mormon Pioneer National Historic Trail,* published by the U.S. Department of Interior and available to the public. The Iowa Mormon Trails Association published (1995) *Iowa Mormon Trails: The Map Guide across the State.* A remarkably detailed guide for one county is Willis M. Heusinkveld, *Mormon Trails across Appanoose County, Iowa* (Centerville, Iowa: Appanoose County Mormon Trails Association, 1995). In 1996 the National Park Service published an accordion-fold-out brochure, "The Mormon Trail," with a detailed highway map showing the entire Mormon Trail with text and information about sites along the trail. See also *The Iowa Mormon Trail,* ed. Susan Easton Black and William G. Hartley (Orem, Utah: Helix Publishing, 1997).

county through which the Mormons' routes passed, and most counties have two (WYW).

**MONTROSE RIVERVIEW PARK

Riverview Park, on the northeast end of Montrose by the Mississippi River marks the beginning of the 300-mile-long **Mormon Trail** in Iowa used by the Saints during their **exoduses from Nauvoo.** During the winter of 1845–46, the Saints in Nauvoo agreed to leave their homes and travel to a new location in the West. They labored feverishly to finish the Nauvoo Temple, receive their temple endowments, construct wagons, and stockpile supplies for their trek. On Feb. 4, 1846, Charles Shumway was the first to depart. His wagon was ferried by flatboat over the Mississippi River.[3] Shumway and those who followed from Nauvoo landed near the shoreline area of **Riverview Park.**

Downriver the Keokuk Dam (1913) has backed up the water of the Mississippi, making the river between Montrose and Nauvoo resemble a lake. In 1846 the width of the river channel between Nauvoo's Parley Street and Montrose's Riverview Park was about the same as it is today—1 mile across. But 1 mile above Riverview Park the river was then half as wide as today and had islands where Saints cut wood and fished. The west shore then was a wide swath of swampy land and sloughs. In the stretch between 1 and 2 miles upriver from Riverview Park (where the east side of today's river on the Nauvoo side bends to the northeast), the river in 1846 was one-third as wide as it is today (AHAI, Lee Co.).

From Montrose and the shoreline north and south of it, the Latter-day Saints from Nauvoo began their fateful trek to the West in February 1846. At Riverview Park's north edge, a **Mormon Trail interpretive panel** tells about the LDS exodus from Nauvoo and the Saints' river crossings to Iowa.

---

3. Good accounts of the Nauvoo exodus are in Russell Rich, *Ensign to the Nations;* Preston Nibley, *Exodus to Greatness;* Wallace Stegner, *The Gathering of Zion;* B. H. Roberts, *Comprehensive History of the Church,* vol. 2; Glen M. Leonard and James B. Allen, *Story of the Latter-day Saints;* Richard E. Bennett, *Mormons at the Missouri, 1846–1852;* and a special issue about Mormons in Iowa in *BYU Studies* 21 (Fall 1981). First-person accounts include the published diaries or writings of Brigham Young, Orson Pratt, Parley P. Pratt, Hosea Stout, Helen Mar Whitney, Horace K. Whitney, Eliza R. Snow, Thomas Bullock, Patty Sessions, and Daniel Tyler, as well as numerous excellent unpublished diaries by such participants as Newel Knight and John Smith.

Crossing the River on the Ice

Almost all of the Saints who left Nauvoo to start west in February 1846 crossed the river on ferryboats. Starting on Feb. 4, ferries constantly carried wagons across the river until freezing weather by Feb. 23 produced flowing ice that made the river too dangerous to cross (see **Sugar Creek Camp**). On Feb. 24 almost everyone going west in Brigham Young's company was in camp and ready to leave. That day, Brigham Young's history noted: "7 P.M., Thermometer 12 degrees below Zero, Fah. Mississippi river frozen over above Montrose." The next day the record says: "About 11 A.M. Captain Charles C. Rich arrived from Nauvoo and reported that he had walked over the Mississippi river on the ice at Montrose" (MHBY). For four more days, people and wagons crossed back and forth over the ice bridge. "We fited up the wagons & broke the catel & got all things ready," **Lorenzo Hill Hatch** wrote, "and on the 27th of Febuay, I baid my friends fare well & we crost the Missippa river on the ice" (DLHH). That same day **John D. Lee,** going back to Nauvoo on an errand, crossed the river in a carriage on the ice (DJDL). **Horace K. Whitney,** riding on horseback, accompanied Cornelius P. Lott, who "with his team left Nauvoo with the women and children crossed the river on the ice and took them to the camp" (JHKW). The ice bridge was short-lived; on Mar. 1 **John D. Lee** "sent 1 waggon & 2 yoke of oxen across the river in crossing on the Ice one yoke of the oxen broke in through the Ice—but was fortunately taken out without injury." By Mar. 3 the ice was unsafe (DJDL Mar. 1 and 3, 1846). Brigham Young said concerning the river crossing:

Crossing the frozen Mississippi River from Nauvoo, IL, to Montrose, IA. (Courtesy of Vernon Murdock, artist, 1973)

> The great severity of the weather and not being able to sell any of our property, the difficulty of crossing the river during many days of running ice all combined to delay our departure,

> though for several days the bridge of ice across the Mississippi greatly facilitated the crossing, and compensated, in part, for the delay caused by the running ice. (MHBY 55)

From the landing area near where Riverview Park is today, the Saints moved inland to their first campsite by Sugar Creek, about 7 miles west of Montrose.

Spring Exodus from Nauvoo—Ferry Crossings

Only one-fifth of the Latter-day Saints who left Nauvoo in 1846 were in Brigham Young's winter company. The vast majority left in the spring, according to the original plan, when "grass grows and water runs."[4] Approximately 12,000 people, including two apostles and several prominent families, left during April, May, and June, intent on catching up with Brigham Young's company. They all crossed the Mississippi River using ferry boats that operated at, above, and below Nauvoo. "During the week four hundred teams have crossed at three points, or about 1,350 souls," the *Quincy Whig* reported on May 20, 1846 (MHBY May 19). Two days later, on May 22, 1846, the *Bloomington Herald* noted that ferries, running day and night, crossed 35 times in 24 hours at Nauvoo, 35 times upriver at Ft. Madison, Iowa, and several times downriver at Nashville, Iowa. Between Montrose and the Des Moines River, the newspaper added, teams numbered about 1,400, with perhaps 7,000 to 8,000 persons, and "the slopes of the hills and the prairie opposite Nauvoo, are still dotted with clusters of tents and wagons."

Several hundred headed south by riverboat to St. Louis, or overland via Quincy on the east side of the river or via Keokuk, Iowa, on the west side. By July fewer than 1,000 Saints were left in

---

4. William G. Hartley, "Spring Exodus from Nauvoo: Act Two in the 1846 Mormon Evacuation Drama," in Black and Hartley, *Iowa Mormon Trail,* 61–84. This article is the only place where source materials dealing with the Spring Exodus are identified. It provides full citations (which space considerations prevent including here). As shown there, the most useful diary accounts are those of Newel Knight, Samuel W. Richards, Joseph Holbrook, Lucius Scovil, Wilford Woodruff, Mary Haskin Parker Richards, and Louisa Barnes Pratt. The last three have been published. Also useful are published biographies of James S. Brown, Edwin D. Woolley, Archibald Gardner, and Robert T. Burton, and life writings related to Lewis Barney, Anson Call, Mosiah Hancock, Isaac Haight, Orson Hyde, and Abraham O. Smoot. Several first-person accounts in Carol Cornwall Madsen, *Journey to Zion,* relate to the Spring Exodus.

Nauvoo. These, mostly **poor Saints** or unhealthy ones, did not depart until September (see **Potter's Slough—Poor Saints Camps**).

■ **POTTER'S SLOUGH—POOR SAINTS CAMPS • SEPT.–OCT. 1846 • MONTROSE

The site of **Potter's Slough,** which once was a Mississippi River inlet on the boggy west shoreline, is about 1.5 miles north of Montrose's Riverview Park and is now covered by the Mississippi River, about .5 mile east of the present-day west bank. It was in Jefferson Township (T66N R5W) in the northeast corner of Section 34 (see map in AHAI, Lee Co.)

The **Poor Saints Camps** were along Potter's Slough. In mid-September 1846 anti-Mormons drove the last Saints from Nauvoo. Many, on their own, found housing or work in eastern Iowa settlements, but between 300 and 600 Saints, poor and ill, camped by Potter's Slough in makeshift shelters. Only the poorest of the poor stayed in the camps. On Sept. 20, after **Robert Campbell** obtained some tent poles, his wife, Joan, and another woman sewed quilts and bedcovers together "that we made considerable of a tent with,

Potter's Slough, IA, beside which the poor Saints camped Sept.–Oct. 1846, after being forced from their homes in Nauvoo, IL. (Photo by George E. Anderson, 1907; courtesy of LDSCA)

not however water-proof." During a storm three days later, the tent "shed little of the rain." For the next two weeks Robert was sick from the "ague"—probably malaria—and his family was ill, too. (Soon after leaving the Poor Camps, Joan Campbell gave birth to a stillborn baby, and she herself died on Oct. 16) (JRLC). Thomas Bullock walked through this campground on Oct. 4 and counted 17 tents and eight wagons and "not a tent or Wagon but [has] sickness in it," and nearly all did not know by what means they could head west (JTB 72).

Three rescue teams transported most of the Saints in the Poor Camps to Garden Grove, Mt. Pisgah, or Council Bluffs before winter (DIA [Winter 1986]: 100–108). **Capt. Orville M. Allen's rescue company** of 22 wagons (joined by six other wagons near the Poor Camps) transported 157 people to Mt. Pisgah and Council Bluffs—a 50-day return trip. Fewer than that number were in the **James Murdock and Allen Taylor rescue company.** The third rescue party, the **Luman Shurtliff rescue company** from **Garden Grove,** picked up about 60 Saints, taking "only the poorest of the poor and the sickest of the sick" and enough well persons to care for the sick and cook for the company. Their journey back to Garden Grove took two weeks (JLAS 69).

The Miracle of the Quail

On Oct. 9, 1846, fatigued flocks of quail landed in the Poor Saints Camp on Potter's Slough, providing needed food for the 125 to 300 souls who still remained in the camps (CHC 3:135–36; DIA [Winter 1986]: 106). A week before the miracle, Robert Campbell mentioned quail and other food in his diary: "Abundance of quail are shot by the Brethren & a good many wild ducks, some fine large fishes are caught here by our tent which weigh 14 lbs." Then, on Oct. 9, he wrote, "Several flocks of quails flew around our wagons and seemed to have lost the power of flying insomuch that many of the Brethren caught them" (JRLC 2, 9 Oct. 1846; spelling standardized). **Thomas Bullock** also recorded the event:

> This morning we had direct manifestation of the mercy & goodness of God, in a miracle being performed in the Camp. A large, or rather several large flocks of Quails, flew into Camp.

Miracle of the quails in the Poor Saints Camp near Potter's Slough, IA. (Courtesy of Vernon Murdock, artist, 1973)

> Some fell on the Wagons—some under—some on the Breakfast tables. The boys & brethren ran about after them & caught them alive with their hands. Men who were not in the Church marvelled at the sight. The brethren & sisters praised God & glorified his name, that what was showered down upon the Children of Israel in the wilderness is manifested unto us in our persecution. The boys caught about 20 alive & as to the number that were killed—every man woman & child had quails to eat for their dinner. After dinner the flocks increased in size . . . A Steam Boat passed down within 5 or 6 rods of our Wagons at the time we were catching the Quails with our hands. (JTB 76, Oct. 9, 1846)

Linger Longer Park has several displays related to the Mormon Trail. The park is reached from Montrose by driving west one block from Riverview Park, then going north on First Street (which becomes Mississippi River Road) for .5 mile to where the street ends at U.S. 61. The park is on the east side of that junction. In it is an **interpretive panel** entitled "A Miracle on the Banks of the Mississippi," which tells about the quail. Also in the park is a

Pioneer Memorial Trail roofed pavilion, inside of which are glass-encased panels, "Nauvoo: From Wilderness to City Beautiful," "From City Beautiful to the Tops of the Mountains," and "Memories," which contain excerpts from personal journals. A display case in the middle of the pavilion features a map of the Mormon Trail across Iowa. From the pavilion, visitors have an excellent view of Nauvoo across the river.

■ ****SUGAR CREEK CAMP • BRIGHAM YOUNG • FEB. 4–28, 1846 • 6.5 MILES • MONTROSE**

Sugar Creek Camp site, called "Kedron" by some Saints (DHS Feb. 15, 123), is 5.5 miles directly west of Montrose (7 by trail route). It is 1.6 miles south-southwest of **New Boston** and 2.5 miles east-northeast of **Argyle.** It is in Sections 11 and 2 of Des Moines Township (T66N R6W). It can be reached from U.S. 218 at a point 1 mile southeast of New Boston and 3.75 miles northwest of the junction of U.S. 218 and U.S. 61 (2 miles southwest of Montrose). From that point, travelers follow 280th Street west .5 mile, south .6 mile, west .5 mile, south .4 mile, and west .5 mile to the bridge that crosses Sugar Creek. If starting from Argyle, the location is 1.5 miles east on 295th Street, then north for .5 mile, and east .5 mile on 290th Street to Sugar Creek. From that bridge location, the 1846 encampment stretched south along the east side of the creek, spanning at least a half square mile.

To reach that camp, Saints in Nauvoo crossed the river in boats and ferries of various sizes and shapes. One large ferry, Hosea Stout noted, carried two wagons, two yokes of oxen, and 20 people (DHS Feb. 9, 113). Once ashore at or near Montrose, people and teams had to move 2.5 miles inland to some bluffs (DHS Feb. 15, 123), go up the bluff slopes, and then travel overland another 5 miles.

Sugar Creek Camp became the **first encampment and staging ground.** Church leaders chose a site along the banks of **Sugar Creek,** in Ambrosia Township, where there was plenty of timber and water (MHBY Feb. 16). Saints camped "on the bottom land on Sugar Creek on either side of the St. Francisville road" (DHS Feb. 13, 122). That road crossed the creek on a bridge, which served as a daily meeting place for leaders and other camp members. "Our camp was formed on the curved bank of the Creek forming a large circle the centre of which was reserved for a parade ground & other public camp purposes," Hosea Stout recorded, "our horses oxen and cows in the rear of our waggons immediately on the bank" (DHS Feb. 16, 123).

On Feb. 9 Lorenzo Snow and his family of seven camped at Sugar Creek with two wagons and a tent. "There were a hundred families gathered in there before us," he said (MUB 264). During February 1846 nearly 500 wagons and about 2,500 Saints gathered at the camp. The large company, led by Brigham Young and other apostles with him, collectively became called the **Camp of Israel.** How some of these displaced Saints felt is glimpsed in Hosea Stout's journal entry Feb. 16:

> About two o'clock I had a white flag raised in front of my tent, as a token of peace but it refused to waive in the air notwithstanding there was a light breeze which seemed to say that it would not proclaim peace in the United States when there was nought but oppression and tyrranny towards the people of God by the rulers of this government and the Saints fleeing from her borders to the wilderness for safety and refuge from her iron yoke. (DHS Feb. 16, 1846, 123)

Brigham Young arrived on Feb. 15 and began organizing the encampment. Three days later he met with men in camp and directed captains to collect money with which to buy "factory drilling & bed ticking—to make waggon covers and Tent ends"; to make a list of everyone in camp; and to have everyone deposit their corn in the commissary store. He wanted men and women to hold night and morning prayers in their tents. He instructed that "order we must & will have!" Later that day he sent three men to nearby St. Francisville, Missouri, to buy materials for tents (DJDL Feb. 18).

Weather turned bad as February progressed. Driving snow fell all day on Feb. 14, putting deep snow on the ground. When **Orson Pratt** reached camp that day he found people "suffering considerably from the storm and cold" (JOP 317). "It is very cold," **midwife Patty Sessions** wrote on Feb. 16. "The wind blows, one can hardly get to the fire for smoke and we have no tent" (JPS 34). On Feb. 19 it snowed all day. "The wind blows the snow in every direction," **Eliza Maria Partridge Lyman** recorded that day, "and our fire is out in the storm so that we cannot get warm by it. I am almost frozen so I shall go into the wagon and make my bed and get into it as that is the only way I can get warm" (JEPL 25). On the 20th the snow stopped, replaced by cold winds that dropped the temperatures drastically. Snow fell again on the 24th. On Feb. 25 President Young moved the meeting with leaders from the bridge down into a deep ravine for shelter from the cold wind. Plans to start the trek west the next day were postponed due to the cold.

Temperatures plunged as low as 12 degrees below zero (HC 7:597). The Saints suffered from the **freezing weather** in their tents and covered wagons. Helen Mar Kimball Whitney recalled that "the youthful portion" held dances by the log fire "to amuse ourselves" and because "it was impossible to keep warm without exercise" (AHMW,h 340–41). During that cold spell the Mississippi River froze over, allowing people and teams to cross on the ice for a few days (see **Crossing the River on the Ice**).

On Feb. 25 an advance company of about 100 **"pioneers"** led by Stephen Markham went ahead from Sugar Creek to prepare the way for those to follow—to improve roads, find campsites, dig wells, and ascertain where hay and corn could be purchased (HC 7:591; MHBY Feb. 18 and 23). Saints were grouped into companies of 100, 50, and 10 able-bodied men with wagons, with or without families (MHBY, 570 note 7; RWCS 316). The **Nauvoo Band,** directed by William Pitt and managed by William Clayton, was to follow behind Markham's **pioneer company,** after which followed the wagon companies according to their numbers—first 50, second 50, and so forth (MHBY Mar. 3, 1846).

Later that year, from April to June, this Sugar Creek Camp site was also used as a staging area for the **Spring Exodus,** involving more than 12,000 Saints from Nauvoo. During that exodus, Newel Knight wrote on Apr. 24:

> We left Mississippi a bout noon we ascended the bluff here we all halted & took a farewell view of our delightful City that we had seen & helped to rear even from its infancy. We allso beheld the magnificent Temple rearing its lofty tower towards the heavens . . . we allso took a farewell look of our Comfortable homes we had labored so hard to rear for the Comfort of our families . . . my heart did swell with in me. (JNK)

Nine Births in One Night?

An account published in 1877 cited **Eliza R. Snow** as saying nine babies were born during "the first night of the encampment" at Sugar Creek (BYUS 21 [Fall 1981]: 441–44), and that episode sometimes appears in more recent histories. The earliest statement about nine births at the Sugar Creek Camp on Feb. 5 was told by Thomas L. Kane in 1850 (NJ [Spring 1995]: 9). But the story lacks other documentation and corroboration, and it challenges common sense—why would nine expectant mothers rush across the river to have babies the next day? Other records show that pregnant women stayed in Nauvoo until their babies came, and then they joined the exodus. The best available evidence points toward the fall of 1846 as the time when this supposed rash of births took place. In a statement notarized in 1883, **Jane Johnston** claimed she was midwife for **nine births** one night in the Poor Saints Camps:

> My husband being in Canada at the time [September–October 1846]. . . . We then ferried across the river into Iowa and remained in Montrose a short time. . . .
>
> Had nothing to eat only half a bushel of meal and half a dozen cucumbers that were given to me by Martin Littlewood. There were a great many sick among the Saints and nothing to comfort them, and nourish them, but corn meal, until the Lord sent quails amongst us, which supplied our wants.
>
> I then got a tent from Brother Johnston and had women that were being delivered of child put in it. I was the mid-wife, and delivered nine babies that night. (BYUS 21[Fall 1981]: 443)

However, partial rosters of the Poor Saints Camp people show but one infant born in Iowa, causing one historian to judge Johnston's account to be "beyond belief" and that the births must have been in February at Sugar Creek after all (DIA 19 [Winter 1986]: 107). So, was it February or fall, or did it really happen at all? We don't know. One other possible source of this story does exist: eight births at a winter camp near the Missouri River occurred two years later (see **Pottawattamie Indian Village**).[5]

---

5. Jane Johnston's notarized statement was dictated May 12, 1883. It is located at the

■ Sugar Creek Camp No. 2 • Brigham Young • Mar. 1 • 4.5 miles • Charleston

The site of **Sugar Creek Camp No. 2** is 4.5 miles northwest of Sugar Creek Camp No. 1 on the northeast side of Sugar Creek, between the junction of Sugar Creek and **Indian Creek** or **Goose Creek.** The site is on private property 4 miles south of **Donnellson** and 2.5 miles west of **Charleston.** The site is .75 mile west and .7 mile south of the junction of State 394 and County Road J62. It is located in the northwest quarter of Section 29 and southwest quarter of Section 20, Charleston Township (T67N R6W).

"Encamp'd in a low, truly romantic valley," Eliza R. Snow wrote of this campsite, while others "tented on the bluff which surrounded us" (JERS Feb. 28 and Mar. 1, 1846). "The snow had to be cleared away to pitch the tents," Helen Mar Kimball Whitney recalled, "and our beds were made upon the frozen ground. We were not blessed with a stove in our tent that night and it was impossible to get warm by the campfire; so that night I laid nothing off, not even my hood" (AHMW,h 344).

On Mar. 1 Brigham Young drove to Sugar Creek Camp No. 2, leading nearly 500 wagons 4.5 miles, thereby starting the journey across Iowa.

In honor of the first full day of travel, Eliza R. Snow penned a song she titled "The Camp of Israel," which contains an "all is well" refrain and reads in part as follows (JERS Mar. 1, 1846):

> Hark! the sound is onward, onward!
>   Camp of Israel! rise & go.
> All at once is life in motion—
>   Trunks and beds & baggage fly;
> Oxen yok'd & horses harness'd—
>   Tents roll'd up, are passing by.
> Soon the carriage wheels are rolling—
>   Onward to a woodland dell
> Where at sunset all are quarter'd—
>   Camp of Israel! all is well.

---

beginning of the Diary of Joseph Smith Black (typescript, BYU Special Collections, Provo, Utah). For an excellent account of the reason for the mix-up in time and place of the "nine births," read Carol Lynn Pearson's "Nine Children Were Born: A Historical Problem from the Sugar Creek Episode," in *BYU Studies* (Fall 1981): 441–44.

Thickly round, the tents are cluster'd
 Neighb'ring smokes together blend—
Supper serv'd—the hymns are chanted—
 And the evening pray'rs ascend.

■ Charleston—Spring Exodus

Charleston, Lee County, is 7.5 miles northwest of Montrose on U.S. 218. It is in the middle of Section 22 of Charleston Township.

Many Saints who left Nauvoo as part of the Spring Exodus went to Charleston and then either to Sugar Creek near Brigham Young's Sugar Creek Camp No. 2 or west to the Des Moines River. On May 25 Wilford Woodruff's group "struck our tents" at the Montrose campsite "and rode to Charlestown & Camped for the night," the campsite being a mile or two northwest of Charleston. A day later he recorded that many Saints "passed us to day" and that Brother Abraham O. Smoot "came up & camped with us for the night" (JWW 50).

■ Lick Creek Camp • Brigham Young • Mar. 2 • 7 miles • Croton

Lick Creek Camp site is 3.75 miles southeast of the center of **Farmington** and .6 mile north-northwest of the center of **Croton.** It is 1.8 miles south of State 2 and .2 miles west of Lick Creek. It is .5 mile north from that creek's junction with the **Des Moines River.** The campsite is centered on the east line of Section 19, Van Buren Township (T67N R7W) at a point .1 mile south of the north line of the section. It is on the north side of the main road that parallels the Des Moines River.

The Camp of Israel left Sugar Creek Camp No. 2 and headed west directly toward the Des Moines River. County Road J62, from a point 3 miles west of Charleston (1 mile west of State 394) and for the next 6 miles westward, closely follows the 1846 pioneers' route to the Des Moines River at present-day **Croton.** During that journey they passed over several tedious hills, reached the river, and turned north along its east side for .5 mile to tent by **Lick Creek** (DHS; JWC; MHBY; JOP; DJDL).

The advance company, the "pioneers," had prepared a campground with piles of split firewood. "When we got into camp about dark," George Whitaker recalled, "there were thirty or forty large fires burning which cheered us up very much. Each family or two or three small families would be put to one fire." His supper was "mush and milk." Around the campfires he saw people talking, singing, dancing, and playing music. "After singing, we had prayers," he said. "The women and children slept in the wagons. We had a large family wagon fixed so that six or seven could lie cross-ways in the wagon. We all slept soundly" (LGW).

■ *FARMINGTON

Farmington, Van Buren County, population about 700, is located on the east bank of the Des Moines River along State 2, which is the official Mormon Trail Highway. Platted in 1839, Farmington is the oldest village in Van Buren County.

Brigham Young's companies passed through the little village of Farmington, starting on Mar. 3, 1846 (MHBY).

William Pitt's Nauvoo Band played a concert there on Mar. 4, while the Saints were encamped at **Reed's Creek** (JWR, Mar. 3). The band arrived at the "principal" **hotel** about 4:30 P.M., where they played. They also performed to a capacity crowd at the **school** until nearly dark. After their concerts they returned to the hotel and were provided with a good supper. **John Kay** sang several songs, and the group received five dollars for their services. They left for camp amid three cheers from the spectators (JWC Mar. 4).

Later, many in the **Spring Exodus** passed through Farmington and crossed the Des Moines River there rather than upriver at Bonaparte, Iowaville, Eddyville, or other ferrying points. "We rode to Farmington," **Wilford Woodruff** wrote on May 28. "The whole company bought there flour at Farmington. I bought flour 4 barrels. We crossed the Desmoin River at the Farmington ferry went out 4 mile & camped" (JWW 3:51). On May 25 **Mary Parker Richards** dined with "bro Palmers famaley" in Farmington and then her company crossed the river there (DMHPR 64).

During the next winter, 1846–47, anti-Mormons in Farmington mistreated some LDS men working in the area. They hanged two men by their heels until the two were nearly dead, cut holes in river ice and held a Mormon or two under water until nearly dead, and arrested some on false charges. **William Gibbs** spent eight weeks in a log jail in Keosauqua until a judge in Iowa City freed him and lectured the Farmington justice of the peace for misconduct (AEDG 111–13).

Five **period houses** that stood when the LDS **pioneers** passed through Farmington are the **State Line House** (or the Von Seggen Farm Home), built in 1838, that served as a stagecoach stop and tavern 1 mile east of Farmington on the south side of State 2; the **Emanuel Miller house** (built in 1840 or before) on the corner of 4th and Pearl; the **Warnock homestead** (1840) at the end of Olive Street; the **Old Perry Place** (1840) at 302 Walnut Hill, built as a home and cigar factory; and **the Pfister home** (built in or before 1845), corner of 4th and Washington (VBCI 1–2). The **First Congregational Church of** Farmington, built in 1848 while some of the Saints were still in the area, is on the southeast corner of State 2 and State Street. Modeled after New England churches, it is the oldest Congregational church building west of the Mississippi River and is home to Farmington's **pioneer museum.**

■ Reed's Creek Camp • Brigham Young • Mar. 3–4 • 8 miles • Bonaparte

Reed's Creek Camp is 3.8 miles north-northwest of Farmington and 2 miles directly east of the Bonaparte bridge over the Des Moines River. It is on the east bank of Reed's Creek .6 of a mile above the point where the creek enters the Des Moines River. It is in the northeast quarter of Section 15, Bonaparte Township (T68N R8W). Here the pioneers camped in a 10-acre field. **Christiana (Mrs. John) Lytle** gave birth here on Mar. 6 to a son they named Charles (MHBY Mar. 6).

The forested setting where the camp generally was is visible from across the river. At the west end of the Farmington bridge across the Des Moines River, turn immediately north on gravel Eagle Drive and go north about 2.5 miles, from which point there is a view of the opposite shore where Reed's Creek enters the river.

■ **Bonaparte (Bonaparte Mills)

Bonaparte, Van Buren County, has a population of about 500 and is located on the north side of the **Des Moines River,** about 25 miles west of Ft. Madison. It is 1.6 miles north of State 2 on County Road W40. It was called Meek's Mills when founded in 1837. A sister village across the Des Moines River was named Napoleon, but it died out before the Civil War.

On Mar. 5 the 1846 Mormon pioneers passed through Bonaparte and **forded the Des Moines River.** Today a bridge spans the general site where they forded the two-feet-deep river from the north to the south sides on a rock bottom. **Mormon Trail signs** at the bridge's north side memorialize the 1846 Mormon crossing. One-half block upriver in the Riverview Park, along Front Street, is a **Mormon Trail Interpretive panel,** "From Mud to Ice." It tells of the Saints crossing the river and struggling along muddy roads on the other side.

"Today the most of the camp moved forward fording the river at Bonaparte Mills," **Orson Pratt** wrote (JOP). "The River was beautiful and had a good ford with a rock bottom," wrote **Hosea Stout** (DHS). While crossing the river, **Eliza R. Snow** "slung a tin cup on a string and drew some water which was a very refreshing draught" (JERS).

The Mormon companies took corn and grain to the **Bonaparte gristmill** to be milled into flour. "There was a splendid Mill on the Des Moines in this town," Stout noted. "The mill dam was built entirely across the river with lock to pass boats up or down" (DHS, Mar. 5). William Meek & Sons built the flouring mill there in 1844, which served until 1878.

Later, many Saints in the **Spring Exodus** passed through Bonaparte. Lucius Scovil said that on May 29 his family reached the "Bonaparte Ferry" but had a long wait because there were "about 40 teams awaiting to get over" (JLNS).

Many men from the Brigham Young company and in later companies found work in Bonaparte and nearby communities. "Wherever the companies stopped," **Helen Mar Kimball Whitney** said regarding that segment of the journey, "our men were able to find employment" (AHMW,h 341–42). Local traditions say that some Mormons remained in this area and that a few are buried 2.5 miles east of Bonaparte (ENS June 1972: 40). One workman was **William Smith** (not the brother of Joseph Smith), a friend of Eliza R. Snow, whom she said had "taken a job near Bonaparte" by July 1846 (JERS July 10). **Curtis E. Bolton** worked in 1846 at a pottery shop near Bonaparte and then chinked and daubed a cabin 45 miles northeast of there (JCEB).

Several Saints died at Bonaparte and were buried near there at sites not yet identified. **Nathaniel Ashby** worked a few days at the gristmill, became ill, died, and was buried in Bonaparte in a rough coffin consisting of "a few boards nailed together." His widow, Susan Hammond Ashby, and her 11 children continued west in their two wagons, she driving one and her 17-year-old son the other (LSHA). John Lowry and his family left Nauvoo in August 1846.

While at Bonaparte their four-year-old daughter **Elizabeth Lowry** died and was buried there (LJL). The Curtis Edwin Bolton family buried newborn **Caroline Bolton** "in [a] grave yard on [a] hill back from Bonaparte" (JCEB).

Riverboats once steamed up the Des Moines River from Keokuk to Bonaparte and beyond. Today the village is part of a federally designated **National Historic District,** containing, among other historic buildings, the **Poe Building** (circa 1850) on the southwest corner of Main and Second Streets (one block north of the bridge); the **Farmers and Traders Bank** (1853), and the **Hopkins Building** (1853).

The **Auntie Green Museum,** one block north of the bridge and one block east on Second Street, was built in 1844 by John and Mary Green as a residence and was the first brick home built in Bonaparte. It was there when Latter-day Saints passed through the town in 1846. In 1855 it was converted into a hotel. Its lower rooms now serve as a public library; the second story is a museum.

A **restored woolen mill** is .5 block west of the bridge, on County Road J40, and beside the river. The first mill was constructed in 1853. It burned in 1863 and was rebuilt four stories high. A huge waterwheel powered the carding machines. Currently the mill is home to Bonaparte Mills Antiques and Collectibles.

Next to the mill is the **Bonaparte's Retreat Restaurant,** housed in a five-story brick building constructed as a gristmill in 1878 on the site of the **gristmill** that the 1846 Mormons used.

In 1996 Bonaparte was selected as one of five communities in the nation to win the Great American Main Street Award. It has been named one of America's Twelve Distinctive Destinations by the National Trust for Historic Preservation.

■ *BENTONSPORT

Bentonsport, Van Buren County, is 4 miles northwest and upriver from Bonaparte on County Road J40, midway between Bonaparte and Keosauqua. It dates from 1836. Originally called the "Ross Settlement," Bentonsport was named for Senator Thomas Hart Benton. Vernon, originally called South Bentonsport, is across the river from it. Ferries linked the towns. By 1845 there were two gristmills and a sawmill in operation. Several 1846 Mormon pioneers found temporary work here, helping to build several structures on both sides of the river and doing other labor.

Mormon workmen in 1846 built the Georgian-style **Mason House Inn,** on the main street running along the river's north side, to serve steamboat travelers going from St. Louis to Des Moines. It is now a bed-and-breakfast inn.

Ruins of a substantial white stone building one block north of the river on County Road J40 are known locally as the **Mormon House.** Uncorroborated local tradition says the two-story house was built by Mormon artisans in 1846 and used as a dormitory for the workmen while they built many brick buildings in the area. Later, the building was used as a wagon factory and a residence.

Portions of Bentonsport were designated a **National Historic District** in 1972. In it are the **Hancock House** (1830s), several 1840s buildings, and the **Greef General Store** (1853).

A one-lane **iron bridge,** built in 1882 and closed in 1985, reopened in 1994 for pedestrians. It is the oldest truss bridge spanning the Des Moines River.

■ **KEOSAUQUA

Keosauqua, Van Buren County's county seat, is on the north side of the Des Moines River on State 1. It is 4 miles north of State 2. Another of the charming "Villages of Van Buren County," boasting a population of about 1,000, it sits on a horseshoe curve of the Des Moines River. *Keosauqua* is a Native American term for "Great Bend."

The **Van Buren County Courthouse** (1843) overlooks Broad Street (State 1), four blocks northeast of Main Street. Its formal address is 902 4th Street. **A must-see for tourists,** it is the second oldest courthouse to remain in continuous use in the United States, and it is the oldest west of the Mississippi to hold this distinction. An excellent example of Greek Revival architecture, it was placed on the National Register of Historic Places in 1977. On the courthouse grounds is a **Mormon Trail interpretive panel,** "Local Concerts Finance Musicians' Trek West."

The 1846 **Camp of Israel** passed south of Keosauqua on Mar. 5, and at the request of the townspeople **Pitt's Nauvoo Band** was paid to perform at the **Van Buren Courthouse** three times, on Mar. 10, 11, and 17. Before playing in the courthouse on Mar. 10, the band dined at the **Des Moines Hotel** and, according to William Clayton,

> after eating we went to the courthouse to prepare for the concert. At seven o'clock the house was crowded and we commenced, playing and singing till about 9:30. The audience seemed highly pleased and gave loud applause. . . . it was the wish of many that we should repeat the concert the following evening. . . . We made nearly $25 clear of all expenses. We started back for the camp soon after ten and arrived about one o'clock. (JWC Mar. 10, 1846, 5)

It was something of a sacrifice for the band to play in Keosauqua because band members were camped at Richardson's Pt., a 10-mile trip each way by wagon.

The **Hotel Manning** is located by the Des Moines River bridge's north end. In 1839 Edwin Manning built at this site a two-story trading post. It burned down and was replaced in 1854. That building burned in the early 1890s, and a hotel was built upon the original foundation. This grand and historic hotel is one of the few surviving examples of classic **Steamboat Gothic** architecture. It is listed on the National Registry of Historic Hotels.

The **Pearson House,** built in 1845–47, is located .5 mile north of the Keosauqua Bridge on the corner of Country Lane Road and Dodge Street. Constructed by Benjamin Franklin Pearson, a skilled stonemason, it once served as a hiding place for slaves on the **Underground Railroad** from Missouri. Owned by the Van Buren County Historical Society, it is open to the public on Sunday afternoons.

On Keosauqua's north end at 1579 North Highway 1 is an LDS Family History Center, housed in an out-of-service LDS chapel. One room is a **Mormon Trail Visitors' Center,** with particular emphasis on Lee, Van Buren, and Davis counties. Its displays include maps, photographs, and art work. The building is open on selected days during the week.

■ Selma

Selma is in the northwest corner of Van Buren County on State 16. A **log cabin park** by the highway features a cabin built in 1846, the year of the Mormon exodus from Nauvoo. In 1969 the cabin was moved there from its original site a few miles east of town and restored.

■ Iowaville Cemetery • Selma

The **Iowaville Cemetery** is 8 miles north of the center of Keosauqua on State 1 and then 12 miles west on State 16. It occupies a hillside on the north side of State 16 overlooking the Des Moines River. It is 15 miles southeast of **Ottumwa** between **Selma** and **Eldon,** exactly .7 mile northwest of **Selma.**

The town of **Iowaville** has disappeared, but its location is along the river about 1 mile northwest of the cemetery. Between 1846 and 1851 several **Nauvoo refugees** lived in or passed through Iowaville. About a dozen died and were buried in this cemetery, and two recent markers honor them. One marks the graves of **Asahel and Elizabeth Smith,** uncle and aunt of Joseph Smith Jr. The other is the **Albert Miner/Mormons at Iowaville Memorial,** erected in 1994, which tells about Albert Miner, Mormons at Iowaville, and Iowaville itself (BiE I:182; CN Sept. 3, 1994; NJ 7 [Spring 1995]: 38–43).

● Eldon

Eldon, 21 miles southeast of **Ottumwa,** is 2 miles west of the Iowaville Cemetery on State 16. In Eldon is the **American Gothic House** (1881), which noted Iowa artist **Grant Wood** painted in the background of his well-known and often parodied "American Gothic" portrait of a dour farm couple holding a pitchfork (1930). Directional signs for finding the house are well posted.

■ Ely Ford/Mormon Crossing/Lacey-Keosauqua State Park

The **Lacey-Keosauqua State Park** entrance is .5 mile southeast of Keosauqua on State 1. One of Iowa's largest state parks and popular for camping and fishing, it covers 1,653 hilly acres of flowers and shrub-filled woods. It is situated along the great 2-mile-long horseshoe bend of the Des Moines River.

Ely Ford/Mormon Crossing marker, on the north side of the park, marks a site that tradition says was used by some Mormons who followed Brigham Young's group. Probably these were Saints in the Spring Exodus rather than in Young's earlier company.

■ Dog Town/Mt. Sterling

Mt. Sterling is 7 miles south of Keosauqua, and 3.5 miles south of State 2 on County Road W20, almost on the Iowa-Missouri border. In the mid-1800s the tiny community was affectionately known as "Dog Town." The first settlers built a sawmill and corn cracker. They had dogs. Patrons of the mill often brought their dogs. Tradition says that one day at the height of a dog rumpus, a stranger asked the name of the place. Told it had no name, he stated, "I think it is a dog town" (VBCG, 36).

In 1853, the **John Forsgren company** (see **Mormon Emigration Routes in 1853**) passed through "Dog's Town" on June 3 (JEFJ June 3, 1853).

■ *INDIAN CREEK CAMP • BRIGHAM YOUNG • MAR. 5–6 • 12 MILES • KEOSAUQUA

Indian Creek Camp site is 4 miles south and .5 mile east of **Keosauqua.** It is .5 mile west of where southbound State 1 meets east-west State 2. The campsite was on the north side of the creek (MHBY Mar. 5–6; GLO 1836).

On Mar. 5 the pioneers moved 2 miles from Reed's Creek, crossed the Des Moines River at Bonaparte, and then moved 3 muddy miles uphill and 7 miles west across the prairie. Snow, cold weather, and rainstorms made muddy roads almost impassable through this part of Iowa, and the result was discomfort and extremely slow movement of the Camp of Israel (HC 7:604–65). "The ground was so wet," one history says, "that we were under the necessity of sleeping in our wagons" (DJDL Mar. 5). That night Patty Sessions's horse became sick, "but they laid hands on him and he is beter to day" (JPS Mar. 6, 36).

Orson Spencer's wife, **Catherine C. Spencer, died** at Indian Creek on Mar. 12 at age 35, leaving six children under age 14

Orson Spencer reading to his wife, Catherine, at their Indian Creek Camp in Iowa. (Courtesy of Vernon Murdock, artist, 1973)

(MHBY Mar. 12). Catherine had written to her parents for financial assistance, which they refused to give unless she denied Mormonism. During her illness she asked her husband to read her parents' letter and then Ruth 1:16–17 ("whither thou goest, I will go") from the Bible. A night or two before she died, she told Orson that "a heavenly messenger has appeared to me tonight, and told me that I have done and suffered enough, and that he had now come to convey me to a mansion of gold." She died in the home of a Mr. Barnes, a nearby resident. Her remains were taken back to Nauvoo, where she was buried next to a daughter who had died six months before. One of her children, **Aurelia Spencer Rogers,** became the LDS Church's first general Primary president (MoP 73–74).

At Indian Creek a horse in William Hall's team became sick with bloating and colic. Elder Hall and Lluellen Mantle gave the horse a priesthood blessing through the laying on of hands on Mar. 14. The horse recovered, pulled for 2 miles, and then became violently ill. Six elders administered to the horse again, causing it to roll over, spring to its feet, squeal, vomit, and purge. The next day it resumed its hauling work (MHBY Mar. 14).

■ Dr. John D. Elbert Farm • Mar. 6 • Keosauqua

The site of **Dr. John D. Elbert's farm** is 4.5 miles west of the center of Keosauqua, 6 miles northwest of the Indian Creek Camp and 5 miles east of the Richardson's Pt. Camp. It is in the northeast quarter of Section 6 of Des Moines Township (T68N R10W) (RA).

On Mar. 6, Dr. Elbert invited the Saints to camp on his property 7 miles ahead where he had designated a quarter section of land for their encampment and where he wanted their help to clear land and cut rails. But good weather the next day caused Brigham Young to move some companies farther than Elbert's site (MHBY Mar. 6, 7). The band and some of the guard camped at Dr. Elbert's that night, where the band split about 130 rails for him in return for corn (JWC Mar. 7, 4).

■ **Richardson's Pt. Camp • Brigham Young • Mar. 7–18 • 11 miles • Lebanon

The **Richardson's Pt. Camp site,** based on close examination of diaries and maps (but challenged by some local lore as being 2 miles too far east) is 3 miles west of **Lebanon** on County Road J40, where that road makes a distinct turn northwest around a hilly, wooded point. The camp was in the southwest corner of Section 33 and in the southeast corner of Section 32, Chequest Township (T69N R11W) (DHS; MHBY; JOP; DJDL; JHKW; GLO 1840).

On Mar. 7 Brigham Young's wagon company moved from Indian Creek Camp 6 miles to Dr. Elbert's campground but decided not to camp there and moved another 5 miles to Richardson's Pt. The two men for whom the point was named, Shadrach and Solomon Richardson, owned about 300 acres, mostly in the southwest quarter of Section 33, Chequest Township (T69N R11W) (RA).

Diarists said this camp was 55 miles from Nauvoo (e.g. DHS Mar. 7, 135) (our calculations show 52). This became a **long stopover and reorganizing camp,** where the Camp of Israel halted for 11 days due to bad weather and muddy roads. While camped here, the **Nauvoo Band** traveled back 10 miles to **Keosauqua** to give concerts on three different days.

On Mar. 8 Heber C. Kimball's wife, **Sarah Ann Whitney Kimball,** gave birth to a son named David in **Bishop Newel K. Whitney's camp** 2 or 3 miles from Richardson's Pt. at a place the Kimballs named "Valley of David"[6] (JHKW). This encampment was 2 or 3 miles beyond Dr. Elbert's campground and probably 1 mile northwest of present-day Lebanon on a branch of Chequest Creek (MHBY).

Buried cannonballs. On Mar. 14 at Richardson's Pt. the artillery men buried about 2,400 pounds of ball and shot to lighten their wagons. Descriptions of the burial site were recorded (DJDL Mar. 9 and 14). What became of the ammunition is not known. Many searches since then have found nothing (RA).

Two Mormons died at Richardson's Pt.: **James M. Tanner,** the 15-month-old son of Sidney Tanner, on Mar. 17 and **Edwin S. Little,** a 30-year-old nephew of Brigham Young, on Mar. 18 (MHBY). Their **grave sites** are 1 mile northwest of Richardson's Pt. (labeled Oak Pt. on present-day maps) in Section 32, Chequest Township (T69N R11W), on the divide between the Fox and

---

6. Pioneers believed the birth at Valley of David took place in Jackson Township, Van Buren County, Missouri (JHKW). At that time Van Buren County extended 6 miles farther west than it does today, so they had the county part right. But according to consensus by diarists, the "Valley of David" was only 2 to 3 miles east of the Richardson's Pt. camps, which puts it 1 mile beyond present-day Jackson Township, or close enough for the Saints to think they were there.

Chequest Rivers. The graves are about 1,320 feet northeast of County Road J40. John D. Lee recorded a precise description of their location (DJDL Mar. 18). Stone markers there were erected in recent times. **The site may be seen with the landowners' permission** (HSM 25; RA).

Feed for animals was a problem for the Camp of Israel. **Hosea Stout** said, "We found feed scarce but I sold a bed stead which I had along for eight bushels of corn which made a feed for the guard tonight" (DHS Mar. 7).

It rained most of Mar. 10. "While making down the beds a quail came fluttering in the top of the tent and lit down in the tent door & I picked it up with out any trouble," **Hosea Stout** recorded. "I had it cooked and it proved a blessing" (DHS Mar. 10, 1846).

Leaders, believing that the danger of being detained by federal troops or attacked by Mormon-haters had passed, released about 30 of the 180-man guard to go back to Nauvoo for their families. They left their wagons but were authorized to receive wagons of equal value from Nauvoo leaders (MHBY Mar. 17).

■ SPENCER GRAVES • TROY

Local tradition says that a **Spencer Cemetery** is located at a point 3 miles north of County Road J40 and about .2 miles east of the Van Buren/Davis county line, on the north bank of Chequest Creek, in the southwest quarter of Section 7 of Chequest Township (T69N R11W). Apparently Samuel Spencer Jr., his wife Elizabeth, and several children are buried there (RA).

■ STRINGTOWN • TROY

The location of **Stringtown** is at a point 1.25 miles south of **Troy** and 3.5 miles north of State 2. The location is near the north side of the Fox River in the southwest quarter of Section 36 of Union Township (T69N R12W).

Stringtown was the first town established in Davis County. First known as **Ox,** it had a post office by 1842. In 1848 it became **Dover,** later **Harpersville,** and then Stringtown from 1853 to 1867 (ATI 35). It had disappeared by 1882 (MPTDC).

On Mar. 15, while the Camp of Israel was encamped at Richardson's Pt., **Horace K. Whitney** and **William Kimball,** "accompanied by several others went to a small place called Stringtown, took dinner and returned home about sunset" (JHKW). Davis

County history materials mention that LDS emigrants camped near or passed through Stringtown, which meant that some took a route west from Richardson's Pt. that dipped slightly south to follow more closely the north side of the Fox River.

James Farrer was a Mormon who worked in Stringtown after leaving Nauvoo during the summer of 1846 (LRF,c). Among LDS companies that outfitted at **Keokuk** in 1853, the **Forsgren company** "passed through String Town" (JJFC), and the **Claudius V. Spencer company** "camped near Stringtown" (JHTK, 193).

The **Stringtown Stagecoach House** is reached by going south from Troy on Wheat Street to 227th St. and then east on 227th about 200 feet. The location is about .25 mile from the Fox River. It is a New England double salt box style house built by 1842. It was a stagecoach stop in the early days. A unique floor plan provided solid-wall separation for lodging male and female passengers. Now dilapidated and needing restoration, it is a historic site listed in the Davis County tourist literature (CEBDC). Very likely this is where Horace K. Whitney and the others dined.

■ EVANS' CAMP • BRIGHAM YOUNG • MAR. 19 • 11 MILES • BLOOMFIELD

The **Evans Camp** is 5 miles east of **Bloomfield** and is .2 mile south of the center of Section 23 in Perry Township (T69N R13W), 1 mile northeast of the Fox River. The pioneers camped on the south side of Chequest Creek on land belonging to a widow named Evans (MHBY; GLO 1843; AHAI 34).[7]

■ BLOOMFIELD

Bloomfield, seat of Davis County, is .75 mile north of State 2 on State 63. **Wilford Woodruff,** in the Spring Exodus, paid $50 for two yoke of cattle in Bloomfield on June 3, 1846 (JWW).

The **Davis County Historical Museum** complex is in Bloomfield two blocks east of U.S. 63 on County Road J40. The museum includes a **Mormon log cabin,** which local tradition says is built of logs hand-hewn by passing Mormons in 1846; a **Mormon Trail interpretive panel,** "Mormon Craftsmen Leave Legacies along the

---

7. W. A. Evans and J. H. Evans are listed as property owners in the middle of Section 23, Perry Township in the Davis County map in *A. T. Andreas' Illustrated Historical Atlas of the State of Iowa 1875* (Chicago: Andreas Atlas Co., 1875). By diary mileage calculations, the Evans Camp must be placed 10.5 to 13 miles from Richardson's Pt. and 10 miles back from the pioneers' upcoming crossing of the Fox River.

Trail"; and the brick Italianate-style **Dr. William Findley house,** built in 1844 and standing when the Saints passed that way in 1846 (MPTDC).

■ **DRAKESVILLE

Drakesville, Davis County, is 3.5 miles north of the center of Bloomfield on U.S. 63 and then 4.5 miles west on State 273.

The pioneers passed through where Drakesville now is and then turned south about .75 mile west. Later, Saints in the Spring Exodus decided against the south-turning route and instead went west on better roads. From a point .75 mile west of Drakesville, the **variant route** headed almost due west towards **Garden Grove** and **Mt. Pisgah.**

The **Drakesville Town Park** is located on Madison Street, two blocks north of Main Street. The park contains a **log cabin** built by the Mormons (according to local tradition) in 1846. In Drakesville a grassy island divides Main Street into two lanes. At the island's east end is a **Mormon Trail interpretive panel,** "A New Route," which honors the **variant Mormon Trail routes** that the Saints in the Spring Exodus took just west of present-day Drakesville. A wooden "Mormon Trail" sign marks the grassy island's west end.

In the Drakesville area live **Amish residents** who drive horse-drawn buggies on the roads. Drivers of automobiles need to be cautious. **Although Amish people do not believe in being photographed, most do not mind if pictures are taken of their animals and buggies. Always request permission first.**

■ FOX RIVER CAMP • BRIGHAM YOUNG • MAR. 20 • 13 MILES • DRAKESVILLE

Fox River Camp is 4 miles southwest of the center of Drakesville and 1.75 miles northwest of the point where U.S. 63 comes north and joins State 2. The campsite is in the northeast quarter of Section 25, Fox River Township (T69N R15W) (GLO 1843).

On Mar. 20, the Mormon pioneers traveled west 3 miles from Evans' Camp to Orson Pratt's camp and then continued 5 miles west and then south 2 miles to the **Fox River.** They struggled through and around a huge mudhole to reach the river and crossed the river on a bridge. Two miles from the bridge they came "on to the **Old Mormon Trail"** (1838) and followed it 1 mile. They turned off to the right and camped (MHBY).

■ *THE "OLD MORMON TRAIL" • DRAKESVILLE

The **Old Mormon Trail** was blazed in late 1838 by Mormons fleeing north out of Missouri into Iowa and then east toward what became Nauvoo. This flight came as a result of the Battle of Crooked River in Ray County, Missouri (HC 3:170–71; DHS Mar. 20, 27, 31, 1846; GLO 1838).[8] Lorenzo Dow Young and Hosea Stout, members of the 1846 Camp of Israel, were two of those who had fled Missouri in 1838. Stout recorded his reactions at seeing the road again (March 20):

> Struck the old Mormon trail. This was the trail which we made when I in company with 27 others fled from Far West, Mo., into the wilderness to escape the vengeance of the mob under executive authority of Gov. Boggs in 1838 when the Saints were expelled from that state. It was with peculiar feeling that I saw this old trail. It was yet to be saw, although a public road now occupied the same ground but was not much traveled. (DHS 140; punctuation standardized)

The 1846 pioneers closely followed the Old Mormon Trail for about 30 miles. On Mar. 31 Stout was on the east side of the **Chariton River** (see **Chariton River Camp and Ford** below) and "found the place where I had encamped when fleeing from Missouri It was but a short distance from the road" (DHS 146).

■ WEST GROVE

West Grove is located on State 2. It is 3 miles west of the junction of State 2 and U.S. 63. West Grove is situated on a prairie ridge that the Old Mormon Trail followed and which the 1846 pioneers passed along.

State 2 here continues to be the **official Mormon Trail Highway,** marked with Mormon Pioneer National Historic Trail signs.

■ COFFMAN'S SETTLEMENT CAMP • BRIGHAM YOUNG • MAR. 21 • 11 MILES • MOULTON

The **Coffman's Settlement Camp site** is at a point 1.5 miles

---

8. Others had fled following the fight at Gallatin a few months earlier. On Aug. 6. 1845, Phineas Young, one of those who had blazed the Old Mormon Road, followed it in reverse. His diary noted a route similar to that which the 1846 pioneers chose (LCS 20–25).

west-southwest of the center of **Moulton,** in Appanoose County. It is in the east half of Section 21, Washington Township (T68N R16W). In 1850 Jacob Coffman owned land in the southeast quarter of the southeast quarter Section 21, on a tributary of the Chariton River, 3 miles away from the Chariton. It is 4.75 miles south of State 2, 1.25 miles west of State 202, then .75 mile south of County Road J51 (GLO 1843; MTAAC 16–17).

The **Mormon Trail** passed through present-day Moulton heading west.[9] The campsite was by a long bluff "at a place called Coffman's settlement where not a house, barn, hut or wigwam or anything else was to be seen, except hills, grass, bushes and trees" (MHBY).

■ ****Chariton River Camp and Ford • Brigham Young • Mar. 22–31 • 5 miles • Exline**

The **Chariton River Camp site** is 5.5 miles southwest of the center of Moulton and 4 miles east of **Exline.** It is 6.5 miles south of State 2 and 1 mile south-southeast of where **Sedan** (now a couple of grain bins) is on current maps. It is barely west of the center of Section 36, Caldwell Township (T68N R17W), which puts it .5 mile southwest of the old Chariton riverbed at the point where Brigham Young and the Saints forded the river, approximately 100 travel miles from Nauvoo (JWR; MHBY; JERS; DHS; GLO 1843; MTAAC 18–19).

Chariton River, IA.

At the campsite, on the ridge overlooking the river, is a **Mormon Trail interpretive panel,** "We Had Considerable Difficulty Crossing That Stream," which tells about the crossing and the camp.

Hampered by rain and mud, the pioneers

---

9. For the Mormon Trail campsites in Appanoose County, an invaluable guide is Willis M. Heusinkveld, ed., *Mormon Trails across Appanoose County, Iowa* (Centerville, Iowa: Appanoose County Mormon Trails Association, 1995). It is available from the Appanoose County Historical Society, 100 W. Maple, Centerville, IA 52544.

struggled to make the **Chariton River crossing.** They crossed just east of the center of the section line between Section 25 and Section 36, Caldwell Township (T68N R17W) (MTAAC 17–19). The river was four rods wide and two feet deep but rising due to the rains. Steep, slippery banks on both sides forced men to lower wagons using ropes attached to the rear wheels.

> Edward P. Duzette and family arrived at Chariton river, this afternoon; in letting his wagon down the bank, the boat broke away, the wagon plunged into the river and upset, but he succeeded in saving most of his goods, although they were thoroughly wet, except his cooking utensils which were left in the river. (MHBY, Mar. 30)

The large wagon caravan needed all day to make the difficult crossing of the Chariton. While Henry B. Jacobs's wagon was waiting, his wife **Zina D. Huntington Jacobs** gave birth to a son on Mar. 22. Appropriately, they named him **Henry Chariton Jacobs.** Zina became the third **general president** of the LDS women's **Relief Society,** succeeding **Eliza R. Snow** in 1887 (DHS Mar. 22, 1846, 141; BiE 1:697).

After crossing the Chariton, the Saints established the **Chariton River Camp,** .5 mile south of the river on a bluff. The soil was clay, and **Eliza R. Snow** reported on Mar. 25 that "the mud of our street and about our fires, in our tents, etc. is indescribable" (JERS). **Hosea Stout** said, "We filled the ridge with our tents & waggons for perhaps half a mile" (DHS, Mar. 22, 1846).

This camp became the **Camp of Israel headquarters** between Mar. 22 and Apr. 1, a long halt necessitated by bad weather. On Mar. 26 the leadership council ordered **James W. Cummings** to go with **John Lowe Butler** to the **James Emmett company** at Camp Vermillion far to the northwest (see **James Emmett Expedition**) and instruct them to meet the Camp of Israel at the Missouri River (MHBY).

In the rainy springtime, mud-plagued pioneers traveled through Iowa.

On Mar. 27 Brigham Young held a leadership meeting 7 miles southwest from the Chariton Camp at **Shoal Creek,** midway between his and Bishop Miller's advance camp. The route from the Chariton River Camp to Shoal Creek was through "one mud hole only, which was about six miles in length" (MHBY).

At this **Shoal Creek conference,** Brigham Young engineered a thorough **company reorganization** (DHS Mar. 27, 1846). Of those companies that left Sugar Creek, "the different divisions have been so far separated from each other by storms, bad roads and other circumstances, that it has hitherto been impossible to affect anything like a perfect organization" (MHBY Mar. 27). Leaders created three companies of 100 wagons each with two sub-companies of 50 wagons each, the nine companies each headed by a president and a captain. The organization was as follows:

Superintendent of Entire Camp:	Brigham Young
Clerk for Entire Camp:	William Clayton
Camp Historian:	Willard Richards

Unit	*President*	*Captain*
1st 100	Brigham Young	Ezra T. Benson
1st 50	Brigham Young	Albert P. Rockwood
2nd 50	Heber C. Kimball	Stephen Markham
2nd 100	Parley P. Pratt	John Smith
3rd 50	Parley P. Pratt	John Harvey
4th 50	Peter Haws	Howard Egan
3rd 100	John Taylor	Samuel Bent
5th 50	John Taylor	Charles C. Rich
6th 50	George Miller	Charles Crisman

The Nauvoo Band was attached to the 4th 50, the Haws company (MHBY, DHS).

During the Chariton River encampment, men worked at odd jobs for farmers in the area and were paid in money, corn, oats, pork, cloth, and a cow (JERS Mar. 31).

■ ****Shoal Creek Camp • Brigham Young • Apr. 1–2 • 6.5 miles • Cincinnati**

The **Shoal Creek Camp site** is at a point 2.2 miles east of the center of Cincinnati, 7.5 miles south of State 2 in **Centerville,**

1 mile southeast of State 5, in the southwest quarter of Section 1, Pleasant Township (T68N R18W). It is on a rise in the prairie 1 mile west of where the Mormon Trail crossed Shoal Creek (GLO 1843; MTAAC 25–26).

On Apr. 1 Brigham Young's 50 and the Nauvoo Band "went to Shoal Creek at the place we held the council on the 27th" and camped (DHS, 147). Earlier, **Capt. Elisha Averett's advance company** had built a 60-foot bridge there over Shoal Creek. From the Shoal Creek encampment, leaders sent wagons into Missouri for supplies, which brought back 65 bushels of corn and 400 pounds of flour from the Chariton Mill, 10 miles away (MHBY Mar. 28).

In a council meeting on Apr. 2, leaders announced a decision made at least as early as Mar. 27, which was that the Camp of Israel should head for a Missouri River crossing at **Banks Ferry** in Missouri, upriver from St. Joseph. This meant they would travel west-southwest, passing through the northern edge of Missouri, rather than west-northwest toward the Council Bluffs region, as they later decided to do (DHS Apr. 2; MoM 36–37).

From the Shoal Creek Camp, the **Mormon Trail** passed through where **Cincinnati** now is and headed directly west for several miles. Cincinnati is on State 5, 7.5 miles south-southwest of Centerville, 3 miles north of the present-day **Missouri border.**

■ HEBER C. KIMBALL'S CAMP • APR. 2 • CINCINNATI

Heber C. Kimball's Camp site on Apr. 2 is .2 mile south of County Road J54, .9 mile northwest of State 5, 1.8 miles west of the center of Cincinnati, and on the north side of a tributary of Little Shoal Creek in the northwest quarter of Section 5 (T67N R18W) (GLO 1843 and 1852).

This camp, 5 miles beyond Brigham Young's Shoal Creek Camp, was in a point of timber on a "prong" of Shoal Creek, 1.5 miles east of the fork of the "**Old Mormon Trail.**" To reach Kimball's camp the next morning, Brigham Young's company moved along a very crooked ridge road over ground so soft that "the heavy wagons cut in deep & was uncommonly hard on the teams" (DHS Apr. 3).

■ *"OLD MORMON TRAIL" FORK • CINCINNATI

Three miles west of the center of Cincinnati on County Road J54 and 7.5 miles south of State 2 is a "Parting of the Ways." Here the **Old Mormon Trail** bent south into Missouri, while the "New Mormon Trail" of the 1846 pioneers headed basically west toward Locust Creek.

Disputed Territory

After the Shoal Creek Camp, the pioneers' west-southwest route took them out of Appanoose County, the last civil jurisdiction in Iowa Territory. They then traveled within 2 miles of today's Missouri state line. This was **disputed territory** claimed by both Iowa and Missouri. Some Camp of Israel diarists recorded that they had now entered Missouri, others that they had entered a disputed zone claimed by both Missouri and Iowa. "Crossed the Missouri State line this afternoon just before coming to this place," Horace K. Whitney wrote (JHKW Apr. 2).

At the time there were two disputed border zones: a wide one containing 10 miles of present-day southern Iowa, and a narrow one involving only 1–3 miles on the Iowa side and 2 or 3 miles on the Missouri side (HMOMc 2:111–13). The 10-mile zone was not of concern—the Saints had been in that zone all the way across southern Iowa except when north of it between Richardson's Pt. and present-day West Grove. But the disputed 3-mile zone worried them. When they left Shoal Creek Camp they entered lands that government surveyors had not surveyed because of the border dispute.

Once inside this border zone, the Saints felt vulnerable to Missouri county officials or residents, and, instead of going across the northern edge of Missouri to Bank's Ferry, they **decided to turn northwest** toward Council Bluffs.

■ ****HICKORY GROVE CAMP • BRIGHAM YOUNG • APR. 3–5 • 14 MILES • SEYMOUR**

Hickory Grove Camp site is 1.6 miles north of the present-day Iowa-Missouri border and is the closest of all the Iowa camps to the border (see Locust Creek, IA, map) (MHBY; GLO 1846, 1852). It is 9.7 miles south of State 2 and 5.2 miles south of the center of **Seymour.** It is reached from the center of Seymour by taking County Road S60 south for 5.2 miles, at which point the site is .4 mile to the west, near a small tributary of East Locust Creek. The campsite is 1 mile east of the East Locust Creek, .75 miles west-northwest of the old Genoa townsite, and in the northeast quarter of Section 14, Monroe Township (T67N R20W).

From Shoal Creek Camp the 1846 pioneers traveled west-southwest 14 miles to a grove of hickory trees and a small stream. They named their camp, which some said was in Missouri and others in the disputed zone, **Hickory Grove. James Dunn** recorded that the pioneers "pitched our tents among the timber, this is in Putnam County, state of Missouri" (JJD Apr. 3, 1846). **Eliza R. Snow** described their camp as "our very beautiful woodland dell" (JERS). Brigham Young's company camped there three nights, Apr. 3–5 (DHS Apr. 3, 1846; MHBY).

On Sunday, Apr. 5, the various companies in and around Hickory Grove held their first Sabbath meeting in which the **sacrament** was administered to the Saints since leaving Nauvoo. Meanwhile, Capt. Averett's company had moved ahead and built two bridges over Locust Creek branches, 70 and 20 feet long (MHBY Apr. 1).

On Apr. 12 company leaders, most of them camped farther ahead by then, gathered at Hickory Grove. Instead of crossing northern Missouri to Banks Ferry, they **decided to turn northwest** toward Council Bluffs.

Apparently they changed course for two reasons: (1) They learned that Sauk and Fox Indians had vacated the "New Purchase" lands west of the Appanoose County line in accordance with the Red Rock Treaty of 1842 that required them to vacate by October 1845.[10] It was now legal and safe for whites to move into and across that vast prairie region of south-central Iowa (IPLD); (2) They feared trouble from Missourians along the Banks Ferry route. Brigham Young remarked: "Who ever thought that the Lord would lead us through Iowa & into Missouri & then back into Ioway again" (DHS May 3). They would "take a North course," Hosea Stout wrote, "until we came into Iowa again" (DHS Apr. 10).

Council members voted to move the Saints to the "New Purchase" on the Upper Weldon Fork of the Grand River. There

10. The U.S. government purchased a large portion of central Iowa from the Sauk and Fox Indians on Oct. 11, 1842—$1,050,000 for seven million acres lying on both sides of the Des Moines River. In this "Red Rock Treaty," the Indians agreed to move to Kansas by 1845. The purchase was divided into two parts by a line running north and south. The west boundary of Appanoose County was that temporary Indian boundary line. By treaty, lands east of the line were to be vacated by May 1, 1843, lands west of the line by Oct. 11, 1845. The eastern part opened to settlement on May 1, 1843 (IPLD).

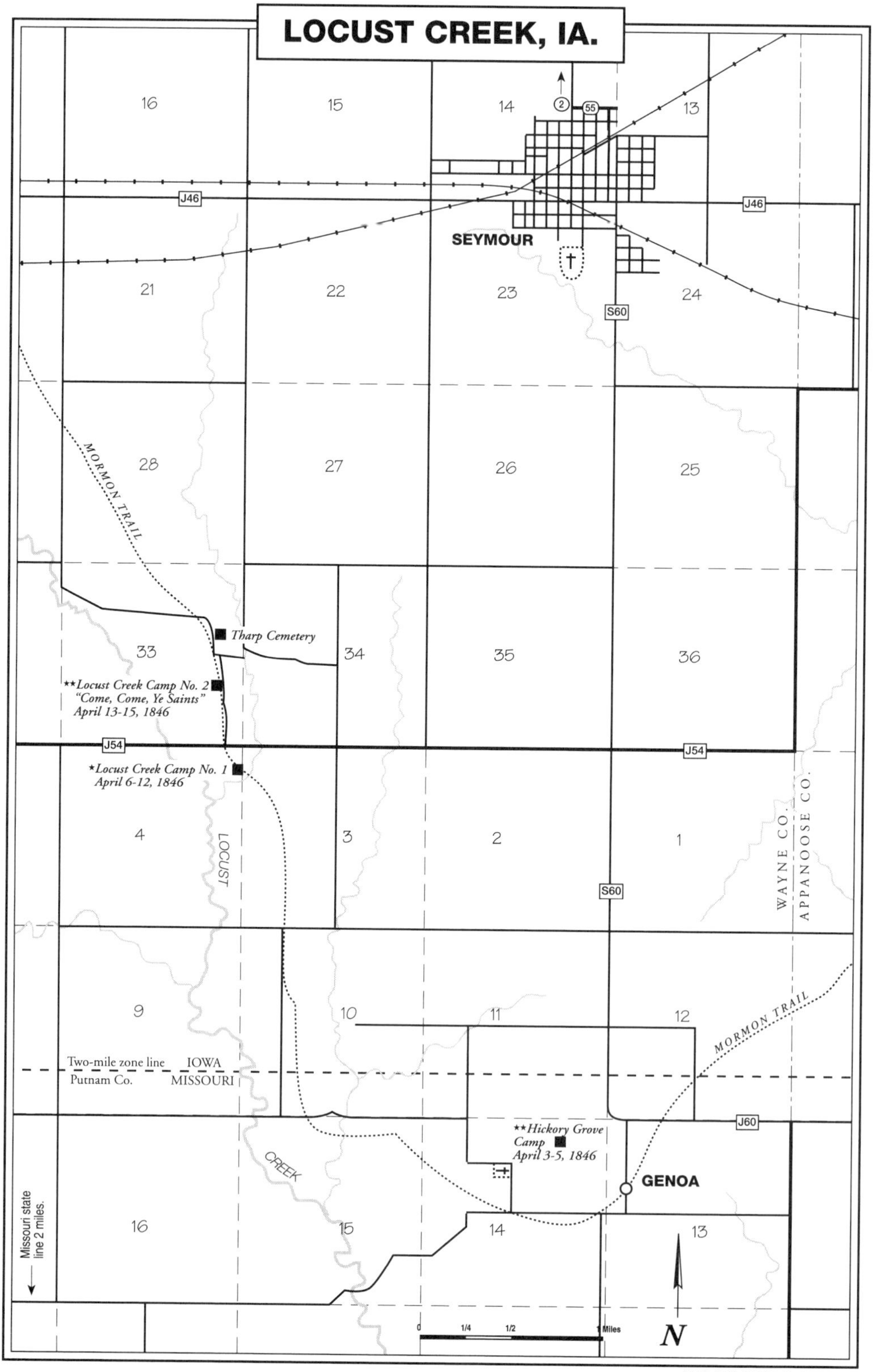

MAP BY LAMAR C. BERRETT

they would fence a field of 2 square miles, build 20 log cabins, plant, and plow. From there, men would return toward Nauvoo to identify a new and better road for the others soon to come that avoided creeks, bad roads, and settlements. They decided to move the main body of Saints only as far as the Missouri River that season and to winter there before continuing on the next spring (1847), except for an advance company of 100 wagons to be sent that summer to "cross the mountains" (MHBY Apr. 12).

■ *Locust Creek Camp No. 1 • Brigham Young • Apr. 6–12 • 3 miles • Seymour

The **Locust Creek Camp No. 1,** just south of **Seymour,** is 2.5 miles northwest of **Hickory Grove Camp,** in the northeast corner of Section 4, Monroe Township (T67N R20W), on the west bank of the Middle Fork of Locust Creek. It is 7.75 miles south of State 2, 3.6 miles south-southwest of the center of Seymour, .1 mile south of County Road J54, and 2 miles west of County Road S60 (see aerial photo and Locust Creek, IA, map; GLO 1846, 1852).

On Apr. 6 Brigham Young traveled about 2 miles from the Hickory Grove Camp to East Locust Creek and then another mile to Middle Locust Creek over a wet, muddy, rough road (MHBY). Hosea Stout wrote, "The road was the worst that I had yet witnessed up hill & down through sloughs on spouty oak ridges and deep marshes raining hard the creek rising. The horses would sometimes sink to their bellies on the ridges teams stall going down hill." They double-teamed some wagons and left others to be retrieved later. Brigham Young camped on the west side of the bridge over Middle Locust Creek on a level bottomland. Here the pioneers found good browse and pasture for their horses and cattle and some dense clusters of trees (DHS Apr. 6; MHBY). Their arrival at the campsites is documented by Hosea Stout:

> At length however we arived at Locus Creek 3 miles & found it a narrow deep stream and muddy banks There was a good bridge built by the pioneers. I camped just across it on a fine ridge & a good place President Young camp with the 50 some two hundred yards below on a level piece of bottom which was before night cut up and tramped into deep mud by the horses & cattle. I had decidedly the best ground. (DHS Apr. 6)

Aerial photo of Locust Creek Camp Nos. 1 and No. 2., near Seymour, IA, 1978. "Come, Come, Ye Saints" was written by William Clayton in Locust Creek Camp No. 2.

On the night of **Brigham Young's arrival** at Middle Locust Creek, a severe storm of rain, thunder, and lightning made a frightening scene. A tree 12 inches in diameter fell across Brother Tanner's wagon (MHBY). Next morning, Apr. 7, water in the creek had risen up to the bridge, and cattle in the pastureland were completely surrounded by water as if on an island. In one camp all the tents but two were blown down (DHS, 150; JWC).

That night **a heroic birth experience** took place. Maria Judd Stewart made a 13-mile wagon ride while "in travail," trying to reach the main camp, and then walked for 2 miles. Rising waters had taken out the bridge, so she crossed the creek on a log in the darkness of night. She was taken to a deserted log cabin. Husband Rufus Putman Stewart rode by horse to the main camp, woke up midwife Patty Sessions about 2 A.M., put her on his horse with him, and they rode through mud and water "some of the way belly deep" to the cabin. They were too late; Maria had given birth to a son (Rufus Putman Stewart Jr.). The father paid midwife Sessions $1.50 for her errand and post-delivery help (MHBY Apr. 7; JPS Apr. 6, 41). Maria was 17 years old. She had married Stewart on May 20, 1845, and they received endowments in Nauvoo on Feb. 3, 1846. During the trek across Iowa she helped care for his two children by a previous wife, who evidently had died (AF, Rufus Putman Stewart).

■ ****LOCUST CREEK CAMP NO. 2 • BRIGHAM YOUNG • APR. 13–15 • .5 MILE • SEYMOUR**

The very important **Locust Creek Camp No. 2** is 3 miles southwest of **Seymour,** 7.25 miles south of State 2, 2.2 miles directly west of County Road S60, 2.25 miles south of County Road J46, .3 miles north of County Road J54, and about .25 mile directly south of the Tharp Cemetery. It was located in the southeast quarter of Section 33, Walnut Township (T68N R20W). In 1997 an old caved-in two-story house was located on or very near the site (see aerial photo and Locust Creek, IA, map; MHBY; JWC; DJDL; GLO 1846, 1852).

The site was only .5 mile north-northwest and up from Locust Creek Camp No. 1. On Apr. 9 John Taylor's No. 5 company of 50 moved to this campsite on the hill on the "edge of the Prairie" (MHBY Apr. 9; JWR Apr. 9). This encampment became the gathering place for all six companies of 50. **Eliza R. Snow** recorded,

"Here I think the whole Camp of Israel once more came together" (JERS Apr. 14).

Writing of "Come, Come, Ye Saints"

Locust Creek Camp No. 2 could be called the "'Come, Come, Ye Saints' Camp" (ENS Sept. 1990, 80). Apr. 15, 1846, was a special day for William Clayton and for the LDS Church because Clayton that day wrote the words for "Come, Come, Ye Saints," a hymn that more than any other expresses the heritage and spirit of the members of The Church of Jesus Christ of Latter-day Saints. The hymn pays tribute to the devotion and faith of the Saints who were wagon train emigrants and the later handcart pioneers. It stirs up feelings of faith in Saints who sing it today. Although Clayton titled the verses "All Is Well," it has been identified in hymnbooks since 1851 as "**Come, Come, Ye Saints.**" Clayton adapted his words to an old English tune that had the refrain "All is well, all is well," words Clayton used to express his feelings (ENS Sept. 1990, 80).

During the 23 years when Mormon pioneers crossed prairie and plains with wagons and handcarts, "Come, Come, Ye Saints" was one of their most popular "marching songs." Of some 70,000 Mormons who used the Mormon Trail, approximately 4,000 to 6,000 died and were buried along the way. The hymn expressed well the general feelings of the hard-pressed pioneers and helped them to "gird up their loins" and "fresh courage take," and even when facing death to "shout praises to our God and King" because "All is well."[11]

For two months Clayton had worried about his young wife Diantha, who stayed behind in Nauvoo because she was pregnant. William wrote to her often, but news from her was sparse. Then, on Apr. 15, Clayton heard good news that made him compose the now-famous verses:

> This morning Ellen [Helen] Kimball came to me and wishes me much joy. She said Diantha has a son. . . . I went over

11. Oscar Winters, son of Rebecca Winters (whose grave is a notable Mormon Trail site in Nebraska), said that one night while on the plains in 1852, members of his camp noticed a sick brother sit down by the fire and weakly sing "Come, Come, Ye Saints." Winters said, "It was a rule of the camp that whenever anybody started this hymn all the camp should join in." No one did this time, hushed by knowing the man was dying. When he finished, hardly anyone had a dry eye. The man died that night (GS 277).

> to [brother] Pond's and he read that she had a fine fat boy on the 30th ult., but she was very sick with the ague and mumps. Truly I feel to rejoice at this intelligence but felt sorry to hear of her sickness. . . .
>
> This morning I composed a new song—"All is well." I feel to thank my heavenly father for my boy and pray that he will spare and preserve his life and that of his mother and so order it so that we may soon meet again. O Lord bless thine handmaid and fill her with thy spirit, make her healthy that her life may be prolonged and that we may live upon the earth and honor the cause of truth. (JWC Apr. 15, 1846, 19–20)

Clayton's concern, gratitude, and faith in God found powerful expression in the words of the song:

> Come, come, ye Saints,
> No toil nor labor fear;
> But with joy wend your way.
> Though hard to you this journey may appear,
> Grace shall be as your day.
> 'Tis better far for us to strive
> Our useless cares from us to drive;
> Do this, and joy your hearts will swell—
> All is well! All is well!
>
> Why should we mourn or think our lot is hard?
> 'Tis not so; all is right.
> Why should we think to earn a great reward
> If we now shun the fight?
> Gird up your loins; fresh courage take.
> Our God will never us forsake;
> And soon we'll have this tale to tell—
> All is well! All is well!
>
> We'll find the place which God for us prepared,
> Far away in the West,
> Where none shall come to hurt or make afraid;
> There the Saints will be blessed.
> We'll make the air with music ring,
> Shout praises to our God and King;
> Above the rest these words we'll tell—
> All is well! All is well!

> And should we die before our journey's through,
> Happy day! All is well!
> We then are free from toil and sorrow, too;
> With the just we shall dwell!
> But if our lives are spared again
> To see the Saints their rest obtain,
> Oh, how we'll make this chorus swell—
> All is well! All is well! (HLDS 30)

That evening Clayton invited a few friends, especially his fellow band members, to his tent for a "social"—a long-distance christening. They named Clayton's new baby boy William Adriel Benoni Clayton (later changed to Moroni). No doubt John D. Lee was referring to Clayton's hymn when he summarized the Saints' worship meeting held four days later:

> At 11 A.M. the Saints asembled [in] a grove a short a distance North of the main Encampment, for public worship The Servises of the mornig commenced by Singing from Elder Pitt & Kay the Hymn or song was composed on the suffering of the camp, while on their Exodus to the West. (DJDL Apr. 19)

When Clayton arrived at Garden Grove a few days later, he sent for Diantha. Six weeks after that, on June 28, when Clayton had reached the Missouri River and returned to **Mt. Pisgah,** he and Diantha were reunited. This prompted Clayton to record in his diary: "Diantha was very glad to see me and burst into tears. My little boy is far beyond all my expectations. He is very fat and well formed and has a noble countenance" (JWC June 28, 51).

■ **THARP CEMETERY/"COME, COME, YE SAINTS" MARKERS • SEYMOUR

The small **Tharp Cemetery** is about 7 miles south of State 2, 3 miles southwest of the center of Seymour, 2.25 miles south of County Road J46, 2.1 miles west of County Road S60, and in the northeast quarter of Section 33, Walnut Township (R20W T68N) (see aerial photo and Locust Creek, IA, map). The cemetery overlooks Locust Creek to the east. Cemetery entrance and fence line are on the east side of the county road.

The cemetery is best reached by driving from the Seymour city park's southwest corner west on Main Street (which becomes

County Road J46) exactly 3 miles to 210th Street, then turning south until 210th elbows east and becomes Fillmore. Follow Fillmore to its end at 220th Street. Turn right on 220th, and a short distance south is Tharp Cemetery on the east side of the road on a slope that goes down from it east to Locust Creek. In front of the cemetery fence is a marker in the shape of a music stand (1990) titled "The Hymn That Went around the World." Beside it is a **Mormon Trail interpretive panel** honoring "A New Son and a New Song."

■ ROLLING PRAIRIE CAMP • BRIGHAM YOUNG • APR. 16 • 6 MILES • SEYMOUR

Experts have difficulty pinpointing the next four campsites the Camp of Israel used after it left Locust Creek Camp No. 2. Diaries of the trek agree about how many miles were between the camps, but the total miles they list between Locust Creek Camp No. 2 and the Garden Grove encampment are too many to fit the mapped route. There are two explanations for the discrepancies: (1) Possibly we have placed the Locust Creek camps in the wrong locations and the actual locations were a few miles farther south in Missouri, which would account for the larger mileage figures;[12] (2) The diarists overestimated the daily mileage because of the mud and difficulties of travel in that stretch.[13]

The **Rolling Prairie Camp** location is estimated by local researchers to be close to the middle of Section 12, Jackson Township (T68N R21W). It is approximately 5.5 miles north-northwest of the location of Locust Creek Camp No. 2. It is 5 miles west of the center of Seymour on County Road J46 and then 1.3 miles north. From that point, the camp was about .5 mile west, on the east bank of Jackson Creek.

While the LDS companies of 50 rolled out of Locust Creek Camp No. 2 on Apr. 16, Brigham Young, Heber C. Kimball, and

---

12. A strong case can be made from diary comments, mileage tallies, and physical terrain for the Locust Creek camps to have been farther downstream, in Missouri. But until more research and on-site work is done that proves convincingly the Missouri possibility, the current locations for the Locust Creek camps in Wayne County, Iowa, best fit the facts now known.

13. Garden Grove Mormon Trail expert Karla Gunzenhauser and Wayne County expert Elbert Pidcock and other local Iowa Mormon Trail Association (IMTA) researchers who have inspected the route on the ground believe the diary mileage counts were overestimated. For our discussion, we rely on the original GLO maps and the IMTA's map and site research to locate the Rolling Prairie, Pleasant Pt., Camp Creek, and Pleasant Grove camps (KG,c).

Willard Richards stayed behind, not wanting to leave until all the Saints were "out of Missouri" (MHBY Apr. 16). Patty Sessions, in the **Brigham Young company,** said they moved 6 miles to the headwaters of Locust Creek, a place **Willard Richards** said they called **Rolling Prairie Encampment** (JPS Apr. 16; JWR Apr. 16). **Eliza R. Snow,** traveling in the **Heber C. Kimball company,** said they moved 6 miles and camped on the prairie, with the 50 wagons arranged double file, creating a public square of sorts between them. By then, rattlesnakes were abundant (JERS). Regarding this camp, **Helen Mar Kimball Whitney** wrote: "I remember that day, and of seeing our men killing snakes in the grass, where our tents were afterwards pitched, and it was enough to give one nervous spasms to see them, and then to think of sleeping in the neighborhood of such dangerous enemies" (AHMW 357).

■ **CORYDON

Corydon is on State 2, 9.5 miles east of U.S. 65. At Corydon's eastern edge, on the north side of State 2, is the outstanding **Prairie Trails Museum of Wayne County.** In front of it is a **Mormon Trail interpretive panel,** "The Trail's Better Half," telling about women's work on the trail. One of the museum's many excellent displays is "**The Hymn That Went around the World**" **exhibit,** which LDS Church Museum experts helped create in 1973. It tells the story of the LDS migration across Iowa and about the writing of "Come, Come, Ye Saints." Most impressive is a replica of a covered wagon pulled by two oxen. With more than 90,000 artifacts of mid-America, it is considered one of the finest small museums in the country.

■ ORSON PRATT'S PARADISE CAMP • APR. 16 • ALLERTON

Local residents estimate that **Paradise Camp** was located in the southwest corner of Section 19, Jackson Township (T68N R21W), near Medicine Creek. The camp is 2.8 miles south and 2.5 miles east of the center of **Allerton.** It is 5 miles south from the east edge of Corydon on County Road S34, .75 mile west on an unnumbered county road, and then .75 mile south on another unnumbered county road.

While the Brigham Young group went to Rolling Prairie Camp, the **Orson Pratt company** and others traveled northwest 4 miles and then west another 4 miles. They moved in total 8 miles and camped near Medicine Creek, naming their campground **Paradise Camp.** The next day Brigham Young's division camped at **Pleasant Pt. Camp,** about 1 mile from Pratt's camp.

■ Pleasant Pt. Camp • Brigham Young • Apr. 17–20 • 7 miles • Allerton

Local residents place the **Pleasant Pt. Camp** site at 1.6 miles south and 1.5 miles east of Allerton's center. It is 5 miles south of the east side of Corydon on County Road S34 and then 1.6 miles west. It is in the southwest quarter of Section 13, Warren Township (T68N R22W). It was about 1.25 miles north-northwest of Orson Pratt's **Paradise Camp.**

From the Rolling Prairie encampment, Brigham Young's 50 headed for Medicine Creek to be near the Orson Pratt encampment. They camped at **Pleasant Pt. Patty Sessions** said the Young company traveled 6 miles, made a bridge over Medicine Creek, then went another 3 miles to camp at Pleasant Pt. **Eliza R. Snow** said they traveled 8 miles and camped on a beautiful timbered ridge, but then the company divided and some, including Brigham Young, crossed the stream and camped on the prairie. From where she camped, Brigham Young's camp was in front, **Bishop George Miller's company** was to her left, and **Amasa Lyman's company** was a day's journey behind. **Orson Pratt** said that the Young and Kimball companies arrived and camped 1 mile north of him (MHBY; JPS; JERS; JOP). Two Boswick children, victims of measles, were buried late that evening (MHBY).

On Apr. 18 priesthood leaders and captains of 100s, 50s, and 10s held a **council meeting** to decide if they should send an advance company to the Rocky Mountains that year. The council authorized Brigham Young to select only those properly outfitted to go. He ordered an inventory to see who was equipped to go, as well as an inventory of "public" property, especially wagons, lent in Nauvoo to Church leaders to help move Church materials west (MHBY 135).

On Sunday, Apr. 19, "the saints assembled in the grove north of the encampment" for a general worship, "a privilege that we had not had since we started, owing to the inclemency of the weather" (MHBY 136). Several of the Twelve and others spoke about sending an expedition to the Rocky Mountains (MHBY; DJDL). They decided they must send some advance teams soon and voted that a farm community must be established just ahead on the Grand River (see **Garden Grove).** That evening, the **Kimball company** and the **Taylor company** held a joint religious meeting (JERS). **Daniel Spencer's company** arrived that night, which meant that the entire Camp of Israel was again close together (MHBY; JPS).

On Apr. 20 another council meeting took place. "Beautiful day," **Horace K. Whitney** recorded, "the birds begin to sing, grass to grow and every thing assumes a pleasing aspect" (JHKW).

■ Allerton

Allerton, population about 550, is 2.5 miles west of the center of **Corydon** on State 2 and 3 miles south on State 26.

Because the **Mormon Trail** passed through present-day Allerton, a **Mormon Trail marker** is posted in town on the north side of the railroad tracks.

The **Inn of the Six Toed Cat** is an elegantly restored Victorian mansion that is now a charming hotel and fine restaurant, well worth a visit. **Nine murals** decorate the town. A rare 50-feet-in-diameter, fully restored **Round Barn** (1912) has been preserved and restored for tourists to see 1 mile east of Allerton. The restored one-room **Williams Country School** (1867) and **Spring Branch Presbyterian Church** (1868) are also at the site.

■ Camp Creek Camp • Brigham Young • Apr. 21 • 5 miles • Allerton

The **Camp Creek Camp site**, according to Iowa Mormon Trail Association experts, is 2.5 miles northwest of the center of **Allerton,** on the north side of **Bob White State Park.** It is located in the northeast corner of Section 5, Warren Township (T68N R22W). The site is reached by traveling west 1 mile on Main Street from the center of Allerton (it becomes County Road J46), turning north for .75 mile and then west 2.2 miles. Inside the park are a generic Mormon Trail panel and a trail-crossing sign.

The Saints stopped beside Camp Creek and made a bridge. Dry prairie grass caught fire, forcing them to set backfires around the wagons. The camps moved to the other side of the river for safety (MHBY; JERS; DHS; JPS; JWR).

The **Camp Creek** site was one of the best camp locations the Camp of Israel used. While stopping there, **Louisa (Mrs. Hosea) Stout** gave birth to a baby girl on Apr. 22, assisted by midwife **Patty Sessions.** They named the baby Louisa (DHS; JPS).

■ **Pleasant Grove Camp • Brigham Young • Apr. 22 • 9 miles • Garden Grove**

Mormon Pioneer Trail sign on Iowa State Highway 2. (1975)

Trail experts in Iowa believe the **Pleasant Grove Camp site** is 2.5 miles north of the intersection of State 2 and U.S. 65, then 1.2 miles west on a level spot not reachable by present-day roads. It is in the northeast quarter of Section 8, Clay Township (T69N R23W).

Brigham Young's company moved 9 miles and camped at **Pleasant Grove Camp.** However, their route was not direct, because a rider rode back from this camp to the previous camp "the nearest way," which was only 6 miles (JHKW, Apr. 22).

Some horses in the companies were bitten by rattlesnakes, including one of Brigham Young's. "I cut the snake into pieces and applied them to the wound," he said. "They drew out the poison, leaving the horse uninjured." Hunters brought in two deer, four turkeys, and one woodchuck (MHBY). A prairie fire threatened wagons and people. Eliza R. Snow described it:

> Towards night saw fire coming towards us with furious rapidity—our men immediately set fires to burn a broader space around our encampment, the wind being so strong that it would have swept across almost instantaneously. After getting ourselves secured we gaz'd with admiration & astonishment at the terrific & majestic spread of the devouring element—the flames rising at times to the incredible height of 30 & 40 feet. I had often listen'd to and read descriptions of "Prairies on fire" & thought them too highly painted, but can now say that the reality "beggars all description." (JERS Apr. 22)

Orson Pratt's company did not stay with the other companies but moved 8 miles that day and set up its own camp (JOP).

By this date the Saints felt excited to see the landscape finally turning green. Near the Pleasant Grove encampment, **Eliza R.**

Snow mentioned "a beautiful green prairie lawn" (JERS Apr. 25). **Horace K. Whitney** described "the grass being of very high and thick growth" (JHKW Apr. 23).

■ **MUDDY CREEK CAMP • BRIGHAM YOUNG • APR. 23 • 1 MILE • GARDEN GROVE**

The **Muddy Creek Camp site** is 4.2 miles east-southeast of the center of **Garden Grove.** It is 2 miles north of State 2, 1.8 miles west of U.S. 65, and in the southwest quarter of Section 5, Clay Township (T69N R23W). The site is on the east side of Steele Creek, where Muddy Creek, coming from the east, meets it (MHBY; GLO 1843).

Brigham Young's 50 traveled 1 mile on Apr. 23 and reached **Muddy Branch (Creek)**. "Encamped at Mudy branch on the N bank," **Willard Richards** wrote. "The Pitching of the Tents were followed immediately [by] a thunder storm & Rain bow but the sun set clear." Hunters brought in two bears, four turkeys, and a bee tree. Workmen built a bridge over the creek the next morning (MHBY Apr. 23–24; JWR Apr. 23–24).

■ ****GARDEN GROVE CAMP • BRIGHAM YOUNG • APR. 24–MAY 12 • 5 MILES • GARDEN GROVE**

The **Garden Grove Camp site,** which served both as a camping place and a temporary LDS settlement from 1846 to 1852, is .8 miles west of present-day **Garden Grove,** in Decatur County. It is 4.5 miles north of State 2 on State 204 and then west on County Road J20 through present-day Garden Grove and another .8 miles west. The site can also be reached from I-35 by taking Exit 18 and going east 11 miles on County Road J20. The site is about 9 miles northeast of Leon, the county seat of Decatur County.

The 1846 pioneers' dairies say the **Garden Grove site** was about 145 miles from Nauvoo. By June it had become the midpoint on the 300-mile-long trail connecting Montrose and Council Bluffs.

Leaders established **Garden Grove** and **Mt. Pisgah** to be stopover places for Saints not properly equipped or healthy enough to continue on toward the Rocky Mountains. When developed, Garden Grove provided rude cabins, land to farm, and access to jobs and trade two days south in the Missouri settlements.

The Camp of Israel camped on the east side of Weldon River (or Creek), a tributary of the Grand River, and south of a stream

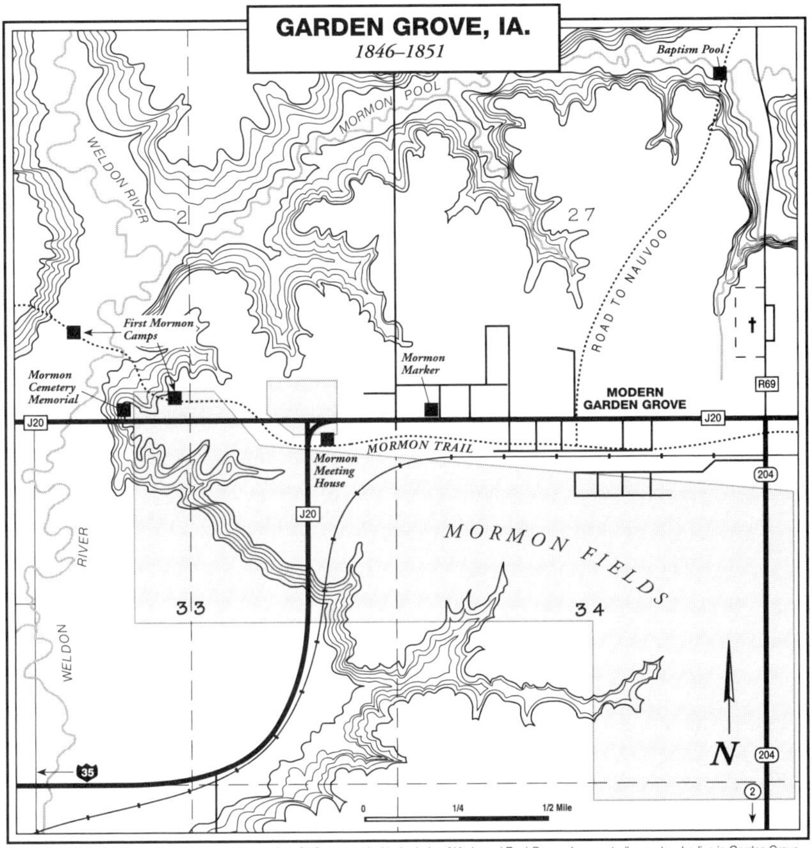

MAP BY LAMAR C. BERRETT, adapted from the 1847 GLO map and with the help of Karla and Paul Gunzenhauser, trail experts who live in Garden Grove

identified on today's maps as Mormon Pool. An original government survey map of 1848 shows the Garden Grove settlement centered in Section 27 and spread out into Sections 28, 29, 33, and 34 of Garden Grove Township (T70N R24W), covering about 2 square miles (see Garden Grove map and aerial photo) (MHBY; GLO 1848).

Brigham Young's 1846 company arrived at the campsite on Apr. 24. "It was a pleasantly situated place" reached by passing into "a beautiful thick wood of tall shell bark hickory" with rich, loose soil, and moving into white oak stands and harder soil (DHS Apr. 27). Grass was eight inches high, and the trees had leafed out (MHBY). Here the Camp of Israel spent a rainy, busy, snake-infested three weeks.

On Apr. 26 Shadrach Roundy arrived with 28 letters from Nauvoo, having made the trip in three and one-half days (MHBY).

In a council meeting on Apr. 26, 359 men were put to work. One hundred were assigned to split rails, superintended by Charles C. Rich, James Pace, Lewis D. Wilson, and Stephen Markham; James Allred supervised 10 men building fences; John Smith directed 48 in house building; Jacob Peart and 12 others dug wells; and A. P. Rockwood and 10 others built bridges. The other men cleared land, plowed, and planted under Daniel Spencer's direction (MHBY 146).

Two weeks later, on May 6, the wind "blew like a huricane," Hosea Stout said, and "trees fell all round the camp some close to my tent one fell on one of Br Lee's Mules and some on some cows." On May 8 Stout reported that "there was a long string of log houses now being put up on the East & on the west of the farm" for those who would stay at the site, "which gave the appearance of a civilized country again" (DHS).

■ **GARDEN GROVE LDS SETTLEMENT, 1846–52

The original **Garden Grove LDS Settlement site** is located northeast, southeast, and south of the cemetery on the top lands

Aerial photo of Garden Grove, IA, looking southeast. City of Garden Grove, top left; Mormon meetinghouse near the Y of the road, center; Mormon cemetery and log cabin sites, lower right. (1978)

and is now farmland. A small park protects the Saints' cemetery site. At the settlement site are **historical markers,** including a **wooden Mormon Trail sign** and two **Mormon Trail interpretive panels.** One panel is "Instant Haven in the Wilderness," telling about the settlement, and the other is "A Snug Home for the Winter," describing the Mormon cabins that stood there.

This settlement provided a way station for those who left Nauvoo later and it started a practice of "planting that others may harvest" (CHC 3:54). "They have made a big field and got it fenced and built sod-houses, will have some to take care of it and put in the crop. The rest of us will go on to another place," Patty Sessions wrote on May 13, the day the Camp of Israel pulled out (JPS). Several hundred Saints stayed behind to rest, mend, resupply, and find better outfits. **Samuel Bent, Aaron Johnson,** and **David Fullmer** were installed as the settlement's presidency. They were responsible to divide the lands among the poor without charge, giving to no one more than he or she could cultivate (BYUS [Fall 1981]: 445–61). Log houses soon lined what became rough streets. That fall the **Garden Grove Branch** sent a **rescue company** of wagons and 18 yoke of oxen to the Mississippi River to rescue **poor Saints** stranded near Montrose (see **Potter's Slough—Poor Saints Camps**) (JLAS 68–70).

Luman Shurtliff said between 500 and 600 people lived there with him at Garden Grove that first winter:

> The three families now in my care ware in log houses rolled up rough and chinked mudded on the outside no floors no windows no doors only what was made of split timber each one had a sort of a place to put or build a fire and their was plenty of wood standing over and around the houses but they would have it to prepare for burning as for food they had but little. (JLAS 71)

Plowing at Garden Grove, IA. (Courtesy of Vernon Murdock, artist, 1973)

Garden Grove cabin sites, according to Paul and Karla Gunzenhauser, owners of Garden Grove, IA, property and friends of the Mormon Trail. Paul is standing in the midst of cabin sites which he and Paula discovered and outlined in the grass about 100 yards east of Garden Grove Cemetery marker. (1997)

President Samuel Bent died in August 1846, so in February 1847 Elder Orson Pratt reorganized the settlement, installing **David Fullmer** as president and Aaron Johnson as counselor. By then the branch had 120 families. Its branch presidency served as the civil authority, too. **Thomas Kington** became the branch president in October 1847 (IOW-W 40–45).

Among signers of a July 1847 commitment to obey the rules of the Church were **Emily Abbott Bunker,** whose husband **Edward Bunker** had enlisted in the **Mormon Battalion,** and her widowed mother and siblings; the Shurtliffs; Isaac Allred; the David and Rhoda Fullmer families; Thomas and Margaret Kington; and large families named Carter, Carson, Demick, Farar, Hawkes, McBride, Mecham, Lamb, Hales, Thomas, Thompson, Valier, Van Buren, Wilson, and Zimmerman. In October 1847 government surveyors said about 30 LDS families lived there (NJ 6 [Fall 1994]: 14–44).

As the Saints living at Garden Grove gradually headed west, non-Mormons moved in and took over the farms and cabins. In 1851 an official **Garden Grove company** moved nearly 100 branch members westward, led by **Capt. Harry Walton.** By 1852 the Mormons' presence in Garden Grove had effectively ended (NJ 6 [Fall 1994]: 14–44).[14]

A Mormon cemetery memorial is located in a **trailside historic park** .8 mile west of today's Garden Grove. From town, travelers need to go west on Main Street (Co. J20) to where the road starts to bend south. On the southeast side of the intersection, according

14. During the 1990s the owners of part of the LDS Garden Grove settlement site, Paul and Karla Gunzenhauser, did major research, site analysis, and artifact recovery. Their interest helped launch the Iowa Mormon Trails Association. For 1996 (the sesquicentennial year of the trail), local chapters of the IMTA in 12 counties produced major mapping, marking, signing, publishing, and publicizing of projects and events.

Garden Grove, IA, cemetery marker, which identifies the location of the cemetery. (1975)

to local tradition, the **Pioneer's Meetinghouse** once stood. Take the road that veers west, for .5 mile. The three-acre **historic park** on the north side features a covered picnic pavilion and a bronze-on-stone monument marking the site of the **Mormon Cemetery.**

Deaths were common among the Garden Grove Saints. On May 2, 1846, **Samuel Thomas,** a Camp of Israel guard since Nauvoo, died and was buried the next day (DHS). On May 7, **Fidelia Green,** who had died at the Grand River settlements in Mercer County, Missouri, was buried near Samuel Thomas (MHBY, DHS). On May 8 **Hyrum Stout,** Hosea Stout's little son, died: "He died in my arms about four o'clock. This was the second child which I had lost both dying in my arms. He died with the hooping cough & black canker." By then the Stout family was ailing and "truly desolate & afflicted and entirely destitute of any thing even to eat much less to nourish the sick" (DHS). On May 12, **William Edwards** died, after being sick for 10 weeks (MHBY). The next day a little child, surname **Gurley,** was buried (JERS).

Gravestone of Mormon pioneer Anna Campbell. It was in the Garden Grove, IA, cemetery when the photo was taken, but the present-day location of the gravestone is now unknown. (Courtesy of George L. Strebel, 1935)

Between April 1846 and the next spring, an estimated 70 Saints died at Garden Grove (MoM, 137). Burials continued at the cemetery until the Saints left in 1851. As time passed, the cemetery was cleared of headstones and the ground farmed. The memorial (1973) now there tells the history of the temporary settlement and honors the Saints buried there.

Present-day Garden Grove has a population of about 250. It, with Humeston and surrounding farm families, are part of the **Mormon Trail School District.** The **Mormon Trail Junior-Senior High School** is located in Garden Grove, and yellow school buses carry the "Mormon Trail School District" name on their sides.

The **Garden Grove town park** near the town's center contains a **memorial plaque** commemorating the Saints' stay at Garden Grove. It was dedicated in 1956 by **apostle Ezra Taft Benson** while he was U.S. secretary of agriculture. His father, **George Taft Benson,** was born in Garden Grove in 1846.

A building in the town center on the north side of County Road J20 features a mural depicting in silhouette a wagon and oxen in brown tones, with the caption, "Mormon Trail 150th Anniversary, 1846–1996." In Garden Grove's center, the restored **J. J. McClung mansion** (1908) is an elegant tourist attraction.

• Lamoni

Lamoni is 3.25 miles north of the Iowa-Missouri border just 2.5 miles west of I-35. It is on U.S. 69/J55 in the southwest corner of Decatur County. Its population is about 2,400.

The **Reorganized Church of Jesus Christ of Latter Day Saints** (RLDS Church; now Community of Christ) was organized in 1860 by former LDS members who did not accept Brigham Young as Joseph Smith's successor as Church leader and who, therefore, did not move to Utah. **Joseph Smith III** served as the church's **first president.**

In 1871 RLDS members established Lamoni, which is named after a Book of Mormon king. They experimented with a communitarian system—an Order of Enoch. Lamoni served as the **RLDS Church headquarters** from the 1880s to the 1930s, until they were moved to Independence, Missouri. In 2001 the church changed its name to **Community of Christ.** In 2005 the church's membership worldwide was 250,000 members in more than 50 nations.

Liberty Hall Historic Center, located at Lamoni's west end at

1300 West Main Street, is a restored 18-room Victorian farmhouse dating from 1881. It was the home of **Joseph Smith III** and his family from 1881 to 1906 and the **birthplace of W. Wallace Smith,** who succeeded Joseph Smith III, his father, as president of the RLDS Church.

The RLDS Church opened **Graceland College** (now University) in Lamoni in 1895. A liberal arts college, Lamoni campus enrollment (2005) is approximately 1,200 undergraduate students.

■ Hickory Thunder Camp • Brigham Young • May 13 • 8 miles • Weldon

The **Hickory Thunder Camp site** is located 2 miles south of Weldon on County Road R48, just west of where that road crosses two small branches of Weldon Creek.

On May 11, **Parley Pratt's 50** was sent ahead to find a route "through a Perfect New Country Where nothing but Red Men Have Ever Resided" (JJoS May 12) and to start the Saints' second farming settlement, this one on the middle fork of the Grand River. Across rain-soaked prairies, slashed by many tiny streams and bogs, Pratt's company blazed a route to reach on May 16 what became **Mt. Pisgah** (JOP May 16).

On May 13 most of the Camp of Israel, after a 19-day layover at Garden Grove, resumed their journey. They traveled about 8 miles west-northwest along a dividing ridge between the Weldon Fork and the Grand River drainage areas. **William Huntington** wrote, "This day on our travels we beheld as beautiful a sight as I ever have seen, the most beautiful rolling prairie spread out in almost every Direction as far as the eye could extend with something like one hundred wagons strung out on the prairie for some 5 or 6 miles" (JWHu May 13, 63; spelling standardized). They camped beside a hickory grove by what they called Hickory Creek, where the scouting company a day earlier had built a bridge. Huts where Indians recently had resided were seen "very plenty" along the creek (JJoS May 12). Willard Richards named the camp "Hickory Thunder" because at dark, before they had put up tents, a storm of thunder, lightning, and torrential rain—one inch per hour for 2.5 hours—battered the emigrants (JWR May 13; MHBY May 13).

The next day Brigham Young and a few others moved on while the majority dried clothes and belongings. From camp they spotted on the "next divide" northeast of them 18 wagons from

Nauvoo—the first group of Saints in the **Spring Exodus** to catch up with the Camp of Israel (JWR May 14).

■ **PETER'S BRIDGE CAMP • BRIGHAM YOUNG • MAY 14 • 4 MILES • WELDON**

The **Peter's Bridge Camp site** is located 2.7 miles west and 1.25 miles north of the center of **Weldon.** It is 3.25 miles north of Van Wert. It is in Clarke County, .5 mile east of I-35 and 1.25 miles north of the Decatur-Clark county line, in the southwest quarter of Section 30, Green Bay Township (T71N R25W), on the south bank of South White Breast Creek.

In the morning of May 14, Brigham Young arrived there with 10 wagons from Hickory Thunder Camp and camped near George A. Smith and Amasa Lyman's groups, who had arrived the night before. The emigrants "laid by" due to rain-soaked ground. Men built a bridge across the creek, which they named "Peter's Bridge," for reasons not known. At the bridge's east end they posted a sign: "Road to California Bridge Built by B. Y. & Co., May 14, 1846." Young, Lyman, and George A. Smith rode ahead to look for another campground (JWR; MHBY; JJoS).

■ **LOST CAMP • OSCEOLA**

The **Lost Camp site** is 6 miles south of present-day **Osceola** on the east side of U.S. 69. Here, **Mormon Trail variant B** heading southwest intersected the Brigham Young route and then aimed northwest (BYUS [Fall 1981]: 422).

Late in 1846 Saints living at **Four Corners** headed west to link up with Brigham Young's companies. Apparently they became lost and camped at what soon was called **Lost Camp.** At least four LDS families wintered there, headed by George Washington Conyer, John Conyer, Mary Conyer and her husband James Langley, and John Langley. Sarah Conyer was born there on Feb. 20, 1847. Perhaps 40 people lived at Lost Camp, and it was a branch of the Church during 1846–47. In February 1848 Elder Jonathan C. Wright preached at Mt. Pisgah, Lost Camp, and Iowaville on his way to Nauvoo. At Lost Camp he found a member preaching false doctrine and corrected one of the Conyers who believed it (JH Feb. 12, 1847).

In the spring of 1848, the Langleys moved from Lost Camp to a site at least 3 miles north of present-day Osceola, in present-day **Fremont Township.** The Conyers stayed and farmed near Lost

Camp until 1854 (CFFC 1–8). A marker telling about Lost Camp is located in **Osceola.**

■ WILLOW BRIDGE CAMP • BRIGHAM YOUNG • MAY 15 • 5 MILES • OSCEOLA

Willow Bridge Camp site (also called **Sprague Encampment**) is on a south branch of White Breast Creek, 4.5 miles directly southwest of the center of **Osceola,** 2 miles west of I-35, and 2 miles south of U.S. 34. It is in the southeast quarter of Section 34, Ward Township (T72N R26W).

On May 15 Brigham Young's company traveled only 5 miles. Near the end of the second mile, they saw a trail formerly used by emigrants bound for Oregon, and on it later that day 11 wagons arrived from Nauvoo on what they termed the "Northern Route"—**Mormon Trail variant B** (JHKW May 14; JJoS May 15). Then, just .25 mile southeast of where they camped, the Saints crossed the **Dragoon Trail** (soldier's trail) that ran from northeast to southwest connecting Raccoon Barracks (present-day Des Moines) with Missouri. Brigham Young's company camped by a "small stream" and built a willow bridge across it, hence the name **Willow Bridge Camp** (JWR; MHBY).

Solomon Hancock's company from Nauvoo joined Young's camp after traveling the Northern Route from the Fox River (JWHu May 15). These newcomers from Nauvoo, Patty Sessions noted wistfully, "have been on the road but 3 weeks and we 3 months" (JPS 49).

Meanwhile, Camp of Israel 50s closely following Brigham Young stopped at **Cream Camp,** 2 miles before the Willow Bridge Camp, and 3 miles beyond the Peter's Bridge Camp. Heber C. Kimball named it Cream Camp because its beautiful prairie and fine pasturage made it the "cream of all the encampments we have hitherto had." His company also passed the Oregon road (JHKW May 15). The **Cream Camp site** is 5 miles south and 2 miles west of **Osceola,** located on the west side of I-35 via Exit 29, .5 mile west on County Road H45, and then .5 mile south.

■ OSCEOLA

Osceola, population about 4,700, is just east of where I-35 and U.S. 34 intersect, midway between Des Moines and the Missouri border. U.S. 69 runs north-south through Osceola. At Osceola's south edge, on the west side of U.S. 69, is the **Clark County**

Historical Museum, outside of which is a **Mormon Trail interpretive panel,** "An Unexpected Winter Home," telling about **Lost Camp.**

■ **WHITE BREAST CREEK CAMP • BRIGHAM YOUNG • MAY 16 • 4 MILES • OSCEOLA**

White Breast Creek Camp site is 5 miles west of the center of **Osceola** on U.S. 35, then .5 mile south on County Road R25, on the southeast side of White Breast Creek. This location is in the northeast quarter of Section 20, Ward Township (T72N R26W).

On May 16 Brigham Young's company "moved on to Whitebreast Creek four miles and built a bridge" (MHBY). Patty Sessions called the creek a "prairia slugh" (JPS 50).

■ **LONG CREEK CAMP • BRIGHAM YOUNG • MAY 17 • 3 MILES • MURRAY**

This **Long Creek Camp site** (once erroneously called **Squaw Creek Camp**) is 7.5 miles west of **Osceola** on U.S. 34 and 1.6 miles north. It is 2 miles east of the north edge of **Murray,** in the middle of Section 12 of Troy Township (T72N R27W).

On May 17 several companies caught up with Brigham Young's party at White Breast Creek camp, including Heber C. Kimball's 50. They held no Sunday meeting. Instead, Young, Kimball, George A. Smith, and Amasa Lyman rode to the prairie, located a road, and then moved the encampment 2 miles to be by a small creek (MHBY; JHKW)—"another slugh" in Patty Sessions's opinion (JPS 50). This small creek, or branch, emptied into the Grand River (DLDY May 17) and that branch now bears the name of Long Creek.

Official Mormon Trail Highways

The designation of State Highway 2 as the official **Mormon Trail Highway** (westbound) terminates at **Leon.** North from Leon to Osceola, U.S. 69 is the next segment of the official **Mormon Trail Highway.** U.S. 34 between **Osceola** and **Creston** is the third segment, from east to west.

■ **MURRAY AND SEVENMILE CREEK CAMP RUTS**

Present-day **Murray,** Clarke County, is about 10 miles west of the center of **Osceola** on U.S. 34 and then 1 mile north on County Road R15. Murray has about 800 residents.

On May 18 Brigham Young's company traveled due west through where Murray now is. In Murray on Fifth Street between Grant and Maple, on the south side, is the **Murray Historical Complex** featuring a restored log rural school and a **Mormon Trail interpretive panel** telling how animal trails on the prairie became wagon roads and then routes for the railroads.

SevenMile Creek Camp ruts are 2.5 miles west of Murray, visible in a never-tilled field. The site is reached by driving north from U.S. 34 on County Road R15 for 1 mile into Murray to the town park. From there, go west two blocks on 5th Street, make the road's quick left-right jag, and travel west on the continuation of 5th Street for 2.5 miles and then southwest .3 mile to the overlook. Signs guide the traveler along this route. The overlook includes an **observation stand** and explanatory display case, from which the visitor can look east and southeast and see **Mormon Trail ruts** in the prairie.

■ ****Mt. Pisgah Camp • Brigham Young • May 18–June 1 • 13 miles • Afton**

Like Garden Grove, **Mt. Pisgah** was both a **campsite and temporary LDS settlement.** The **Mt. Pisgah site** is approximately 18 miles west of **Osceola,** 5.5 miles northeast of the center of **Afton** and 4 miles northwest of **Thayer.** The site is 1.8 miles north of U.S. 34 and 1.25 miles west of U.S. 169. The location is 32 direct miles northwest of Garden Grove. The Mt. Pisgah camp and settlement spread out, having cabins and farms in Sections 5, 6, 7, 8, and 9 in Jones Township (T72N R28W). Much of the settlement was in Section 8 on a long ridge running north and south, but west of it were farms and cabins in the river bottoms of the Middle Fork (Thompson River) of the Grand River (see Mt. Pisgah, IA, map and aerial photo) (GLO 1847, Notes, 47).

Traveling in advance of the Camp of Israel, **Parley P. Pratt's 50** blazed a route to this site. Elder Pratt picked the Mt. Pisgah site two days before Brigham Young's arrival:

> Riding about three or four miles through beautiful prairies, I came suddenly to some round and sloping hills, grassy, and crowned with beautiful groves of timber; while alternate open groves and forests seemed blended in all the beauty and harmony of an English park. While beneath and beyond, on the

west, rolled a main branch of Grand River, with its rich bottoms of alternate forest and prairie. As I approached this lovely scenery several deer and wolves, being startled at the sight of me, abandoned the place and bounded away till lost from my sight amid the groves. Being pleased and excited at the varied beauty before me, I cried out, "this is *Mount Pisgah.*" (APPP 307–8)

In the Old Testament, Mt. Pisgah is the elevation from whose summit Moses viewed the promised land (Deuteronomy 3:27).

On May 18, 1846, men in the main camp (from various LDS companies) worked on a bridge while Brigham Young and four others rode out to find Parley P. Pratt's trail to the Grand River. While these men were gone, the companies ignored Young's instruction not to move. After finishing the bridge they advanced across it and "went on without a pilot & took a very crooked route." They stopped at noon at a creek where they had to build another bridge (JWR). Meanwhile, Brigham Young and the scouts discovered the right trail 2 miles away from their last camp, so they returned and met up with their company just after noon, to show it the right course.

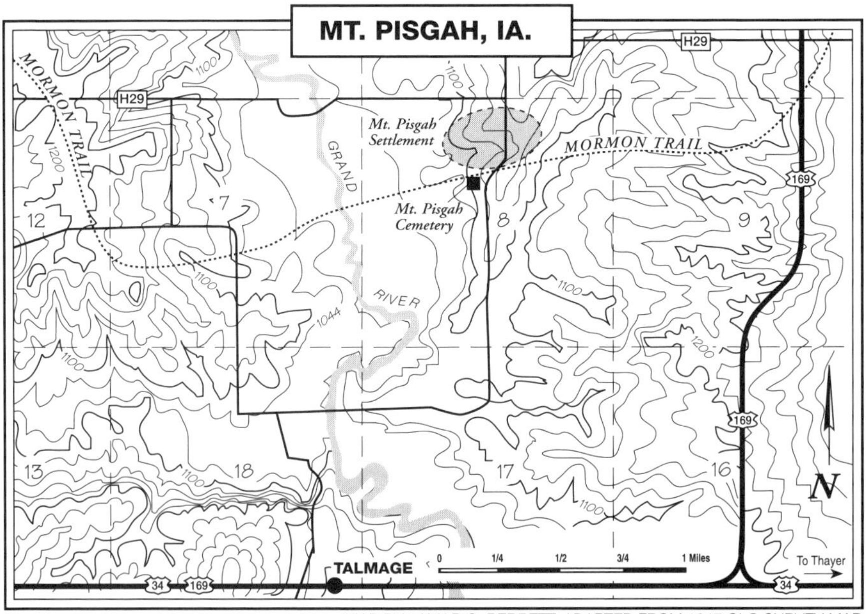

MAP BY LAMAR C. BERRETT; ADAPTED FROM 1847 GLO SURVEY MAP.

Aerial photo of Mt. Pisgah, IA, looking south-southwest; U.S. 34 and 169 lead east-west at the top; turnout on the dirt road in the center at the Mt. Pisgah Mormon Cemetery; east-west County Road H29 is at the bottom right; and the tree-lined Grand River is at the top right center. (1978)

The Young-led companies then crossed the just-completed bridge and ascended a hill, there to discover a natural curiosity, an **immense split granite rock** in an open, rockless prairie. It resembled an ancient altar that was split apart, the parts having fallen in various directions (JWR). It was "a rock of an immense size in the open prairie. It was a curiosity" (DLDY). It "had the appearance of having been rent in pieces either by the Indians setting fire to it, or by some convulsion of Nature" (JHKW). "This is a curiosity," Brigham Young noted, "in a country where there is no rock" (MHBY). Patty Sessions "broke of some of it and kept it" (JPS 50). Years later a farmer named Grandfield called that part of his farm "Castlerock Farm." In time he dynamited the rock to obtain foundation stones for a house, buried part of the original rock, and plowed away the rise. Nothing remains today of the rock. It was located in the southwest quarter of Section 24, New Hope Township (T73N R28W) (KR,c).

On May 18 Parley and Orson Pratt rode back to look for the overdue main company and spotted it 3 miles too far north. They sent out Lorenzo Snow, who guided the wagon caravan 5 miles to Mt. Pisgah (JOP; MHBY).

Mt. Pisgah Encampment

At Mt. Pisgah the main company camped for two weeks, until June 1, constructing a **temporary settlement** like the one at Garden Grove. President Young ordered those lacking proper outfits and provisions not to go farther west until they were better prepared. He arranged for a properly equipped, smaller company to push toward the Rocky Mountains, sent provision wagons south into Missouri to trade for needed supplies, had a bridge built across the Grand River, ordered all the men to help fence 500 to 1,000 acres for a farm and begin plowing. He held a kneeling prayer session with leaders on the prairie 3 miles north of Mt. Pisgah, after which they returned "with renewed assurance that the Lord was with us and were comforted" (MHBY May 30).

At Mt. Pisgah the six companies of 50 were joined day after day by Saints who had left Nauvoo in early May. To help evacuate more Saints from Nauvoo, the Camp of Israel sent back as many teams from Mt. Pisgah as could be spared. "Thus the Camp of Israel had become a veritable marching, industrial column: founding settlements as it marched; planting for others to harvest, and leaving behind them within easy reach bases of supplies that insured their own safety in case of emergency" (CHC 3:55).

On June 2 the Camp of Israel, leaving many Saints at Mt. Pisgah, resumed its trek toward the Missouri River.

Mormon Battalion Recruitment

After Brigham Young's party reached the Missouri River in mid-June, an invitation came from **President James K. Polk** for a battalion of 500 soldiers to serve in the Mexican War. (On May 13, 1846, the United States had declared war against Mexico for invading a disputed border zone in Texas.) Five uniformed army soldiers carried the enlistment request from Ft. Leavenworth (now in Kansas) to Mt. Pisgah, thinking Brigham Young was still there. Their arrival on June 26 caused great fear, even after they met with Mt. Pisgah branch president **William Huntington** and **Elder Wilford Woodruff.** Next day **Capt. James Allen,** First Dragoons, U.S. Army of the West, arrived. Mt. Pisgah leaders sent these soldiers to Council Bluffs to present the proposal to President Young (see **Mormon Battalion**

enlistments). On July 6 Brigham Young and others arrived from the Missouri camps to recruit enlistees at Mt. Pisgah for the battalion. At a general meeting the next day, President Young preached a rousing call for volunteers "to go to California in the U S service" (JERS July 7, 1846). Sixty-six enlisted and left for the bluffs the next day (MHBY July 7–8, 1846).

Brigham Young enlisting men for the Mormon Battalion. (Courtesty of Vernon Murdock, artist, 1973)

Hosea Stout wrote that the Saints were indignant at the requisition of the government to serve in the military and said, "I confess that my feeling was uncommonly wrought up against them. This was the universal feeling at Pisgah." When Brigham Young and other Church leaders arrived in Pisgah, the Saints became more willing to comply with the call to serve. Stout said, "Their presence seemed to give new life to all the camp who flocked around them" (JHS June 28, 1846).

■ **Mt. Pisgah LDS Settlement, 1846–52

William Huntington was placed in charge at Mt. Pisgah, which by early June 1846 was a busy place:

> The main settlement was situated on a long ridge running North & South. To the west was a large deep valley or bottom land of good prairie and was now being plowed & planted while all the adjoining glades and groves were teeming with men & cattle engaged in the busy hum of improving and planting. The whole woods & prairie seemed alive to business & a continual stream of emigration pouring in which looked like the entire country would be inhabited as a city in a short time (DHS June 1, 1846; spelling standardized).

On June 4, **Eliza R. Snow** described the cabin she moved into:

> Moved into a house built of logs some peeled & some with bark on, laid up cob fashion from 3 to 8 inches apart—the roof formed by stretching the tent cloth over the ridge pole & fastening at the bottom on the outside, which with carpeting, blankets, &c. fasten'd up at the north end to prevent the wind which is almost cold as winter, we find ourselves very comfortably & commodiously situated. (JERS 304; spelling standardized)

After the Camp of Israel departed from Mt. Pisgah, Nauvoo Saints flowed through the budding settlement. "Every day brings the arrival of saints from the City (Nauvoo) and the departure of saints from Mount Pisgah," Eliza R. Snow noted on June 11 (JERS 305).

When President Huntington died that August, **Charles C. Rich** became the presiding elder. **Lorenzo Snow** succeeded him in 1847. Mt. Pisgah saw a **continual turnover** of residents. At its peak about 2,000 to 3,000 Saints lived there, cultivating several thousand acres of fenced prairie land (EnH 546).

Five years later, in 1851, a small company of LDS emigrants crossed southern Iowa, bound for Utah. The company included **Jean Rio Baker,** whose diary recorded their progress. They reached Mt. Pisgah on June 6. "Only five families left in Pisgah," she noted. The graveyard there, she said, "tells a sad tale of the sufferings of the Church in the driving from Nauvoo" (DJRB June 7, 1851). Saints totally vacated Mt. Pisgah by 1852.

Mt. Pisgah Mormon Cemetery is located on the hill in the center of this photo, looking southeast. The Memorial Monument is in the center of the photo, in front of a small tree. (Courtesy of George L. Strebel, 1935)

Many Saints died at Mt. Pisgah and were buried in the **Mt. Pisgah LDS Cemetery.** Lorenzo Snow, who suffered a "severe fit of sickness" such that he had a near-death, out-of-body-type visionary experience, reported:

> The latter part of July and August [1846] witnessed a general and almost universal scenes of sickness throughout Pisgah. Well persons [could] not be found to take care of the sick; it was indeed a distressing scene. A great number of deaths occurred and it was often very difficult to get their bodies decently interred. In one or two instances bodies were put into the ground without any coffin or box. Scarcely a family escaped sickness and very few where death did not make an inroad. A general spirit of lamentation and sorrow prevaded Pisgah. (MUB 269–70)

One of the first deaths was that of **Noah Rogers,** who had recently returned from a South Seas Island mission. He died there on June 15 (MHBY). An estimated 80 people died that first year, including **Joseph Knight Sr.** and **Leonora Snow,** daughter of Lorenzo and Charlotte Snow (MoM 137). Today the nine-acre **Memorial Park,** maintained by the LDS Church and Union County, features a tall white obelisk (1888) containing 60 names of approximately 150 Saints who died there through 1852.[15] The park also has a 1923 **DAR memorial** honoring Mt. Pisgah as the first white settlement in Union County, displays telling about the LDS settlement and the

Mt. Pisgah Obelisk Memorial Monument, in the Mt. Pisgah Mormon Cemetery on one acre of ground purchased by the LDS Church in 1884. The monument was erected in 1888 in memory of the Mormon pioneers. Visiting in Sept. 1936 were (L to R) Andrew Jenson, asst. Church historian; George Albert Smith, apostle (1903) and president of the Church (1945); John D. Giles, one of the Church's Mutual Improvement Association workers. (Courtesy of Wilford C. Wood)

15. A large but incomplete list of those who died at Mt. Pisgah is found in Preston Nibley, *Exodus to Greatness,* 168–69.

Mt. Pisgah Obelisk Memorial Monument, Mt. Pisgah, IA. (1975)

Mormon Battalion recruitment, a replicated log cabin, a **Mormon Trail interpretive panel,** and picnic and rest room facilities. Other improvements are underway.

The Saints' huts, cabins, and farms once spread across the toplands and wooded slopes to the north, south, and east of the cemetery and on the bottomlands to the west dotted both sides of the Grand River (BYUS [Fall 1981]: 445–61).

Mt. Moriah Settlement

A few Mormon emigrants made a temporary settlement about 2.5 miles northwest of the heart of Mt. Pisgah in what is now Section 31, New Hope Township (T73N R28W). On a hill immediately east of the Grand River, they built temporary shelters, cleared a small piece of land, and cultivated it until they left in 1852. They gave the hill and their settlement the biblical name of Mt. Moriah, the sacred hill in Jerusalem upon which a temple was built (UGHM Oct. 1916, 162–63).

Winterset

Winterset, the county seat of Madison County, is 20 miles north of the Mt. Pisgah turnoff from U.S. 169. It is 18 miles southwest of Des Moines, 39 miles northwest of Osceola, and is situated where U.S. 169 and State 92 intersect.

Some Saints who moved across Iowa following the Camp of Israel passed through where present-day Winterset is now located (BYUS 21 [Fall 1981]: 426, 429). Also, some wagon companies that outfitted in **Keokuk** in 1853 passed through Winterset, including the **Joseph W. Young company**: "June 25. The company proceeded across the prairie and encamped at Winterset. Sister **Elizabeth Griffiths** of Pembrokshire . . . Wales died about 12 miles east of Winterset, age 64 years. She was buried on the prairie" (JWYCJ) (see **Mormon Emigration Routes in 1853**).

Madison County, with Winterset as county seat, is famous for its **six historic covered bridges** dating from the 1870s and 1880s and hosts a Covered Bridge Festival during the second full weekend in October.

Mormon Trail Variant Routes and Sites to Garden Grove and Mt. Pisgah

The vast majority of Saints left the Nauvoo area not with Brigham Young's Camp of Israel but according to the original plan—in spring when the grass grew and the water ran. During April, May, and June these Saints migrated as individual families or in small wagon companies they formed, manned, and led themselves. Because their livestock could feed on the prairie grass and plants, they had no need to follow the Camp of Israel's difficult route through southern Iowa (taken to be near Missouri settlements to buy feed). So they found and were shown better, more northerly, **variant routes** that took them to the trail of the Camp of Israel at either **Garden Grove** or **Mt. Pisgah.**

While Brigham Young was at Garden Grove, he sent men back "to look out a new and better road, to pilot the next company so they may avoid the creeks, bad roads and settlements through which we have passed" (MHBY Apr. 12, 1846). By late April he had sent instructions to Nauvoo Saints to travel a more northerly course up the main divide along the east side of the Des Moines River before turning west (DJDL Apr. 30, 1846).

Many Saints in the Spring Exodus stopped at towns or farms along the way to work or for health reasons, staying for days, weeks, months, or even years. Several of Iowa's southern counties through which the Camp of Israel did not pass have important sites and trail segments too, produced by Saints following variants of the trail or finding their own courses across southern Iowa.

Some Saints crossed the **Des Moines River** upriver from **Bonaparte,** where the Camp of Israel crossed, at such places as **Iowaville, Ottumwa, Eddyville** (AJH 43), and even **Des Moines** (ALB 53).

Mormon Trail Variant A: Drakesville to Garden Grove

From **Drakesville's** west edge, what trail experts today call **Mormon Trail Variant A** (HSM 35–36) bypassed the Brigham Young route, which turned south there across the Fox River, and instead continued west along a high ridge road between the Fox River and **Soap Creek.**

Unionville is 12 miles west of Drakesville via State 273 and County Road J3T and 7 miles north of State 2 on County Road T61. At 1.5 miles north of Unionville, County Road J3T crosses **South Soap Creek.** Where County Road J3T doglegs north 1 mile west of Unionville, the Mormon variant trail ran parallel about .75 mile to the east, until it dropped down to South Soap Creek. Approximately 1 mile up that creek (east) from where County Road J3T crosses it is a **Soap Creek Camp site** used by Saints in the **Spring Exodus** and the **Fall Exodus.** It is in the middle of Section 28, Union Township (T70N R16W). Soap Creek is one of the few Iowa landmarks LDS diarists mentioned. On some maps a branch of North Soap Creek, 4 miles east-northeast of **Moravia,** is shown as **Mormon Creek.**

A day's journey beyond Soap Creek, Newel Knight, part of the Spring Exodus, beheld with awe the prairie's beauty:

> The rich & variegated Prairie looks as if nature had done her best to Cheer the weary & attract the admiration of the traveler while our Children amuse themselves with the sweet & beautiful flowers which grow spontaneous it gives a refreshing fragrance to all & serves to Cheer us on our way. (JNK, May 11, 1846)

That fall **Capt. O. M. Allen's rescue company** with Saints from the **Poor Camps** encamped on the west bank of Soap Creek Oct. 25–27. About bedtime the first night, five Saints responded to cries for assistance and helped put out a prairie fire threatening a farmer's field and fence. For a reward, the farmer gave each man a pumpkin (JTB 85–86, Oct. 25–27, 1846).

Variant trail A then left Soap Creek and looped away from County Road J3T, following higher ground to the northwest until 2 miles southeast of present-day **Moravia,** where the trail and

County Road J3T are the same and pass through where **Moravia** now is.

For the next 7 miles west from Moravia, the trail ran within 1 mile north of and parallel to State 142, passing through what is now the town of **Iconium.** Just west of Iconium the trail branched, with one part crossing the Chariton River where **Rathbun Lake** now is and continuing west to Garden Grove—passing through where **Confidence, Millerton,** and **Humeston** now are. **A Mormon Trail interpretive panel,** "A Short Cut to Zion," is located at an overlook just beyond where State 142 bends southward to cross a neck of Rathbun Lake. The other branch (**Mormon Trail Variant B**) went directly to Mt. Pisgah.

Mormon Trail Variant B: Drakesville to Mt. Pisgah

Variant B (HSM 37–39) let Saints bypass Garden Grove and go directly to Mt. Pisgah (HSM 35). This route branched off from Variant A just past present-day **Iconium.** Instead of crossing the Chariton River, it pursued high ground northwest along the river to Chariton Pt. near present-day **Chariton** in Lucas County.

Chariton is on U.S. 34, 25 miles east of **Osceola** and 17 miles north of Corydon on State 14. Two **Mormon Trail interpretive panels** are in the Chariton area. One, "Why Take the High Road," is in the middle of the town square on the Lucas County Courthouse grounds (916 Braden St.). The other, "Tragedy along the Trace," is on the U.S. 34 East Bypass, .5 mile east of the town square. **Historic markers** (1917) with bronze plaques on large stones are located on the courthouse grounds and on Blue Grass Road (ask locally for directions).

Local histories say that some Mormons who left Nauvoo late in 1846 reached the northern bend in the Chariton River, 2 miles southwest of the present-day courthouse in Chariton, and camped for the winter. They stayed long enough to plant and grow a crop before rejoining the Saints at the Missouri River (HoLC 378–79).

From present-day Chariton, the route to Mt. Pisgah followed the high ground between the Chariton River and **White Breast Creek** through Lucas and Clarke Counties, intersecting the main Mormon Trail about 6 miles south of present-day **Osceola** (on U.S. 69).

Last Camp/Last Chance Camp, Garden Grove. Called "**Last Chance**" on current maps, this uninhabited site is about 14 miles west-southwest of **Chariton.** It is best reached by driving 8 miles north from **Garden Grove** on 320th Ave. (Co. R69) and then east on Mormon Trail Road (Co. H50) to the Lucas County line. The site was located about where that road now is, within the first mile eastbound into Lucas County. It is in Lucas County in Union Township (T71N R23W) along the Section 7 south boundary. Just to the north is the Stephens State Forest.

The Albert Merrill family left Nauvoo in mid-June 1846 and traveled with others along one of the alternate routes. They were about 16 miles east of Garden Grove when they stopped on Aug. 6 for Albert's wife, Margaret Ann, to give birth to a son. They moved forward only 4 miles and then stopped because Margaret was too ill to travel. Their company moved on, leaving them "alone on the prairie." Some men agreed to move them to Garden Grove but instead took them to a place known as "Last Camp," where a few LDS families were living in newly built houses. Albert's writings show that the place was about 12 miles from Garden Grove on one route and 35 miles from Mt. Pisgah on another. Illness swept through the Merrill family. Of their five children, three died (ages 9, 7, and 2 months) in October and November and were buried "at the point of a hill at 'Last Camp'" (AMBS, 3–5).

In January 1847 **Elder Orson Pratt** was sent from Winter Quarters to read a revelation called "The Word and Will of the Lord" (D&C 136) to the Saints in the Mt. Pisgah and Garden Grove settlements and organize Saints in both places into companies for the westward journey. He organized 110 families at Mt. Pisgah, 120 families at Garden Grove, and "a small company at Lost Creek east of Garden Grove," which he also termed "Lost Camp" (not to be confused with Lost Camp referred to above) (MHBY Feb. 12, 1847). Albert Merrill said he accompanied Elder Pratt from there to Winter Quarters, obtained cattle, and drove them back to the camp. Albert twice traveled to present-day Des Moines to trade for food and supplies. In the spring of 1847, the Merrills moved west to Winter Quarters, but others waited until later (AMBS, 4–5).

It seems certain that what Albert termed "Last Camp" is the place called "Last Chance" on current Iowa maps. On the alternate Mormon trail, it was the last camp before the trail forked and people had a last chance to decide whether to turn off to Garden Grove or continue directly to Mt. Pisgah.

The **Last Chance Cemetery** is located in the southwest corner of Union Township, near the Clarke County line. It contains the grave of Lafayette Sherwood, whose headstone says he was an "Emigrant Killed by Oxteam" in 1851. It is not known if he was a Latter-day Saint. It is likely the three Merrills were among the first people buried there.

After 1846 Mormons continued to use this **Variant B** route. Jean Rio Baker, crossing Iowa in 1851, said her small LDS company passed through Drakesville, camped along Soap Creek, had a child die near Dodge's Pt. (now Iconium), forded the head of the Chariton River, camped by Little White Breast Creek, and reached Mt. Pisgah (DJRB June 19 and 20, 1851).

Mormon Trail Variant in Monroe County

Yet another of the 1846 Saints' routes stayed east of the Des Moines River until **Eddyville** and crossed there. On May 29 Joseph Holbrook's group "camped on the Des Moines River at a little town by the name of Edville," where they waited until June 2 "for the chance of ferrying" (AJH 43).

The Saints then moved on to **Cedar Creek** where **Albia** (the Monroe County seat) is now located (22 miles north of Centerville on State 5, 21 miles west of Ottumwa on U.S. 34) and connected with **Variant B.**

Monroe County is 11 miles north of Centerville and State 2. It is intersected by State 5 and U.S. 34. In 1848 Mormons living as far away as **Kanesville** by the Missouri River were eligible to vote in Monroe County's **1848 election.** Mormons voted solidly Whig (for Zachary Taylor for U.S. president), creating local folklore still circulating that the Whig Party offered them a bigger bribe than did the Democrats.

Monroe County histories tell about the "**Hairy Nation,**" a group of early settlers from Indiana as well as some Mormons or friends of Mormons originally from New England who became disaffected during the Missouri Mormon War period and moved north into present-day Monroe County. Fiercely independent, they were called the "Hairy Nation" because of their unshaven and wild appearance. "Hairy Nation" soldiers represented Iowa valiantly in the Civil War (HMCI 379).

Resuming the Trail of Brigham Young's Camp of Israel

■ GRAND RIVER CAMP • BRIGHAM YOUNG • JUNE 1, 2 • 4 MILES • AFTON

The **Grand River Camp site** is 2.5 miles north and 1.75 miles west of the center of **Afton.** The campsite is in the southeast quarter of the northeast quarter of Section 3, Union Township (T72N R29W) on the east side of **Two-Mile Creek** (GLO 1850).

Some of Brigham Young's 50 left Mt. Pisgah on June 1 (his 45th birthday), crossed the Grand River, traveled 4 miles and camped on the east side of the West Fork of the Grand River (**Two-Mile Creek**). Young joined his company the next day by traveling "on roads somewhat muddy but improving," and then returned to Mt. Pisgah, but he rejoined and camped with his 50 that night (JHKW).

This **restarting of the trek west** occurred in spurts, with various companies leaving one after another on June 2 and during the next few days. Brigham Young's 50 generally took the lead.

Six miles west of Mt. Pisgah by Threemile Lake is a **Mormon Trail interpretive panel,** "The Naming of Threemile Lake," which tells about how Mormon Trail streams were named. The panel is located 2.75 miles north of **Afton** on County Road P53 (Creamery Road) and .4 mile west on County Road H33 or Three Mile Campground Road.

On June 29 **Wilford Woodruff** left Mt. Pisgah and camped about 5 miles away. He had six wagons, one carriage, and 42 head of livestock. The next day he came to the top of the rolling prairie and beheld "a splendid view":

> I could stand and gaze to the east west north & south & behold the Saints pouring out & gathering like clouds from the hills & dales, grove & prairie with their teams, wagons, flocks, & herds by hundreds & thousands as it were until it looked like the movements of a great nation. (JWW June 30; spelling and capitalization standardized)

Note for westbound travelers following the Mormon Trail: The best way to stay close to the next 60 miles of the Mormon Trail west from Mt. Pisgah is to drive east from Mt. Pisgah to U.S. 169, south to State U.S. 34/169, west on it 16 miles to **Creston,** then north on State 25 for 11.5 miles to **Orient** in Adair County.

■ Twelve-Mile Prairie Camp • Brigham Young • June 3 • 7 miles • Creston

Twelve-Mile Prairie Camp site is 6 direct miles east-northeast of the center of **Creston** in the southeast quarter of the northeast quarter of Section 26, Lincoln Township (T73N R30W). The campsite location is centered at a point 3 miles north of U.S. 34 and 7.75 miles east of State 25 (GLO 1850).

On June 3, 1846, Brigham Young's 50 left the Grand River Camp about noon with Willard Richard's company who had joined them at 9 A.M. That afternoon Young's wagons "traveled seven miles and encamped on the prairie." This camp was 12 miles from Mt. Pisgah (MHBY; JHKW).

■ Orient

Orient, Adair County, is located on State 25, 10.5 miles north-northwest of the center of Creston. It is approximately 45 miles southwest of Des Moines.

Patty Sessions recorded that on June 4 the company stopped 9 miles from their last camp on "Platte water," which spot is 3 miles south of **Orient** on State 25 and then 2.2 miles east on the east-west township line in the northwest quarter of Section 1, Spaulding Township (T73N R31W). That site is 6 miles north of Creston's north edge via State 186 and then .2 mile east along the east-west section (and township) line dividing Section 1 in Spaulding Township (T73N R31W) and Section 36 in Orient Township (T74N R31W) (JPS 53; GLO 1853).

The 1846 **Mormon Trail,** heading northwest, passed .5 miles southwest of present-day **Orient.** A 1917 DAR bronze plaque **Mormon trail marker,** set in red sandstone, stands on the south end of the town on the east side of State 25 in front of the public school. At the southeast corner of East First Street and Broad Street is a **Mormon Trail interpretive panel,** "Growing Up on the Trail," telling about children during the trek west. Across the street is the **Bank of Memories,** an 1894 bank building serving as a museum, which contains a **Mormon Trail mural, exhibit, and replicated handcart.**

Orient, population about 400, has a welcome sign boasting of its Mormon Trail location and its being the **home of Vice President Henry A. Wallace** (1941–45) and of **Dazzy Vance,** a Hall of Fame baseball player.

■ BROMBERRY HILL CAMP • BRIGHAM YOUNG • JUNE 4 • 18 MILES • ORIENT

The **Bromberry Hill Camp site** is in the southeast quarter of Section 23, Richland Township (T74N R32W). It is reachable by going 4 miles west of the center of Orient on County Road G61, 1 mile south on County Road P13, and about .2 mile west on the section line road (JWR; GLO 1850).

On a cold, cloudy, windy June 4, Brigham Young's company traveled 18 miles over one continuous stretch of prairie, "the longest days journey since we left Nauvoo," and camped there (JHKW).

■ GREENFIELD

Greenfield, county seat for Adair County, is located midway between I-80 and U.S. 34 on State 25, approximately 40 miles southwest of Des Moines.

Greenfield is home to the **Adair County Historical Museum.** Open during summers, it contains several Iowa Mormon Pioneer Trail exhibits, including two original 1935 **wooden trail markers** crafted as part of a statewide WPA project. The site also contains an authentic **covered wagon.**

Greenfield lies along Iowa's **Great Divide**: east of the divide Iowa waterways flow toward the Mississippi River, and west of the divide they flow toward the Missouri River.

■ *MORMON TRAIL COUNTY PARK AND LAKE • BRIDGEWATER

Adair County's **Mormon Trail County Park** is located 1.75 miles southeast of Bridgewater. It is centered east to west in the north portion of Section 3, Washington Township (T74N R33W). It is reached by turning south off State 92 just east of Bridgewater on Delta Ave (Co. N54) and driving 1.25 miles to the park entrance.

In the park is the .5 by .25 mile **Mormon Lake.** The 160-acre park and lake are named to honor those Saints who traveled on the Mormon Pioneer Trail, which ran .5 mile south of the center of the lake. In the park is a **Mormon Trail interpretive panel,** "The Iowa Prairie—How the Mormons Saw It," placed next to recently planted patches of native prairie grasses. These grasses grow taller than the back of a horse and display a beautiful mix of "switchgrass, big bluestem, lead plant and coneflowers . . . the bright magenta of downy phlox and the delicate pink blooms of native wild roses" (WYW 68). In the 1800s and earlier, prairie Indians burned the tall, dry prairie grasses in the late fall or spring to drive out game that they could hunt for food.

Brigham Young's company passed by here on June 5, 1846, during that day's 14-mile trek (MHBY).

Mormon Trail wagon ruts, among the few still existing in Iowa, are deeply eroded and visible in the pasture 1 mile south-southwest of Mormon Lake, in the southeast quarter of Section 4, Washington Township (R33W T74N), near County Road G53. From the western end of Mormon Lake turn south on Delta Avenue (Co. N54) for .75 mile to an intersection with 290th Avenue (Co. G53). Turn right (west) on County Road G53 (290th Street) for about .2 mile. From the first house on the north side of the road, the ruts run east and west and are about .25 mile west of the house. The ruts are visible from the road, near a **Mormon Trail sign** and **Original Trail Ruts sign,** but **if a close-up observation is desired, permission must be obtained from the landowner.**

■ Small Creek Prairie Camp • Brigham Young • June 5 • 14 miles • Massena

Small Creek Prairie camp (misnamed in some records as Shoal Creek Camp) is just south of the center of Section 15, Victoria Township (T74N R34W). It is 4.75 miles southwest of Bridgewater. It is 3.2 miles south and 1 mile east of **Massena.** The site is .6 mile east of State 148 on County Road G61 and then .3 mile north.

On June 5, two hours into their travel day, Brigham Young's company "found the Indian trail to Council Bluffs" from Raccoon Barracks (present-day Des Moines) which they followed westward. They forded the Middle Nodaway River—Brigham Young thought it might be "the west branch of Grand river" (MHBY). That day they saw the remains of "a great many Indian wigwams" (JHKW). After traveling 14 miles they camped on the prairie near a small creek (MHBY). Patty Sessions said that poison ivy was "thick all around" the camp (JPS 53).

Near this Middle Nodaway River site—within the area between **Mormon Trail County Park** and the **West Nodaway River**—Brigham Young met with Indians three weeks after he reached the Missouri River in mid-June. He returned from the Missouri camps to Mt. Pisgah to recruit men for the Mormon Battalion, and, during his carriage rush back to the Missouri, he met "Musqaukoe" (Mesquakie) Indians on July 10 who wanted him to talk with **Chief Poweshiek.** (Poweshiek County in Iowa is named for this important leader.) That evening President Young, Heber C. Kimball, Willard Richards, and others met for a half hour in a Mormon's tent with Poweshiek and his chiefs and braves. The Indian leader wanted to know where the Mormon chief had come from and where the Mormons were going. He said his people were going off with the Pottawattamies, but he would like to go with the Mormons. However, he would lose his government annuity if he did not locate on land the government had appointed his people. Brigham Young gave the chief an invitation:

> I told him to come over the mountains and see us when we got located and bring his men to hunt for us. . . . Powsheek said he would like to go. I told him I would send a messenger in two or three years, or as soon as I could, to bring them to us. . . . I said, when they came to see us, I would tell them a great many things. . . . Powsheek spoke of Joseph Smith, the prophet, who had been murdered and with whom he had been acquainted; said, the Prophet was a great and good man.

When the LDS leaders left the tent, "Baquejappa, a Pottawatomie chief, called us aside, and presented a paper, counselling the Indians not to sell their lands." Jonathan Dunham, a Mormon emissary to the Indians during the Nauvoo years, had given him that note, along with "two sheets of hieroglyphics, from the book of Abraham" (MHBY July 11, 1846).

■ ***Ring (Circled Wagons) Camp • Brigham Young • June 6 • 8 miles • Lyman**

The **Ring (Circled Wagons) Camp site** was on the south shore of the **West Nodaway River,** barely west of where Whistlers Branch flows into the Nodaway from the north. This site is 4 miles south of State 92 and 5 miles east of U.S. 71. It is 5 miles east and 2 miles south of **Lyman.** It is also 5 miles south and 1 mile west of

Cumberland. It is in the far southwest corner of Section 16 and the extreme northwest corner of Section 21, Edna Township (T74N R35W). It is on the down-sloping north edge of the **Reno Methodist Cemetery.** Convenient for drivers to find, the Reno Cemetery is on the northeast corner of the T intersection where County Road G61 (Victoria Road), coming from the east, ends at 680th Street, a north-south county section line road (MHBY; GLO 1852).

On June 6 the Mormon wagons advanced 14 miles and camped along the bottoms of "quite a large creek" (JHKW). Visiting Pottawattamie chiefs told the pioneers that the creek was the **Nodaway River** (DJDL June 7), Patty Sessions heard it called the "ottoway" river (JPS 54); in fact, it is the West Nodaway. To leave the camp the next morning, Patty Sessions said they had to "cross a bad place," where men had to "gather grass to put in to the mud instead of timber" (JPS June 7, 54).

As protection against Indians, the 72 wagons and buggies parked that evening in a circle about .25 mile in circumference. "Form a circle with our waggons," Patty Sessions wrote, "pitch the tents and build our fires out side put the catle inside the circle." Speaking of circling the wagons, she said it was "the first time we have camped this way." Another 15 vehicles parked in sight of the circled wagons (JPS June 6, 54; JWR; JHKW).

Before leaving camp the next day, Sunday, they held a meeting inside the circle, where a temporary stand was erected. Eight Indians were present. Heber C. Kimball and Brigham Young preached and gave practical advice about the trek. President Young recommended that men be selected to go south into Missouri for supplies and that the Camp of Israel travel by companies of 10s, in order to set up and leave campsites more quickly (MHBY). "A number of Indians and squaws came in to see us," Horace K. Whitney said, "mounted on their ponies and horses, and decorated and painted in their peculiar manner—they are of the Pottawatamie tribe—they have a camp some 4 or 5 miles from here" (JHKW).

The **Pottawattamie Indians** had been living on a five-million-acre reservation granted to them in 1833, which covered much of southwest Iowa. When the Saints arrived on their lands, the Pottawattamies were in the process of negotiating away their Iowa territory—that month they would formally cede the land to the U.S. government, under pressure, and begin relocating to the Kansas River region. When the LDS refugees from Nauvoo encountered them, the Pottawattamies, like the Saints, were uprooting and looking for a new start elsewhere. These Indians sympathized with the plight of the Mormons (BJI 38).

The **Reno Cemetery** is a remnant of a post-1846 non-LDS community called **Reno** that has since disappeared. About 200 feet east of the cemetery gate and inside the fence line beside County Road G61 is a sandstone marker (with its bronze plaque missing), placed there in memory of the pioneers who traveled the Old Mormon Trail (HSM 30–31).

Nodaway River—Hosea Stout Encampment • June 23–29

Three weeks behind Brigham Young's company, **Hosea and Louisa Taylor Stout** left Mt. Pisgah on June 20, 1846. They struggled to advance three wagons, one of them carrying Church arms. Hosea drove one team; a black boy, Peter Manning, voluntarily drove another; and a girl drove the third until it was hitched to one of the other wagons (DHS June 17–20). On June 23 they camped by the Nodaway River, about where Brigham Young's **Ring (Circled Wagons) Camp** had been on June 6. That day they saw "several Indians which was the first that we had seen since we left Nauvoo." Other Saints arrived from Mt. Pisgah and joined them, creating "**a very large encampment**" (DHS June 24). Rain, wind, and high water prevented their crossing for four days. The Nodaway's banks were 20 feet high. A bridge crossed about eight feet below bank level. "Quite a number of Indians came to camp to day some we fed They were all friendly" (DHS June 25). By nightfall on June 25, the river overflowed it banks, spreading a sea of water around some wagons and tents. The next day **William Clayton** arrived back from the bluffs and had to float his wagon box and swim his horses across. That day "many friendly Indians came & went" and "there was a continual crossing of the Indians all day swimming their horses which seemed to be but little disadvantage to them to come to a stream out of its banks" (DHS June 26). On June 27 the river receded slowly, but the bridge remained submerged. "Plenty of Indians here today," Stout noted. "They were going to the Buffalo country to kill their winter meat It is about one hundred miles and among the Souix Indians with whom all other tribes are at war These are Pottawottamies & Musquakas. They not only expect to kill all the buffalo they can but also all the Souix. So it is a war expidition as well as a buffalo hunt" (DHS June 27).

By then Hosea and Louisa's son William Hosea, age three, was deathly ill. He had developed whooping cough symptoms seven weeks before, when his little brother Hyrum, not quite two, had died of the disease on May 8 at **Mt. Pisgah.** Little Hosea died on Sunday, June 28, at 7:40 A.M. Father Hosea's lengthy lamentations in his diary break the reader's heart. One reads: "Thus died my only son and one too on whom I had placed my own name and was truly the dearest object of my heart. Gone too in the midst of affliction sorrow and disappointment In the wild solitary wilderness." He and Louisa felt "utterly destitute & disconsolate." Camp members proffered every kindness, and someone constructed a good coffin. That morning the company moved on—Stout did not say if the bridge had survived or not—to about 1 mile northwest of the Nodaway, where they stopped for a burial (DHS June 28).

■ Burial Site of Stout and Smith Children • Lyman

The burial site of **William Hosea Stout** (born April 16, 1843; died June 28, 1846) and **Isabella Smith** (June 12, 1846) is approximately 1 mile northwest of the Ring (Circled Wagons) Camp site in the middle of Section 17, Edna Township (T74N R35W). It is approximately .5 mile north of the Reno Cemetery via an unnumbered country road on a hill about .5 mile west of there. If driving east from Lyman, the traveler should go east on County Road G53 for 5 miles and then turn south on that same unnumbered county road for 1.5 miles. The site is on a hill about .5 mile west from that point.

The Stouts crossed the river and buried their child "on a hill in the prairie about one mile from the Nodaway where there was the grave of an infant of Br John Smith." Then the company "pursued our journey leaving the two lovely innocents to slumber in peace in this solitary wild" (DHS June 28).

Two weeks earlier **Father John Smith's company** (Joseph Smith's uncle) had camped by the Nodaway. Due to an accident, Smith's daughter-in-law **Augusta Bowen Smith** gave birth early to a baby, who died. Her family made a small coffin, buried the child, put a mound of earth over the grave, and on a board at the head of the grave wrote: "June 12, 1846, Infant Daughter of John S. & Augusta B. Smith, Isabella's Grave." Heartbroken parents John Lyman Smith and Augusta Bowen had been married but 11 months (JJS June 12, 1846).

■ LYMAN

Lyman, Cass County, is .2 mile east of where State 92, coming from the west, meets U.S. 71 at a point 7.5 miles southeast of **Lewis** and 12 miles south and 2 miles east of **Atlantic.** There a **Mormon Trail interpretive panel,** "Trail Builders, Also Bridge Builders," is by a highway pull-off east on County Road G53 from where State 92 intersects U.S. 71 from the west.

During travels on June 6, 1846, Brigham Young's company followed a course that crossed where the tiny town of **Lyman** now is, and they camped 2.5 miles northwest of there. A **"Mormon Trail Crossed Here"** sign is on Main Street in Lyman.

■ PLEASANT VALLEY (PLEASANT PRAIRIE) CAMP • BRIGHAM YOUNG • JUNE 7 • 7 MILES • LEWIS

Pleasant Valley (Pleasant Prairie) Camp is 2.5 miles northwest of Lyman and 5 miles southeast of **Lewis.** It is in the northwest quarter of Section 32, Bear Grove Township (T75N R36W), on the west side of **SevenMile Creek.** It is 1.75 miles east of U.S. 71 and 1.5 miles north of State 92. It is reachable by driving north of Lyman 1 mile, turning west and driving 2 miles on the section road, and then turning north .5 mile on a section road (Co. N16).

On Sunday, June 7, after a church meeting and visits at **Ring (Circled Wagons) Camp** by mounted Pottawattamie Indians who were camped 4 or 5 miles away, Brigham Young's company moved northwest 7 miles and stopped on the prairie by a small creek near timber, after crossing a bridge built by **Bishop Miller's advance party** over present-day SevenMile Creek. Miller named the bridge "**Lost Fork Bridge**" (JHKW). John D. Lee called the camp **Pleasant Prairie Encampment.** Patty Sessions said her part of the company camped "on pleasant prairie valley," a "splended place," where the halted wagons "form a line a quarter of a mile in length" (JPS). The Brigham Young 50 lined up on one side of the road, and the Heber C. Kimball 50 on the other (JHKW).

■ **LEWIS/MORMON TRAIL AND HANDCART ROUTES

See **Iowa Historic Route 2** discussion below for the **handcart route near present-day Lewis.**

On June 8 the **1846 Mormon pioneers** moved 14 miles, during which they passed 2 miles southwest of present-day **Lewis.** Lewis, population about 450, is 40 miles east of Council Bluffs. It is 1 mile south of U.S. 6 on County Road M56, which is Lewis's main north-south street.

The **Lewis town park** is four blocks west of County Road M56 on Main Street. In the park is a **Mormon Trail marker** erected in 1917 by the Iowa DAR. The marker originally was located 1.5 miles west of town commemorating the site of **Indiantown.**

Lewis, platted in 1853, became the county seat of Cass County and received a post office in 1854.

The **1856 and 1857 handcart and wagon pioneers** passed through Lewis and about 1 mile west of town began following the route that the **1846 pioneers** had taken to Council Bluffs.

Cold Springs County Park, 1 mile south of Lewis on the west side of County Road M56, has a **Mormon Trail** panel and route sign in the upper picnic area. The trail passed 1 mile southwest of where this park now is.

● ****POTTAWATTAMIE INDIAN VILLAGE • LEWIS**

The **Pottawattamie Indian Village site** is 2 miles west of Lewis on a ridge overlooking the spot where Indian Creek flows into the East Nishnabotna River. It is 1 mile south of U.S. 6 and .75 mile east of State 48. It is in the northeast corner of Section 17 and southeast corner of Section 8, Cass Township (T75N R37W). The village site is 2 miles west of the center of Lewis, reachable by driving north of the Lewis town park two blocks to Minnesota Street and then west across the East Nishnabotna River and then Spring Creek. The Indian Village was by the creek and along the slopes on the other side.

On June 8, soon after starting 14 miles of travel, the Camp of Israel saw an Indian village on a eminence about 5 miles distant. While they plodded along towards the village, an Indian rode up and demanded that they pay a duty for passing through the village and for the grass their cattle would eat. But Church leaders explained the good that the Mormons would do, including the building of bridges, so the Indian "readily consented" to let the Mormons pass without a toll. Brigham Young instructed the captains of tens to "see that the guns and pistols in their companies were all cleaned and conveniently placed" (MHBY).

The wagons reached the **East Nishnabotna River** and crossed on a new bridge barely finished by Bishop George Miller's advance **pioneer party.** The river has since been rechanneled, but the site of the crossing, a subject of recent archaeological probes, is on the north side of the East Nishnabotna River, .3 mile west of the east section line of Section 17, Cass Township (T75N R37W). **It is not accessible by car.**

Across the bridge, the Mormon pioneers passed in view of the **Pottawattamie Indian Village of Mi-Au-Mise,** where the tribal chief lived (NJ 6 [Spring 1994]: 16). The village was less than a mile to the north and "situated on a very beautiful ridge skirted by timber and beautiful rolling prairie" (JWC June 10, 44). John D. Lee said the village had 50 wigwams and that "some few lots of grounds were enclosed by Pole fenses & tilled by the squaws" (DJDL June 8). Horace K. Whitney said Indians told the Mormons they had 130 "wigwams" (JHKW June 8).

Two months earlier John Lowe Butler and James Cummings, in advance of the Camp of Israel and heading for the **James Emmett Encampment** at Camp Vermillion in present-day South Dakota, stayed at this village (see **James Emmett Expedition**). They found wickiups, or huts, built of bark and "shaped considerable like a house but very irregularly situated, no two of them fronting the same way." Wickiups, they said, were frames covered by mats made of "flag"—like cattails—except for a hole in the top to let smoke out (DJC Apr. 14, 1846).

Once across the East Nishnabotna, the Camp of Israel moved northwest and immediately crossed what today is **Indian Creek** and halted to rest the cattle. They were visited "by a great number of the tribe." Horace K. Whitney said, and while Saints and teams rested, they watched Indian horse races. He observed that the Indians "have very fine horses and ponies among them" (JHKW). After resting, the companies resumed their day's journey.

Traveling three weeks behind the Camp of Israel, **Hosea Stout's company** camped on June 28 on a hill from where they could see the Indian Village some 4 miles away. The recent rains had turned the "Nishanabotothany," which ran by the Indian Village, into "a very large stream and now out of its banks and very deep and muddy" (DHS June 28, 172). Gone was the wood bridge Bishop Miller had built there earlier, so Stout and others spent three days laboring to replace it and one just beyond, on Indian Creek. Indians "thronged around us all the time we were building the bridge," Stout said, "& at times would come in droves to the camp but they were very civil friendly & good natured. . . . They would amuse themselves sometimes by swimming in the creek in large numbers and sometimes at playing cards at which they seemed to be very dexterous." Bridge building "seemed to be a great novelty to them" (DHS July 2, 173).

Before Stout and others could finish the bridges, Elder **Parley P. Pratt** and **Solomon Hancock** came from Council Bluffs, bound for Mt. Pisgah. On June 30 Pratt tried to swim his mule across **Indian Creek,** west of the Indian village, and both he and the mule nearly drowned. Pratt "floted to shore," Hosea Stout heard, "and was so much exhausted that he could not get out. After resting awhile he attempted it again and came near being drowned the second time. I believe he was finally assisted over by some indian boys." Meanwhile, more wagons were arriving from Mt. Pisgah and Nauvoo. "Our encampment now was very large," Stout reported on July 1, "the hills were full of our tents & waggons and seemed to be nearley as large as the first camp [Sugar Creek] when it started in February" (DHS June 28 to July 1, 171–73).

Seven weeks later **Eliza R. Snow's group** reached this point on Aug. 22. She penned an interesting description of the Indian village:

> We came in sight of an Indian Settlement of about 100 wigwams of the Pottawattamie tribe—when in about a mile of the first huts, we were amus'd to see them riding at full speed to meet us—bringing sacks of corn & beans which they were vary anxious to sell for money or 'swap' for meat baskets &c. They were all pretty well cloth'd & well decorated—talk english some—appear happy and friendly. Their improvements [gardens] are small but neatly cultivated—being done by the females—the business of men being hunting. (JERS Aug. 21, 141)

Two years later, in the late fall of 1848, 15 LDS families that had left Nauvoo in the fall of 1846 and stayed in the Montrose area finally were able to move west. But they had to stop at this Indian village on account of deep snow. That winter and spring, while these families occupied abandoned Indian wickiups, eight babies were born (SPP). Possibly it was stories about these births that gave rise to the "**nine births in one night**" legend currently linked to the **Sugar Creek Camp.**

■ Indiantown • Lewis

Indiantown, an LDS settlement, sprang up late in 1846 when some 20 families of Saints built log cabins about 1 mile to the northeast of the Indian village. The site is in the southeast quarter of the northwest quarter of Section 9, Cass Township (T75N R37W) and is reachable from Lewis via Minnesota Street (two blocks north of the city park), driving 1 mile west to where that road crosses Spring Creek. From that bridge Indiantown was on the north side of that road and east of Spring Creek.

Indiantown was **Cass County's first white settlement** and the **first white settlement between Des Moines and Council Bluffs.** From 1847 to 1853 its post office name was **Cold Spring.**

Indiantown was located at the **junction of two trails—the Raccoon Forks Trail,** coming from the northeast from Raccoon Forks (Des Moines), and the **Pottawattamie Indian Trail** (NJ 6:18)—and was 1.5 miles northeast of where the Mormon Trail from Mt. Pisgah crossed the Nishnabotna River and met the Indian Trail. From these junctions the trails became one and ran west along the Pottawattamie Indian Trail into present-day Council Bluffs.

Indiantown was a Mormon settlement from 1846 until 1852. In 1850, a stagecoach traveler noted that his coach crossed the East Nishnabotna River and "went down the creek about a mile to Indian Town a Mormon Settlement of 7 families." That year a little daughter of a Mormon widow named Beeker was so severely burned by playing with embers from an emigrant party's fire that she died. At one point **James Ferring** was the bishop. Visitors said they observed Mormon preachers and also Mormon dances on many evenings. In 1851 Jeremiah Bradshaw arrived at Indiantown and found seven Mormon families there—two Pettengill families and others named Marsh, Bunnell, Warner, Ferrin, and Wicks. Most Saints had left by 1852 (NJ 6 [Spring 1994]: 18–19).

A Mormon Trail marker in the **Lewis town park** once stood at the Indiantown site, for which reason the marker's text says: "At this point was Indiantown and the Junction with the Trail from Raccoon Forks."

Just west of Indiantown was another short-lived tiny settlement called **Iranistan.** Started in 1852, it had a sawmill and stood near oak and walnut trees. It had a post office between 1854 and 1857 but died out in favor of Lewis. Handcart companies passed by Iranistan (NJ 6 [Spring 1994]: 21–22).

Near Lewis the route of the **Mormon handcart companies of 1856 and 1857** merged into the **Mormon Trail** route. To reach this point, the handcart companies had followed a road from Iowa City in eastern Iowa to Des Moines, in Iowa's center. Then they traveled on a road that had replaced the Raccoon Forks Trail to this spot and passed through Indiantown. Their route from Iowa City to this point, where it joined the 1846 Mormon Trail, is described below in **Iowa Historic Route 2,** but the handcart story is included here with Mormon Trail site descriptions between Indiantown and Council Bluffs.

The **Willie handcart company** moved through Indiantown on Aug. 7, 1856. In that company were **Elders James G. Willie, Milan Atwood, and Levi Savage,** who had been on this route 10 years before while traveling with the 1846 companies from Nauvoo (JJGW). "We traveled about seven miles to a small village called Indian Town," Levi Savage Jr. wrote. "We drove through about a mile and took dinner. Here we met with a brother from Pennsylvania by the name of Joseph Seltcer [Pelzer?]. He gave Brothers Willey, Atwood, Woodard, Chislet, Cox and myself dinner. He is strong in the faith and intends to dispose of his property and gather with the Saints this fall. . . . As we passed through Indian town several of the Saints stopped and purchased some necessary provisions" (JLS Aug. 7). On Aug. 19, 1856 the **Martin handcart company** passed through "Indian Town" (LHWJJ).

After **Lewis** was established in 1853, it absorbed Indiantown and Iranistan by the end of that decade (NJ 6 [Spring 1994]: 16–24).

Almost immediately after leaving Lewis by going west on Minnesota Street, today's traveler will see the reconstructed **ferry house** (originally built in the 1850s), located where handcart pioneers crossed the East Nishnabotna River. At this location is a **Mormon Trail interpretive panel** that tells about the coming together of the several trails near here.

The historic **Hitchcock House,** open to the public (except in winter), is 2 miles west of Lewis via Minnesota Street and .5 mile south on a gravel road. Travelers are guided by directional signs. In 1856 (the first year for handcarts) the **Rev. George B. Hitchcock,** a Congregational minister, built a fine red sandstone home high on this hill. The house became a hiding place on the **Underground Railroad** for Missouri slaves fleeing to Canada. **John Brown,** the fiery abolitionist, is reported to have sung and preached there. **A Mormon Trail interpretive panel** stands on the south side of the Hitchcock House on an overlook, telling about the Mormons passing the Pottawattamie Indian Village and showing where, from that overlook, the village once was.

■ **PLEASANT VALLEY (WALNUT CREEK) CAMP • BRIGHAM YOUNG • JUNE 8 • 14 MILES • LEWIS**

The **Pleasant Valley (Walnute Creek) Camp site** is 7 miles west and .5 mile south of the center of Lewis. It is 3.3 miles west of the Pottawattamie-Cass county line, 1.4 miles south of U.S. 6, and .75 mile east of County Road M47. It is on the west side of Walnut Creek in the northeast quarter of Section 16, Wright Township (T75N R38W).

After passing the Indian village on June 8, Brigham Young's company traveled 7 more miles and crossed present-day **Walnut Creek** to camp near timber "in a beautiful valley which we called Pleasant Valley" (JHKW; DJDL). This was their first campsite in present-day Pottawattamie County.

■ **NISHNABOTNA MIDDLE FORK CAMP • BRIGHAM YOUNG • JUNE 9–10 • 16 MILES • MACEDONIA**

The **Nishnabotna Middle Fork Camp** is located .75 mile west of today's **Macedonia** on the east side of the **West Nishnabotna River.** It is approximately 20 miles east of Council Bluffs and in the southwest quarter of Section 22, Macedonia Township (T74N R40W). It is 2.2 miles west of U.S. 59 on County Road G66 (Pioneer Trail Road).

On June 9 Brigham Young's company traveled 13 miles and halted in a creek bottom (**Graybill Creek**) while workmen finished a bridge. They then moved west 3 more miles, through where today's **Macedonia** is, to the place where Bishop Miller's company had halted to build a major bridge across what they called the **Middle Fork of the Nishnabotna River.** They camped there through June 10, while workers finished the bridge (MHBY; DJDL).

Meanwhile, Heber C. Kimball's company stayed at Graybill Creek to keep their livestock from mixing with that of the Young and Miller groups. During the two-day stop, the Saints in both camps enjoyed visiting back and forth. Some women rode out in a carriage to pick strawberries. Pioneers had a "pleasant time" that evening, "which we spent in dancing on the green grass till bed-time, the bright orb of night shining in all its glory over our heads" (JHKW).

On June 10, **black Saint Jane Manning James gave birth to Silas F. James** between 1:00 and 2:00 P.M. at the Young camp (DJDL). "Put black Jane to bed with a son," midwife Patty Sessions noted that day. "Paid me 24 pounds of flour." Jane and Isaac were traveling, she said, with a Brother Dikes—probably George P. Dykes (JPS June 10, 54). Jane Elizabeth Manning, born in the 1820s, grew up in Connecticut. She was a freeborn black who earned her living as a domestic and servant in Wilton, Connecticut. She and other family members converted to Mormonism there. In 1843, eight of the family started for Nauvoo. Refused passage on a boat at Buffalo, New York, because they were black, they walked the rest of the way to Nauvoo, a distance of some 800 miles. Joseph Smith welcomed them into his home. Jane Manning helped Emma Smith with household work. In Nauvoo Jane married another black Mormon, Isaac James, a native of New Jersey and an 1839 convert. Silas was their first child (JMJ 28).

■ *MACEDONIA LDS SETTLEMENT

In the fall of 1846, Saints established a small settlement called **Macedonia** on the west bank of the Nishnabotna River, across the river from where Brigham Young's camp was. That site is 1 mile west of today's Macedonia on the west bank of the West Nishnabotna River in Old Towne Park, on the south side of County Road G66 (Pioneer Trail Road). It is 2 miles west of U.S. 59 on County Road G66 (Pioneer Trail Road) (2.5 miles south of State 92) near the center of Section 21, Macedonia Township (T74N R40W). It is 19 miles east of Council Bluffs.

Saints from the Macedonia (Ramus) Branch in Illinois, 22 miles southeast of Nauvoo, joined the **Spring Exodus** on May 8, 1846, traveling as the "Macedonia Company" of 31 wagons led by Andrew H. Perkins (JWW June 2, 9, 1846, 51–52). They encamped by the West Nishnabotna River. On Feb. 14, 1847, the 140 members became the Macedonia Branch, with Perkins as branch president. Perkins also served as a stake high councilor and a delegate to the Iowa State legislature (JNM). On June 28, 1851, Jean Rio Baker's small LDS company ferried across a river swollen half a mile wide by constant rains and camped on a hill "at Macedonia, a Mormon town containing 5 houses" (DJRB June 29, 1851). On June 16, 1852, the Macedonia Saints left as a company for Utah (JNM), after which non-Mormons kept Macedonia alive to the present, relocating it less than a mile to the east.

Old Towne Park is a small riverside park honoring the site where the LDS town of Macedonia first stood, 1 mile west of present-day Macedonia. Mormons lived there off and on between 1848 and 1852. The 1846 **Mormon Trail** passed .5 mile south of this park. The 1856–57 **handcart route** passed within .25 mile of the north edge of the park. **A Mormon Trail interpretive panel** is in the park.

New Macedonia

The 1846 **Mormon Trail** and the 1856–57 **handcart route** (both the same trail here) headed westerly through the southern edge of present-day **Macedonia,** crossed the river, and passed about where **Old Towne Park** is.

When the Chicago, Burlington, and Quincy Railroad laid tracks .75 mile east of the old town site, a new town, also called Macedonia, was laid out near the tracks in 1880, and the new Macedonia developed there. Its population is close to 300.

A Mormon Trail interpretive panel, "Macedonia, Transplanted Twice," is .4 mile west of downtown Macedonia on County Road G66 (Pioneer Trail Road) on the north side. By it is a 10,000-pound red granite boulder with a metal plaque telling about Old and New Macedonia and the Mormon Trail.

■ ***West Fork Nishnabotna Camp (Silver Creek Camp) • Brigham Young • June 11 • 8 miles • Treynor**

The **West Fork Camp site** is 4.75 miles south-southeast of Treynor on the east bank of Silver Creek. It is in the southwest quarter of Section 32, Silver Creek Township (T74N R41W). (Today, the Middle Fork of Silver Creek flows into Silver Creek below the pioneers' campsite, which would have cost them two stream crossings within a quarter mile; but the GLO 1852 map shows the Middle Fork entering Silver Creek .5 mile upriver from the campsite.) The campsite is 5 miles south of State 92 on County Road L63 and then west on an unnumbered county road 1 mile, at which spot the campsite spreads north to Silver Creek.

The Camp of Israel resumed its trek on June 11. Across the **West Nishnabotna River** they ascended a hill, from where "a more grand & sublime scene was seldom witnessed. The high Rolling green Elevated Prariries were lined with waggons & almost covered with heards for Miles" (DJDL). They traveled 10 miles and camped near Bishop Miller's pioneer company by what they called the **West Fork of the Nishnabotna River** (today's **Silver Creek**), where workmen built a bridge. The Kimball 50 camped on the south side of the Young 50, and Bishop Miller's company camped south of Kimball's. Capt. Daniel Spencer's company camped "in front" of all the camps, on the bottoms close to Silver Creek (JHKW).

During that June 11 travel day, riders **James Cummings** and **William Potter** arrived, bringing word that **John Lowe Butler** had led the **Emmett company** from **Camp Vermillion** down to a site on the Missouri River about 30 miles south of present-day **Council Bluffs** (MHBY; DJDL).

Ten years later the **Martin handcart company** camped at Silver Creek on Aug. 20, 1856, after pulling for 21 miles. John Jaques described the site as a "good camping place, very little wood, plenty of feed and muddy water" (LHWJJ).

County Road G66 (Pioneer Trail Road)—Mormon Trail/handcart route. Pottawattamie County Road G66 (Pioneer Trail Road) between **Macedonia** and the south edge of **Council Bluffs** closely parallels and sometimes follows exactly the **1846 Mormon Trail route** and the **1856–57 handcart route.**

■ KEG CREEK CAMP • BRIGHAM YOUNG • JUNE 12 • 12 MILES • TREYNOR

The **Keg Creek Camp site** is 4.6 miles southwest of Treynor, 3 miles south of State 92, in the center of the south edge of Section 21, Keg Creek Township (T74N R42W). It is reached by driving 1 mile west of Treynor on State 92, 3 miles south on County Road L55, and 2.6 miles west on County Road G66 (Pioneer Trail Road) to the Keg Creek bridge. The **Keg Creek Camp** site is on the north side of County Road G66 (Pioneer Trail Road) on the east side of the creek.

On June 12 Brigham Young's company moved 9–10 miles and camped on the east bank of a "small stream" (**Keg Creek**), which they thought was a west fork of the Nishnabotna River. There, workmen had to build yet another bridge. The banks were miry, and 40 to 50 cattle had to be pulled from the mud (MHBY). The company was now within one day's travel of reaching the bluffs overlooking the Missouri River.

The **1856 and 1857 handcart companies** followed this same route from Indiantown to Council Bluffs and passed or stopped at some of the same trail sites as did the 1846 pioneers. For example, on Aug. 9, 1856, thc **Willie handcart company** traveled 10 miles from the **West Nishnabotna River** to **Silver Creek,** rested two hours, and then moved on here to Keg Creek (JJGW).

■ **MOSQUITO CREEK HILL CAMP • BRIGHAM YOUNG • JUNE 13 • 9–10 MILES • COUNCIL BLUFFS

The **Mosquito Creek Hill Camp** is on the southeast side of present-day Council Bluffs, 6 miles east of the Missouri River via I-80 and 1.8 miles north-northeast of the Iowa School for the Deaf. It is 2 miles east-southeast of present-day downtown Council Bluffs in the northeast quarter of the southeast quarter of Section 32, Kane Township (T75N R43W). The 1851 GLO map shows a settlement called Carterville in this location (GLO, 1851). The site is reached from I-80 by taking the Madison Ave./Mall of the Bluffs exit, driving southeast and east on Madison until it crosses Mosquito Creek .25 mile away, turning left (northeast) on Valley View Drive for .5 mile and then turning southeast on Franklin Avenue, which immediately ascends what the pioneers called Mosquito Creek Hill.

On June 13, 1846, builders finished the Keg Creek bridge at 10 A.M., so Brigham Young's company traveled 10 miles and camped on a hill near **Mosquito Creek,** where they stopped to build another bridge. Three other companies camped near the creek.

Missouri River and Council Bluffs, IA, 1853. (Steel engraving by Frederick Piercy)

Early that evening Brigham Young and Willard Richards went fishing for an hour (MHBY).

The **Miller, Spencer, and Parley Pratt camps** were down in the valley by Mosquito Creek, in the same location where Saints picked about 10 bushels of wild strawberries (DJDL; MHBY).

The **Kimball company camp** was established 1.5 miles south of the Brigham Young camp. Horace K. Whitney said that just before reaching the campsite, they "could perceive the grand and lofty hills on the opposite side of the Missouri River," and from there they could see the Missouri River "which is about 2 miles from us, a swampy wet bottom intervening" (JHKW). Two days later their camp would become the headquarters campsite for two weeks, after the Missouri River Camp site posed too many problems (see **Mosquito Creek Camp No. 2**).

■ **MISSOURI RIVER CAMP • BRIGHAM YOUNG • JUNE 14–15 • 7 MILES • COUNCIL BLUFFS

Because the course of the Missouri River has since shifted eastward, the **Missouri River Camp** site is now located on the Nebraska side of the river, 1 mile west of the present location of Long's Landing County Park—southwest of Council Bluffs and south of Lake Manawa. To reach the park and obtain a fine view of the river about where the Saints' campsite was located, drive on U.S. 275/State 92 to its intersection with the South Expressway, turn south on what then is called Piute Street for .4 mile, turn left (east) on Comanche and then south on Navajo Road. Stay on that road as it bends around Lake Manawa's east shore and turns south, to its end at **Long's Landing County Park** site (see 32 below and Council Bluffs, IA, map). The Saints' camp was about 1 mile west of this point, now across the Missouri River. That site is also about where the **White Catfish Camp** was on the **Lewis and Clark National Historic Trail.**

At about 11 A.M. on June 14, when the Mosquito Creek bridge was ready, Brigham Young led the companies from their hilly encampments for 7 miles on a circuitous route across the Missouri River flatlands to a campsite near the river he had selected earlier that morning. By nightfall, "all the companies came together and we formed a hollow square on the bank of the Missouri river" (JHKW; MHBY). This encampment was about 1 mile above **Traders (Trading) Pt.,** the location of American Fur Company agent Peter

Sarpy's subtrading post, the Pottawattamie Indian agency, and a village inhabited by French, Indians, and "half-breeds" (JHKW). Across the river the Saints could see Sarpy's principal post, "quite a settlement" of Indians and three trading posts, where Bellevue, Nebraska, now is (see Council Bluffs, IA, map and site 32) (DJDL; JOP June 17).

The leadership council met and decided that one or two men from each company of 10 should herd cattle, one man in four should help build a ferryboat, which work millwright Frederick Kesler should supervise; Bishop Whitney, Bishop Miller, and Capt. Albert Rockwood would be a committee to coordinate with the local traders and agents; and no person should trade with outsiders without permission (MHBY; DJDL; JHKW).

John D. Lee recorded that in the evening on June 14, "several Indians of different Tribes were around our Encampment—among which were the Mohaws [Omahas] who had lately been subdued by the Seus [Sioux] & robbed of all they Possesed, & left to starveation almost naked, they were objects of Pity." He added that "the Potawatomies are civle & will do us no harm, but the Mohaus [Omahas] are suspicious" (DJDL June 15).

On June 15 several men and wagons went "into the country," south into the state of Missouri, to trade—the state line was approximately 50 miles away. Brigham Young, Heber C. Kimball, and Bishops Whitney and Miller made trade arrangements with the "trading house" (JHKW). After one full day in the river camp, Brigham Young decided the encampment should move "back to our old quarters on the bluff, that we last had before coming here," where they "could get good spring water," find better fuel, control the cattle better, and be away from the "Omaha" Indians (JHKW; MHBY; DJDL).

"Learned that there are 2200 Indians (Pottawatomis) and 100 families of white traders a number of halfbreeds, that reside on the pt. below us," Horace K. Whitney noted on June 15. "Among those on the other side of the river are some Mohawks [Omaha], Sioux and other tribes" (JHKW).

■ **MOSQUITO CREEK HILL CAMP NO. 2 • BRIGHAM YOUNG • JUNE 16 • 5 MILES • COUNCIL BLUFFS

The **Mosquito Creek Hill Camp No. 2** was established where the Kimball company had camped on June 13. This triangular site amid "hills and dales and murmuring rivelets" was where Little Pony Creek on their left flowed into Mosquito Creek on their right (JHKW June 13). The site is approximately where the Lewis Central High School building is on the west side of U.S. 275 (Co. L35), across from the Iowa School for the Deaf. The company ranged their cattle in the low area, including where the Iowa School for the Deaf campus is, but camped eastward on higher ground. The site is in the southeast corner of Section 7 and spread through the middle of the west half of Section 8, in Lewis Township (T74N R43W). They occupied a V-shaped area between where the creek once emptied into Mosquito Creek—before both creek beds were rerouted (GLO, 1852; Map EDCB 7).

Disliking the **Missouri River Camp** site, Brigham Young led the companies back to this site on June 16. The last wagons arrived after dark. Bishop Miller brought a "large quantity of fish," including catfish and buffalo fish, and some 100 pounds were distributed among Heber C. Kimball's company. The plan was to stay encamped for two or three weeks until a ferryboat could be built and made operational (JHKW June 16).

While waiting, the emigrants built a bridge across Mosquito Creek, and people soon camped along both sides of that creek. After two weeks, **Church headquarters** were moved to the northwest side of Mosquito Creek (see site 22 **Redemption Hill**). For the next six weeks Saints from the Nauvoo area arrived by the hundreds and established a long string of temporary encampments extending eastward almost to present-day **Treynor** (see site 21 **Pioneer Grand Encampment**) while they waited to cross the Missouri River.

On June 29 the Mormon ferryboat was launched, and from then until fall some 4,000 to 5,000 Saints crossed the river to locate in Nebraska camps (see **ferry** discussions below). The others, numbering 5,000 to 8,000 or more, found campsites all over southwestern Iowa.

■ **MILLER'S HOLLOW/KANESVILLE/COUNCIL BLUFFS, 1846–1852

Council Bluffs, Pottawattamie County, is located on the east side of the Missouri River opposite **Omaha, Nebraska,** on I-80. It is nearly 1,000 feet above sea level and had a population of 58,268 in 2000 (see Miller's Hollow, Kanesville, Council Bluffs, IA, map).

For centuries Native Americans held ceremonial powwows in this area. In 1804 the Lewis and Clark expedition, during their historic exploring journey to the Oregon country, moved through here and conferred on the Nebraska side with the Oto/Missouri Indians where Ft. Atkinson (later Ft. Calhoun) was. By 1852 more California gold seekers used Council Bluffs as their departure point than any other outfitting post along the Missouri River.

The Council Bluffs area is rich in sites related to LDS history. By June 14, 1846, the **Mormon pioneer advance parties** reached the Missouri River here, followed by thousands more of the Nauvoo refugees by fall. At the Pioneer Grand Encampment area, near Council Bluffs, the **Mormon Battalion** assembled and departed.

In late summer 1846, after leaders cancelled plans to reach the Rocky Mountains that year, they moved one-third of the people across the river and by October established **Winter Quarters.** The rest remained on the east side and set up scores of tiny settlements, including **Miller's Hollow,** which is now Council Bluffs. Miller's Hollow became the Mormon city of **Kanesville** and existed from 1848 to 1852. LDS voters and office holders dominated Pottawattamie County by 1849. When almost all Mormons left the area in 1852, the population of **Kanesville** dropped drastically. The city was renamed **Council Bluffs** in 1853. The **1856 and 1857 handcart pioneers** passed through it.

Entrance to Kanesville (Council Bluffs, IA). (Steel engraving by Frederick Piercy, 1853)

In 1863 President Abraham Lincoln, who had visited Council Bluffs in 1859, designated the city as the **eastern terminus for the transcontinental railroad,** soon to be built. Local resident **Grenville Dodge** became the chief engineer of the project. Crews from Council Bluffs and Omaha helped construct the railroad westward to Utah until its completion in 1869. A railway bridge spanning the Missouri was not completed until 1873, however. The city, being a transportation hub for trains and riverboats, became an important agricultural shipping, commercial, and industrial center and continues to be the county seat for Pottawattamie County.

The Mormon Battalion Enlistments

To make proper sense of **Mormon Battalion sites in the Council Bluffs area,** it seems appropriate to include here a brief history of the Battalion's enlistment. On July 1 Capt. James Allen arrived from Ft. Leavenworth (after looking for Brigham Young at Mt. Pisgah), to present him with an invitation from **U.S. president James K. Polk** to enlist a battalion to serve in the Mexican War. The war had formally started on May 13 because of disputes about a border zone claimed by both Mexico and newly independent Texas. For months Church emissaries had lobbied with President Polk for the federal government to help the Saints move west through contracts to do various kinds of work. President Polk's call for a battalion was a favor to the Church. But it came at a bad time.

The government wanted four or five companies of 73 to 109 men each—men ages 18 to 45—to serve for 12 months. The battalion was to receive equipment at Ft. Leavenworth, 200 miles south, and then march to Santa Fe and on to California as part of Gen. Stephen Kearny's Army of the West. Companies could choose their own officers. They would be allowed to keep their guns and other equipment when released from service. Twenty women, or four per company, could be enlisted as laundresses (CHMB 113–15).

In return for the battalion's service, the Church would receive several benefits: (1) the legal right to live on Indian lands that winter; (2) income from the clothing allowance of $42 per man plus paychecks during the march; (3) badly needed income, because once in California the men could earn wages and then take those earnings back to their families; (4) improved public opinion of the Saints; (5) the possibility of more government work in the future; and (6) the assurance that the federal government would not interfere with the Saints' westward march (MoM 58–59).

To recruit 500 men was a hard task. Some men feared this offer was a "plot laid to bring trouble on us as a people," Hosea Stout said, adding that the "universal feelings" among the Saints were "wrought up" against the government (DHS 28 June 1846, 172). "To say the least of it," battalion historian Sgt. Daniel Tyler wrote, "it was a very severe test of their loyalty" (CHMB 117). Few wanted to march 2,000 miles. Few wanted to leave their hard-pressed families in the midst of a rather desperate search for a place to live.

For the Church to give up 500 of its best and needed men on short notice was a major hardship. At the time there were only 800 wagons near the Missouri River, so to remove 500 men from 800 families would have badly crippled the migration effort. To find more manpower, Brigham Young headed back on the trail and counted wagons. From the Missouri River to Mt. Pisgah he found 1,805 wagons (MHBY July 7). He recruited as he went (see **Mormon Battalion Recruitment** in connection with **Mt. Pisgah**) and sent appeals to Garden Grove and on toward Nauvoo for volunteers to rush to the bluffs and enlist.

On July 16, 450 men signed up, filling four of the five companies. Their soldiers' pay started that day. The companies marched about 7 miles to Sarpy's post, where each man received one blanket and food. For the next week the soldiers came and went between their camp by the Missouri River and the Mormon encampments along Mosquito Creek. On July 18 Brigham Young and four apostles met with the officers and urged them to be fathers to the men and to govern by priesthood power, not military methods. He promised them they would not have to do any fighting (MHBY July 16–18).

On July 21 companies A, B, C, and D began the long march to Ft. Leavenworth. Company E finally filled up and caught up with the rest. This war-caused separation of families exacted high tolls emotionally, as shown in Sgt. William Hyde's comments:

> The thoughts of leaving my family at this critical time are indescribable. They were far from the land of their nativity, situated upon a lonely prairie with no dwelling but a wagon, the

> scorching sun beating upon them, with the prospect of the cold winds of December finding them in the same bleak, dreary place. My family consisted of a wife and two small children, who were left in company with an aged father and mother and a brother. The most of the Battalion left families, some in care of the Church and some in care of relatives, with some in their own care. (CHMB 128)

The Mormon Battalion reached Ft. Leavenworth on Aug 1. From there the unit, despite sizeable releases of sick detachments along the way, marched from Ft. Leavenworth, Kansas, to Santa Fe, New Mexico, and arrived in San Diego, California, on Jan. 29, 1847. After their year of service ended in July 1847, Battalion members returned from California by various routes to meet their families in Utah, on the Mormon Trail, or in the Council Bluffs area.

Accepting such a loss of manpower from the 1846 Mormon wagon trains, President Young cancelled plans to send a pioneering party to the Rocky Mountains in 1846.

Miller's Hollow and Kanesville (Early Council Bluffs)

Miller's Hollow, the original tiny Mormon settlement that became the nucleus around which Kanesville grew, was centered where present-day Broadway and 4th Streets intersect (see Miller's Hollow, Kanesville, Council Bluffs, IA, map).

Henry W. Miller and his brother **Daniel A. Miller** cofounded **Miller's Hollow** in 1846, and Henry became the bishop of the little settlement. He later served as a delegate to the Iowa legislature, the first Mormon to do so. Miller's Hollow became known as **Kane** in 1847 and **Kanesville** in 1848 (NJ [Fall 1996]: 75).

The settlement snuggled along **Indian Creek** within a hollow surrounded by hills and bluffs. Indian Creek now flows through underground culverts in downtown Council Bluffs.

In 1848, keeping their prior commitment to Native Americans, the Saints abandoned Winter Quarters on the west side of the Missouri River. They made **Miller's Hollow,** soon renamed **Kanesville,** the new hub of activity in that area and one of the Church's main stopping places for Saints to outfit themselves before heading west (ENS Aug. 2002:14–21). Kanesville was named

Thomas L. Kane, friend of the Saints.

to honor **Thomas L. Kane,** a friend to the Mormons. Born in 1822, Kane was part of a prominent Pennsylvania family. He completed college training in Philadelphia, studied in England, and became an attorney. He arrived among the Mormons on July 11, 1846, as an emissary of President Polk to help recruit the Mormon Battalion. He gained the Saints' trust immediately. Horace K. Whitney said of Kane:

> This young gentleman became acquainted with some of our presiding elders in the east, particularly Bro. Little with whom he held several interviews, and obtained a knowledge of our persecutions, &c., and having sympathy for us he was anxious to do something for our benefit, and being intimately acquainted with the President of the U.S. he went to the city of Washington, and laid before him our case. . . . This young man appears to be an instrument in the hands of the Lord to bring about our salvation at the present time. (JHKW July 12)

Kane developed deep sympathy for the plight of the Mormon refugees. Back east he became an unofficial adviser to President Young ("Kane," EnM).

To memorialize Kanesville, a main street in downtown Council Bluffs today is named **Kanesville Boulevard.**

Kanesville's main intersection was two blocks south of present-day Kanesville Boulevard, where today's Pierce Street and South 1st Street intersect. Kanesville's commercial district spread two blocks southward up **1st Street** (then called **Hyde Street**) and east and west from that intersection for 10 or 12 blocks along Pierce Street and the next street north, Main Street (now Broadway).

A county history published in 1907 made several observations about the Kanesville period of Council Bluffs history:

> No more industrious, frugal and temperate community was ever known. Among them were mechanics of almost every kind, and they proceeded to build a city here, which they called Kanesville. . . . Not only did they build the city, but the rich

Kanesville (Miller's Hollow or Council Bluffs), IA, 1849–51. (Sketch by George Simons; courtesy of Council Bluffs Public Library)

> valleys became hives of industry; good crops were raised, which enabled them to assist their fellow pilgrims who were passing through. . . . At this time everything was controlled by the church. Idleness and dissipation were not tolerated. There was no jail nor need for one. A newspaper was published by Orson Hyde called the *Frontier Guardian,* and although the buildings were mostly of logs, good stocks of goods were kept by as honorable merchants as you will find anywhere. . . . At this time the whole of Pottawattamie county, which was much larger than at present, as well as considerable adjoining territory, was under exclusive control of the Mormons. They made public sentiment, controlled election of all public officers, and representatives of their faith sat in two sessions of the state legislature. (HPCF 8–9)

In early 1852 the city had 1,200 to 1,500 residents, about 300 houses, 16 mercantile establishments, two drug stores, two printing offices, five hotels, four groceries, two jewelers shops, one harness maker, eight wagon shops, two livery stables, two tinsmiths, two cabinet shops, one mill, five boot makers and shoemakers, three barber shops, four bakeries, seven blacksmith shops, two daguerrean rooms, one gunsmith, one cooper, several ministers of different denominations, five physicians, and nine attorneys. Several ferries operated nearby to take travelers across the wide Missouri (FG Apr. 15, 1852).

Kanesville became the **Church's eastern headquarters** for the United States regions east of the Rockies, with **apostle Orson Hyde** as **president.** For more than three years Church concerns were promoted in the ***Frontier Guardian,*** a weekly and semiweekly Kanesville newspaper edited and published by Elder Hyde.

The town served as an **LDS hub community** for western Iowa. Mormons waiting to go to Utah created nearly 90 tiny villages and settlements (branches) within a 60-mile radius of Kanesville. At its peak Kanesville and these surrounding clusters had a population of more than 7,000 in 1852 (FG Apr. 15, 1852).

Kanesville served as an **outfitting and transportation center** for LDS emigrants and returning missionaries heading for Utah. From 1848 to 1852, an estimated 46 Mormon wagon trains left from there, involving about 2,900 wagons and more than 25,000 Mormons (HRSMT 134–41). In 1851 traveler Jean Rio Baker described Kanesville as "quite a pretty town, and the surrounding scenery very beautiful" (DJRB, July 2, 258).

During its four-year existence, Kanesville was a **missionary depot** for missionaries from the Utah Territory going to their fields of labor.

Thousands of **gold rush travelers** outfitted in Kanesville in preparation for their treks to California—about 10,000 in 1849 alone—and their purchases brought prosperity to Saints in the area:

> In 1849 a great wave of California immigration set in, and hundreds of trains and thousands of men assembled here and camped while laying in supplies, and Kanesville became a great outfitting point, and the merchants reaped a rich harvest. The farms furnished abundance of grain, while steamboats arrived almost daily with large stocks of goods for the merchants, and the rush was so great that at times emigrants had to wait for days for their turn to be ferried across the river. Not only that, but the Mormons saw money in it and proceeded to establish ranches along the trail, and ferries across the rivers. (HPCF 9)

On Sept. 21, 1851, the LDS First Presidency wrote a letter instructing "all the Saints in Pottawatamie" to move to Utah the next season "and fail not." "What are you waiting for? Have you any good excuse for not coming? No!" "We wish you to evacuate

Pottawatamie, and the States, and next fall be with us." Those who make the sacrifice "shall be blessed" (MFP 2:75–76). In response, during 1852 almost all the Saints left **Kanesville and southwestern Iowa** and became a massive stream of emigrants flowing to Utah (HRSMT 134).

The next year the local residents renamed the city **Council Bluffs** (ENS Aug. 1988:54–57; EnH 160–61). "The natural influx of Gentiles," a county history states,

> so changed matters that its character as a Mormon community was lost forever. . . . Whether this change was morally beneficial is debatable. Under the old dispensation the saloon, gambling and bawdy house were not tolerated, but now blossomed out in full vigor, and . . . the city was what would now be called a wide-open town. (HPCF 10)

See the Miller's Hollow, Kanesville, Council Bluffs, IA, map for the locations of the following sites and downtown buildings: (1) Kanesville Log Tabernacle site, (2) Replicated Log Tabernacle (3) Old Blockhouse, (4) Hyde Street, along which were the

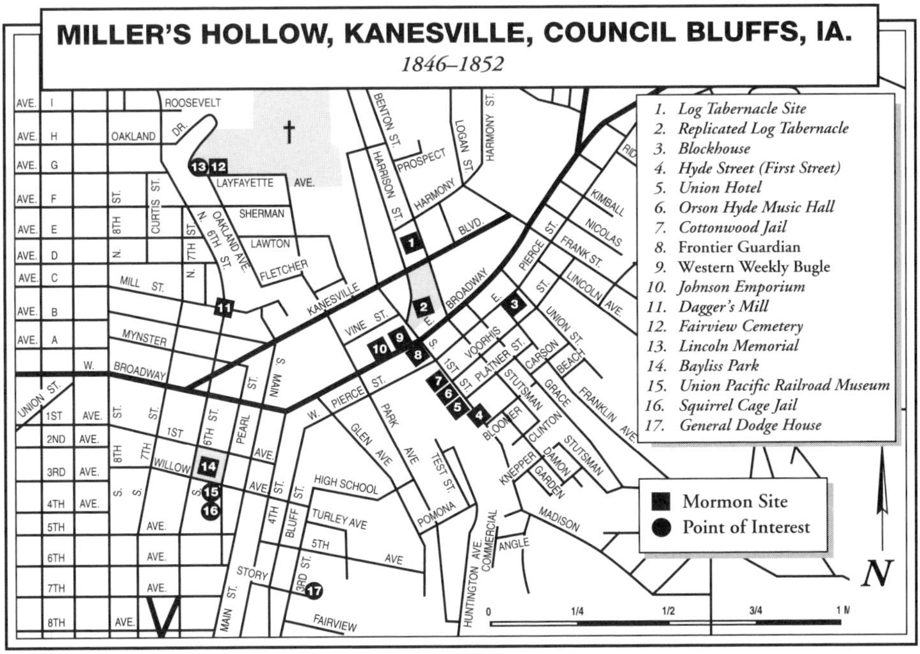

(5) Union Hotel, (6) Orson Hyde Music Hall, and (7) Cottonwood Jail; (8) *Frontier Guardian* newspaper office, (9) *Western Weekly Bugle* newspaper office, (10) Johnson Emporium, (11) Dagger's Mill, (12) Fairview Cemetery (originally Kanesville Cemetery), (13) Lincoln Memorial, (14) Bayliss Park, (15) Union Pacific Railroad Museum, (16) Squirrel Cage Jail, and (17) Historic Gen. Dodge House. Most of these sites lack markers, and none of the original buildings has survived. The location of an important Kanesville building called the Council House is not known. The following sites relating to Miller's Hollow and Kanesville (now Council Bluffs) are of particular interest.

■ **1. Original Kanesville Log Tabernacle Site.** The site of the original Kanesville Log Tabernacle is in downtown Council Bluffs. Travelers can see where it once stood by proceeding from the intersection of South 1st Street and Kanesville Boulevard northeast two blocks on Kanesville Boulevard and then turning north on Benton Street for half a block. There, on the west side, mid-block, is where the tabernacle once stood.

The Kanesville Log Tabernacle was the **first tabernacle in LDS history.** With Henry W. Miller as construction superintendent, Saints built the tabernacle in just three weeks in December 1847 so that an important Church conference could be held. The cottonwood log building measured at least 60 feet west to east and 40 feet north to south and could seat a large number of people. A fireplace covered the entire west end. Two four-foot doors, about 14 feet apart, were in the middle of the long south side. From the 13-foot-high walls, the pitched roof rose 20 feet.

Approximately 1,000 Saints gathered at the tabernacle for a **historic conference and tabernacle dedication** held Dec. 23–27, 1847. The key business during the conference was the **reconstituting of the LDS First Presidency** for the first time since Joseph Smith's death, with **Brigham Young** as president and **Heber C. Kimball** and **Willard Richards** as counselors. The First Presidency was sustained by the congregation on Dec. 27 (HC 7:622–24).

The tabernacle served as Kanesville's main meetinghouse for more than a year and was used extensively for conferences, elections, balls, socials, and meetings of the Blockhouse Branch and the Pottawattamie Stake High Council. The tabernacle was dismantled in 1849, however, because by then logs from the green cottonwood trees used in its construction had begun to shrink, causing it to leak badly. Apparently, some of its logs were reused to help construct the Pigeon Creek Branch tabernacle, the exact site of which is unknown (MoM 309).

At a **jubilee** in January 1848, LDS members enjoyed a five-day gathering at the tabernacle for celebrating, worship, preaching, and dancing. Plans for the town's development were drawn up then (JH Jan. 16–21, 1848; MoM 212, 217).

■ 2. KANESVILLE HISTORIC PARK/REPLICATED LOG TABERNACLE. Located a long block southeast from where the original once stood, the replica is in the Kanesville Historic Park, 222 East Broadway, filling most of a city block between Broadway and Kanesville Boulevard, one block east of 1st Street and just west of Benton Street.

The snug replica tabernacle, built by Kanesville Restoration Inc., was dedicated by **LDS Church president Gordon B. Hinckley** on July 13, 1996. It became an **LDS Visitors' Center** in 1999. It measures 40 feet by 60 feet inside with an extension 12 feet by 20 feet on the north side. At the back of the extension is a Bill Hill (Mendon, Utah) painting depicting the Twelve Apostles at the time the original tabernacle was dedicated and the First Presidency reconstituted. Displays depict LDS history, including the trek of the Mormon Battalion. The uses of the replica tabernacle are similar to those of the original—religious services, musical programs, debates, social events, receptions, group meetings, and historical reenactments.

Also in the park is a **visitors' center** where the story of the tabernacle is depicted in wall displays and exhibits, and a film about the Mormon Battalion is shown. On the grounds are a wayside panel depicting the building of the log tabernacle; a Stan Watts sculpture of the 1847 First Presidency; a Bob Keiser **statue of Henry W. Miller,** the founder (with his brother David) of Miller's Hollow, which became Kanesville; a **Families Are Forever Court of Memories and Gardens,**

Replica of the Kanesville Log Tabernacle. (1997)

which features Bill Hill's **sculpture of a pioneer family** entitled "The Family, an Everlasting Heritage"; and standing plaques that contain (1) the LDS Church's 1995 **Proclamation on the Family,** (2) facts about the reconstituting of the First Presidency in December 1847, (3) the text of the "Word and Will of the Lord" revelation of Jan. 14, 1847 that gave directions for organizing the LDS trek west; and (4) "The Living Christ: The Testimony of The Apostles." A heroic-sized statue of Thomas L. Kane is planned.

■ **3. Blockhouse.** At the southeast corner of East Pierce and Franklin Streets a **historical marker** (1971) designates the approximate location of the old log Blockhouse. Built in 1837 by U.S. troops to protect Pottawattamie Indians, the Blockhouse is considered to have been the **first building in Council Bluffs.** Between 1838 and 1841 it served as the **St. Mary/St. Joseph Catholic Mission.**

Around the corner from Pierce Street on Franklin Street is another **historical marker** that tells about the LDS connection to the blockhouse.

In 1846 LDS **Bishop Henry Miller** purchased the Blockhouse from the Pottawattamie Indians, and around it grew up **Miller's Hollow** (1846) and then **Kanesville** (1848). The Blockhouse became the meeting hall for the LDS **Blockhouse Branch.** The building was torn down in 1857.

On Dec. 3–4, 1847 LDS Church leaders attempted to hold a conference in **Silas Richards**'s double blockhouse, near the Blockhouse, but the Saints congregated in such large numbers and so clamored at the windows for admission that the conference was adjourned for three weeks in order to build a new **log tabernacle** to house Church gatherings (HC 7:620–22).

■ **4. Hyde Street (now 1st Street).** A block and a half southwest of the replicated Log Tabernacle is the intersection of 1st Street and Broadway. South of that intersection, 1st Street used to be called **Hyde Street,** named for LDS apostle **Orson Hyde.** Hyde Street was Kanesville's main north-south street. Several important "downtown" buildings lined Hyde Street as well as Broadway (then Main Street) and Pierce Street (GGH 22). Two blocks south on 1st Street from Broadway, opposite where Platner Street now intersects 1st Street from the east, are the locations where three historic LDS buildings once stood next to each other.

■ **5. Union Hotel Site.** Directly opposite present-day Platner Street, the hotel housed travelers, diners, and professional offices.

■ **6. Orson Hyde Music Hall.** Next door to the Union Hotel on the north was the Orson Hyde Music Hall. Choral and band concerts, music lessons, and plays took place there, as did civic and social activities. The hall served later as the Pottawattamie County's first courthouse.

■ **7. Cottonwood Jail.** Next to the Music Hall on its north side stood the county jail, required by law once Pottawattamie County was formed. It had few if any occupants.

■ **8. *Frontier Guardian* Newspaper Office.** With offices located on the southwest corner of Broadway and South 1st Street (Main Street and Hyde Street in those days), this LDS four-page bi-weekly newspaper was first published on Feb. 7, 1849, and continued until early 1852. The ***Frontier Guardian*** kept Saints in the area informed about the progress of the Church and promoted Kanesville's development and overland trail outfittings. It contained much advertising, names of passing gold rush travelers, and news about trail conditions, ferry crossings, and Indians (HFG).

■ **9. *Western Weekly Bugle* Newspaper Office.** Directly north across the street from the *Frontier Guardian* office site and one building to the west is the site of another early LDS newspaper. Published briefly during the Kanesville period, the ***Western Weekly Bugle*** was edited by Almon G. Babbitt and then by Joseph E. Johnson.

■ **10. Johnson Emporium.** A store was operated by Joel H. Johnson two building sites west of the *Western Weekly Bugle* office on the north side of Broadway in the middle of the block between 1st Street and Park Avenue.

■ **11. Dagger's Mill.** The Dagger's Mill site is located at the edge of the bluff where **Mill Street** now intersects with North 6th Street (six blocks west of 1st Street).

Madison Dagger built a gristmill about 1848, powered by an overshot waterwheel turned by water brought in a long ditch from Indian Creek. The millrace ditch began where Benton Street and

Kanesville Boulevard (Greene Street or Race Street then) now intersect, and followed along the south side of Kanesville Boulevard to near present-day Mill Street. Mormons at Kanesville used this mill (EDCB 87).

■ **12. Fairview Cemetery.** The southwest entrance to **Fairview Cemetery,** 308 Lafayette, is four blocks north and uphill from Kanesville Boulevard via Oakland Avenue (two long blocks west of 1st Street). This was the **Kanesville Cemetery** from 1846 to 1863, when it was replatted and reopened as Fairview Cemetery. To the right of this main entrance is a **historical marker** telling about the Kanesville Cemetery.

Kanesville Mormon Cemetery, IA, 1846–52. It was renamed Fairview Cemetery in 1863 and given to the city of Council Bluffs in 1974. Only a few marked graves date back to LDS times. (1997)

Between 1846 and 1852 several hundred Saints were buried in the Kanesville Cemetery, probably more than at the better-known Winter Quarters cemetery across the river in present-day Florence, Nebraska. A Mormon visitor to the cemetery in 1876 said regarding the LDS section:

> The surface of the ground was in such a shape that no reliable estimate could be formed of the number buried. The boards and billets of wood which had been placed at the heads of graves, the former in some instances with the indistinct remains of lettering in memory of the departed, were gradually disappearing, leaving only little knobs of earth covered with rank grass, scarcely distinguishable from the surrounding surface, to indicate where weary wanderers found a resting place.
>
> No carving was found in memory of the dead dating farther back than 1850. The corroding influence of the elements had obliterated everything of earlier date. One inscription on a head board . . . bore the following inscription: "John P. Greene,

infant son of Evan M. and Susan Greene, died March 3rd, 1852, aged 8 months and 16 days." (KSLL 254–55)

Near the cemetery's southwest entrance are graves of the Bloomer family. In 1855 Council Bluffs became the home of famed suffragette **Amelia Jenks Bloomer,** a magazine editor who introduced to the world the "bloomer girl" look, featuring heavily gathered "skirt pants" or "bloomers." Many women on the overland trails—but few if any in Mormon wagon trains—appreciated wearing "bloomers," which were practical clothing for women walking across the plains.

At the cemetery's southeast corner, on Lafayette and North 2nd Streets, is the famous **Black Angel Statue** (1920), sometimes called "The Angel of Death," sculpted in solid bronze by Daniel Chester French, best known for his statue of the Minute Man in Concord and the Lincoln Memorial in Washington, D.C. Daughters of Ruth Anne Dodge, wife of railroad construction engineer Grenville Dodge, commissioned the heroic-sized statue in memory of their mother. According to tourist literature, it depicts what Mrs. Dodge reportedly dreamt during the three nights preceding her death in 1916—the bronze angel in the prow of a boat extends a vessel of water, offering Mrs. Dodge "the water of life."

Early headstones in the cemetery (none are yet documented as being LDS-related) are found in Sections JE and E, dating from 1852, and Section CC, dating as early as 1853. Mormon pioneer graves were primarily on the high east side of the cemetery.

● **13. Lincoln Memorial.** One block west of the Fairview Cemetery's southwest entrance at the top of Oakland Avenue is a **Lincoln Memorial** (1911). This stately pylon marks the site where presidential candidate Abraham Lincoln stood in 1859 to nominate the city as the **eastern terminus for a** future **transcontinental railroad** (see Miller's Hollow, Kanesville, and Council Bluffs, IA, map).

Downtown Council Bluffs

■ **14. Bayliss Park.** A downtown city block contains **Bayliss Park,** located one block south of West Broadway on 1st Avenue between Pearl Street and South 6th Street.

Among its several monuments is a massive boulder on the

north side facing 1st Avenue, to which are attached **DAR plaques** commemorating the **Mormon Trail in Iowa.** Other monuments in the park honor veterans of the Civil War, Spanish-American War, and the Vietnam War. At the park's center is a **computerized fountain** that is constantly changing in form and, at night, in lighting. **Black squirrels,** found mostly along the east side of the Missouri River from northwestern Missouri to Council Bluffs, are frequent park visitors.

● **15. Union Pacific Railroad Museum.** A restored Carnegie Library building (1903) at 200 Pearl Street houses the **Union Pacific's historical collection** of artifacts, photographs, and documents that trace the development of railroads in the American West and of the nation's first transcontinental railroad. Council Bluffs was the eastern terminus of the Union Pacific, the starting point for tens of thousands of westward-bound emigrants.

In 1862 **President Lincoln** created the **Union Pacific Railroad** and directed that it and the **Central Pacific Railroad** build America's first **transcontinental railroad** from Council Bluffs to Sacramento. The project began in 1863 in Omaha and was completed in 1869 with the driving of the **golden spike** at **Promontory Summit,** in **Utah Territory.** The Union Pacific quickly became the nation's primary east-west mover of passengers and freight. In 1875 the Union Pacific opened a bridge between Council Bluffs and Omaha. In 1971 Amtrak took over operations of the nation's passenger train service. In 1996 Union Pacific and Southern Pacific merged, reuniting the original transcontinental partnership.

● **16. Squirrel Cage Jail.** This unusual old **Pottawattamie County Jail** is located half a block south of Bayliss Park at 226 Pearl Street. Its interior contains a three-story steel cage with wedge-shaped cells. The entire cage had to be rotated, like a Lazy Susan, to access each cell. Built in 1885 and closed in 1969, it is now a tourist attraction.

● **17. Historic Gen. Dodge House.** Located at 605 3rd Street (corner of 3rd Street and Story Street), this restored, elegant 14-room, three-story Victorian mansion was built in 1869 and is a National Historic Landmark and a house-museum open to the public.

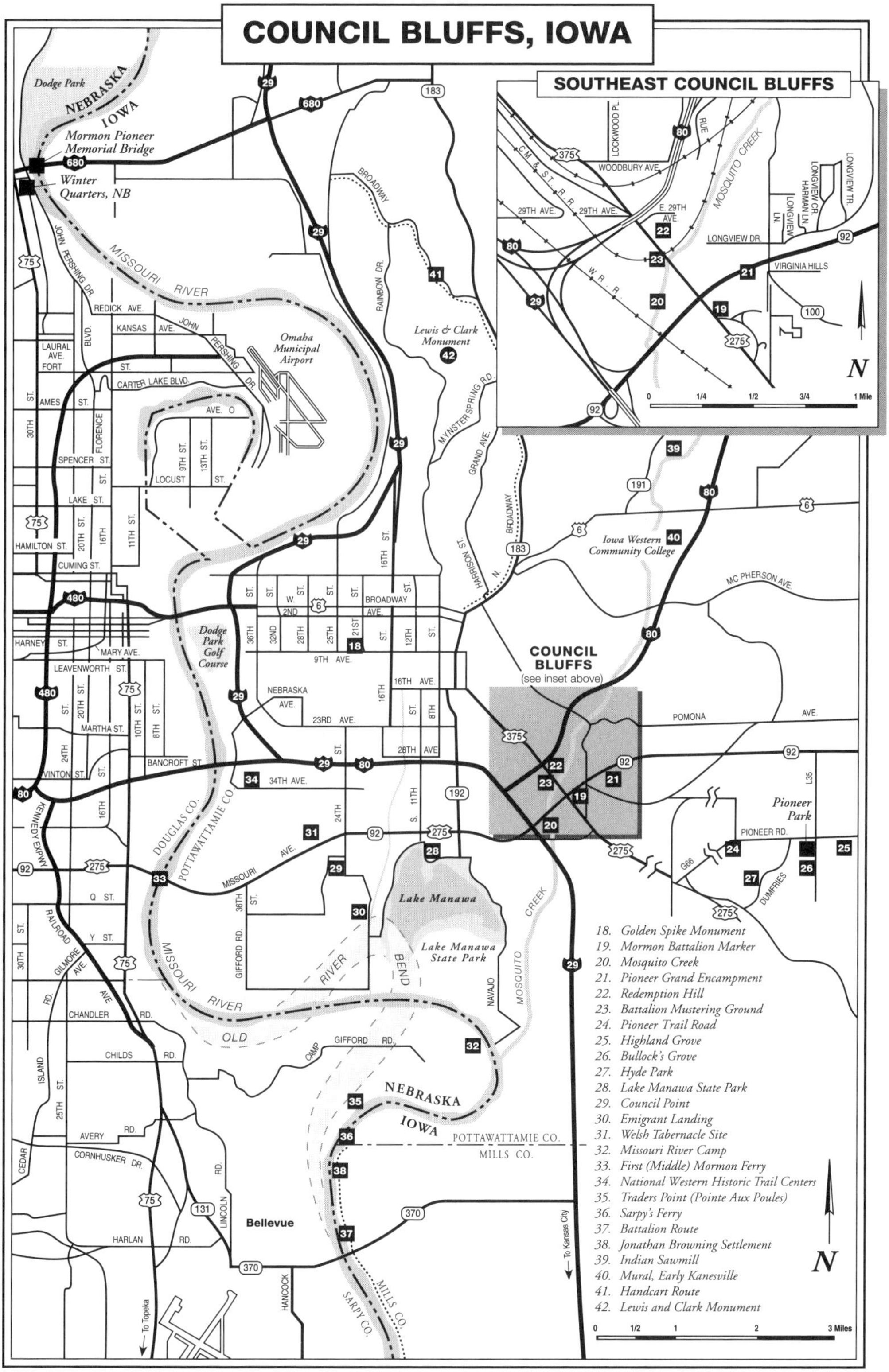
COUNCIL BLUFFS, IOWA
SOUTHEAST COUNCIL BLUFFS
Dodge Park
NEBRASKA
IOWA
Mormon Pioneer Memorial Bridge
Winter Quarters, NB
MISSOURI RIVER
Omaha Municipal Airport
Lewis & Clark Monument
Dodge Park Golf Course
Iowa Western Community College
COUNCIL BLUFFS (see inset above)
Pioneer Park
Lake Manawa
Lake Manawa State Park
OLD RIVER BEND
MOSQUITO CREEK
DOUGLAS CO.
POTTAWATTAMIE CO.
MILLS CO.
SARPY CO.
Bellevue
To Topeka
To Kansas City
18. Golden Spike Monument
19. Mormon Battalion Marker
20. Mosquito Creek
21. Pioneer Grand Encampment
22. Redemption Hill
23. Battalion Mustering Ground
24. Pioneer Trail Road
25. Highland Grove
26. Bullock's Grove
27. Hyde Park
28. Lake Manawa State Park
29. Council Point
30. Emigrant Landing
31. Welsh Tabernacle Site
32. Missouri River Camp
33. First (Middle) Mormon Ferry
34. National Western Historic Trail Centers
35. Traders Point (Pointe Aux Poules)
36. Sarpy's Ferry
37. Battalion Route
38. Jonathan Browning Settlement
39. Indian Sawmill
40. Mural, Early Kanesville
41. Handcart Route
42. Lewis and Clark Monument
N
0 1/2 1 2 3 Miles

Sitting high on a terrace overlooking the Missouri River Valley, it was built as the residence of Civil War general **Grenville M. Dodge.**

Dodge also was the chief engineer for constructing the Union Pacific's half of the transcontinental railroad between Council Bluffs and Promontory Summit, Utah. He was considered a great railroad builder and was an author, financier, and friend and counselor to seven United States presidents.

Southern Council Bluffs Area

● **18. Golden Spike Monument.** A 56-foot concrete golden spike located at South 21st Street and 9th Avenue was erected to mark the eastern terminus of the **Union Pacific Railroad.** The dedication of the monument on Apr. 28, 1939, coincided with Omaha's premiere of the black-and-white movie *Union Pacific.* The spike stands as a towering reminder of the grit and determination that built the first transcontinental railroad (see Council Bluffs, IA, map).

■ **19. Mormon Battalion Marker/Iowa School for the Deaf** (see **Mormon Battalion Enlistments** and sites 22, 23, and 37). The **Iowa School for the Deaf** is located at the south edge of Council Bluffs, east of the point where U.S. 275 intersects State 92. **A Mormon Battalion marker** (1986) at the school's northwest entrance honors the Battalion's enlistment site (see Council Bluffs, IA, map).

In July 1846 the **Mormon Battalion** recruits assembled .5 mile northwest of this marker (see site 23). The unit of 489 men, organized into five companies, was accompanied by 34 women and 44 children—most of the women served as laundresses and some teenage boys as aides to the officers (MRB-R 28; EnM 935). During late July 1846 the battalion left for Ft. Leavenworth, Kansas, some 200 miles away, marching south along the Missouri River's east shoreline (see site 37).

■ **20. Mosquito Creek** flows south-southwest through the southeast part of Council Bluffs. I-80 parallels the creek for much of that length.

The 1846 pioneers had two camps along Mosquito Creek. They established **Mosquito Creek Hill Camp** on the southeast side of present-day Council Bluffs, 6 miles from the Missouri River

Mosquito Creek, IA.

and 1.8 miles north-northeast of the Iowa School for the Deaf. They also moved back from the Missouri River to set up a camp headquarters at **Mosquito Creek Camp No. 2,** just west of where the Iowa School for the Deaf is now.

Mosquito Creek became the central geographic feature of the 1846 encampments and of the headquarters camp.

When **Oliver Cowdery** returned to the Church (see site 27), he was baptized in Mosquito Creek.

Starting in 1846 and continuing until 1852, Saints built cabins and farms and small cluster settlements upstream along the creek for 30 miles. One such place was the **Mosquito Creek Settlement,** its precise location along the creek unknown.

■ **21. Pioneer Grand Encampment.** When the 1846 Saints arrived, their first camps were along Mosquito Creek and then, as campsites filled up, ever more eastward from it. Soon this **Pioneer Grand Encampment,** a wagon-and-tent city of thousands of Saints, stretched 9 miles east and southeast of Mosquito Creek. Some of the camps straddled or bordered today's east-west State 92 from Council Bluffs almost to **Treynor.** This highway now has several **Mormon Trail signs** along it.

On the northwest side of the **Iowa School for the Deaf,** about one block east of U.S. 275 (Co. L35) and just south of State 92, is a **Mormon Trail interpretive panel** honoring the **Pioneer Grand Encampment.** This marker is on the **scenic nature trail** that crosses U.S. 275 (Co. L35) from the southwest corner of the Iowa School for the Deaf campus. Heading south near U.S. 275 (Co. L35), the nature trail passes the Lewis Central High School and joins the **Wabash Trace,** a roadbed for the old Wabash Railroad. From there the crushed rock trail heads southeast, and about 5 miles later passes the **Hyde Park** site (see site 27). This scenic hiking, biking, and equestrian trail continues south-southeast into Missouri. A second **Iowa Mormon Trail panel** on the School for the Deaf grounds depicts the building of cabins on the Missouri River.

"We came to some camps," late arriver Hosea Stout said on July 5, "which were the outer camps of the main encampment although the Ferry across the Missouri was yet twelve miles." He called this lineup the "first part of the **Grand encampment**" (DHS July 5, 174). On July 12, when Brigham Young returned from his quick recruiting trip to Mt. Pisgah, he counted 30 to 40 different companies camped between Keg Creek and Redemption Hill (MHBY). On July 13, after almost all of the LDS refugees from the Nauvoo area who were coming had arrived, John Smith said, "There is probably 2,000 wagons Here in the camp" (DJS).

The **Pioneer Grand Encampment** existed for several weeks while the Saints, as they could, were either ferried across the river to merge with Brigham Young's advance companies in July and August or until they could find and move to better sites on the Iowa side.

■ **22. Redemption Hill, Bowery, Post Office, LDS Headquarters.** North of the Iowa School for the Deaf, northeast of where Harry Langdon Boulevard crosses Mosquito Creek, is a distinct hill on and along which the 1846 pioneer companies headed by **John Taylor, Parley P. Pratt,** and **Wilford Woodruff** had camped. Saints named this hill **Redemption Hill** (JWW July 12, 1846).

This site is reached by going .7 mile north of the Iowa School for the Deaf on Harry Langdon Boulevard just north of where it crosses Mosquito Creek, to a very short street on the right (east) called East 29th Avenue, which runs steeply uphill toward the east, up what was called Redemption Hill. "I pitched my tent & encampment on a Bluff near Elders Taylor & P P Pratt," Wilford Woodruff wrote on July 9 (JWW). He described part of the Redemption Hill layout:

> Elder Taylor's company was encamped on the South of Chime rid[g]e of Redemption Hill & mine on the North about 4 rods apart. Elder P. P. Pratts was 10 rods north of my Company. We built a Bower[y] between Elder Taylors Tent and my own. (JWW July 12)

Along this hill the **1846 pioneers** set up a temporary **Church headquarters** while waiting to cross the Missouri River. Church leaders met here often. The Saints erected a **bowery** for meetings, assemblies, and socials and opened a **post office** in **Willard Richards's tent.** In the vicinity they also erected a **liberty pole** from which they flew a white sheet and under it a United States flag (AGW July 1846).

Here is where **U.S. Army Capt. James Allen** found Brigham Young in July and formally requested of the Church four or five companies of recruits for service in the Mexican War (see **Mormon Battalion Enlistments** and sites 19, 23 and 37).

During the evenings of July 13 and 14, the Saints gathered at the bowery for a **concert and dance.** Thomas L. Kane gave a colorful description of the dance held on July 13, which he and subsequent historians have confused with the actual farewell ball that took place later near Traders Pt. on July 18. Kane seems to have merged the two occasions into one in his word picture:

> The afternoon before [the Battalion departed] was appropriated to a farewell ball; and a more merry dancing rout I have never seen, though the company was without refreshments, and their ball-room was of the most primitive. It was the custom, whenever the larger camps rested for a few days together, to make great arbors, or Boweries, as they called them, of poles, and brush, and wattling, as places of shelter for their meetings. . . . In one of these, where the ground had been trodden firm and hard by the worshippers of the popular Father Taylor's precinct, was gathered now the mirth and beauty of the Mormon Israel. . . .
>
> With the rest attended the elders of the church within call, including nearly all the chiefs of the High Council, with their wives and children. . . . Their leading off the dancing in a great double cotillion was the signal bade the festivity commence. To the canto of debonnair violins, the cheer of horns, the jingle of sleigh-bells, and the jovial snoring of the tambourine, they did dance! None of your minuets or other mortuary processions of gentles in etiquette, tight shoes, and pinching gloves, but the spirited and scientific displays of our venerated and merry grandparents, who were not above following the fiddle to the Fox-Chase Inn, or Gardens of Gray's Ferry. French Fours, Copenhagen Jigs, Virginia reels, and the like forgotten figures, executed with the spirit of people too happy to be slow, or bashful or constrained. Light hearts, lithe figures and light feet,

> had it their own way from an early hour till after the sun had dipped behind the sharp sky line of the Omaha hills. (MOR 29–31)

On Saturday, July 11, Thomas L. Kane had first arrived in the Mormon camps. "A man came here by the name of Kane," Hosea Stout noted that day. "He was from Washington. He said that we had nothing to fear and all was right between us and the Government &c. He was quite an intelligent man notwithstanding he was uncommonly small and feminine" (DHS July 11, 176). The next morning, Sunday, Guy M. Keysor and others erected a "large bowery" in front of John Taylor's camp, near Redemption Hill, where, Keysor said, a large congregation met that day (DGMK July 12 [13]). Speakers were Elder Wilford Woodruff, newly returned from a mission to England, and Elder Parley P. Pratt (DHS July 12, 177). At the call of President Young that evening, all available men gathered to the bowery on Monday, July 13. There, speakers spent the afternoon meetings discussing the Battalion call and seeking recruits. By 5:00 P.M. nearly three companies had been recruited. That evening the big concert and dance that Kane described took place. According to Brigham Young's history,

> about six, the Council, Captn. Allen, Col. Kane and a large party of the Saints assembled inside the Bowery and danced to the music of the band until near dark, when the concert closed with a song "The Maid of Judah" by Susan Divine, and benediction by Prest. Young. (MHBY July 13)

The Battalion's **farewell dance** is discussed in connection with site 33.

■ **23. Mormon Battalion Mustering Grounds** (see **Mormon Battalion Enlistments** and sites 19, 22, and 37). The site of the **Battalion**'s mustering, gathering, and organizing place was near the base of Redemption Hill by Mosquito Creek. Drive .5 mile northwest of the Iowa School for the Deaf and its Battalion Marker (site 19) on Harry Landon Boulevard onto that road's bridge spanning Mosquito Creek. The site is on the flatlands along the northwest side of the creek (see Council Bluffs, IA, map). Elder Wilford Woodruff described their **departure meeting**:

> [July] 16, [1846.] Four Companies of the volunteers were ready for marching. They were brought together into a Hollow square by there Captains And there addressed by several of the quorum of the Twelve. . . . At the Close of the Addresses they marched in double file from redemption Hill for 7 miles across the Missouri River Bottom to the ferry [site] (JWW).

■ **24. Pioneer Trail Road.** From the Iowa School for the Deaf, U.S. 275 (Co. L35) runs southeast for 1.75 miles to its intersection with County Road G66 **(Pioneer Trail Road).** From that intersection, County Road G66 **(Pioneer Trail Road)** loops northeast and then southeast for 3.3 miles to its intersection with County Road L35.

■ **25. Highland Grove.** A traveler standing at the intersection of County Road G66 **(Pioneer Trail Road)** and County Road L35 looking east about .5 mile will see where the LDS settlement of **Highland Grove** was during the Kanesville period. On the south side of County Road G66 **(Pioneer Trail Road),** just west of County Road L35, is a small **Pioneer Park** planted in native prairie flowers and grasses. In it is a **Mormon Trail interpretive panel,** "Arrival," describing the Mormon pioneers' arrival at the Missouri River and the several LDS settlements that sprang up nearby, including Bullock's Grove, Highland Park, Keg Creek, and Hyde Park.

■ **26. Bullock's Grove.** By driving 1 mile south on County Road L35 from that same intersection at G66 **(Pioneer Trail Road),** visitors reach Aspen Road on the west side. About .12 mile west on that road is the general area where the LDS settlement called **Bullock's Grove** was located during the Kanesville period (see Council Bluffs, IA, map).

■ **27. Hyde Park (Orson Hyde Home).** Visitors can see the site where **Hyde Park** was by driving east 3.5 miles on Pioneer Trail Road (G66) from its intersection with County Road L35 and turning south on the gravel Dumfries Avenue, continuing .75 mile to a bridge, going west over the bridge and then southerly for nearly

Hyde Park, IA, where Orson Hyde lived. He was the apostle who first dedicated the Holy Land for the return of the Jews. Looking northwest across the site of Hyde Park. (1997)

1 mile to a sizeable marker adjacent to 11212 Dumphries Avenue. The white gate identifies the entrance to the site where Hyde Park once was. The site is practically on the section line between Section 25 and Section 26, Lewis Township (T74N R43W).

Apostle **Orson Hyde** presided over the Kanesville area between 1848 and 1851. He selected **Hyde Park** for his family residence in June 1846 before going on a mission to England. His home and farm were part of a small farming settlement there (OHH 492–93).

At Hyde Park the Quorum of the Twelve voted on Dec. 5, 1847, to **reconstitute the First Presidency** with Brigham Young as president of the Church and Heber C. Kimball and Willard Richards as counselors (HC 7:621). Elder Hyde later said:

> I must say that I feel not a little proud of the circumstance, and also very thankful, on account of its happening in my own little retired and sequestered hamlet, bearing my own name. We were in prayer and council, communing together; and what took place on that occasion? The voice of God came from on high, and spake to the Council. Every latent feeling was aroused, and every heart melted. What did it say unto us? "Let my servant Brigham step forth and receive the full power of the presiding Priesthood in my Church and kingdom." This was the voice of the Almighty unto us at Council Bluffs, before I removed to what was called Kanesville. (JD 8:234)

Three weeks later, Church members sustained the new First Presidency at a conference at the **Kanesville Log Tabernacle.** Also at Hyde Park **John Smith** was confirmed as the Church Patriarch (HiR).

Oliver Cowdery returned to the Church and spoke at a special conference at Hyde Park on Oct. 21, 1848. Listed in the front of the Book of Mormon as one of the Three Witnesses who viewed the gold plates from which the Book of Mormon was translated, he testified about that event: "Friends and brethren my name is Cowdery, Oliver Cowdery. In the early history of this church I stood identified with her, and one in her councils. . . . I wrote with my own pen the entire Book of Mormon (save a few pages) as it fell from the lips of the Prophet, as he translated [it] by the gift and power of God." He stated, "I beheld with my eyes and handled with my hands the gold plates from which it was translated" and testified, "That book is true. Sidney Rigdon did not write it. Mr. Spaulding did not write it. I wrote it myself as it fell from the lips of the Prophet." He added, "I was present with Joseph when an holy angel from God came down from heaven and conferred or restored, the Aaronic Priesthood," and "I was also present with Joseph when the Melchizedek Priesthood was conferred by the holy angels of God." Then, referring to his calling to help select the first Twelve Apostles in the LDS Church in 1835, he pointed to Elder Hyde and said, "I conferred upon him this Priesthood. . . . He was also called through me [by the prayer of faith] an apostle of the Lord [Jesus] Christ" (CHC 1:139; spelling and capitalization standardized; DHOC 4:480–90).

Next, Oliver spoke to the high priests quorum in the area on Nov. 5 in the Tabernacle, and on Nov. 12, 1848, was baptized in Mosquito Creek by Elder Hyde (ROC 117, 154). Cowdery told the high priests, in part:

> Brethren, for a number of years I have been separated from you. I now desire to come back. I wish to come humbly and be one in your midst. I seek no station; I only wish to be identified with you. I am out of the Church. I am not a member of the church; but I wish to become a member of it. I wish to come in at the door. I know the door. I have not come here to seek precedence [presidency]. I come humbly and throw myself upon the decision of this body. (DHOC 4:495)

■ **28. Lake Manawa State Park.** One mile beyond the south end of Council Bluffs is **Lake Manawa State Park.** Its entrance is 2 miles west of the Iowa School for the Deaf on the south side of State 92/U.S. 275 and is accessible from I-29/I-80 via the Lake Manawa

Exit. The park, with its 660-acre lake, is a popular boating, camping, and picnicking spot.

State 92/U.S. 275, which runs east-west between the School for the Deaf and the Missouri River, has signs designating it the **Mormon Pioneer National Historic Trail highway.**

■ **29. Council Pt.** Located near a former bend of the Missouri River, 4 miles southwest of Kanesville and west of present-day Lake Manawa, the settlement site is in the center of the northeast quarter of Section 15 (T74N R44W).

Council Pt. was the support town for construction and later operation of the **Middle Mormon Ferry.** Brigham Young moved there from Redemption Hill to oversee construction of the ferry. Council Pt. was a stop for **Missouri River steamboats** carrying Saints and gold rush passengers and ever-increasing loads of merchandise from St. Louis and taking passengers down river. Council Pt. was the first established and **second largest LDS settlement,** after Kanesville, in Iowa. It served as a support community for river arrivals and departures. Here, **Reuben F. Allred** established a ropewalk to manufacture ropes for use in the LDS ferrying operations as well as ropes, cords, and lines for other purposes (FG May 15, 1859; GGH).

Travelers can see the Council Pt. site by driving west from the Iowa School for the Deaf on State 92/U.S. 275 (S. Omaha Bridge Road) for 3.2 miles to 24th Street (or 2.7 miles east of the South Omaha Bridge) and turning south on 24th Street as it jogs right (west) for .25 mile and then goes due south for .5 mile, where it elbows left (east), becoming Gifford Road. At 100 feet beyond the elbow, on the south side of Gifford Road, is a **historical marker** honoring the Council Pt. settlement, **Emigrant Landing,** Allred's Ropewalk, and the **Welsh Tabernacle** site (see site 31 below). Council Pt. was about .25 mile west-northwest of the marker.

■ **30. Emigrant Landing.** The site of **Emigrant Landing** is .5 mile southeast of Council Pt. in the southwest quarter of Section 14 (T74N R44W). From the Council Pt. observation location just noted, look southeast to see where Emigrant Landing was—now a field.

At the landing, which was on a bend of the Missouri River before it changed course, riverboats loaded and unloaded freight and passengers. The landing was first built, apparently, by the U.S. government, to serve a farm they had established for the Pottawattamie, Ottawa, and Chippewa Indians (ENS Aug. 2002, 20). This landing became the unloading site for thousands of LDS emigrants, mostly from the British Isles, and provided a warehouse where travelers' goods were stored. Presidential candidate **Abraham Lincoln** apparently arrived at this landing when he visited Council Bluffs in 1859 (GGH 44–46).

■ **31. Welsh Tabernacle Site.** The **Welsh Tabernacle site** was located about where Twin City Drive leads north from State 92/U.S. 275 into a cluster of streets, .5 mile west of South 24th Street. This site is northwest of Council Pt. within 1 mile. This tabernacle served Welsh Saints living in the area during the Kanesville period (GGH 45).

■ **32. 1846 Pioneers' Missouri River Encampment/Long's Landing County Park.** Because the river has changed course, the Camp of Israel's **Missouri River camp site** of June 14 and 15, 1846, is now on the Nebraska side of the river, 1 mile west of the present-day location of Long's Landing County Park—southwest of Council Bluffs and south of Lake Manawa (see **Missouri River Camp,** site 32 on Council Bluffs, IA, map).

■ **33. South Omaha Bridge/First Mormon Ferry/Battalion Camp.** Between the Iowa School for the Deaf and the Missouri River, State 92/U.S. 275 extends for 6 miles west across a wide expanse of Missouri River bottomlands. State 92/U.S. 275 crosses the Missouri River on the **South Omaha Bridge (Veterans Memorial Bridge)** and enters what Omahans still call South Omaha, Nebraska. The bridge, including the eastern approach to it, is actually in Nebraska—the Missouri River has moved west since the state boundary lines were drawn. This bridge opened in 1936.

Between 1848 and 1852, **LDS settlements** avoided the flood-prone bottomlands that bordered the river north and south of present-day State 92/U.S. 275, except for **Council Pt., Ferryville,** and **Bethlehem**—the support towns for the Middle, North, and South Mormon ferries.

About .5 mile south of the east end of today's South Omaha Bridge is where the **First, or Middle, Mormon Ferry** operated. The river's east shore has moved about .25 mile west from where it was when the ferry was there. Half a mile farther downstream, on the west side of the Missouri River, was the landing place for the ferry. The return ferry left from about where the west end of the South Omaha Bridge is now. The South Omaha Bridge provides travelers an excellent view of the wide Missouri, giving a feel for what kind of river the ferryboats had to cross in those days.

On June 21, 1846, Brigham Young put men to work building a large ferryboat, supervised by **Frederick Kesler.** They used planks Young had arranged to be sawed at the Pottawattamie Indian Mill, operated by S. E. Wicks (see site 39). The ferry location was near their "old camping ground on the river" (JHKW June 30). On June 28 spadesmen dug a launching ramp, and the next day, after workmen caulked the boat, it was launched. By early July, Saints moved from the Grand Encampment camps down close to the ferry, waited their turn, and crossed over into Nebraska. Perhaps one-third of the Saints crossed, and the rest, by leaders' orders, stayed on the Iowa side that winter.

Saints waiting to use the ferry sometimes camped within .75 mile of the Traders Pt. settlement. It appears that Saints came to or through the trading post village before they reached the ferry (DHS July 31, 1846, 182). "Before we reach'd the ferry we pass'd a village of perhaps 50 huts or houses," Eliza R. Snow noted (JERS Aug. 28, 1846). Horace K. Whitney said they used a boat capable of holding three wagons at a time. "The current is quite favorable, setting in almost to the opposite shore, where there is quite an eddy" (JHKW July 8). Once across, they had a steep and very difficult passage up ravines and bluffs.

On July 16, the four and a half companies of men enlisted in the **Mormon Battalion** marched double file for 7 miles from their mustering-in grounds near Redemption Hill along Mosquito Creek to the small ferry location by **Traders Pt.** They camped nearby without tents (JWW). This was the **Mormon Battalion headquarters** and army camp while they waited for the ranks of the fifth company, Company E, to fill up before continuing their march to Ft. Leavenworth (JWW). During those waiting days, the soldiers were allowed to visit the camps near Redemption Hill. "We have been marched down to headquarters on the bank of the missouri river & for the first time i have drawn rations from uncle Sam, a pound of flour, a pound of beef, some salt, & coffee, sugar per day," wrote Pvt.

Guy M. Keysor in Company B. Six men composed a "mess" to eat together. The next day the soldiers drew blankets, knives, caps, pantaloons, shirts and other necessaries, emptying the stores (DGMK July 16, 17).

On July 16 Brigham Young returned by ferry from a short visit across the river and started out for the Redemption Hill camp. However, just .5 mile east of the river he "met most of the volunteers ready to be delivered into Captn. Allen's care." He then went to Elder Orson Pratt's tent, located near the soldiers and on the flats near the bank of the river. There, at 4:30 P.M. he held a council meeting with the Twelve. They prayed and then approved and **ordained Ezra T. Benson an apostle.** He replaced John E. Page, who had been dropped from the quorum the previous February (MHBY; HC 7:582).

The **Battalion Farewell Ball** took place on Saturday, July 18, in the Battalion Camp beside the Missouri River under open skies. After breakfast that day "we cleared A piece of ground eight Rods square for the purpose of concert or if you please to here it a Military ball," Pvt. Keysor wrote. The companies then positioned their camps on one of the four sides of this square. At 2 P.M. the dance started with a "double French four," which the officers and their ladies danced, "occupying several portions of the square." After that number, everyone else was invited to join in dancing—officers, soldiers, citizens, and "natives." There was no disorder, Pvt. Keysor said, and "all was still & quiet & nothing was heard but the Musick, except now & then a soft breeze Steeling over the tops of lofty coten woods" (DGMK July 18). "We have a ball in the afternoon some of the 12 was there and danced," Pvt. Franklin Allen of Company B recorded. "It was a good performance" (DFA). Brigham Young did not attend, but at about 6 P.M. he met with the Battalion officers "in the cottonwoods near the bank of the river" to give them important and pointed counsel about how to lead. He also gave them a blessing (MHBY July 18).

■ **34. National Western Historic Trails Center.** This center, opened in 1997, is located by the Missouri River in bottomlands at 3434 Richard Downing Avenue—just south of I-80 via Exit 1-B (South 24th Street). The State Historical Society of Iowa owns and operates the center. It was designed and built by the National Park Service and local partners. Its extensive museum portrays the

American movements west, focusing especially on the **Lewis and Clark Trail,** the **Oregon/California Trails,** and **the Mormon Pioneer Trail,** as well as on **Native Americans.**

The walkway to the main building is a "Path of Names," granite pavers carved with the names of emigrants and Indian nations once on or crossing the plains. Beside the walkway is a long wall depicting the changes in elevation migrants traveled from the Mississippi River to the Pacific. The main center, the Lied Historical Building, is surrounded by 400 acres of natural flora and fauna, and walking trails to the Missouri River's shore.

■ **35. Traders (Trading) Pt., or Pointe Aux Poules.** The **Traders Pt.** site is 3 miles south of the **Council Pt.** site and about 1 mile north of the present-day Bellevue Bridge across the Missouri River. In 1846 Mormons traveled 9 miles from Miller's Hollow to reach the outpost.

American Fur Company agent **Peter Sarpy** operated a trading post consisting of three trading houses at **Traders** (or **Trading**) **Pt.,** or, in French, *Pointe Aux Poules* (JHKW June 14, 1846) and a larger trading center (the American Fur Company post) directly across the river where Bellevue, Nebraska, now is. Sarpy used a small dinghy to ferry people and goods back and forth across the Missouri River.

In 1846 U.S. Indian subagent Robert B. Mitchell, under the supervision of Maj. John Miller on the Nebraska side of the river, had his **Pottawattamie Indian Agency headquarters** at Traders Pt., beside which was an Indian village. Traders Pt., which was 50 rods from the river, consisted of about 20 to 40 houses, mostly of hewn logs. The houses looked "very respectful," Guy Keysor said, "being white washed out side" (DGMK July 17). The houses had no glass in the windows (JWC June 17, 1846, 47). The people there included Americans, French, Indians, and "half-breeds," in total "not amounting to many" (DHS July 6, 1846). Peter Sarpy, Richard Pearson, and John D. Linfleu held government licenses to trade with the Indians, who had settled all around that place "from 3 to 5, 10 & 15 miles." Some Indians had modest gardens growing corn, potatoes, and beans (DGMK June 17, 1846).

A few days after arriving at the bluffs, the Twelve and a large Mormon contingent accepted Agent Mitchell's invitation and on June 20, 1846, enjoyed a social at the agency:

> Many Indians and others were assembled. Halfday [Op-te-gee-shuck] and Hoby, two chiefs, were introduced to the Presidency and band. After a few tunes the Presidency, Ladies and band dined with Major Mitchell, Twelve at a table, six tables; thereafter music and dancing and a few songs by John Kay till about half-past six when the party started for Camp . . . all parties appeared highly delighted with the repasts and amusements of the day, and the best of feelings were manifested by the citizens and Indians toward the saints. (MHBY)

Fifteen days earlier, at the agency, Halfday and 56 other Pottawattamie chiefs and leading men had signed a treaty by which they sold all their southwest Iowa lands to the U.S. government, promising to vacate the area within two years and relocate in Kansas (PP, 341).

The Pottawattamie Indians were hospitable to the Latter-day Saint refugees. At some point the Indian agent summoned the chiefs for a council at Sarpy's log trading house at their village. The chiefs signed formal articles, a land use agreement, "with their unpronounceable names," Thomas L. Kane observed. At a meeting with Mormons, which Kane attended, a chief or at least a spokesman named Pied Rioche but called **Le Clerc** because of his education, arose and **spoke eloquently and sympathetically** to the Church leaders. Le Clerc, or La Clair, was part French, and he spoke English well (MHBY June 18; CHC 3:137). Kane, no doubt embellishing a little, wrote down the essence of the speech, based on Le Clerc's retelling of it to him afterwards in French:

> The Pottawatamie came sad and tired into this unhealthy Missouri Bottom, not many years back, when he was taken from his beautiful country beyond the Mississippi, which had abundant game and timber and clear water everywhere. Now you are driven away, the same, from your lodges and lands there, and the graves of your people. So we have both suffered. We must help one another, and the Great Spirit will help us both. You are now free to cut and use all the wood you wish. You can make all your improvements and live on any part of our actual land not occupied by us. Because one suffers, and does not deserve it, is no reason he shall suffer always: I say. We may live

to see all right yet. However, if we do not, our children will.—Bon Jour. (MOR 59)

Brigham Young's daily history makes no mention of a meeting like this, which suggests that he was not present; however, on July 15 he did appoint Jesse C. Little to visit with Capt. Allen and get a recommend from him allowing the Saints to tarry on Indian lands along the Missouri River. Possibly this meeting was the occasion when Le Clerc made his sympathetic speech (MHBY July 15).

A **Pointe Aux Poules marker** stands on the Pottawattamie/Mills County line at Allis Road and Applewood Avenue, .6 miles west of I-80 but only reachable by way of Co. L31 (192nd Street). The sign commemorates one of several locations in the early and mid 1800s of the French and Native American village of Pointe Aux Poules (French for "Prairie Chicken Crossing").

■ **36. 1846 SARPY'S FERRY AND CROSSING SITE.** Peter Sarpy operated a dinghy ferry from his post at **Traders Pt.** The **ferry crossing site** today is about 1.5 miles north of the Bellevue Bridge, which crosses the Missouri River from Bellevue, Nebraska, to Iowa. This ferry was only a small dinghy, or rowboat, that Sarpy operated between his posts on both sides of the river.

■ **37. MORMON BATTALION ROUTE FROM COUNCIL BLUFFS** (see **Mormon Battalion Enlistments** and sites 19, 22, and 23). The **Battalion's marching route** in Iowa started on July 16, 1846, at the **mustering grounds** near the present-day Iowa School for the Deaf. Under the command of Lt. Col. James Allen, who helped recruit the men, the soldiers marched that day 7 or 8 miles and camped at the **Traders Pt. Ferry** near **Peter Sarpy's trading post** for four days "to purchase blankets and other necessary articles" for the march and to wait for the fifth company to arrive (CHMB 128).

On Tuesday, July 21, President Young traveled to the ferry and found that four companies of the Battalion had marched away at 3:00 P.M. (MHBY). The next morning, Company E started off to catch up with the other companies. Col. Allen requested the company musician, Levi W. Hancock, to play "The Girl I Left behind Me" as march music for the men (MHBY).

Their line of march took the enlisted men south along the east side of the Missouri River bottomlands. Today's **I-29 from Council**

Bluffs to the Missouri border follows fairly closely their route, which hugged the base of the bluffs. They passed through where present-day **Glenwood** is now located, 15 miles south of Council Bluffs, and near present-day **Thurman** and **Hamburg,** before entering Missouri on their way to receive equippage at Ft. Leavenworth, Kansas.

■ **38. JONATHAN BROWNING SETTLEMENT.** The **Jonathan Browning gunshop** was located 7.5 miles south of Kanesville on Mosquito Creek (along its old course, which then flowed much farther south before it emptied into the Missouri River), 1 mile south of Traders Pt., at a site about .5 mile south of the Pottawattamie/Mills county line on the east bank of the present-day Missouri River. In his advertisement in the ***Frontier Guardian*** on Apr. 4, 1849, gunsmith-inventor Browning offered to manufacture or order "improved Fire-arms" that included revolving rifles and pistols and "slide guns" that fired from five to 25 shots. A small settlement developed around his shop.

Northern Council Bluffs Area

■ **39. POTTAWATTAMIE INDIANS' (WICKS) SAWMILL.** The site of the **Pottawattamie Indians' Sawmill, or Wicks Mill,** was on Mosquito Creek some 3 to 4 miles northeast of Kanesville. To reach the site today, the traveler can drive 2.5 miles northeast of downtown Council Bluffs via U.S. 6 to an interchange at which College Road goes south and Washboard Road goes north. Take Washboard Road north .75 mile until it ends in a T at Follet Road, then turn west on Follet and travel .1 mile. There the road follows the south side of Mosquito Creek. Wicks Mill once stood on the opposite side of the creek at that spot (see Council Bluffs, IA, map).

This gristmill and sawmill, built by S. E. Wicks, a miller and interpreter for the Pottawattamie Indians, was operating when the 1846 Mormon pioneers reached the Missouri, and it continued in use during the Kanesville period. According to Brigham Young, the mill provided **planks for the ferryboat** the Saints were constructing. On June 21, 1846, President Young arranged for 12 yoke of oxen to haul logs "to the Indian saw mill" and two wagons to haul planks from the mill to the boat. The next day he rode in his carriage "to Mr. Wick's, at the Indian Sawmill," where he "purchased boards" (MHBY June 21, 22). Hosea Stout visited the mill on July 7, 1846, by traveling "about four miles" from the Mormon encampments on "an uncommon rough road" (DHS).

■ **40. Grant Wood Mural of Early Kanesville.** Iowa's **famous artist Grant Wood** painted a large 19-foot by 6-foot mural, "The Early Days of Kanesville," based on Council Bluff artist George Simon's pencil drawings. The mural once adorned the Chieftain Hotel in Council Bluffs. Its current home is the Looft Continuing Education Center main lobby on the Iowa Western Community College campus. The college is in east Council Bluffs at 2700 College Road, just south of U.S. 6 and .5 mile from the U.S. 6 and I-80 interchange.

■ **41. 1856/1857 Handcart Pioneers' Route, Council Bluffs to Upper Ferry. The 1856 and 1857 handcart pioneers** entered Council Bluffs on the 1846 **Mormon Trail route** which by then was part of the Des Moines-to-Council Bluffs Road. Some handcart pioneers apparently moved into Council Bluffs by way of present-day Madison Street, which borders the Mall of the Bluffs on its southwest edge and becomes 1st Street after it crosses the crest of the bluffs. They then went northeast up present-day Broadway and turned north on present-day North Broadway, which is County Road L20. It appears they traveled the route where today's County Road L20 goes from Council Bluffs north to **Crescent,** and they camped between Crescent and the river.

"After traveling about three miles we came to Bluff City," said Levi Savage on Aug. 12, 1856, speaking of the **Willie handcart company.** "Here, like all other towns through which we have passed, the people thronged the street sides and gazed upon us with apparent great surprise. They were civil, except a few fellows who endeavored to make sport of us, the cripple and lame not excepted. They were reprimanded by better chaps" (JLS Aug.12).

On Aug. 21, 1856, the **Martin handcart company** "passed Pony Creek about 7 miles to Mosquito Creek, baited [rested]. . . . Three miles to Council Bluffs, then 8 miles to Missouri bottom," and then "we camped about three miles from the Florence Ferry" (LHWJJ). From there they pulled to the Missouri River and crossed on ferryboats near where I-680 now spans the river (see **Mormon Pioneer Bridge** on Council Bluffs, IA, map).

- **42. Lewis and Clark Monument.** Located at Rainbow Pt., in north Council Bluffs on 8th Street and overlooking the broad Missouri River, the monument honors the 1804 expedition of Lewis and Clark and their meeting with the Otoe Indians. It was dedicated in 1936.

Southwest Iowa

■ Keg Creek Settlement

The LDS **Keg Creek settlement,** which was contemporary with Kanesville, was located near the mouth of Keg Creek, where it enters the Missouri River close to where U.S. 34 crosses the river to Plattsmouth, Nebraska.

■ Bethlehem—the Plattsmouth Ferry

Plattsmouth, aptly named, is in Nebraska, 3 miles south of where the Platte River flows into the Missouri. It was an important ferrying site between Plattsmouth in Nebraska and a Platteville trading post on the Iowa side, near where the U.S. 34 bridge spans the river.

In 1850 Mormons established a town just below the ferry and called it **Bethlehem.** Mormon **Shadrach Roundy** was president of the town company. From 1848 to 1852 Brother **Labbeus T. Coons** operated a **Bethlehem ferry** there, a simple flatboat propelled by long oars. Many Mormons used the ferry during the Kanesville period and the mass exodus from Kanesville in 1852. Bethlehem was renamed Sharpsville in 1858 and then East Plattsmouth when it became the terminus for the Burlington and Missouri River Railroad. The village was gone soon after the turn of the century (MCI 14, 20; RRH,c).

■ Mills County

Mills County, Pottawattamie County's neighbor to the south, was first settled by Mormons in 1846. It was part of Pottawattamie County until August 1851.

Glenwood, through which Keg Creek passes, was originally called **Coonsville** for early settler Labbeus T. Coons. When Mills County was formed from Pottawattamie County in August 1851, Glenwood became the county seat (HMC 558–60).

The first settlers of Glenwood, including **Labbeus Coons,** moved to this site from **Rushville,** a Mormon settlement (which has disappeared without a trace) that was located on Keg Creek about 3 or 4 miles south of Glenwood. Coons presided over a branch of the Church here (ARC 15). Coons was the town's first postmaster and a Mills County prosecuting attorney (RRH,c).

In the fall of 1847, Mormons established **Silver Creek Grove** at a site that is about halfway between present-day Malvern and Silver City, in today's Silver Creek Township, which is a few miles northeast of Glenwood, in Mills County. It was known as **Cutler's Camp,** named for **Alpheus Cutler,** who was a prominent elder in the LDS Church before he and a small flock of followers left the Brigham Young-led Church. These settlers built a mill, using the waters of Silver Creek, and planted and harvested for several years, although the settlement was established only to be a temporary stopping place during the Mormon migration (GTMC 26).

LDS families named Cox, Whiting, Baker, Fisher, Murdock, Patten, and others located there. One early settler in that area was **Warren Follett,** son of King Follett, about whom Joseph Smith delivered the famous King Follett discourse in Nauvoo (HMC 628). Another settler was **Joseph Smith Black,** who wrote: "We located twenty miles below Kanesville on Silver Creek where we remained until the spring of 1850" (JJSB 262). In about 1852 the Cutler group left Silver Creek, apparently seeking better resources, and founded **Manti,** 25 miles to the southeast. Their cabins at Silver Creek Grove were moved to other locations and used by later farmers (AnI 58 [Spring 1999]: 143).

■ FREMONT AND PAGE COUNTIES

Fremont and Page counties, in Iowa's southwest corner, had settlements of Saints who were moving out from the Council Bluffs/Kanesville area.

Fremont County is Iowa's most southwestern county. It was organized from Pottawattamie County in 1847. In late July 1846 the newly enlisted **Mormon Battalion,** marching south from Traders Pt. to Ft. Leavenworth, Kansas, passed through where **Hamburg** is today (at the county's south end, on U.S. 275). By late 1846 Mormons had settled near **Austin,** which once existed 8 miles south of **Sidney** and 2.5 miles north of present-day **Hamburg,** on U.S. 275. Also, 3.5 miles east of Hamburg on today's State 333 and .5 mile north, Mormon Battalion veterans **Edward Bunker, William A.**

Follett, and John Spidle each bought a quarter-section of farmland in 1850, using their Mexican War bounty land warrants.

From Winter Quarters many Saints seeking supplies or temporary employment moved back and forth between Winter Quarters and towns in Missouri, passing through present-day Fremont County.

In February 1847 Winter Quarters resident **Mary Haskin Parker Richards** visited friends living near **Austin** for several weeks. Austin was thought to be in Atchison County, Missouri, until later that year when Iowa created Fremont County, which included Austin. Mary stayed with the **Robert T. Burton family** (he became a counselor in the Presiding Bishopric in Utah) and the **John Haven Family.** Robert and Maria Burton's daughter Theresa Hannah was born in their log cabin before Mary visited there. Living nearby, Mary said, was an **LDS family named Duel** and Brother **Priddy Meeks's family.** At the Meeks's, Mary and seven other LDS girls danced with five non-LDS gentlemen. Mary was invited to attend a dance 8 miles north in **Sidney,** but she lacked transportation (MHPR 111–15).

Manti, named for a Book of Mormon city, was on **Fremont County**'s eastern border, next to **Page County,** about where east-west State 2 intersects the county line. Manti's location was about 2 miles south of present-day Shenandoah. A cottage, house, and barn mark what was Manti's main street, which is now a gravel road.

Manti was founded by 20 families who followed **Alpheus Cutler** after he pulled away from Brigham Young's leadership. On September 19, 1853, they formally organized the independent **Church of Jesus Christ (Cutlerite)** at Manti. By that year 102 "Cutlerites" lived there, most of whom later joined the RLDS Church after its start in 1860. Alpheus Cutler died at Manti in 1864 (NJ [Fall 1994]: 97–111).

Manti became a crossroads for two heavily traveled **stage roads.** But a railroad line bypassed it to the north, causing the town to shrivel and officially cease to exist in 1878. Abandoned Manti buildings were hauled away to nearby Shenandoah.

The **Manti Cemetery** is all that remains to memorialize the Manti settlement. It is reachable by driving west 1 mile on State 2 from **Shenandoah**'s south edge, turning south on Manti Road and then traveling 1 mile to the **Manti Memorial Park.** A pleasant .4 mile nature trail reaches the cemetery near the hilltop. Father Cutler's headstone and those of several other Manti residents are in that cemetery. The headstones were removed from their graves by vandals but have been placed back in the approximate location, although not on the exact gravesites, where the cemetery once was on that hill (AnI 58 [Spring 1999]: 161).

Thurman is in northwest Fremont County, 30 miles south of Council Bluffs, 3 miles east of I-29 on State 145. Some wives and children of Mormon Battalion soldiers settled near a beautiful creek bounded by growths of native fruit. They named the place **Plumb Hollow,** later renamed Thurman. These families' surnames included Huston, Study, Ewell, Benner, Ettleman, Clapper, Forney, and Dyke. When the men returned from Battalion service, some stayed there and built cabins on the north creek bank. Leonard C. Study conducted a school there in 1847 with five students. Some of the settlers went on to Utah. Others stayed behind, most of whom became members of the RLDS Church after 1860.

■ Corning, Adams County

Adams County is three counties east of the Missouri River and the second county north of the Iowa-Missouri border. **Corning,** the county seat, is located where U.S. 34 and State 148 intersect.

Early in the twentieth century, George Bickford grew up near Corning on a farm marked by wagon ruts through never-plowed prairie, ruts that his family said were tracks made by Mormon wagons. Their claim could well be true, because some Mormons crossing Iowa after 1846 could have gone directly west to the Missouri River from Mt. Pisgah rather than staying on the Mormon Trail. As a college student in the 1930s, Bickford published a poem he wrote called "**Mormon Monument**" that expressed his pondering while inspecting those ruts as a boy. To him, the ruts were "A monument to faith." Part of the poem reads:

> And as the summer rains rush down
> Leaving the clay of red and brown
> The trail on the slopes is growing deeper.
> And here and there where men have plowed
> And cut the sod across the trail
> The tasseled corn grows tall and proud. (LFH,c)

■ Blockton (Mormontown), Taylor County

Taylor County is on Iowa's south border and the third county east of the Missouri River. **Blockton** is located in the county's far southeast corner, on the Platte River in the northwest part of Section 12 in present-day Jefferson Township. In 1858 Elder Alpheus Cutler and two others scouted out this location, 50 miles east of Manti, for a new settlement for Cutler's followers.

In 1861 a dozen Mormon families from the **Manti** area built a few log dwellings along the river and established gardens, farms, shops, and a flour mill. They did not succeed with their enterprises and, admitting failure, returned to Manti in 1865 (AnI 58 [Spring 1999]: 150–51). Local residents called the settlement **Mormontown.** After the "Cutlerites" left, Mormontown was the largest village in Jefferson Township. In 1888 Mormontown's name was changed to **Blockton** (HTC 597–99; BLI 10–11).

North of Council Bluffs

■ Mormon Pioneer Memorial Bridge

The **Mormon Pioneer Memorial Bridge** is 8 miles northwest of Council Bluffs, where I-680 crosses the Missouri River. The bridge, once a toll bridge, has two spans. The original span, now the south one for eastbound traffic, was dedicated by **LDS Church president David O. McKay** and opened on June 1, 1953. The span of the newer bridge, which carries westbound traffic, was dedicated by **Church president Spencer W. Kimball,** who paid the last toll (CN 10 June 1972; HRSMT 81–82).

After travelers cross the bridge westbound, they are in Nebraska, close to the **LDS Winter Quarters Memorial.**

■ Upper Ferry

Mormon Pioneer Memorial Bridge over the Missouri River between IA and NE, looking west. (1958)

Latter-day Saints operated a ferry near the Mormon Pioneer Memorial Bridge location during the 1847–53 period. This was the **Upper Ferry.** The boat was the one used during 1846 to move Saints from near

Traders Pt. to the Nebraska side. In connection with the Upper Ferry, the LDS settlement of **Ferryville** developed. The site today is near the east shoreline of the Missouri River and on the north side of I-680. In 1853 Mormon traveler Frederick Piercy used this ferry:

> The company being ready we drove down to Ferryville, or Council Bluffs Ferry, 12 miles distant, and just opposite Winter Quarters, at which point we crossed the Missouri into Indian Territory, now Nebraska. (RFL 100–101)

The **1856 and 1857 handcart companies** crossed the Missouri near here by ferry.

On July 8, 1856, the first handcart company, the **Ellsworth company,** halted at midday at Pigeon Creek, cooked dinner, rested, and then "crossed the Missouri by the steam ferry-boat a little below Florence" (HCZ 203).

Ellenor Roberts Lewis, a young Welsh woman in the **Bunker handcart company,** prided herself on keeping her shoes shiny and clean. At the Missouri River, she took them off and set them on the bank of the river. After she ferried across, she discovered she had left the shoes behind, which caused her to cross the plains barefoot (HCZ 87–88).

Council Bluffs Ferry, IA, known also as "Upper Ferry" or "Mormon Ferry," was located near present-day Mormon Pioneer Memorial Bridge. Cottonwood trees, shown here, were favorites along the Mormon Trail. (Steel engraving by Frederick Piercy, 1853)

James McGaw, the Church's emigration agent at Florence, met the **Willie handcart company** and went with it north towards the ferry. At a house where some of the company stopped for refreshments, "some of the gentiles and apostates commenced to abuse the Saints and curse the handcart system and those that instituted it." Elder McGaw defended the system, and "consequently got into a fist fight with them. He whipped one or two of them, but received no material injury to himself except getting his hair well pulled" (JLS Aug. 11).

On Aug. 11, 1856, the **Willie handcart company** reached the ferry, which ran from sunrise to sunset and could carry six wagons and teams at once, crossing the river in about one minute (DSL-H). Once the handcart travelers were across, LDS emigration agents met their boat and guided them to a campground where they would rest and prepare for the journey west.

■ Honey Creek

Honey Creek is 13 miles north of downtown Council Bluffs on County Road L20. It is 5.5 miles east of the Mormon Pioneer Memorial Bridge via I-680 and then 6 miles north on County Road L20.

Honey Creek was one of about 90 LDS satellite settlements that grew up around Kanesville before 1852. After the Saints left, Honey Creek continued to exist and today is a tiny, unincorporated community.

The site of the **Honey Creek Mormon Pioneer Cemetery** is a few yards south of State 183 (Co. L20). It is accessible by walking south along an unpaved road between the last two buildings at the west edge of Honey Creek. Through a narrow, overgrown, and easily missed drive on your left, you may walk in and see the huge hole carved out of the hillside where the LDS cemetery was located. In about 1960 the cemetery was part of land that was sold, dug up, and hauled away as fill dirt for the construction of I-29 west of Honey Creek. The site is called by some local residents the "purloined cemetery" (GGH).

● Desoto Bend National Wildlife Refuge and Riverboat *Bertrand* Museum

The **Desoto Bend National Wildlife Refuge** is a large preserve and is 8 miles west of the town of **Missouri Valley** on U.S. 30. The refuge is a stopover sanctuary for ducks and geese migrating south each autumn. Its visitors' center contains a display of thousands of artifacts recovered from an 1864 sternwheeler, the *Bertrand,* which sank on its first trip upriver while fully loaded. The salvaged array of clothing, tools, implements, housewares and household goods are contemporary with the **Utah Pioneer period** of LDS history.

■ Harrison County

Harrison County is bordered by the Missouri River on the west and Pottawattamie County on the south. Several small Mormon settlements dotted Harrison County during the 1848–52 period, capitalizing on it creeks, fertile soil, and impressive groves of oak, hickory, black walnut, ironwood, elm, and basswood. Several of today's Harrison County communities were founded by Mormons (HDHC 11–23).

The **Missouri Valley Welcome Center,** .5 mile northeast of the town of Missouri Valley on State 30, is a good starting place to find Mormon sites in the county. The center includes the **Harrison County Historical Museum** and a gift shop that sells published histories and maps, several of which identify some of the Mormon sites. The museum's complex of eight buildings includes a country store, a blacksmith shop, a log cabin dating from 1853, an Indian burial ground, an 1868 school, and a cooper's room. On the grounds is a corn museum and exhibits of farm machinery, fur trapping history, firearms, and Indian artifacts.

■ Tennessee Hollow

Within 4 miles south or southeast of present-day Missouri Valley, at a site not yet pinpointed, was the Mormon settlement of **Tennessee Hollow.** Saints held meetings there in 1850 and apparently built a tabernacle for their branch (HHCI 204; ENS Aug. 1988: 57[map]).

■ Harris Grove

Harris Grove is 7 or 8 miles east of the town of Missouri Valley. The site can be reached by going 2 miles northwest from Missouri Valley, turning east on 296th Street (Co. F58) for 4 miles to where it intersects with Overton Avenue (Co. L34). From that intersection continue east on 296th Street (Co. F58) for 1.2 miles, at which point the road crosses **Harris Grove Creek.** For the next 1.2 miles after that point, the land on the south side of County Road L34 (Overton Ave.) is the general area where the Harris Grove settlement once was located. A Harris Grove memorial chapel is on the north side of County Road F58 and the Harris Grove Cemetery on the south side.

A Mormon named **John Harris,** to get away from illness and 49ers' bad behavior at Kanesville, moved north with 30 other families and settled at **Harris Grove** amid 10,000 acres of hardwood trees—oak, hickory, and walnut. His group found an abundance of walnuts, hazelnuts, wild strawberries, gooseberries, blackberries, raspberries, deer, and wild turkeys. They built some 30 cabins, each with gardens and surrounded by a rail fence. During its three-year-life, the settlement had 12 wagon shops, two mills, a **double log cabin tabernacle,** and a school. When Harris and others went west in 1852, the area was gladly taken over by non-Mormon settlers (MHGI).

■ SIX-MILE GROVE

North of Harris Grove 6 miles, at a site not precisely located yet but within 5 miles southeast of present-day **Logan,** was another LDS settlement called **Six-Mile Grove.** In 1848 Lewis Barney, seeking farmland, "made a location in the Six Mile Grove" on the Boyer River "about 50 miles north of Kanesville." The settlement sometimes was referred to as "Barney's Grove." Other Saints joined the Barneys, including Tunis Rappleye and Bryant Jolley (LTLB 120–24). In June 1853 two wagon trains with 404 people left from there to go to Utah (TPH 3:3; LTLB 117–136).

■ WOODBINE

Woodbine is 17 miles northeast of the town of Missouri Valley on U.S. 30. That 17-mile stretch forms a segment of Iowa's **Western Skies Scenic Byway.**

The **Lorenzo Dow Butler family,** Mormons in the 1846 migration from Nauvoo, first settled Woodbine. Wife Ann Binnall Butler named the place Woodbine after a flowering vine that grew at her English home (MBK 238–39). Lorenzo, Ann, and other Butler relatives are buried in the **Woodbine Cemetery.**

Woodbine is Iowa's "**apple capital,**" and a "Town of Brick Streets." Lincoln Way in Woodbine is a rare surviving stretch of the **Lincoln Highway,** the nation's first transcontinental highway that dates from the 1920s. An original Lincoln Highway marker is displayed at 210 Lincoln Way, outside the **Merry Brook School Museum,** a one-room school built in the 1890s (HCVG 10–11).

■ TWELVE-MILE GROVE

Twelve miles north of **Harris Grove,** at a site near Woodbine but not yet identified, was another Mormon settlement called **Twelve-Mile Grove** (HDHC 11).

Travelers can discover what these original groves were like by driving through an impressive one near where the Twelve-Mile

Grove settlement was. Drive 1.5 miles east on County Road F32 (194th St.) from where it intersects U.S. 30 just south of Woodbine. Turn south on Sawyer Trail Road and follow it for another 1.5 miles while it meanders through remnants of what once was Twelve-Mile Grove, a 5-mile stand of timber along the creek bottoms.

■ Bigler's Grove

Another Mormon settlement near Woodbine, within 5 miles of it, apparently to the southwest, was **Bigler's Grove** (HDHC 11–13).

■ Shelby County

Shelby County is north of Pottawattamie County and east of Harrison County and bisected by U.S. 59 and State 44. **Harlan,** the county seat, is located where those highways intersect in the middle of the county.

Grove Township, in the county's northwest corner, is where **Galland's Grove** was settled by relatives of **Isaac Galland,** the man who sold the Mormons land near Montrose. Part of the Texas colony led by apostate **apostle Lyman Wight** settled here in 1861, after Wight's death in March 1858.

Located in **Harlan** is **Potter's Park,** on the corner of Pine Street and Morse Avenue. In the park is the **Shelby County Historical Settlement** that features two log cabins built by Mormons who did not migrate west: the **John A. McIntosh Cabin** (1857) that originally stood in Galland's Grove, and the **Benjamin Leland Cabin** (1856) that was originally farther west in Persia, Harrison County.

The **Dinesen Prairie Wildlife Area** is 4 miles northeast of Harlan, near Kirkman. Here, visitors can see a rare preserve of virgin prairie grasslands and sense what Iowa prairies looked like when the 1846 pioneers crossed Iowa and many of them turned southwestern Iowa prairielands into farms.

At the county's southeast corner is **Elk Horn,** 7 miles north of I-80 via Exit 54. It is also reached from State 44 by driving south 3 miles on State 173 from **Kimballton** (which is barely outside of Shelby County, in Audubon County). Both Elk Horn and Kimballton are becoming known as **America's Danish capital.** Thousands of Danes immigrated there between 1880 and 1910.

A National Danish Immigrant Museum is on the west edge of Elk Horn at 2212 Washington Street, 10 blocks west of Main Street

(State 173), which includes LDS displays. In Elk Horn tourists can go inside a working 1848 **Danish windmill** with 66-foot blades, located in the Danish Windmill Museum and Welcome Center at 4038 Main Street.

In **Kimballton City Park** at 310 North Main—the north end of the business district—is a "**Little Mermaid**" **fountain,** featuring a replica of the **Little Mermaid statue** in the harbor of Copenhagen, Denmark. The Little Mermaid is based on Hans Christian Andersen's fairytale.

Emmett Company's Return

In March 1846, when the Camp of Israel was at the Chariton River Camp, Brigham Young delegated **John Lowe Butler** and **James Willard Cummings** to go to the **Emmett company** at **Camp Vermillion** (near present-day Burbank, South Dakota; see **James Emmett Expedition**) and instruct them to travel down the Missouri River to meet the Camp of Israel near the Missouri border. Butler's family was at Camp Vermillion, where he had been second in command until Nauvoo authorities called him home late in 1845, so he was anxious to rejoin them.

On Mar. 30 Butler and Cummings started on a dangerous journey over uncharted and gameless prairie to the Missouri River. They reached the **Indian village** by the **Nishnabotna River** on Apr. 14, seven weeks before the Camp of Israel did, and arrived at the location of present-day **Council Bluffs** on Apr. 16, two months before Brigham Young. Butler and Cummings bear the honor of being the first members of the Camp of Israel to reach the Council Bluffs area.

To their surprise they found seven Emmett company families from Camp Vermillion comfortably encamped by the bluffs, led there by **Lyman Hinman** a month before. Butler and Cummings instructed those families to move south to the Missouri state line to await the Camp of Israel (not realizing that the plan Brigham Young approved at Richardson's Pt. to cross the Missouri River at Bank's Ferry, Missouri, had been changed in favor of crossing at Council Bluffs).

On Apr. 19 Butler and Cummings started north for Camp Vermillion, apparently following part of a route for ox-drawn two-wheeled carts used in 1838 and perhaps other years, by fur traders from Pointe aux Poules up to the Big Bend of the Missouri River in present-day South Dakota. They **blazed some of their route up the Missouri River's eastern shore** (GGH). With difficulty they crossed **Pigeon Creek,** the **Boyer River, Soldier Creek,** the **Little Sioux River, Willow Creek** (where Sioux City is now), and the **Big Sioux River** near its mouth. They reached Camp Vermillion after an arduous eight-day trip covering some 130 miles.

On May 5 Butler and Cummings led the Emmett company south, trying to follow the route they had taken on the way north. The **Emmett caravan** included 14 wagons, 12 families, and 59 people. They camped by the Big Sioux River on May 6, Willow Creek (Floyd River) on May 11 (5 miles from its mouth), came up on the bluffs near Sergeant Bluff, followed the river bottoms for 25 miles, and camped by the Little Sioux River on May 14. Unable to cross that river until May 17, they camped by what they called Lighthouse Lake (possibly today's Round Lake). On May 18 they camped by Willow Creek and crossed it the next day. They camped by the Boyer River on May 20, and due to high water caused by rain, they could not cross for a week, until May 28. By then their provisions were depleted, and they had to dig "Sioux roots" for food.

On May 28 they camped 9 miles above **Traders (Trading) Pt.** and the next night camped just below that post, on Mosquito Creek near its mouth. After doing some trading, they crossed Mosquito Creek on May 30 on a bridge already there and camped by Keg Creek, which also was bridged. Finally, on May 31, the company reached the Hinman group of Emmett Saints and set up camp with them, probably near present-day **Hamburg,** at the south edge of Fremont County. Meanwhile, they sent messengers to the Camp of Israel to report their location and received word to move back north to Traders Pt. to meet the Camp of Israel and be ready to push for the Rocky Mountains.

By mid-July 1846 they had crossed the Missouri River and merged with other companies, ending their 22-month experience as a separate LDS emigrating company that had started in August 1844 (MBK 187–208; DJC).

Iowa Historic Route 2

Across Central Iowa along I-80

I-80 is Iowa's main east-west artery, passing through central Iowa and connecting **Davenport** on the east with **Council Bluffs** on the west. I-80 parallels and at times follows the same general route that the **1856 and 1857 handcart and wagon train companies** used. It also is close to other sites important to LDS history, including those connected with the **James Emmett Expedition.**

Eastern Edge: Davenport to Iowa City

■ Davenport

Davenport is a Mississippi River port city on I-80 at Iowa's eastern border. The **first LDS handcart emigrants,** heading for the handcart outfitting camp in Iowa City, arrived from the east by railroad and crossed the **Mississippi River** here in April 1856. Because a river steamer knocked out the new railroad bridge spanning the river, the rail travelers had to cross the river by ferryboat and then resume their journey by train. U.S. 6, which joins I-80 for 20 miles, follows their train route closely between Davenport and Iowa City.

■ West Branch and Herbert Hoover National Historic Site

The **Herbert Hoover National Historic Site** is located at **West Branch,** 10 miles east of Iowa City on I-80, Exit 254. Mr. Hoover was the 31st president of the United States. One of 13 presidential libraries operated by the National Archives, the site has the **Herbert Hoover Presidential Library,** birthplace cottage (1874), his grave (1964), a Quaker meetinghouse, and a blacksmith shop.

● Kalona—South of Iowa City

Kalona, 20 miles south of Iowa City on U.S. 1, is the largest **Amish-Mennonite settlement** west of the Mississippi River. Its

historic village includes two museums (one is the Iowa Mennonite Museum and Archives), a restored depot, schoolhouse, Grandpa House, a log house, and several antique shops. Many residents of Kalona are Mennonites; many Amish live in the rural areas.

Four groups evolved from a religious group that began in Switzerland in 1525 during the Protestant Reformation. The **Mennonites** were called Anabaptists because they opposed baptizing infants and were against military service. From the Mennonites have come Old Order Amish, Beachy Amish, Conservative Mennonites, and Old Mennonites. Members of all four groups came to America, seeking religious freedom.

The **Old Order Amish** broke from the Mennonites in 1693, calling for stricter practices. Many arrived and settled near Kalona in 1846. Today, the Amish live on farms and do not use electricity or gasoline-powered cars or farm equipment. They drive horse-drawn black buggies and wear simple, homemade clothes. Amish farms are identifiable by buggies in the driveways and a lack of electrical wires to their homes. The Amish do not swear oaths, vote, or serve in the military, and they defend their right to educate their own children. They do not believe in violence. They use shunning as a way to punish their own who break from their traditions. They are friendly people, but they **dislike having their pictures taken without permission. Always ask permission first.**

■ Osterdock—North of Iowa City

Osterdock is 102 miles north-northeast of Iowa City and 4 miles from the Mississippi River. It is 32 miles west-northwest of **Dubuque** by State 3 and then 8 miles north of **Colesburg** via County Road X3C (Colesburg Road) and County Road 43 (Osterdock Road).

The Prophet Joseph Smith's brother **William Smith** died in Osterdock on Nov. 13, 1893, and is buried there. He was an LDS apostle from 1835 to 1845 and was ordained Presiding Patriarch on May 24, 1845. Before he was sustained as Church Patriarch, however, he was dropped from that position and from the Quorum of the Twelve; he was excommunicated on Oct. 6, 1845 (CHC 2:432–35).

● Dyersville's *Field of Dreams*—Northeast of Iowa City

Dyersville is approximately 65 miles northeast of Iowa City. It is 25 miles west of Dubuque on U.S. 20. Three miles northeast of

Dyersville at 29001 Lansing Road is the farmhouse, baseball diamond, and cornfield that were the movie set for the 1989 movie *Field of Dreams.* The site is popular even with international visitors. The diamond is reached by going north from State 20 on State 136 through Dyersville, turning east on 3rd Ave. NE, then left or northeast on 12th St. NE, and then east and north on Dyersville East Road to Lansing Road, and east on Lansing Road to the site. Near the ball field are gift shops, refreshment stands, and batting cages which are open April through November. Balls, bats, and gloves are available for tourists to use on the field. "Ghost Players" make several appearances each year. An annual "Field of Dreams Festival" takes place in mid to late August, featuring recent all-star major league players and baseball memorabilia shows.

Dyersville is known as the **farm toy capital of the world** for its three toy companies and because it hosts the National Farm Toy Museum, featuring 30,000 toys and exhibits. It is just off U.S. 20 and State 136, at 1110 16th Ave. Ct. SE.

■ Iowa City

Iowa City is in eastern Iowa on I-80, 56 miles west of Davenport. It was Iowa's capital city from 1846 to 1857. Its population in 2000 was 62,220.

Iowa City is connected to LDS history by (1) the **1844 James Emmett Expedition,** (2) the **1846 pioneers' official messages** to the Iowa Territory's government while they were traveling through that territory, and (3) the **1856–1857 handcart companies** and some **1856, 1857, and 1858 wagon companies.**

1. The James Emmett Expedition. In 1844 James Emmett led more than 150 Saints from the Nauvoo area into the Iowa wilderness, seeking to fulfill an assignment given to him by Joseph Smith just weeks before the martyrdom. Starting in August and September 1844 and continuing in the subsequent months, people who enlisted in this expedition left Nauvoo, crossed the Mississippi, and reached Iowa City via Ft. Madison or by following the **Iowa River.** Once assembled in Iowa City, they moved 30 miles up the **Iowa River** and wintered where **Marengo** now is.

Early in 1845 they moved farther up the north side of the **Iowa River** and encamped near present-day **Marshalltown.** There a posse from Iowa City arrested six men on false charges and took them back to Iowa City for trial. Charges were eventually dropped. That summer, 1845, the Emmett company proceeded northwesterly across present-day Iowa to the southeastern tip of what is now **South Dakota** and established Camp Vermillion as their winter camp. In June 1846 they left Camp Vermillion and moved down the Missouri River (see **Emmett Company's Return**) to meet the westbound companies of Saints coming from Nauvoo (MBK 135–77, 187–208).

2. The 1846 Pioneers Official Message. When the Saints started leaving Nauvoo in early 1846, Brigham Young wrote a **letter to Iowa governor James Clark** at Iowa City, requesting permission for the Mormons to pass through Iowa Territory and be protected while doing so (MHBY Feb. 28, 1846). There is no record that the governor answered the letter.

3. Handcart Outfitting. For the first two years of handcart travel, 1856 and 1857, the handcart outfitting site was in Iowa City. Travelers arrived in Iowa City by train and waited until handcarts were made available and companies were organized and sent off.

The **Iowa City Railroad Depot site** is .5 mile north of U.S. 6 on Gilbert Street and two blocks east, near the intersection of Bowery and Johnson Streets. It is .5 mile southeast of Iowa City's central business district where Iowa Interstate Railway tracks pass through southeastern Iowa City, parallel to U.S. 6. The depot grounds stretched .5 mile eastward along these tracks from Gilbert Street.

In 1856 and 1857 LDS handcart emigrants arrived by train in Iowa City from **Davenport** at the Mississippi and Missouri Railroad's "depot grounds." The first handcart Saints arrived in Iowa City on May 12, 1856. They stayed two days in depot buildings and then hauled luggage by wagons and carts across the **Iowa River** to the **outfitting grounds.** During the next month, more Saints arrived and moved to the encampment.

University of Iowa. A Big Ten school, the university has nearly 30,000 students. The campus of some 90 buildings is located on both sides of the picturesque Iowa River. **Mormon Trek Boulevard** is a main north-south street on the campus's west edge, named to honor the handcart outfittings in 1856 and 1857.

The heart of the campus is the stately **Old Capitol Building,** one of Iowa Territory's earliest seats of government. It became operational in 1842 and served until 1857, when it became the University of Iowa's first building. Built of limestone blocks and topped by a gold dome, this national historic landmark is a fine example of Greek Revival architecture. It is open to the public for tours.

Plum Grove Historic Home is at 1030 South Carroll Street, off Kirkwood Avenue. It was the home of **Governor Robert Lucas,** Iowa Territory's first governor (1838–41) at the time the Saints were establishing Nauvoo. He and his wife, Friendly, built this home in 1844 (the year of Joseph and Hyrum Smith's martyrdom) of soft red brick made in Iowa City. The home is surrounded by a grove of plum trees, the source of its name. It is furnished with period pieces from the 1844–53 period.

■ **CORALVILLE—HANDCART PARK/OUTFITTING GROUNDS

Coralville, on Iowa City's northwest shoulder, contains the site of the **1856 and 1857 handcart outfitting grounds.** The site is 2 miles west-northwest from Iowa City's Central Business District. The .25 mile site stretches east and west from a spot one quarter of the way south on the section line dividing Sections 7 and 8, West Lucas Township (T79N R6W).

In 1976, in connection with the U.S. Bicentennial Celebration, a several-acre Mormon Handcart Park was developed in Coralville on ground owned by the University of Iowa, through funds provided by the LDS Church. Now called the **University of Iowa Mormon Handcart Park and Nature Preserve,** it is .5 mile southwest of U.S. 6 on Mormon Trek Boulevard (north of that intersection the boulevard is named 1st Ave.), and then three blocks west on Hawkeye Park Road (in the Hawkeye Student Housing complex), then north on Hawkeye Court to the end, where the park's parking lot is. From there a paved .5 mile path goes westerly up to the northern edge of a vast level field, now a giant soccer complex, where the 1856–57 handcart outfitting campground once was. Along the path are **three interpretive signs** (erected 1979) that explain the 1856 "handcart brigades."

One mile northwest of the handcart park, a shopping complex built in 2002 caused a DAR **handcart marker** (1936) to be moved six blocks west. It is now in Coralville's **S. T. Morrison Park** in the 1600 block on 5th Street (5th Street is parallel to and one street north of U.S. 6.) The park is adjacent to and west of Coralville's city hall. The marker, a bronze plaque on a large stone, stands next to 5th Street and is in front of a pond. Its inscription (with referents now out of place) reads:

The Mormon Handcart Brigade Camp

South of this boulder on the banks of Clear Creek is the site of the "Mormon/Handcart Brigade Camp." In 1856 some thirteen hundred European immigrants, converts to the Mormon faith, detrained at Iowa City, the end of the railroad. Encamped here, they made handcarts and equipment for their journey on foot to Salt Lake City. 1936.

The 1856 and 1857 Handcart Companies

In 1856 the LDS Church implemented a system of **handcart companies** in which emigrants who could not afford covered wagons could pull small, inexpensive handcarts almost 1,300 miles to Utah faster than wagons could travel. One advantage was lower cost; disadvantages of the handcarts were that people had to power the carts themselves, the small carts could carry only bare essentials, and the travelers had no protection from sun, wind, and rain like that provided by covered wagons (although they did have big tents to sleep in each night). Between 1856 and 1860, 10 handcart brigades were organized and traveled to Utah (seven crossed Iowa), involving 2,962 LDS travelers, mostly from Europe (HCZ 193).

Elder Daniel Spencer had on-site responsibility for the handcart outfitting, with advisement from **Elders John Taylor and Franklin D. Richards. Chauncey Webb** was the camp's main wheelwright. Directions for the design and fabrication of the carts came from Church headquarters. LDS workers at the outfitting camp as well as wheelwrights in Iowa City and St. Louis constructed the two-wheeled handcarts, usually of hickory or oak. The first companies employed four different **handcart designs**—experimenting to see what worked best. In the first year, 100 carts were built at St. Louis, 100 in Iowa City, and about 172 at the campground. Green wood was used in some hubs,

Building handcarts in Iowa City, IA, 1856–57, seven companies. (Courtesy of Vernon Murdock, artist, 1973)

in response to Brigham Young's direct orders to do so (DSL-H).

The covered family carts each had a small wagon box about 54 inches by 32 inches with side and end boards about eight inches high. The larger, open carts had fabric floors, and no covers or sideboards. Carts were designed with an extended rectangular handle in front by which two people could push the cart. One journal entry provided this description of the carts:

> The carts which are delivered to us are well constructed and light. They have very strong wooden wheels, four feet high. The rim is made of two steam-bent fellies around which is fastened an iron tire. They have wooden axles upon which are attached two shafts eight feet long and five matching cross pieces. The carts are four feet wide and weigh 60 pounds. (DPM)

Each cart was built to carry about 100 pounds of clothing and equipment, although another 100 pounds of flour was added to some carts in Nebraska. Each handcart traveler was limited to 17 pounds of baggage. Five persons were assigned to each cart, with 20 assigned to each large, round tent that the LDS agents provided. Each company included a wagon and ox-team for each 20 carts, used to carry tents, food, and incapacitated travelers (HCZ 58–59).

On Aug. 2, 1856 the *New York Evening Post* published a non-Mormon's description of the outfitting camp when it was near its busiest time:

> The camp, as viewed from the brow of a neighboring hill . . . presents a fine spectacle. Over one hundred tents, and perhaps as many covered wagons, with their spires and arches of dazzling white—contrast well with the green sward of the prairie and the sparkling ripples of the river running close beside. . . . In all about three thousand have rendezvoused in this spot, of whom some eighteen hundred still remain. . . . The tents are arranged in rows, with wide streets between them—the wagons generally in rings, with the entrance at one side, and sleeping tents on the outside. . . . There are in all four hundred and forty-five oxen, twenty mules, and a few horses. . . . There is seen, as you enter camp, a smithery, a workshop

and a store, all full of business and industry. . . . I have made acquaintance of their leaders, and have found them courteous, cultivated, and in business transactions, uncommonly "sharp." (ThM Aug. 2, 1856, 2)

The **first two handcart companies,** captained by **Edmund Ellsworth** and **Daniel McArthur,** left the outfitting grounds on June 9 and 11, 1856, respectively, and traveled close together all the way to Utah. Together, they contained 497 people, 100 handcarts, five wagons, 24 oxen, four mules, 25 tents, and provisions to last the group until they reached Florence, Nebraska Territory, 275 miles away, where they would be reprovisioned. The Ellsworth company arrived in Florence 27 days after starting; the McArthur company in 25 (HCZ).

On some days the pioneers walked and pulled 20 miles or more. On July 1 diarist **Archer Walters** noted that he had "traveled about 15 miles. Walked very fast,—nearly 4 miles an hour." **Patrick Twiss Bermingham,** in the McArthur company, noted on July 3 that the company started at 5 A.M. and traveled "a long and tedious journey of 25 miles" before camping at 7:15 P.M. "Some of the brethren fainted on the road and were carried into camp in the ox-team. I nearly fainted myself from exhaustion." Bermingham said the company reached Florence City on July 8, "generally very fatigued. Found some of Brother Ellsworth's company lying insensible on the road." These travelers had dust-stained clothes and sunburned faces (HCZ 62–63; JPTB; ThM Aug. 2, 1856, 2).

The third handcart brigade, the **Edward Bunker company,** contained mostly Welsh Saints—300 persons, 60 handcarts, and five wagons pulled by mule teams. They left the outfitting camp on June 28 and reached Florence July 19—taking only 22 days. They encountered some "heavy rain and wind storms which blew down our tents and washed away our handcarts," Bunker recalled. **Priscilla Evans,** in that

Original handcart temporarily on display at the Museum of Science and Technology, Washington, D.C. (1975)

company, said that "people made fun of us as we walked, pulling our carts," and that although "we were very tired at night, still we thought it was a glorious way to go to Zion." She noted that among those in her tent group was a man with one leg (her husband), two blind men, a man with a missing arm, and a widow with five children (HCZ 85–86).

John D. T. McAllister, one of the elders who disbursed equipment and supplies at the outfitting camp in 1856, wrote a **handcart song** that was sung by many handcart pioneers and has been sung by Saints ever since (HCZ 65–66):

> Ye Saints that dwell on Europe's shore
> Prepare yourselves with many more
> To leave behind your native land
> For sure God's Judgments are at hand.
> Prepare to cross the stormy main
> Before you do the Valley gain,
> And with the faithful make a start
> To cross the plains with your handcart.
>
> *Chorus:*
>
> Some must push and some must pull
> As we go marching up the hill,
> And merrily on the way we go
> Until we reach the Valley, oh!

Of the five handcart companies that left Iowa City in 1856, the Ellsworth, McArthur, and Bunker companies made the long trek to Utah successfully, arriving respectively on Sept. 26, Sept. 28, and Oct. 2. But the last two, the **James G. Willie** and **Edward Martin handcart companies,** left late because they were inundated with unexpected passengers, requiring that agents find additional handcarts and supplies. (Six handcart companies, not five, crossed Iowa. The **Jesse Haven company** traveled separately from the Martin company, but at Florence, Nebraska, the Haven and Martin companies merged.) The **Willie company** had about 500 people, 100 carts, and five wagons; and the **Martin company,** 665 people, 133 handcarts, and seven wagons. The Willie company reached Florence, Nebraska, in 27 days and the Martin company in 25 days, the same pace, respectively, as kept by the Ellsworth and McArthur handcart companies.

Trapped by severe blizzards in Wyoming, many of the 1,162 members of the Willie and Martin companies lost their lives. For the journey from Iowa City to Salt Lake City, 165 died in both companies; 196 died in all five handcart companies (HCZ 193; DSP).

In 1857, the **Israel Evans** and **Christian Christiansen** handcart companies were the last of the seven groups that used Iowa City as their departure point (BZ 125–44). The final three handcart brigades, which made the trek in 1859 and 1860, started from Florence, Nebraska Territory.

In addition to the seven handcart companies, nine **LDS-sponsored wagon trains** outfitted at Iowa City in 1856, 1857, and 1858. These nine companies were named after their captains. The (1) William B. Hodgetts and (2) Dan Jones (later John A. Hunt) companies left in 1856. Four 1857 companies were led by (3) Jesse B. Martin, (4) Matthias Cowley, (5) Jacob Hoffheins, and (6) William G. Young. Three small 1858 companies were captained by (7) Horace S. Eldredge, (8) Iver N. Iverson, and (9) Russell K. Homer (HRSMT 143–44).

The 1856–57 Handcart Route, Iowa City to Des Moines

Between **Iowa City** and **Des Moines,** the 111-mile stretch of U.S. 6 follows or parallels closely the old river-to-river route along which the 1856 and 1857 handcart trains traveled.

■ *South Amana

South Amana is on U.S. 6, 7 miles north of I-80 and 22 miles west of Iowa City. It is one of seven historic villages composing the **Amana Colonies,** dating from 1855. LDS **handcart and wagon companies** in 1856 and 1857 passed where South Amana now is.

The Amana Colonies. In 1714 a religious movement in southwest Germany known as the Community of True Inspiration was founded. This movement evolved into today's **Amana community.** Ancestors of the Amana people came to the United States in 1842 and settled near Buffalo, New York. In 1855 they moved to Iowa and established the Amana Colonies, which were being built when the handcart companies passed by. In America the believers adopted a communal way of life, holding all property in common.

That communal lifestyle, including central dining houses, lasted until 1932, when the religious and economic spheres were separated. The Amana Refrigerator Company is no longer a community-owned industry. The people of Amana are *not* related to the Amish or Mennonite people, and they are modern in lifestyle.

The Amana Colonies today are one of Iowa's most popular tourist attractions because of their charming period restaurants, old brick houses, shops, and craft operations that produce quality furniture, cheese, wool products, and bakery goods.

■ Marengo—Emmett Company Encampment, Handcart Route

Marengo, 5 miles west of **South Amana** on U.S. 6, is 8 miles north of I-80 via County Road V66. Its population is about 2,300.

Where Marengo is now was once a wilderness area when it served as the first major **James Emmett Expedition encampment** (see **Iowa City, James Emmett Expedition**) from September 1844 to January 1845. Within months of the Emmett group's departure, the first white settler arrived and occupied a deserted Mormon cabin. The town of Marengo developed from that tiny beginning.

The **1856–57 handcart route** passed 1 mile south of Marengo. Several handcart diarists mentioned seeing Marengo in the distance, including **John Jaques** in the Martin handcart company:

> Sun. 3 [August, 1856], Traveled 7 miles and camped east of Hilton Creek, plenty of timber, water, and feed. Three miles from Marengo, on our right . . . two wagon loads of rough men came to our camp from Marengo with the intention of creating a disturbance, but they were unable to and went away in a short time shouting and yelling.
>
> Mon. 4 [August]. . . . at 4 P.M.we started, crossed the creek, took left hand road, (the right leading to Marengo), passed through the woods, kept Marengo in sight for 2 or 3 hours. (LHWJJ 120)

Two **log cabins built by Henrich Meyer,** one in the handcart year of 1856 and the other in 1861, have been relocated to a park at the corner of South Street and Wallace, two blocks east of Marengo's main north-south street.

■ *MORMON RIDGE—EMMETT COMPANY ENCAMPMENT • ALBION

Mormon Ridge, a Marshall County landmark, is 3.75 miles west-northwest of Albion, a suburb of **Marshalltown.** Albion is 45 miles northeast of Des Moines via U.S. 65/State 330 and then 5 miles north on County Road S75. The ridge stretches out southeast to northwest in Sections 20, 29, 33, and 34 in Bangor Township (T85N R19W). **Mormon Ridge Road** runs along the ridge.

Mormon Ridge is reached by driving 5 miles west of the south end of Marshalltown on U.S. 30, turning north on County Road S75 (becomes Co. S330) for 5 miles, going west on 190th Street (Co. E29) for 4.5 miles, then north on Hopkins Ave. (Co. S62) for 4.2 miles, and east on 148th St. (Co. E23) for .5 mile up the hill to **Mormon Ridge Road.** Turn right on Mormon Ridge Road and within .25 mile, on the left (northeast) is **the Historical Log Cabin on Mormon Ridge,** a restored cabin believed to have been built in 1856 and moved to its present site in 1991 from elsewhere on the ridge. Mormon Ridge Road goes 1.25 miles southeast until it ends at 160th Street. From there, drivers can go 1.5 miles west and return to Hopkins Ave. (Co. S62).

The **James Emmett company** (see **James Emmett Expedition**) camped from mid-February to April 1845 at the southeast tip of this ridge, near where Minerva Creek flows into the Iowa River (southeast quarter of the southeast quarter of Section 34, Bangor Township [T85N R19W]). These Saints built rude huts or cabins and tapped maple trees for sugar. Five leaders were falsely arrested by a posse from Iowa City, taken there, and released uncharged. In early May the expedition, reduced to 22 wagons, continued northward and then west-northwest until June 7, 1845, when they reached the **Missouri River** near present-day **Vermillion, South Dakota** (MBK 147–68).

A **mystery of Mormon Ridge** circulates in Marshall County. Local folklore claims that a Mormon company, unknown to history, wintered on the ridge and suffered numerous deaths, so that the ridge contains many Mormon graves. No excavation to find graves has been tried yet. The myth is a strange combining of elements: the Emmett company's camp there, LDS deaths at Winter Quarters, and LDS handcart companies passing through Iowa and suffering death in Wyoming winter snows (MBK 161–62).

■ **HANDCART COMPANY GRAVE OF JOB WELLING JR. • GRINNELL

The **Job Welling Jr. grave marker** is about 50 miles east-northeast of **Des Moines.** The site is .25 mile north of I-80, Exit 182 (Grinnell exit), on State 146, then west 2.25 miles on Stagecoach Avenue/410th Avenue to a sharp bend to the south. The grave marker is in the sloping yard on the northwest side of the bend. Just past the bend is a parking area that is the Ahrens Access to the Jacob Krumm Nature Preserve, including a small lake.

The only specific grave marker in Iowa connected to the **Mormon handcart companies** honors the Welling boy, not quite two years old, who was part of the **Ellsworth handcart company.** He died June 17, 1856, about 10 miles east of this spot and was buried here the next day. The marker was erected in recent times by Welling family descendants, with the property owner's permission. According to the Ellsworth Camp Journal:

> June 17th. At four A.M. the bugle was blown for all to turn out, and at quarter to seven the camp moved off. Traveled ten miles and rested two hours. At twenty past two we pitched our tents. The journey was performed without any accident. No wood, plenty of water. About twenty minutes past three Job Welling, son of Job Welling, died, age one year and seven months. Died of canker or inflammation of the bowels.
>
> June 18th. At four A.M. the bugle sounded for all to turn out. At twenty minutes past five the camp rolled out; and traveled ten miles without any accident. Pitched tents at thirty-five past eight A.M., to give the Sisters an opportunity of washing the clothes. Today the body of Job Welling was interred three feet from the Northeast corner of Mr. Watrous' Farm, Township 80, Range 17, Section 25 (HCZ 200).

■ NEWTON

Newton is 35 miles east of Des Moines and 3 miles north of I-80 on Highway 6. Its population is approximately 16,000.

The **Mormon handcart route** passed through Newton. On June 20, 1856, the **Ellsworth handcart company** "passed through the city of Newton" (HCZ 201). On July 28 the **Willie handcart company** also passed through Newton, where, it had been rumored, the inhabitants were prepared to mob them. But the Saints moved in close order formation without incident, according to Capt. Willie:

> It appeared as if the residents of the entire city and the country round about were lining the streets as they walked along. No one molested them but snide remarks such as gee and haw were directed toward the company. These words, commonly used to direct oxen to the right or to the left, were uttered to make them appear as beasts of burden. The greater majority, however, just gazed upon them with a look of surprise. (JJGW)

On Aug. 8, 1856, the **Martin handcart company** "passed through Newton, town of about 2000 inhabitants. Two or 3 miles further camped at 8 P.M. in a valley through which a creek ran" (LHWJJ 121). That campsite was in present-day Westwood Park, 2 miles west of Newton on the south side of State 6.

Newton, "the home laundry center of the world," is the **home of Maytag Appliances.** About 1900 **Fred Maytag** began manufacturing washing machines, giving the town an economic base. The Maytag story is told in the **Jasper County Historical Museum,** near Exit 164 from I-80.

■ MITCHELLVILLE

Mitchellville is 12 miles east of Des Moines and 1 mile south of I-80 on County Road S27.

The **Mormon handcart route** passed through today's Mitchellville, following closely where County Road S27 passes through town.

The **Thomas Mitchell Park** is 2.5 miles south of Mitchellville. Between 1846 and 1854 Thomas Mitchell opened cabins and rented them to travelers at his "Apple Grove Inn"—perhaps America's first motel. **Handcart pioneers** mention passing apple orchards in this area, and orchards still are found 2 miles south of the park along County Road S27 (112th St). On July 30, 1856, **James G. Willie** recorded that his company passed through

Mormon handcart emigrants passing through Iowa. (Old print)

a recently established settlement about noon which appears to have been west of today's **Apple Grove** (JJGW). They camped along **Camp Creek.** In Section 26, whose east border is County Road S27 between mile 1 and mile 2 north of State 163, handcart pioneer **James Bowers** of the **Ellsworth handcart company** was buried June 22, 1856 (HCZ 201).

■ Rising Sun

Rising Sun is 8 miles east of **Des Moines** on State 163. The **Mormon handcart route** passed through Rising Sun and through present-day Ellis Park (between Rising Sun and Pleasant Hill). "Passed through Rising Sun," John Jaques in the **Martin handcart company** noted Aug. 13, 1856, and they halted for a midday rest "1 mile east of Fort Des Moines" (LHWJJ 121).

■ *Des Moines

Des Moines is located near the center of Iowa. I-80 and I-35 intersect there. The city lines both sides of the beautiful **Des Moines River** at this point.

Des Moines, **Iowa's capital,** has approximately 200,000 people, and is the nation's second leading insurance city. Some 50 insurance companies have home offices there. Des Moines began in 1843 as a military garrison called **Raccoon Barracks.** Two years later this part of Iowa Territory opened up for settlement by whites, and **Ft. Des Moines** became the county seat of Polk County. In 1857 Des Moines replaced Iowa City as the **state capital.**

During the **Spring Exodus from Nauvoo** in 1846, some Saints journeyed here and then crossed the Des Moines River.

The **1856 and 1857 LDS handcart companies** crossed the **Des Moines River** (east to west) .5 mile south of the present-day **Walnut Street Bridge** in downtown Des Moines (then called **Ft. Des Moines,** population about 1,100). Today, four blocks south of that bridge, near where Riverside and SW First Street intersect, is the partially restored **Old Ft. Des Moines** on the west bank of the river. Handcart pioneers passed by the fort.

"Passed the River des Moin at the town of Des Moins," Ellsworth handcart company member John Oakley wrote on June 24. "2800 inhabitants some of the people here raged with the spirit of Cain against us" (DJO June 24).

On July 31, 1856, the **Willie handcart company** left camp at

6:30 A.M., crossed the Des Moines River on a floating bridge, and passed through the city before it came to life. A mile beyond the fort they stopped at a small store near a creek and made some purchases. Mr. Charles Good presented them with a gift of 15 pairs of children's boots, which they accepted with gratitude (JJGW).

On Aug. 13, 1856, the **Martin handcart company** left its camp 1 mile east of Ft. Des Moines and "passed fort and river and baited [halted] 4 miles from fort. Made 12 miles" (LHWJJ 121).

Leaving Ft. Des Moines, the handcart pioneers' route was westbound, close to present-day University Avenue to today's community of **Waukee,** on the west edge of Des Moines.

Martin Harris, one of the Three Witnesses to the Book of Mormon, testified at an LDS meeting in Des Moines in August 1870 about his seeing the gold plates, being visited by an angel, and taking a copy of Book of Mormon characters to Professor Anthon for verification (BiE 1:273–74).

The **State Capitol Building,** completed in 1886, is in downtown Des Moines 4.5 miles south of I-80 and seven blocks east of the Des Moines River at East 9th and Grand Avenue. It is noted for its main dome and four smaller ones covered with 23-karat gold leaf and for the ornate ceilings, mosaics, murals, and wood carvings inside. An impressive **Korean War Memorial** stands on the south grounds of the capitol.

The beautiful **State Historical Society Building,** one block west of the capitol, contains books and manuscripts relating to LDS history in Iowa and a small scale-model of the famous Torleif Knaphus's **Handcart Family Statue.**

■ Polk City—North of Des Moines

Polk City, population about 2,100, is 15 miles north of Des Moines on State 415. This town is where **John C. Bennett,** former mayor of Nauvoo and an assistant to the First Presidency before he apostatized, died in 1867. His tombstone is one of the largest in the Polk City Cemetery. Bennett arrived in Polk City from Plymouth, Massachusetts, where he had moved after defecting from **former Mormon James J. Strang**'s movement. Bennett served in the Tenth Iowa Infantry during the Civil War (LJCB 184–86).

The 1856–57 Handcart Route, Des Moines to Council Bluffs

■ *ADEL

Adel is 13 miles west of Des Moines on U.S. 6. The **1856 and 1857 handcart pioneers** passed directly through this early Iowa town and forded the **North Raccoon River** there, two blocks north of U.S. 6.

On Aug. 2, 1856, the **Willie handcart company** pulled for 6 miles and reached Adel, population then about 126. To enter the town they forded the North Racoon River, which was knee-deep. Many residents turned out to watch them pass through town. A few tried to dissuade some of the sisters from continuing west (JJGW).

On Aug. 14 the **Martin handcart company** crossed the knee-deep river "close by the town of Adel" (WMHC 103).

In Adel at 415 River Street at the west entrance to a bridge crossing the river is a **historical marker,** "North Raccoon River," noting the old state highway route and ferry crossing.

■ WISCOTTA • REDFIELD

Wiscotta is on U.S. 6 at 23 miles west of Des Moines and 1 mile south of **Redfield.** The **handcart pioneers** pulled along the South Raccoon River bottoms through what is now **Wiscotta,** probably passing where the **Wiscotta Cemetery** now is.

■ *DALMANUTHA CEMETERY • CASEY

Dalmanutha Cemetery is north of **Casey,** which itself is 2 miles north of I-80 at a point 41 miles west of Des Moines and 7 miles east of **Anita.** The cemetery is reached by going 2.5 miles northwest of Casey on Sherman Street (Co. F65), north 3 miles on Juniper St. (Co. N72), crossing 310th St (Co. F63), continuing north 1.5 miles, turning east on 295th Street/Lost Trail Road (a gravel road), and following it as it elbows for .6 mile to the cemetery.

This well-maintained cemetery is all that remains of **Dalmanutha,** a **stagecoach town** laid out in 1855. The **1856 and 1857 handcart pioneers** passed this site. First burials in the cemetery date from 1849. Signs on the cemetery's south side contain histories of Dalmanutha, the cemetery, the handcarts (inaccurately told), and a map showing the supposed handcart route from Des Moines. The **Martin handcart company** camped at a good site

.75 mile south-southwest of Dalmanutha by what is today the Middle River (near where 310th Street crosses the river) on Aug. 16, 1856, a fact recorded by **John Jaques**: "Traveled 17 miles. Three or four old houses at commencement, one at 14 miles. Camped on a hill past Mud River, good water and feed, timber scarce, hilly. [At] Dalmanutha" (LHWJJ 122).

■ Anita

Anita is approximately 60 miles west of downtown Des Moines and 75 miles northeast of Council Bluffs. It is 3 miles south of I-80 via Exit 70 on State 148. **Turkey Creek** runs along the south edge of Anita, flowing in a west-southwest direction. At a point 1 mile upstream from Anita and then for 4.5 miles downstream from Anita, the **handcart route** closely followed the north side of Turkey Creek.

The **Ellsworth and McArthur companies** passed here on July 1, 1856. John Jaques reported that the **Willie handcart company** reached a stage station beside **Turkey Creek** on August 17, apparently 1 mile west-southwest of present-day Anita. The next day they moved along the creek for 3.5 miles, following closely present-day State 83. There, 4.5 miles west-southwest of Anita, they crossed Turkey Creek. They halted 10 miles later "along Turkey Creek," a stopping place 4 miles south of present-day **Atlantic** on U.S. 71, near where U.S. 71 now crosses Turkey Creek in Grove Township, Section 27 (LHWJJ 122).

On July 1, the **Ellsworth and McArthur handcart companies** covered 14 miles, moving part of that time between where **Anita** and **Wiota** now are. That day, and somewhere along that stretch, there occurred what has become **an oft-told handcart story about a lost boy** (often erroneously placed in Nebraska; TPH 5:240–41). In the McArthur company were Robert and Ann Parker and four children ages 12, 10, 6, and 1. While the company took a rest break on July 1, a storm approached, causing them to hurriedly start moving again. Six-year-old Arthur Parker, who had been resting with other children, had fallen asleep and, unnoticed by his parents, was left behind. When the McArthur company camped with the **Ellsworth company** at the "head of Turkey Creek" later that afternoon, some 14 miles from the last camp, the Parkers discovered Arthur was missing. Men in both handcart companies began a vigorous search. The Parkers' company stayed camped all day on

July 2 while searchers looked in vain for the boy.

Diarist Archer Walters noted on July 2: "Brother Parker's little boy, age six, was lost. The father went back to hunt him" (HCZ 61). Ann pinned a bright red shawl around Robert's shoulders before he left, telling him that if he found the boy dead he could wrap him in the shawl; if he found him alive, he could use the shawl to signal that the boy was all right. The next day, July 3, the McArthur company, including Ann Parker and the children, moved on (TF May 2004, 4–7).

Pushing and pulling a handcart. (Courtesy of Vernon Murdock, artist, 1973)

Heading the other direction, Robert Parker retraced the trail, calling, searching, and praying. At a mail and trading station 10 miles back—possibly the one mentioned above in the Willie company account, which was perhaps 1 mile west-southwest of present-day Anita—he learned that Arthur had been found and cared for by a farmer and his wife. Robert learned from the boy that he had spent the stormy night under a tree and then had wandered for what Robert determined was nine miles until he found the farmhouse.

Meanwhile, for two nights Ann and the McArthur company, on the move, watched for Robert to return. On July 5 the McArthur company was camped at **Silver Creek,** about 60 miles beyond where the boy had disappeared and 14 miles east of Council Bluffs. By sunset light Ann saw the red shawl waving. She rejoiced. "Brother Parker brings into camp his little boy that had been lost," diarist Walter wrote. "Great joy through the camp. The mother's joy I can not describe" (HCZ 61).

■ ATLANTIC

Atlantic is 57 miles east of Council Bluffs and located on U.S. 6. The **handcart companies** passed 3 miles south of Atlantic. In Atlantic U.S. 6 intersects with U.S. 71 (southbound), and at a point 4 miles south from that intersection, on U.S. 71, the handcart companies passed, heading southwest.

■ **LEWIS

At Lewis, which is 40 miles east of Council Bluffs via U.S. 6, the handcart companies joined the **1846 Mormon Trail** route. For the rest of the handcart route and sites, please see **Iowa Historic Route 1** concerning the **1846 Mormon Trail from Lewis to Council Bluffs.** Included are details relating to the handcart pioneers' connections to Mormon Trail sites from there to the Missouri River. Also see **Council Bluffs** sitc 41, concerning the handcart route through **Council Bluffs** to **Upper Ferry,** as well as the **Upper Ferry** entry, which deals with the site where handcart pioneers' crossed the Missouri River to Florence, Nebraska Territory.

Nebraska

William G. Hartley

A. Gary Anderson

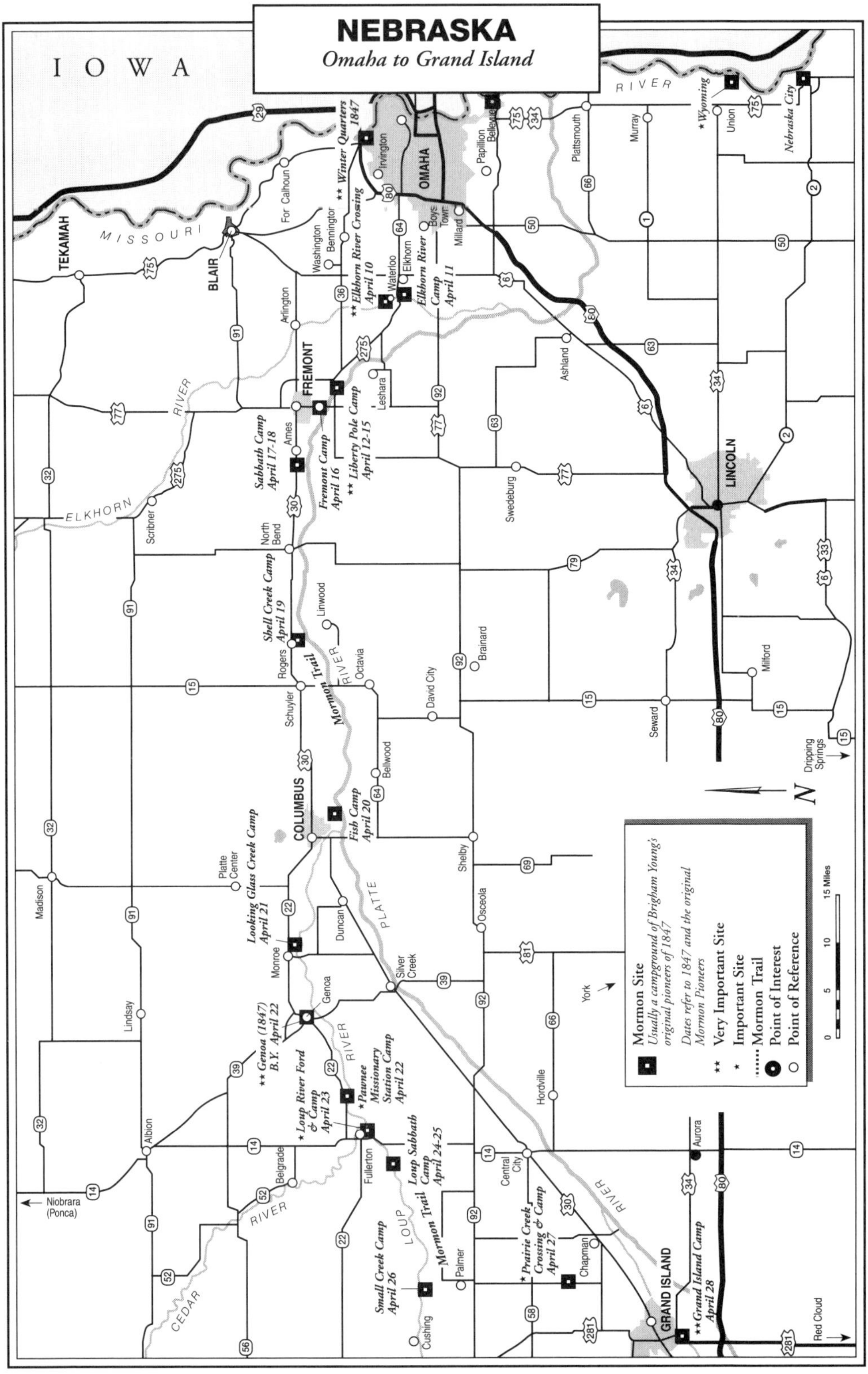

NEBRASKA
Omaha to Grand Island
IOWA
MISSOURI
RIVER
ELKHORN
PLATTE
LOUP
CEDAR
TEKAMAH
BLAIR
FREMONT
COLUMBUS
OMAHA
LINCOLN
GRAND ISLAND
For Calhoun
Washington
Bennington
Arlington
Irvington
Waterloo
Elkhorn
Boys Town
Millard
Papillion
Bellevue
Plattsmouth
Murray
Union
Leshara
Ames
Ashland
Swedeburg
Scribner
North Bend
Linwood
Rogers
Schuyler
Octavia
David City
Brainard
Bellwood
Platte Center
Madison
Duncan
Monroe
Genoa
Silver Creek
Shelby
Osceola
Lindsay
Albion
Belgrade
Fullerton
Central City
Chapman
Palmer
Cushing
Hordville
York
Aurora
Seward
Milford
Dripping Springs
Red Cloud
Niobrara (Ponca)
** Winter Quarters 1847
** Elkhorn River Crossing April 10
Elkhorn River Camp April 11
** Liberty Pole Camp April 12-15
Fremont Camp April 16
Sabbath Camp April 17-18
Shell Creek Camp April 19
Mormon Trail
Fish Camp April 20
Looking Glass Creek Camp April 21
** Genoa (1847) B.Y. April 22
* Paunee Missionary Station Camp April 22
* Loup River Ford & Camp April 23
Loup Sabbath Camp April 24-25
Small Creek Camp April 26
* Prairie Creek Crossing & Camp April 27
** Grand Island Camp April 28
* Wyoming
Nebraska City
N
Mormon Site
Usually a campground of Brigham Young's original pioneers of 1847
Dates refer to 1847 and the original Mormon Pioneers
** Very Important Site
* Important Site
Mormon Trail
Point of Interest
Point of Reference
0 5 10 15 Miles

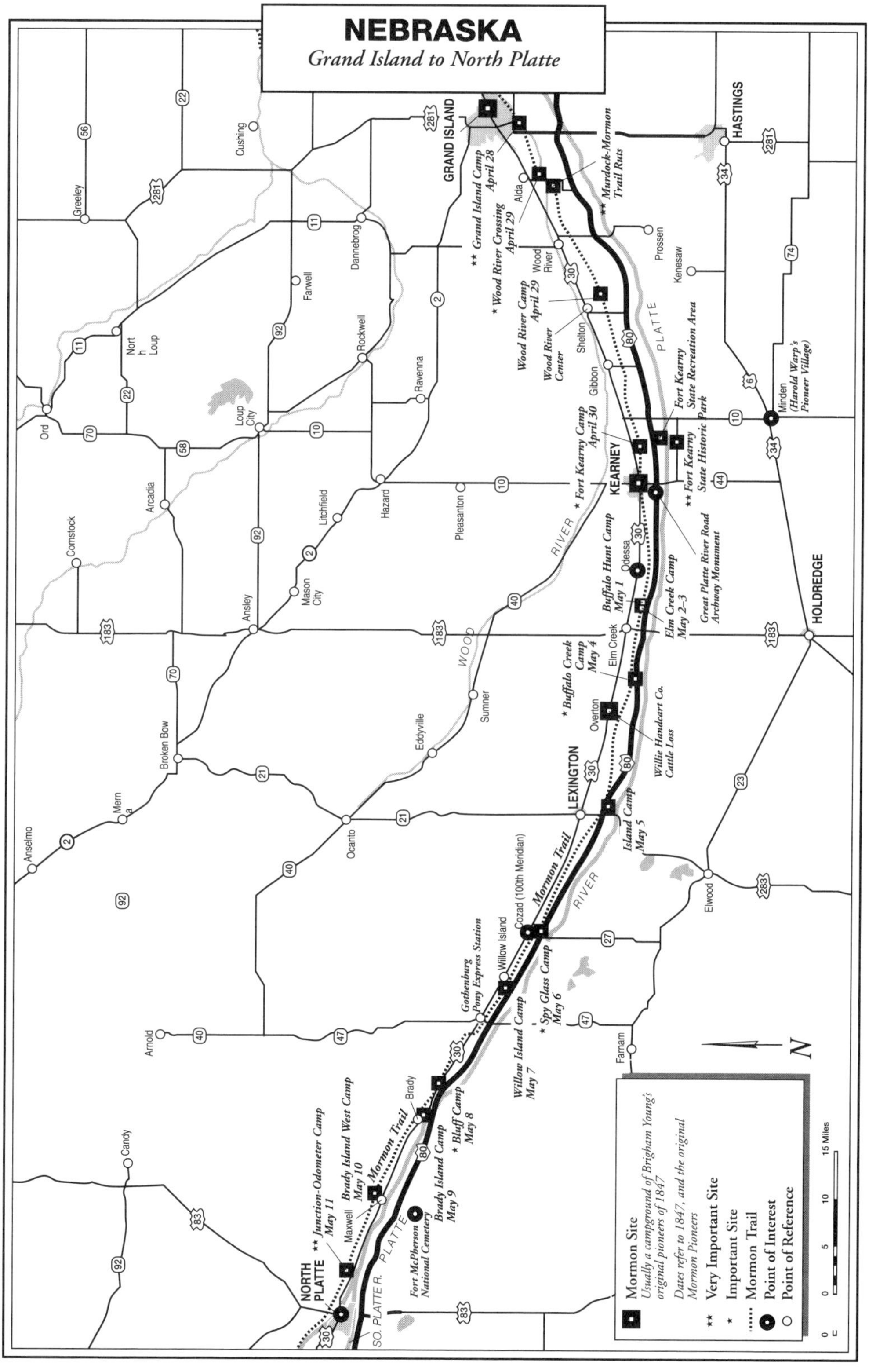

NEBRASKA
Grand Island to North Platte
GRAND ISLAND
** Grand Island Camp April 28
** Wood River Crossing April 29
** Murdock-Mormon Trail Ruts
Wood River Camp April 29
Wood River Center
Fort Kearny State Recreation Area
** Fort Kearny State Historic Park
* Fort Kearny Camp April 30
KEARNEY
Great Platte River Road Archway Monument
Buffalo Hunt Camp May 1
Elm Creek Camp May 2–3
* Buffalo Creek Camp May 4
Willie Handcart Co. Cattle Loss
LEXINGTON
Island Camp May 5
Cozad (100th Meridian)
Mormon Trail
Gothenburg Pony Express Station
* Spy Glass Camp May 6
Willow Island Camp May 7
* Bluff Camp May 8
Brady Island Camp May 9
Brady Island West Camp May 10
** Junction-Odometer Camp May 11
Fort McPherson National Cemetery
NORTH PLATTE
SO. PLATTE R.
PLATTE
RIVER
WOOD RIVER
HASTINGS
HOLDREDGE
Minden (Harold Warp's Pioneer Village)
Cushing
Greeley
Dannebrog
Farwell
North Loup
Rockwell
Ravenna
Ord
Loup City
Arcadia
Comstock
Hazard
Litchfield
Mason City
Ansley
Pleasanton
Alda
Wood River
Shelton
Gibbon
Prossen
Kenesaw
Odessa
Elm Creek
Overton
Sumner
Eddyville
Broken Bow
Merna
Anselmo
Ocanto
Willow Island
Arnold
Farnam
Elwood
Brady
Maxwell
Candy
N
Mormon Site
Usually a campground of Brigham Young's original pioneers of 1847
Dates refer to 1847, and the original Mormon Pioneers
** Very Important Site
* Important Site
Mormon Trail
Point of Interest
Point of Reference
0 5 10 15 Miles
0 Km

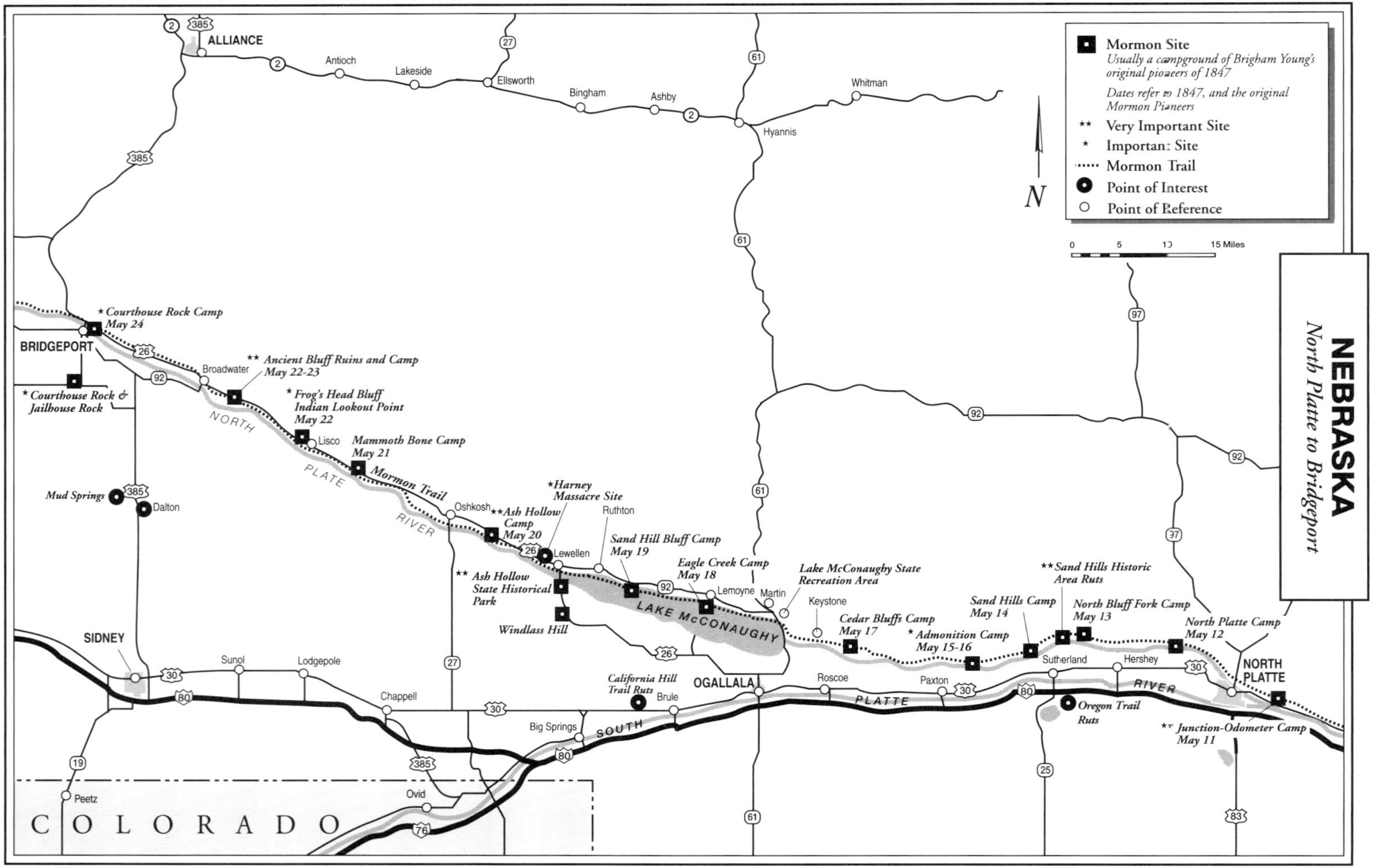
NEBRASKA
North Platte to Bridgeport
Mormon Site
Usually a campground of Brigham Young's original pioneers of 1847
Dates refer to 1847, and the original Mormon Pioneers
★★ Very Important Site
★ Important Site
Mormon Trail
Point of Interest
Point of Reference
0 5 10 15 Miles
N
ALLIANCE
Antioch
Lakeside
Ellsworth
Bingham
Ashby
Hyannis
Whitman
★ Courthouse Rock Camp May 24
BRIDGEPORT
★ Courthouse Rock & Jailhouse Rock
Broadwater
★★ Ancient Bluff Ruins and Camp May 22-23
★ Frog's Head Bluff Indian Lookout Point May 22
Lisco
Mammoth Bone Camp May 21
Mormon Trail
NORTH PLATTE RIVER
Mud Springs
Dalton
Oshkosh
★★ Ash Hollow Camp May 20
★ Harney Massacre Site
Lewellen
Ruthton
★★ Ash Hollow State Historical Park
Windlass Hill
Sand Hill Bluff Camp May 19
Eagle Creek Camp May 18
Lemoyne
LAKE McCONAUGHY
Martin
Lake McConaughy State Recreation Area
Keystone
Cedar Bluffs Camp May 17
★ Admonition Camp May 15-16
Sand Hills Camp May 14
★★ Sand Hills Historic Area Ruts
North Bluff Fork Camp May 13
North Platte Camp May 12
NORTH PLATTE
★★ Junction-Odometer Camp May 11
SIDNEY
Sunol
Lodgepole
Chappell
California Hill Trail Ruts
Brule
OGALLALA
Big Springs
SOUTH PLATTE RIVER
Roscoe
Paxton
Sutherland
Hershey
Oregon Trail Ruts
Peetz
Ovid
COLORADO
2
385
27
61
92
97
37
26
30
80
19
76
25
83

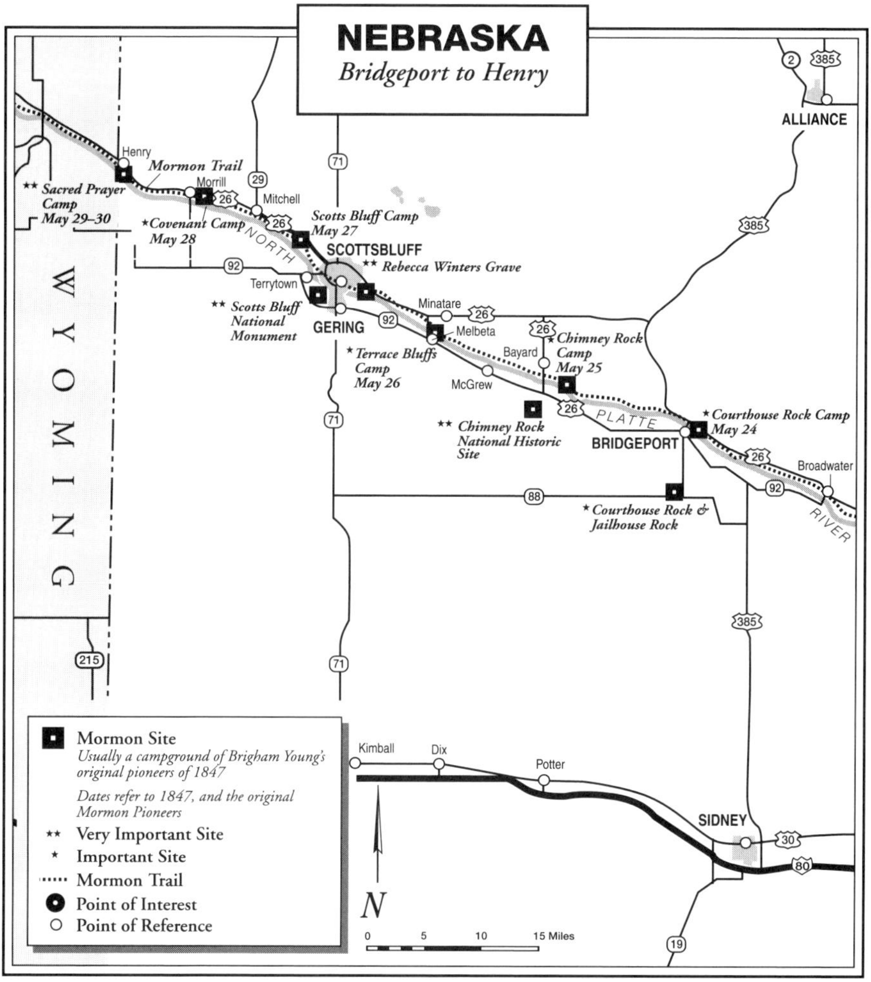

NEBRASKA
Bridgeport to Henry
ALLIANCE
Henry
Mormon Trail
Morrill
Mitchell
★★ Sacred Prayer Camp May 29–30
★ Covenant Camp May 28
Scotts Bluff Camp May 27
SCOTTSBLUFF
★★ Rebecca Winters Grave
NORTH
Terrytown
★★ Scotts Bluff National Monument
GERING
Minatare
Melbeta
★ Terrace Bluffs Camp May 26
Bayard
★ Chimney Rock Camp May 25
McGrew
★★ Chimney Rock National Historic Site
PLATTE
BRIDGEPORT
★ Courthouse Rock Camp May 24
Broadwater
RIVER
★ Courthouse Rock & Jailhouse Rock
WYOMING
Kimball
Dix
Potter
SIDNEY
N
0 5 10 15 Miles
Mormon Site
Usually a campground of Brigham Young's original pioneers of 1847
Dates refer to 1847, and the original Mormon Pioneers
★★ Very Important Site
★ Important Site
Mormon Trail
Point of Interest
Point of Reference

Mormon Trail Auto Route

Winter Quarters (Florence) to Fremont (Liberty Pole) (32 miles)

From the Winter Quarters Pioneer Center return to N. 30th St., go left to State 36 (left at light before I-680), which is McKinley Street. Proceed northwest to the North Omaha Airport, where the road becomes Bennington Road (still State 36) and turns west. (5) Continue westbound and veer right (northwest) to stay on State 36 when Bennington Road continues due west. State 36 will pass through Glen Cunningham Lake Recreation Area and continue until it ends at U.S. 275. (22) Go north on U.S. 275, which becomes U.S. 30 (5) and loops around and bypasses Fremont on the north.

Fremont to Grand Island (127 miles)

From Fremont continue west on U.S. 30 to Columbus. (47) In Columbus, where U.S. 30 intersects U.S. 81, turn north on U.S. 81. Go northwest to State 22 (6), turn left or west, and drive to Genoa (16). Take State 22/39 south out of Genoa (1) and when 22/39 forks, take 22 to the west, and stay on it southwesterly to Fullerton (14). In Fullerton turn south on State 14 to Central City (17), and from there take U.S. 30 southwest to Grand Island. (25)

Grand Island to Ogallala (187–194 miles)

Option 1 From Grand Island, take U.S. 30 southwest to Kearney (40), and continue northwest to North Platte (96). (From Kearney to North Platte U.S. 30 follows rather closely the 1847 Mormon Trail route.) Continue west on U.S. 30 to Ogallala (51).

Option 2 From Grand Island drive south on U.S. 281 to I-80 (7), then take I-80 southwest past Kearney (39), northwest past North Platte (96), and west to Ogallala (52).

Ogallala to Henry (131 miles)

Option 1 Stay on U.S. 30 through Ogallalla to the U.S. 26 bypass west of town. (2). Take U.S. 26 all the way to Henry—through Lewellen, Broadwater, and Bridgeport (75). At Bridgeport U.S. 26 crosses from the north to the south side of the North Platte River. Continue northwest on U.S. 26 to Scotts Bluff National Monument (33) and then to Henry (21). Occasionally U.S. 26 and State 92 are the same.

Option 2 If on I-80, take exit 126 north on State 61 to U.S. 30 (2) and then follow the same directions as in option 1.

Option 3 At Ogallala take State 61 north around the east end of Lake McConaughy. At Martin turn west on State 92 and go to Lewellen (35), and from there take U.S. 26 west to Henry, as in Option 1.

Total miles: 477–84

MAIN SITES ALONG THE MORMON TRAIL

The main sites along the Mormon Trail are listed from east to west, in the order in which the Saints established or encountered them. In the site identifications and narratives that follow, LDS sites of particular importance historically are marked * and those considered very important are marked **. Be certain to obtain permission from the landowner before visiting any sites that are privately owned.

**Winter Quarters, Apr. 1847
**Elkhorn River Crossing, Brigham Young, Apr. 10–11
Elkhorn River Camp, Brigham Young, Apr. 11
** Liberty Pole Camp, Brigham Young, Apr. 12–15
Fremont Camp, Brigham Young, Apr. 16
Sabbath Camp, Brigham Young, Apr. 17–18
Shell Creek Camp, Brigham Young, Apr. 19
Fish Camp, Brigham Young, Apr. 20
Looking Glass Creek Camp, Brigham Young, Apr. 21
**Genoa, (1847) Brigham Young Apr. 22; 1857 YX Settlement
*Pawnee Missionary Station Camp, Brigham Young, Apr. 22
**Loup River Ford and Camp, Brigham Young, Apr. 23
**Ponca Winter Camp, Niobrara, Nebraska
Loup Sabbath Camp, Brigham Young, Apr. 24–25
Small Creek Camp, Brigham Young, Apr. 26
*Prairie Creek Crossing and Camp, Brigham Young, Apr. 27
**Grand Island Camp, Brigham Young, Apr. 28
*Wood River Crossing, Brigham Young, Apr. 29
**Murdock—Mormon Trail Ruts
Wood River Camp, Brigham Young, Apr. 29
Wood River Center (Shelton)
Harold Warp's Pioneer Village
Great Platte River Road Archway Monument, Kearney

*Ft. Kearny Camp, Brigham Young, Apr. 30
**Ft. Kearny State Historic Park
Ft. Kearny State Recreation Area
Buffalo Skulls and Mail, Odessa
Dripping Springs—Little Blue River, near Fairbury
Rock Creek Station State Historical Park, near Fairbury
Buffalo Hunt Camp, Brigham Young, May 1
Elm Creek Camp, Brigham Young, May 2–3
*Buffalo Creek Camp, Brigham Young, May 4
Willie Handcart Company Cattle Loss, Overton
Island Camp, Brigham Young, May 5
*Spy Glass Camp, Brigham Young, May 6
Cozad and the 100th Meridian
Willow Island Camp, Brigham Young, May 7
Gothenburg Pony Express Station
*Bluff Camp, Brigham Young, May 8
Brady Island Camp, Brigham Young, May 9
Brady Island West Camp, Brigham Young, May 10
Ft. McPherson National Cemetery
**Junction-Odometer Camp, Brigham Young, May 11
North Platte
North Platte Camp, Brigham Young, May 12
North Bluff Fork Camp, Brigham Young, May 13
**Sand Hills Historic Area Ruts
Sand Hills Camp, Brigham Young, May 14
*Admonition Camp, Brigham Young, May 15–16
Cedar Bluffs Camp, Brigham Young, May 17
California Hill Trail Ruts, Brule
Lake McConaughy State Recreation Area
Eagle Creek Camp, Brigham Young, May 18
Sand Hill Bluff Camp, Brigham Young, May 19
Ash Hollow State Historical Park and Windlass Hill
**Ash Hollow Camp, Brigham Young, May 20
*The Harney Massacre Site
Mammoth Bone Camp, Brigham Young, May 21
*Frog's Head Bluff Indian Lookout Pt., May 22
**Ancient Bluff Ruins and Camp, Brigham Young, May 22–23
*Courthouse Rock Camp, Brigham Young, May 24
*Courthouse Rock and Jailhouse Rock
Mud Springs, Dalton

*Chimney Rock Camp, Brigham Young, May 25
**Chimney Rock National Historic Site
*Terrace Bluffs Camp, Brigham Young, May 26
**The Rebecca Winters Grave
Scottsbluff
**Scotts Bluff National Monument
Scotts Bluff Camp, Brigham Young, May 27
*Covenant Camp, Brigham Young, May 28
**Sacred Prayer Camp, Brigham Young, May 29–30

Introduction to Nebraska

Nebraska, once claimed by Spain and then by France, became part of the United States in 1803 when the United States acquired more than 500 million acres of territory from France for $15 million (approximately $232.5 million in 2003 dollars). The **Louisiana Purchase** included all or part of what became 11 states, including Nebraska, or one-quarter of today's continental United States. In 1804 President Thomas Jefferson commissioned Meriwether Lewis and William Clark to lead an expedition to explore the headwaters of the Missouri River in the hope of finding an overland route to the Pacific Ocean by way of the Columbia River. This "Corps of Discovery," or **Lewis and Clark Expedition,** traveled up the Missouri River using a keelboat and two "pirogues." In an epic journey that would become one of America's most fabled expeditions, the company journeyed along the eastern and northern border of present-day Nebraska and on through today's Dakotas, Montana, Idaho, Washington, and Oregon. They reached the Pacific Ocean in November 1805, where they built Ft. Clatsop near present-day Astoria, Oregon. In the spring of 1806 they returned, again moving along Nebraska's edge, reaching St. Louis on Sept. 23. Their reports, including maps and descriptions, influenced later developments in the Louisiana Purchase region, including in Nebraska.

During Lewis and Clark's westward journey up the Missouri River in 1804, they participated in the first council between the United States and the Indians of Nebraska—the Oto and the Missouri. The name *Nebraska* comes from the Oto word "nebrathka." The word means "flat" or "shallow" water and was the Native American name for Nebraska's chief river, the Platte, which flows through the length of Nebraska west to east. The Platte River Valley was the popular route that fur traders used to travel to the western mountains. Subsequently, missionaries and other emigrants to Oregon used that route. Between 1840 and 1866 an estimated 350,000 emigrants to Oregon, California, and Utah crossed Nebraska in covered wagons.

Stephen H. Long's 1820 expedition named the region west of the 100th meridian to the Rocky Mountains "the Great American Desert," a name that continued until after the Civil War. Today it is called the Great Plains. Yet Nebraska has more miles of river than any other state. The eastern boundary of the state is delineated by the Missouri River. Of its main tributaries, the Platte is by far the largest. From the city of North Platte, where the Platte River's northern and southern branches converge, the river curves eastward, draining half the state before it joins the Missouri south of Omaha.

The **Kansas-Nebraska Act,** passed on May 30, 1854, created the **Territory of Nebraska.** Its initial boundaries extended from Kansas to Canada and from the top of the Rocky Mountains to Minnesota and Iowa, making it five times as large as Nebraska is now (HSN). Once the territory was announced, lands on the west bank of the Missouri River quickly gained attention from developers. The passage of the Homestead Act of 1862 and the building of the transcontinental railroad, which began its route west from Omaha in 1865, led to the development of Nebraska and to its statehood in 1867. Nebraska became the 37th state in the Union.

Of all the United States, Nebraska ranks 16th in land size and 38th in population. Its 1,740,000 residents (2003) are found in 93 counties. Nebraska is the only state to have a unicameral state legislature of 49 nonpartisan representatives rather than the division of senate and house used by other states. **Omaha** is Nebraska's largest city, and **Lincoln** is the capital. Nebraska's nickname is the "Cornhusker State."

Although Nebraska enjoys a reputation for agriculture, with ranching in the west and fruit and general farming in the east, a growing proportion of its income comes from sources outside the farm. A wide variety of commodities are manufactured in the state. Food processing is the largest industry, with flour, dairy, and meat products being prominent. The expanding manufacture of durable goods includes electrical machinery, farm equipment, metal and prefabricated buildings, automotive parts, and energy conversion systems.

Nonmetallic minerals such as clays, gemstones, limestone, sand, gravel, and pumice account for over half the state's mineral production. Crude petroleum, natural gas, and natural gas liquids are also produced. One of the world's largest lead refineries is in Omaha, along with the headquarters for the Union Pacific Railroad.

Well-known native Nebraskans include several born in Omaha: **Gerald Ford,** the 38th president of the United States; billionaire **Warren Buffet;** Hall of Fame baseball pitcher **Bob Gibson;** boxer **Max Baer;** black activist **Malcolm X;** TV newsperson **Paula Zahn;** and actors **Fred Astaire** (Frederick Austerlitz), **Dorothy Maguire, Marlon Brando,** and **Nick Nolte.** Among famous persons born elsewhere in Nebraska are Ponca chief **Standing Bear,** Oglala Sioux leader **Red Cloud,** Hall of Fame pitcher **Grover Cleveland Alexander** (Elba), movie producer **Darryl Zanuck** (Wahoo), TV talk show personality **Dick Cavett** (Gibbon), and actors **Henry Fonda** (Grand Island), **David Jannsen** (Naponee), **Sandy Dennis** (Hastings), and **Marg Helgenberger** (Fremont). Although not born in Nebraska, TV talk show celebrity **Johnny Carson** grew up in Norfolk and graduated from the University of Nebraska. Author **Willa Cather** moved to Red Cloud when she was young and graduated from the University of Nebraska. Move-in **William Jennings Bryan,** the "Boy Orator of the Platte," ran unsuccessfully for U.S. president three times, was secretary of state under President Woodrow Wilson, and gained fame in the "Monkey Trial" for prosecuting Tennessee schoolteacher John Scopes for teaching evolution. **George W. Norris** was a congressman for 40 years. **Gen. John J. Pershing,** World War I general, came to Lincoln in 1891, became a cadet instructor at the University of Nebraska, and considered Lincoln his home. Wild West legends **James Butler ("Wild Bill") Hickok** and **William Frederick ("Buffalo Bill") Cody** were also residents of Nebraska. The latter made his home in North Platte for more than 30 years.

Latter-day Saints in Nebraska

Members of The Church of Jesus Christ of Latter-day Saints who left Nauvoo, Illinois, under the direction of Brigham Young in 1846 intended to migrate to the Great Basin that same year. Because of difficulty in crossing Iowa, lack of preparation, and the departure of 500 volunteers to help fight the war in Mexico, the scattered Saints spent the winter of 1846–47 in the Iowa-Nebraska area to prepare for the exodus to the West in 1847 and subsequent years.

Winter Quarters, located in Nebraska on the west bank of the Missouri River, became the headquarters of the Saints' winter encampment. The exodus began in the spring of 1847 when a pioneer company led by **Brigham Young** crossed the plains of Nebraska, basically following the Platte River Road. Other Latter-day Saints followed that same year, and thousands more during the next two decades until the railroad provided easier transportation after 1867. Most of the Latter-day Saints who migrated by wagon train to Utah between 1847 and 1867 passed through Nebraska.

After the trail emigration period ended in Nebraska in 1867, LDS Church connections to Nebraska were limited to train transportation through it and to sporadic missionary labors. In 1877 a branch was established in Fremont, which was part of the Northwestern States Mission. In 1896 the Nebraska Conference was organized, and by 1900 a branch had been established in Omaha. In 1935 President **Heber J. Grant** negotiated a 50-year lease of the Winter Quarters Cemetery site. By 1950 branches existed in Omaha, Lincoln, North Platte, Bridgeport, Scotts Bluff, and Grand Island, with Sunday Schools in several other towns. In May 1953 general authorities dedicated the new Mormon Pioneer Memorial Bridge across the Missouri River. In 1960 the Winter Quarters Stake was created, with wards in Omaha, Bellevue, Lincoln, Fremont, Grand Island, Kearney, and Hastings. It was later renamed the Omaha Nebraska Stake. Stakes formed since then include Lincoln (1974), Omaha Papillion (1986), and Kearney (1991). As of 2003, LDS Church membership had reached 20,203 in four stakes, 36 wards, and 23 branches (DNCA 2005:208–9).

The Missouri River and Mormon Emigration

The Missouri River is the longest river in the United States (approximately 2,700 miles in length). It was first discovered by Europeans in 1673 by French-Canadian explorer Louis Joliet and the French missionary and explorer Jacques Marquette. In the winter the river almost comes to a standstill, and parts freeze over. The

Missouri defines Nebraska's eastern border and is designated a **National Wild and Scenic River.**

During the 19th century the Missouri served much the same purpose as modern interstate highways do. **Steamboats** made it a major transportation artery for passengers and freight. Prior to construction of the transcontinental railroad, several **Mormon wagon train outfitting camps** were located along the Missouri River in Nebraska or across the river. In Nebraska they were **Winter Quarters** (1846–48), **Florence** (1856–63), and the town of **Wyoming** (1864–66). Between 1848 and 1852 the main outfitting center was in Iowa just across the river from Omaha, at **Council Bluffs (Kanesville).**

Steamboats transported thousands of **Mormon emigrants** up the Missouri River to these staging areas. Between 1840 and 1855, at least 89 emigrant ships unloaded European converts at the port of New Orleans. From there, riverboats carried the emigrants up the Mississippi River to Nauvoo until 1846, when the Saints fled Nauvoo and settled in Council Bluffs, Iowa, and Winter Quarters, Nebraska. Between 1847 and 1855, the emigrants steamed up the Mississippi and then the Missouri to the outfitting sites. In 1854 Brigham Young announced that the emigrants' ship arrival port would be changed in 1855 from New Orleans to east coast cities. The emigrants would then travel across "the States" by train and by river steamboats to the outfitting camps.

The Platte River and the "Great Platte River Road"

The **Platte River,** a tributary of the Missouri River, rises in the Rocky Mountains and is formed by the junction of the North and South Forks of the Platte in western Nebraska, in Lincoln County. The Platte flows easterly and enters the Missouri River 15 miles below Omaha, after a course of 1,000 miles. The Platte was a source of amazement to travelers. It is from one to 3 miles wide but so shallow that it is not navigable and is hard to cross because of quicksand. Travelers and locals describe it as being "a mile wide, a foot deep, too thin to plow and too thick to drink." Above Grand Island the Platte was braided with islands and was full of sandbars. Only the river's islands offered a wood supply. Away from the river's edge, the Platte River Valley lacked trees because frequent prairie fires burned off the seedlings (GPRR 238–241; EmG 46–7).

Mormons were participants in a massive westward migration that took place in the 1840s, 1850s, and 1860s, which crossed the Missouri River to travel on either the north or south side of the Platte. During the 1840s **Independence, Missouri,** was the main crossing place for most emigrants; in 1849 to 1850, **St. Joseph** was the principal crossing; and 1850–63, **Council Bluffs** served this purpose. The Mormon emigrants from Nauvoo in 1846 crossed at present-day Council Bluffs (OJ Fall 1985: 38).

The **"Great Platte River Road"** refers to trails on both sides of the Platte River from Ft. Kearny (halfway across Nebraska) westward. The **Oregon Trail** initially reached the Platte River near the Ft. Kearny location and then followed the south side of the Platte. Most emigrants to Oregon and California used that south side route.

Mormon emigrants beginning in 1847 favored the north side, where a poorly developed route already existed. The first military exploration of the **north side** of the Platte River was directed by **Maj. Stephen H. Long** in 1820. Fur trappers, including **Thomas Fitzpatrick, Jim Clyman,** and **Jedediah Smith,** and others had followed the northern side of the river. In 1844 **Elisha Stevens** led the **first emigrant wagon train** (13 wagons) to California along the **north side** of the Platte River. The 1847 Mormons generally followed that route. Many emigrants besides the Mormons used that side. What is now termed the **Mormon Trail** was referred to in trail days by most non-Mormons as the **Council Bluffs Road.** In 1849 it became commonly called the north branch of the **Great Platte River Road** or the **northern branch of the Mormon-Oregon-California Trails** (GPRR).

Beginning in 1849 a substantial number of Mormon wagons chose to follow trails on the south side instead. Of an estimated 350,000 emigrants using the **Great Platte River Road** between 1841 and 1866, about 35 percent chose the northern route (OJ Fall 1985: 35–36). Although thousands other than Mormons used the northern route before and after they did, the Mormons had the largest organized group that ever left the Missouri River to settle in the West. Because of this, the northern route they used became known as the **Mormon Trail.**

THE HISTORIC NEBRASKA MORMON TRAIL

The Mormon Pioneer National Historic Trail extends from Nauvoo, Illinois, to Salt Lake City, Utah, and was established by law in 1978 as a part of the National Trails System. In Nebraska that designated trail is the route the **1847 Brigham Young company** used on the north side of the Platte. This route, at least across Nebraska, also served the overland stage, transcontinental telegraph, Union Pacific Railroad, and U.S. 30 or Lincoln Highway—the nation's first transcontinental highway. In total, the basic Mormon Trail extended for approximately 1,300 miles, of which nearly 500 miles are in present-day Nebraska.

During the lifetime of the Mormon Trail, 1846 to 1868, its travelers used **various types of wagons** and carriages but mostly ordinary, reinforced farm wagons, which were about 10 feet long and arch-covered by canvas or other cloth. Because wagons had to cross rivers, owners caulked or covered bottoms with canvas so the wagons could float. For pulling the wagons, most emigrants favored oxen to horses or mules. Oxen, although slower, could pull more weight and graze better; being castrated steers, they were more docile. Most wagon train emigrants walked instead of riding in the wagons.

An estimated 329 LDS Church-organized wagon and handcart companies went west, led by Church appointed or approved captains. About 10,000 wagons were involved. Wagon trains averaged about 2 miles per hour. To go from the Missouri River to Salt Lake City required six to eight weeks of travel. Between 1856 and 1860, in addition to the annual wagon trains, ten companies of handcart pioneers with nearly 3,000 Saints set out for Utah. Estimates for all overland trail travel show that by 1868 about 300,000 emigrants went to California or Oregon; about 60,000 Mormons went to

Utah. Mormon deaths on the trail are estimated to be about 6,000 (MPNHT).

Scholars have noted a number of "uncommon aspects" of the Mormon migration compared to that of other travelers on the overland trails. These include the following: (1) the movement of a community centered at Nauvoo; (2) a religiously motivated migration; (3) the migration of families; (4) the system of organizing Mormon wagon trains; (5) the lack of professional guides; (6) the caring for fellow passengers, making improvements for people coming later, and Church financial assistance; and, (7) abiding respect for life and death. A number of LDS wagon train captains returned to lead other companies in subsequent years (MPNHT 9–10).

LDS Handcart Companies in Nebraska

Between 1856 and 1860, ten LDS handcart companies crossed the plains to Utah, and one missionary company went by handcart brigade from Utah to the Missouri River. They all pulled across Nebraska. LDS wagon companies were also on the trail during those years (HCZ).

In 1856 six handcart companies outfitted in **Iowa City, Iowa,** about three-quarters of that year's LDS emigration. They pulled across Iowa and stopped briefly at **Florence (Winter Quarters), Nebraska,** to rest, repair, and resupply. Two companies merged into one. Then, the five companies individually moved across Nebraska that summer and early fall. Generally they followed the **Brigham Young company's 1847 route** on the north side of the Platte River but deviated occasionally to use stretches of newer, better trail and to avoid natural impediments. They did not blaze any new trails. In western Nebraska the last two handcart brigades that year, the ill-fated **Willie and Martin companies,** left the Mormon Trail and crossed to the south side of the Platte River and briefly followed the Oregon Trail (EJWM). (See **1856 Handcart Companies**).

The first three handcart companies in 1856—the **Edmund Ellsworth, Daniel D. McArthur, and Edward Bunker companies**—reached Utah in reasonably good time and condition. But the last two, **the Willie and Martin companies,** due to a late start, larger size, and various travel difficulties, suffered tragedy when caught in early blizzards in Wyoming. (See **The 1856 Handcart Companies** discussion below.)

In 1857, to demonstrate continuing faith in the handcart system, the LDS Church had missionaries, who were heading east, pull handcarts instead of using wagons. That year, in addition to the **missionary handcart company,** the **Israel Evans and Christian Christiansen handcart companies** made the journey from Iowa City to Utah, transporting 40 percent of that year's LDS emigration (HCZ, BZ).

In 1858 the annual LDS emigration flow dried up because of the Utah War but it resumed in 1859. That year the Church moved the outfitting site from **Iowa City** to **Florence,** which served as the starting point for Mormon companies until 1864. In 1859 the **George Rowley handcart company** left from Florence (with about 17 percent of that year's LDS emigration). The next year the **Daniel Robinson and Oscar O. Stoddard handcart companies** departed from Florence with about 20 percent of that year's emigration. They were the last two handcart companies (HCZ).

In total, the ten handcart companies started out with nearly 3,000 people, but scores dropped out along the way, dozens died during the normal course of travel, and about 150–170 died in the Wyoming snows (HCZ).

From Prairie to Great Plains

The overland trails in Nebraska started in **prairie country,** like that around **Winter Quarters.** Rain and humidity produced prairie grasses taller than a man. Due to the absence of trees on the prairie, wood houses or log cabins were hard to come by, so settlers, including Mormons at Winter Quarters, built some **sod homes,** which were cheap to build. Sod is the top layer of ground soil with the grass and roots still in it. To cut sod, men plowed ribbons about three to six inches thick and then cut them into "bricks." Roofs were timber frames covered with sod, which posed dangers from falling sod and leaked during rains. Snakes and bugs liked sod walls. Nebraska prairie lands bordering the Platte River were riddled with creeks and streams.

Along the trails in mid-Nebraska, **prairie game** ranged "from the lordly buffalo to the comical prairie dog, the soaring buzzard to the earthbound snipe." Some **prairie dog towns,** many of which the Mormon pioneers passed, extended from 100 to 500 acres (GPRR 250). Wagon train emigrants encountered **buffalo,** which roamed the praire and plains by millions. The Platte River Valley, containing "the largest open grassland in the world" and a seemingly endless supply of river water, served as the center of buffalo movements. Buffalo approaching the Platte River made grooves in the ground—their hoofprints measuring about 15 inches across and 4 inches deep, creating a washboard pattern on the trails that broke many wagon axles. "Sometimes we would see the Plain black with them [buffalo] for ten miles in width," John Pulsipher reported in 1848. Two years later another traveler saw a buffalo herd he estimated numbered two million traveling in a solid phalanx, thick as sheep. Buffalo males stood about seven feet tall at the shoulders and weighed up to 2,000 pounds; females weighed less than half as much. Buffalo were a great resource for Indians and for emigrants, providing meat, hides, tallow, and burnable buffalo chips (GPRR 243–54).

In mid-Nebraska the overland trails entered the **Great Plains,** which were higher in elevation and dry. Clear air made distant objects seem near. Grasses were shorter, and notable rock formations, including **Chimney Rock** and **Scotts Bluff,** dotted the route.

Native Americans along the Platte routes were Pawnee, Sioux, and Cheyenne (GPRR 260).

Brigham Young's 1847 company traveled close to 500 miles in today's Nebraska (EmG 56–57). The National Park Service (NPS) and Nebraska Mormon Trails Association (NMTA), in partnership, have erected a series of **Mormon Pioneer National Historic Trails interpretive panels** along that 1847 route. These tell key stories and facts about the trek of the 1847 Brigham Young company across Nebraska. The panels consist of a title, text, visuals, a map of the Nebraska Mormon Trail, and quotations from pioneer diaries relevant to the historic site featured on the panel. Locations of these panels are noted in Mormon Trail site discussions as **NPS/NMTA Mormon Trail interpretive panels.**

In addition, more than a dozen smaller **NPS/NMTA Mormon Trail** panels entitled **"The Road to Zion"** are being installed. Those already in place are located in or at the following sites:

Omaha/Florence, across from the old mill
The Schuyler City Park
Columbus City Park
Genoa, near trail ruts
Gothenburg, in Ehman City Park by the Pony Express station
Kearney, in the Great Platte River Road Arch Complex
Lake McConaughy, outside the Games and Park Information Center near the dam
Rebecca Winters's gravesite

Winter Quarters Area

In 1846 the Mormons left the Nauvoo, Illinois, area and crossed Iowa to where **Council Bluffs,** Iowa, now is, on the east side of the Missouri River. Brigham Young's Camp of Israel arrived there on June 14, nine days after Pottawattamie/Ottawa/Chippewa chiefs returned from Washington, D.C. The chiefs were preparing

to sell southwestern Iowa back to the American government and remove all 2,250 tribal members to northeastern Kansas. In July 1846 some LDS companies crossed the Missouri River and started for the Rockies. A general lack of progress coupled with the loss of about 500 men to the Mormon Battalion caused the Twelve to halt the vanguard's trek west and find quarters for the winter. By then, several thousand Saints had crossed the river into Nebraska. After meeting with Native American leaders and receiving permission from the federal government, Church leaders decided to halt the push west and make a major encampment for winter by the Missouri River. They established headquarters camps first at **Cold Spring Camp** (July 1–Aug. 6), then at **Cutler's Park** (Aug. 6–Dec.), and finally at **Winter Quarters** (Sept. 1846–June 1848).

Meanwhile, as wood, water, and grass ran out in the Grand Encampment on the Iowa side (south and west of present-day Council Bluffs), thousands of LDS refugees scattered to form dozens of settlement clusters all around southwestern Iowa. The main settlement was **Kanesville,** later renamed **Council Bluffs,** which served as the leadership hub for Mormon settlements in the Middle Missouri River region until 1852 (MoM; ENS Aug. 2002, 19, 21).

The 1847 company of Mormon pioneers left Winter Quarters in the spring. They followed the slightly used north branch of the Oregon Trail that went along the north side of the Platte River. In Wyoming they traveled on the Oregon-California Trail and entered Utah using the route of the Donner Party. After starting a community near the Great Salt Lake, half the company, including Brigham Young, returned to Winter Quarters for one more winter. The next year, 1848, when Church leaders closed Winter Quarters, many Saints moved west to Utah; others moved back across the river to Kanesville, which served as the Church's headquarters for "the States" until 1852 (ENS Aug. 2002).

Places of interest in the Winter Quarters area include the following sites. An asterisk (*) denotes a place of special importance.

Sites in Winter Quarters

■ **1. *MORMON PIONEER MEMORIAL BRIDGE.** This steel-girder bridge is located on I-680 as it crosses the Missouri River between Florence,

Mormon Pioneer Memorial Bridge Toll Station, west end of the bridge in Nebraska. (1958)

Nebraska, and Iowa. The bridge was dedicated June 1, 1953, by LDS Church president **David O. McKay** and called **Mormon Bridge** because it spanned the Missouri near where a **Mormon ferry** existed as early as 1846. The bridge now accommodates only eastbound traffic, and another bridge was built in 1975 for westbound traffic (CN May 16, 1953:3).

In 1953 a **marker** describing the Mormons' presence in Winter Quarters was placed at the west end of the bridge on the south side of the road. It is best to walk to the marker.

■ **2. *Mormon Ferry or Upper Ferry Site.** A ferry that once operated near where the Mormon Bridge now is was known as the **Upper Ferry, North Ferry,** or **Mormon Ferry.** It was not the "original" or "first" ferry site of the Mormons, which is described below as site 26 (in **Sites near Winter Quarters**). That ferry was moved to this site by the end of September 1846. John S. Higbee was appointed ferryman (WiQ 59).

Mormon Ferry (Upper Ferry) on Missouri River looking northeast from Winter Quarters (Florence, NE). (Old print)

The ferry operated between **Ferryville,** on the Iowa side of the river, and Winter Quarters, on the Nebraska side. During the gold rush, many people heading for California used a ferry operating at this site. Because more overland trail traffic preferred the Oregon Trail south of the Platte, the number of crossings by those travelers at St. Joseph or Weston-Leavenworth exceeded usage at this north ferry. Later, this north ferry was moved downriver to Bethlehem, Iowa, south and across from the confluence of the Platte and Missouri Rivers.

In 1853 artist Frederick Piercy crossed on a ferry at this upper location and described the venture:

> The ferry-boats are flat-bottomed and large enough to carry 2 wagons of the ordinary size. The starting point is usually chosen a considerable distance up the stream, so that the current may assist in conveying the boats to the landing place on the opposite side of the river. Ferrying is hard work. When the boat is pushed from the bank the rowers are obliged to ply their oars most vigorously, as it is no slight matter to row across a river a quarter or half a mile wide, with a current running at the rate of 4 or 5 miles an hour. Six or 8 stout fellows are required to do the work. (RFL 101)

A **marker** telling about the Mormon Ferry is located on Pershing Drive north of the Mormon Bridge on the Nebraska side, near the Coast Guard compound fence at 9980 Pershing Drive.

■ **3. *OLD MORMON/FLORENCE/WINTER QUARTERS MILL/WEBER MILL.** The **original mill,** much added to, is not now at its original site. It is in Florence southwest of the Mormon Bridge and south of Exit 13 from I-680. At Exit 13, go south on U.S. 75 (North 30th St.) for 1 block and then turn east on McKinley Street a short block to the mill.

Construction of the mill started in October 1846, directed by Mormon pioneer millwright **Frederick Kesler Jr.** An overshot mill powered by Mill Creek, it was operational by March 1847 and was one of the first mills built in Nebraska. Church funds financed the $3,000 project. The mill used two sets of millstones. Basement timbers were of oak and walnut, and cottonwood was used above the first floor. Wooden pegs helped keep foot-square beams in place.

Old Mormon Mill, or Weber Mill, at Winter Quarters, NE. The corrugated iron tower is a more recent addition. (Courtesy of George L. Strebel, 1935)

The mill ground corn and grain into flour and employed about 150 men (ENS Sept. 1997, 47). It also served as a sawmill to provide Winter Quarters with lumber. The mill was abandoned when the Mormons departed from Winter Quarters in 1848.

In 1856 **Alexander Hunter** rebuilt around the deteriorating frame and began milling. His flour aided new residents of **Florence,** then being founded, as well as many Mormons outfitting or re-outfitting for the trek west. In 1870 **Jacob Weber** acquired the mill, and it was changed from water to steam power in 1880. The mill continued to produce flour under the direction of the Weber family. An elevator was added to the mill in 1915.

The original mill was located on Turkey (Mill) Creek, about two blocks southwest of its present-day location on the west side of North 30th Street near the overhanging Interstate sign. Mill Creek, which originally powered the overshot mill, is now piped underground to the Missouri River. After a severe flood in 1939, the mill was dismantled and moved to its present-day location (CN July 18, 1992:9). The present-day building contains a few timbers from the original mill. A **historic marker** in front of the mill tells its history. In 1998 a local artist opened an art gallery in the building.

■ **4. Brigham Young Home and Council House Sites.** The **Brigham Young home,** a two-story building with a brick chimney, was located at 9102 N. 30 Street, which is south-southwest across the street from the Old Mormon Mill in Florence. Young's home was a few yards northwest of the present-day fire station. By Nov. 8, 1846, Brigham Young said he had a house "with doors but no windows, and chimneys built of brick obtained from the ruins of an old fort [Ft. Atkinson] at Council Bluffs, but no floor" (MHBY Nov. 8, 1846, 445). His home was completed Nov. 12, 1846. Living quarters were on the second floor, and the first floor served as a home as well as for church and civic functions.

The fire station just across the street south of the mill was built where the Mormon **Council House** stood. The foundation of the Council House was commenced near the southeast corner of Brigham Young's house on Dec. 22, 1846. The building was 22 feet by 32 feet in size (CN Sept. 19, 1935:5). Though small, thc building served as a civic and religious center. An **NPS/NMTA Mormon Trail interpretive panel** at the site of the Council House is entitled "A Meeting House for the Saints." It tells about streets and blocks in Winter Quarters and the Council House, which was the social center of Winter Quarters.

Dr. Willard Richards's Octagonal House, location not pinpointed, was used as a council house before the "new" Council House was built. It served as Elder Richards's residence, a post office, doctor's office, hospital, and a meeting place for the Twelve and the High Council. In it Brigham Young recorded a revelation on Jan. 14, 1847, **Doctrine and Covenants 136,** known as "The Word and Will of the Lord" (CHC 3:154–57; JH Jan. 14–15, 1847). The revelation related to the forthcoming exodus of Mormon pioneers in 1847.

■ **5. *Florence Park (Mormon Park).** On the west side of N. 30th Street between State and Mormon Streets, **Florence Park** was on the western edge of Winter Quarters until a picket fence was built around the city and some log cabins were moved a quarter of a block west of the present-day park to reinforce the palisade. What is now the park was reported in 1856 as having been a Mormon corral for Winter Quarters.

A **historic marker** in the northern part of the park reads: "Winter Quarters location of the Camp of Israel / Pioneer Mormon Cemetery 1/3 of a mile west." Another **historical marker** located in the southeast part of the park tells about "Winter Quarters." Note that the street on the south side of the park is Mormon Street, and the one two blocks south is Young Street.

■ **6. **Winter Quarters.** The site of the city of **Winter Quarters,** Church headquarters for 18 months, is reached by taking Exit 13 from I-680 and traveling south on U.S. 75, or N. 30th Street. The city extended from the **Old Mormon Mill** south about 1 mile and was about .33 mile wide. It was situated near the Omaha Waterworks of today on the tableland overlooking the river.

Winter Quarters, NE, bronze plaque at the Winter Quarters Cemetery, made from a painting by C.C.A. Christensen. (1975)

Streams ran out of the hills on both the north and south side of the community, a little more than a mile apart. There was a high bluff to the north where artillery might have been defensively placed.

Early in September 1846 the Saints vacated **Cutler's Park** and established **Winter Quarters** where present-day Florence now is. This new settlement served as the headquarters of the Church from September 1846 to May 1848, while the Mormons prepared to emigrate to the valleys of the Great Basin. In May 1848 the Saints relocated the headquarters across the river to **Kanesville** (**Council Bluffs**).

Before building shelters, the Saints' first concern was food for the winter for both man and beast. They collected tons of prairie hay, gathered hundreds of bushels of berries, and salted and dried meat. Having missed the growing season, they lacked vegetables and had to trade downriver for grain. Brigham Young and a surveying crew platted Winter Quarters into five-acre blocks with 20 lots per block. A full-sized block could accommodate 20 houses and a population of from 150 to 300 persons. South of the city was a large section with haystacks and livestock yards.

The city was apportioned into large sections with prominent large families forming the nucleus of each division. **Brigham**

Young's division occupied most of the center of the city. **Heber C. Kimball's** company was on the south; **Wilford Woodruff** and his families occupied an entire block, presumably along Woodruff Street; **Alpheus Cutler's** families' lots overlooked the river, where most of the community's sheep were stockaded and haying operations were conducted.

Winter Quarters was organized into 22 Church wards. It had a **council house** for public meetings and public worship, a **gristmill,** and a **welfare store.** Funds donated by volunteers in the Mormon Battalion were pooled for bulk purchases of food, clothing, and medicine downriver in St. Joseph and St. Louis, Missouri. The **population** of Winter Quarters by Christmas 1846 was 3,483, including 757 men and boys over age 10 (population 5,000 by spring 1847). The Saints lived in 538 log (mostly cottonwood) cabins and 83 sod (dugout) houses. **Thomas Bullock,** secretary to Brigham Young, arrived from Nauvoo in late November 1846 and reported:

> [I] went through the City—where nine weeks ago there was not a foot path or a Cow track, now may be seen hundreds of houses, and hundreds in different stages of completion—impossible to distinguish the rich from the poor. The Streets are wide and regular and every prospect of a large city being raised up here. (MoM 80–81)

The quality of the homes varied widely from large, sturdy, two-story log buildings with solid floors throughout to cabin shanties inadequately finished. Many were without doors or floors, and some had only partial roofs. Some were not cabins but dugouts snugly built into the first rise of bluffs to the west (ENS Sept. 1997, 45).

Winter Quarters was occupied for about 20 months (Sept. 1846–May 1848). Those who were still unable to migrate west in the spring of 1848 moved back across the Missouri River to **Council Bluffs** (**Kanesville**) or to other LDS communities in Iowa. Frederick Piercy reported the burning of the last house at Winter Quarters by "some person" in the spring of 1853 (RFL 81). Timber from the Winter Quarters Mill was left standing.

In 1856 other settlers moved to the area and named it **Florence** (see site 10 below), hoping to build a commercial center. Florence was eventually annexed to Omaha in 1916 and is now known as North Omaha.

■ **7. *Mormon Trail Center at Historic Winter Quarters.** This center is located at 3215 State St., across the street to the east from the **Mormon Pioneer Cemetery.** LDS Church president Gordon B. Hinckley dedicated the center on Apr. 18, 1997—the sesquicentennial year of the 1847 pioneer company's trek west to Utah. Artwork, artifacts, maps, video and sound clips, and interactive exhibits tell the history of the Saints in the Middle Missouri River area between 1846 and 1852 and about the Mormon Trail and westward migration. The displays include a detailed model of what Winter Quarters looked like, a replicated log cabin, a covered wagon, and a handcart.

Mormon Trail Center at Historic Winter Quarters, NE. (1997)

■ **8. **Mormon Pioneer Cemetery.** This historic cemetery is on State Street, three blocks west of N. 30th Street and the northeast corner of Florence Park. It is across the street from the **Mormon Trail Center,** which is on the corner of State Street and North Ridge Drive. It is the burial site of 56 Saints from **Cutler's Park** and 304 from Winter Quarters who died between September 1846 and May 1848. The abandoned cemetery was rediscovered when State Street was cut through its upper

Memorial plaque with names of Saints buried in the Mormon Pioneer Cemetery at Winter Quarters and other cemeteries.

reaches in the 1930s. In 1936 the LDS Church leased the cemetery from Omaha City. The peaceful hilltop cemetery features a magnificent heroic-sized bronze statue, *Tragedy of Winter Quarters,* sculpted by **Avard Fairbanks.** It portrays the agony of pioneer parents buffeted by wind as they pause with shovel in hand over their infant in an open grave. It was dedicated by President **Heber J. Grant** on Sept. 20, 1936. **A memorial plaque** in front of the sculpture lists the names and ages of 365 Saints who are buried in the cemetery (CN July 18, 1992:7). Other plaques tell about Winter Quarters.

Bronze statue, Tragedy of Winter Quarters, *in the Mormon Pioneer Cemetery at Winter Quarters, NE, sculpted by Avard Fairbanks.*

Some estimate that 600 Saints died in the Council Bluffs–Winter Quarters area from 1846 to 1848 (MoM 131–47).

■ **9. *WINTER QUARTERS TEMPLE.** The **Winter Quarters Temple** is on the south side of the Mormon Pioneer Cemetery and across the street and just south of the Mormon Trail Center. It was dedicated on Apr. 22, 2001, by President Gordon B. Hinckley. At the same time, the cemetery property was rededicated as part of the temple grounds. The temple has 18 scenic stained-glass windows that depict historic Winter Quarters sites and events, reminding visitors of the pioneers who found refuge there and paid the ultimate price for their faith (DNCA 208).

Sites near Winter Quarters

The following places of interest (sites 10–28) near Winter Quarters, though not shown on a map in this book, are listed numerically in a logical visiting sequence.

■ **10. POST-WINTER QUARTERS: FLORENCE.** Named after **Florence Kilbourne,** daughter of an early town promoter, Florence is one of Nebraska's oldest settlements. In 1854, when Nebraska was opened for settlement, businessmen created the Florence Land Company that established the town where **Winter Quarters** had been.

Florence as LDS outfitting center, 1856–63. During eight emigration seasons, nearly 10,000 Saints outfitted or re-outfitted in Florence. At least 60 well-organized wagon and handcart companies, more than 1,000 wagons, and thousands of cattle were involved. To assist the emigration, LDS agents established stores, storage buildings, a bowery, weighing machines, corrals, and river landings. Florence proved to be an acceptable outfitting point because of its access to Missouri River steamboats; its nearby streams, grasses, and woods, which allowed for wagon camps, corrals, and pastures; its easy access to the Mormon Trail; and its proximity to merchants in Council Bluffs and later in Omaha City.

In contrast to the troubled Winter Quarters story, the Florence LDS emigration story is a positive and successful one. In 1856 and 1857 Florence served as an outfitting center for LDS wagon trains and as a resupply place for **7 handcart companies.** After 1857 Florence replaced Iowa City as the starting point for handcart companies and wagons because travel by railroad across Missouri and by boat upriver to Florence was easier than traveling overland from the Iowa City rail terminus.

Outfittings in 1861 and "down-and-back" wagon trains. To help the needy to emigrate, the LDS Church instituted a **Perpetual Emigrating Fund** in 1849 and then in 1856 tried out the low-cost handcart system. Drained of money, the Church in 1861 introduced a new system for assisting the needy. It sent four wagon trains *down* from Utah to take emigrants *back,* a 2,200-mile round trip. These Church trains consisted of wagons, teams, and men lent to the six-month effort in return for tithing credits. In mid-April 1861 four such down-and-back companies left Salt Lake City, consisting of 203 wagons, 217 teamsters, 1,699 oxen, and 18 guards. Together they transported 136,000 pounds of Utah flour, which they deposited at four stations along the trail for use on the trip back: Rocky Ridge, North Platte Bridge, and Deer Creek, all in Wyoming, and at **Wood River Center** in present-day Nebraska. Their trip to Florence took two months.

For three months of 1861, LDS agents operated a bustling outfitting campground at Florence. For the wagon companies, Church agents procured bulk supplies from stores in Omaha City and Council Bluffs, including 13,000 pounds of sugar; 3,000 pounds of apples; 3,300 pounds of ham; and 15,000 pounds of bacon (GFF 359). During May, June, and July, four large groups of LDS emigrants from the eastern United States and Europe converged at Florence, disembarking from river boats at Florence (precise landing site not identified). "The boat was densely crowded," said one Saint aboard the *Omaha,* "and every available spot was occupied by men, women, children, and baggage" (GFF 355). When a riverboat unloaded LDS emigrants on June 3 after dark, most of the luggage was left on the shore and guarded until morning. The *Sunshine* arrived on June 14, bringing about 30 Saints, mostly from Pittsburgh and St. Louis (GFF 357–8). On June 20, the *Omaha* unloaded Saints from the eastern states. Among them was Thomas Griggs, who noted that Saints were occupying many "deserted and unfinished houses" in Florence. Three days later he changed his clothes for the first time in thirteen days. He said that the days were "spent by the emigrants, teamsters, and presiding officers in arranging the details of the company organization, purchasing supplies, oxen, wagons, manufacturing tents, breaking in cattle, collecting such cash from the emigrants that they could advance to purchase needed groceries, bacon, &c." He found the "country very destitute of wood of any kind"; he had to hike two miles to find some (GFF 360–61).

When July began, Florence—a tent-and-wagon city near a few buildings—held its largest population of the year, exceeding 2,500 Mormons. They were a rich mixture of Germans, Swiss, Italians, Danes, Swedes, Norwegians, Scots, Welsh, English, Irish, Canadians, and Americans. Thirteen wagon trains rolled successfully to Utah from Florence that year—624 wagons and just over 3,900 emigrants (1,700 traveled in the down-and-back companies). A final letter from the camp, dated July 17, reported to Brigham Young that "every Saint who reached Florence, and desired to go home this season, has had the privilege. The sending down of waggons from Utah to Florence is a grand scheme." The 1861 wagon trains required an average of 73 days for the trek and averaged 14 miles per day (GF 366–68).

Down-and-back wagon trains continued to move LDS emigrants during the rest of the 1860s, until the transcontinental railroad reached Utah in 1869.

Florence itself enjoyed two more outfitting seasons, in 1862 and 1863, again helped by down-and-back wagon trains from Utah.

Then, in 1864, because transcontinental railroad tracks had pushed west of the Missouri River, the outfitting site changed to **Wyoming, Nebraska.** The down-and-back system, because of its 1861 success, was repeated during six of the next eight emigration seasons, involving 1,956 Utah teams, for an average of 326 wagons per year. The opening of the **transcontinental railroad** in 1869 essentially ended wagon train travel to Utah (DBWT 23–25).

After 1863 Florence reverted to being a town that never boomed. The 1870 census taker counted but 395 Florentines, 800 fewer than in 1860.

Thomas B. Marsh, former president of the Quorum of the Twelve Apostles, arrived in Florence in 1857 after being out of the Church for 18 years. He requested baptism, and Andrew Cunningham baptized him on July 16, 1857, in Big Papillion Creek. Marsh went to Salt Lake City shortly thereafter (BiE 1:74–76; ABM 182–86; JD 5:206–13; CN Oct. 1, 1960:20).

● **11. Bank of Florence Museum.** The Bank of Florence Museum is located at 8502 N. 30th Street. It is the oldest bank in Nebraska. Gambling that Florence would become the capital of Nebraska Territory, investors opened the two-story Bank of Florence in 1856, having built it around a large walk-in vault. The bank issued Nebraska's first paper currency, in denominations of $1, $2, $3, and $5. It was in business when LDS wagon and handcart companies passed through Florence in 1856 and 1857. Very likely LDS agents or individuals did some business there.

Due to the national financial panic of 1857, the bank closed sometime between 1858 and 1860. It was an empty building when LDS wagon trains were outfitting in Florence in the early 1860s. Vacant for years, the bank was restarted in 1890. The building was eventually donated to the Florence Historical Foundation, and now is a museum open to the public.

■ **12. Cutler's Park.** Church headquarters for two months, **Cutler's Park** is located on the high ground on both sides of Mormon Bridge Road and south of Young Street in northeast Omaha. It is easily reached by traveling west on State Street 1.5 mile from the Mormon Pioneer Cemetery (State Street becomes Young Street west of the cemetery). It can also be reached by taking I-680 Exit 12 and going 1.2 miles south on Mormon Bridge Road.

When the advance group of 1846 LDS refugees from Nauvoo arrived in this area, they first camped at **Cold Spring Camp** (in present-day Omaha; see site 27 below) 8 miles south of Cutler's Park. They stayed there from July 1 to Aug. 6, 1846, and then moved to **Cutler's Park.** From Cutler's Park they moved to **Winter Quarters** in September 1846.

A memorial marker with historical narrative is located on Mormon Bridge Road just north of the Young Street junction. It tells the story of Cutler's Park, Nebraska's first organized community. Although composed of only tents and wagons arranged in orderly squares, the short-lived community had a mayor and city council, 24 policemen and fireguards, various administrative committees, and a town square for public meetings.

Alpheus Cutler, master builder of the Nauvoo Temple, found this location and became president of its municipal council. By popular vote in a public square, residents of Cutler's Park passed Nebraska's first anti-pollution ordinance: open burning was banned. All residents were required to build sod fireplaces and chimneys to keep smoke and sparks out of the wagons and tents of their neighbors. Corrals were built, wells dug, and a spring was "developed," probably with a wooden walk and water lift. Crews of men and boys were sent out to put up 800 tons of hay before building cabins.

The **Oto** had hunted on these lands since about 1700. The **Omaha** people came here when they fled from the Dakota Sioux in 1845. Eighty **Omaha** and a smaller number of **Oto** met with LDS leaders at **Cutler's Park** Aug. 27, 1846, to determine what payment should be made by the Mormons to stay on Indian lands. **A treaty** allowed the Mormons to remain on the Otos' land at least two years while preparing to remove to the Rocky Mountains. The Saints also agreed to move 3 miles east and settle on the banks of the Missouri River. That settlement became **Winter Quarters** (MoM 68–72).

● **13. Gen. George C. Crook House Museum.** This house is part of the **Ft. Omaha Historic District,** which also serves as the Metropolitan Community College Campus. It is located at 30th and Fort Streets and is reachable from Florence by driving south about

1 mile on Historic Main Street, or U.S. 75, which becomes North 30th Street.

In 1862 Omaha became headquarters for the Military District of Nebraska. By 1868 barracks for a new army post were completed. Gen. George C. Crook (1828–90) was a distinguished Civil War officer, and his campaigns in the West earned him recognition as the army's greatest Indian fighter. The post was named Ft. Omaha in 1878. He lived there as commander of the U.S. Army's Department of the Platte from 1875 to 1882 and again from 1886 to 1888. He moved into the Italianate style two-story residence, commonly known as the Crook House, after its completion in 1879. Presidents **Ulysses S. Grant** and **Rutherford B. Hayes** were among prominent guests entertained there. An adjoining building houses the Douglas County Historical Society Library and Archives.

The fort's historic district includes a group of structures around the Gen. Crook House: department headquarters and storehouse (1879), and a guardhouse, magazine, and officers quarters built in the 1880s.

Historic and Other Sites North of Winter Quarters

■ **14. The Mormons' First Camp Marker and Kimball Monument.** The **Kimball monument** at the **"First Camp"** was located north of the Winter Quarters site on one of the trails leading from Winter Quarters. The location is north of I-680, near the North Omaha Airport. It is reached by driving west on I-680 to 72nd Street (Exit 9), going north on N. 72nd Street for 2.7 miles to Bennington Road, and then turning east .2 mile (past the airport on the north side) to N. 69th Street (coming from the south). The marker is just east of that junction, on the south side of Bennington.

On Apr. 5, 1847, apostle Heber C. Kimball and a few others started for the Rocky Mountains. Six wagons departed Winter Quarters. The group was called, variously, the Advance Company, the Discovery Company, and the Pioneer Band. The group camped for two nights near present-day Highway 36 and 69th Street, waiting for others to join in. The Kimball Monument was erected in 1947 by the Daughters of Utah Pioneers (HSM 54; DBD Apr. 5, 1847).

■ **15. Heber C. Kimball Farm.** The site of **LDS apostle Heber C. Kimball's farm** is reached by traveling 2.1 miles north on Pershing Drive from the junction of Pershing Drive and McKinley Street, just east of the Mormon Mill. At the northeast entrance to **Hummel Park** is a marker commemorating **John Pierre Cabannes's Trading Post** and **Ft. Lisa.** Ft. Lisa was about 1 mile north of the marker, a little north of the Douglas/Washington County line, and well north of Cabannes's trading post. The fort was named after **Manuel Lisa,** trader and Indian agent, who helped the Native Americans remain loyal to the United States during the War of 1812, although Lisa himself called it Ft. Henry. The **Kimball farm** was in the vicinity of Ft. Lisa (1812–23).

On the farm 30 families lived in homes built around a square. They planted several hundred acres and operated a good gristmill (MoM 164).

● **16. Ft. Atkinson State Historical Park—Old "Council Bluffs." Ft. Atkinson** is a State Historical Park 9 miles north of Omaha on U.S. 75 and on the east edge of the city of Ft. Calhoun.

Its story begins with the **Lewis and Clark expedition,** which set up camp in the area. On Aug. 2, 1804, Lewis and Clark met with six Oto and Missouri chiefs and their warriors. The next day the Americans informed the them that the land now belonged to the United States and that the expedition was a peaceful one. Because of this council, the location became known as **Council Bluffs.** The expedition reported that Council Bluffs was an ideal site for an army fort.

In 1819 President James Monroe dispatched the **Yellowstone Expedition** to establish forts in the Upper Missouri area to counter British influence among Native Americans, who then included the Pawnee, Omaha, Iowa, Oto, Missouri, Osage, and Sauks. Col. Henry Atkinson's Sixth Infantry linked up with the Rifle Regiment near St. Louis and moved upriver. A scientific and exploring party led by **Maj. Stephen H. Long** of the Army Corps of Engineers accompanied them. They reached a spot near this site aboard the sternwheeler ***Western Engineer,*** the first successful ascent of the Missouri River by a steamboat.

Stopped by funding cuts and winter, the groups established a post along the river bottoms about 1 mile north of the Council Bluffs site. To survive the winter, the 1,120 men built **Cantonment**

Missouri. Some 160 persons died that winter of scurvy and fevers. Spring 1820 brought high waters that flooded the camp and forced troops to move atop Council Bluffs and establish what became **Ft. Atkinson** (1820–27). The bluff was about 100 feet higher than the river and perpendicular on the side where the river flowed at its base.

Ft. Atkinson became the nation's largest and most western military post. Its population of more than 1,000 included soldiers, their families, and other civilians. The fortification consisted of a rectangular arrangement of one-story barracks fashioned of horizontal logs around a parade ground. Exterior walls, with mid-wall gates and loopholes, protected the fort, as did cannons mounted in the northwest and southeast bastions. A large powder magazine stood near the center of the fort. Outside the fort's walls, the troops erected a large council house where negotiations with Native Americans took place. Also outside were a gristmill, sawmill, schoolhouse, and other buildings, some of which were built with bricks produced by the post's brick kiln.

Active from 1820 to 1827, the fort protected the burgeoning western fur trade and controlled access to the Upper Missouri country and the Platte Valley overland route. Abandoned in 1827, the fort fell subject to time, weather, Indians, and settlers. In 1841 the river shifted to the east; it currently flows some 3 miles east of the Council Bluffs it once touched. By the time the **Latter-day Saints** arrived in 1846, they found only brick and masonry remnants of the fort and used some of those for building (FAN).

Restoration of the site began in 1961. At **Ft. Atkinson State Historical Park,** most of the fort has been reconstructed, and an interpretive center explains the fort's history to visitors. A Nebraska **historical marker** at the site provides a good historical summary.

■ **17. Summer Quarters.** A Church farm that helped supply Winter Quarters, Summer Quarters was about 2 miles northwest of present-day Ft. Calhoun City, which is 10 miles north of Omaha on U.S. 75. This farm occupied land between Mill Creek and Moor Creek in Washington County.

Today's Ft. Calhoun City sits near what was the north-south dividing line between traditional Oto-Missouri and Omaha tribal hunting grounds. Just north of that dividing line, several LDS families opened 600 acres of farmland. **Isaac Morley** managed this

"Brigham Young Farm," which became termed "Summer Quarters," with **John D. Lee** as foreman. They built homes and other facilities, which the Omaha were to receive after the Mormons left, on land that was not contested by the Oto-Missouri Indians. The flatland is between two streams and has good soil. It is said this was the largest and best tract of farmland within easy reach of Winter Quarters. It included some of old (1820) Ft. Atkinson's farmlands (HSM 71).

John D. Lee began building near the bluff on the south bank of Mill Creek. Houses and pens formed a fort-like unit with guarded gates. The company cut logs by hand to provide timber and hauled brick from the ruined Ft. Atkinson. About three dozen families worked the farm. While the farmers plowed and planted, a large herd of Winter Quarters cattle was moved into the rush bottoms about 20 miles farther north. Summer Quarters produced an abundance of corn, beans, cabbage, melons, and other foodstuffs (MoM 164). Sickness struck the camp in midsummer 1847, and about 18 persons died. They were buried on high ground .5 mile south of the settlement. In the spring of 1848, wagons hauled the 1847 harvest of corn to Winter Quarters. Then, because Winter Quarters had to be closed down per agreement with the government in 1846, Summer Quarters was vacated, too. On Apr. 26, 1848, teams from Winter Quarters moved the families and equipment, ending the operation.

● **18. Bertrand Museum and Excavation Site.** Located 30 miles north of Omaha on U.S. 75 and then 6 miles east on U.S. 30, the **Bertrand Museum and Excavation Site** are part of the **DeSoto National Wildlife Refuge.** Though once in Nebraska, it is now in Iowa because the Missouri River has changed course. The ***Bertrand*** was one of 400 steamboats that sank in the Missouri River during the mid-1800s. It is of interest because freight and other articles from it were recovered and placed in the museum (see **North of Council Bluffs** section in Iowa).

Historic and Other Sites in and around Omaha

Interstate I-80 links **Omaha,** Nebraska, with **Council Bluffs,** Iowa. **Omaha** ranges in altitude from 970 feet at the Missouri River to 1,245 feet at the top of its wooded hills. It has been called the "**crossroads of the nation**" because of historical north-south river traffic on the Missouri and east-west emigrant traffic along the Great Platte River Road and later along the Union Pacific Railroad.

Omaha was founded in 1854 with a ferry business which grew into the politically powerful Council Bluffs-Nebraska Ferry Co. Omaha was the starting point for the laying of tracks for the **transcontinental railroad.** The headquarters of the **Union Pacific** are in Omaha at 1400 Douglas Street. In 1995 the U. P. merged with the Chicago and Northwestern Railroad.

Stimulated by the railroad construction project during the 1860s, Omaha grew rapidly. After a meatpacking plant opened in 1871 and the Union Stock Yards began operations, Omaha came to dominate the industry. By 1955 it had become the nation's largest livestock market. That market has since declined. More than 20 insurance companies, including Mutual of Omaha, have their home offices there. As of 2003, Omaha's population was 404,267, but the greater Omaha area has more than 800,000 residents.

Omaha's cultural resources include the Omaha Symphony, Opera Omaha, and the Omaha Community Playhouse, which is the largest community theater in the nation and was a venue where such luminaries as Henry Fonda and Dorothy McGuire began their acting careers. In Omaha are **Creighton University,** the **University of Nebraska–Omaha, College of St. Mary, Metropolitan Community College,** and **Grace College of the Bible,** as are the **Joslyn Art Museum** and other fine galleries.

● **19. Old Market.** Located on the eastern side of downtown Omaha, Old Market covers an area three blocks long and three blocks wide. Bounded by 10th and 13th Streets on the east and west and by Farnam and Jackson Streets on the north and south, it is five blocks south of I-480 via 13th Street, just west of the **Heartland of America** scenic park. It is Omaha's historic **Old Warehouse District,** which once thrived with fruit and vegetable warehouses and markets. Revitalized during the 1960s, the district features rustic cobblestone streets and quaint brick buildings that now house specialty shops, restaurants, taverns, and galleries. **The Old Market District** is listed as a Historic District in the National Register of Historic Places.

● **20. Durham Western Heritage Museum.** Located at 801 So. 10th Street in the grand Art Deco Union Station, **Durham Western**

Heritage Museum has historic Indian and pioneer photographs, the historically important Byron Reed Collection of coinage, and exhibits dealing with Omaha from 1880 to 1930.

- **21. Joslyn Art Museum. The Joslyn Art Museum**, at 2200 Dodge Street, is a Georgia pink marble art deco building with ancient to contemporary paintings and sculpture. It was built as a gift to Omaha from Sarah Joslyn in memory of her husband George, a prominent Omaha businessman and community leader.

The Joslyn Museum is especially noted for its displays of art of the American West. It is world-renowned for its collection of works by Swiss artist **Karl Bodmer,** whose watercolors and prints document his 1832–34 journey in the Missouri River Valley with the German naturalist, Prince Maximilian of Wied. The art works are owned jointly by **Brigham Young University** and the Joslyn Museum. Another collection contains watercolors and paintings by **Alfred Jacob Miller,** based on Miller's experience in the West of the 1830s. Joslyn's Western American collection also includes paintings and sculpture by **George Catlin, Frederic Remington,** and **William Robinson Leigh.**

- **22. President Gerald R. Ford Birth Site and Gardens.** The site of President Ford's first home is at 32nd Street and Woolworth Avenue, four blocks west of I-480. It is an outdoor park with the **Betty Ford Rose Garden,** a scale model of the house where President Ford was born, busts of him and of his wife Betty (Elizabeth Ann Bloomer), and displays of White House articles.

President Ford was born July 14, 1913, and named Leslie Lynch King Jr. His parents then lived in a three-story, fourteen-room, elegant Victorian house that once stood at this site. When his parents divorced, his mother took him to live with her parents in Grand Rapids, Michigan. She remarried, and his stepfather adopted him, renaming him Gerald Rudolph Ford Jr. After a quarter century of service in Congress, Mr. Ford was elected vice president and then served as the **38th president of the United States,** 1974–77, in place of President Richard M. Nixon, who resigned the presidency because of the Watergate scandal.

In 1971 President Ford's first home was razed following a fire. In the 1970s this birth site memorial was established. The birth site and gardens are administered by the City of Omaha. In Omaha I-480 is the **Gerald Ford Commemorative Freeway.**

● **23. Malcolm X Birthplace.** Located at 3448 Pinkney Street, the site is about 3 miles west of Omaha's airport, Eppley Airfield, and is 4 blocks west of U.S. 75 (North Expressway). It is reached driving north from Bedford Avenue (1 block west of Adams Park) on North 36th Street for 2 blocks, then turning east on Pinkney Street to where it ends at the railroad tracks. An upright white marker telling about "Malcolm X Shabazz" now stands on the vacant site of his birthplace.

He was born on May 19, 1925, and named Malcolm Little. He became a spokesperson for the Nation of Islam and was a militant activist in behalf of blacks in America. On Feb. 21, 1965, he was assassinated in New York City.

■ **24. Prospect Hill Cemetery, Ahmanson Graves.** The Prospect Hill Cemetery (founded in 1858), which is Omaha's pioneer cemetery, is located at about 32nd and Parker Streets (roughly 10 blocks south of Malcolm X's birthplace). It is reached from I-29 or I-80 by going north on U.S. 75 and exiting on Hamilton, going left to North 30th, turning right to Parker, turning left on Parker and going 1.5 blocks to the cemetery entrance on the right.

Johan August Ahmanson's grave is part of a walking or driving tour of markers for important persons buried there. Ahmanson, a Swedish LDS convert and missionary, was a captain of hundred in the 1856 Willie handcart company (see **1856 Handcart Companies**). He became disenchanted with Mormonism and left Utah in 1857. He moved his family to Omaha by 1861, where he was first a hardware merchant and then a grocer. He represented Douglas County in the Eighth Nebraska State Legislature and was highly regarded as a leader of the Republican Party. He successfully sued Brigham Young for loss of property during the handcart experience. In 1876 he published an expose of Mormonism in Swedish (*Muhammed of Our Time*). He became a central figure among Scandinavian former Mormons in eastern Nebraska and western Wyoming. At the age of 40, he went to Chicago to study Homeopathic Medicine, returning to practice in Omaha until his death in August 1891 (HmTZ 184; OPHC; UTC,p).

● **25. Creighton University.** This prestigious Catholic Jesuit university occupies a 108-acre campus adjacent to the downtown business district. It is located on the north side of the junction where I-480 separates from north-south U.S. 75 and turns east. It is best reached from U.S. 75, using the Burt and Cuming Streets exit just north of the I-480 separation, then going west on Cuming Street to 24th Street, and driving south on 24th to Cass Street where there is a visitors' parking lot.

Brothers **Edward and John Creighton** came to Omaha in the 1850s. Edward was primarily responsible for the laying of the **transcontinental telegraph lines** from Omaha to the west coast, and his financial interests played a major role in the economic development of Omaha. John was successful in many mining and agricultural enterprises. After Edward's death, his family honored his request that his estate establish a Catholic school in Omaha in his name. It opened in 1878 and today enrolls more than 6,700 students.

Elder **Jacob Gates,** in charge of the 1861 LDS wagon train outfittings in Florence (see above) received a manpower request from John Creighton, who was desperate to complete construction of his telegraph lines to Utah. Mr. Creighton contracted to hire **75 LDS men** and agreed to give them half their salaries in advance, to aid the men's families, and to give them the other half in November in Utah. As LDS wagon trains rolled west in 1861, they passed some of these Mormon men helping erect telegraph poles and string wires in western Nebraska (DBWT 25).

■ **26. Original, or Middle, Mormon Ferry Site.** The original or first Mormon ferry site across the Missouri River in 1846 was located within the mile of shoreline south of South Omaha Bridge, which conveys U.S. 275 between South Omaha and Iowa. Since then the river's course has altered a little.

By July 1846 the 1846 Mormon pioneers established a ferry to move Nauvoo refugees across the Missouri River to the Nebraska side. In time this ferry became identified as the Middle Ferry. Basically it involved a landing on the Iowa side and two landings on the Nebraska side. From the Iowa side the ferry crossed, going a bit downriver and landing at the south dugway. Then the ferry was moved upriver to the north dugway. From there eastbound people and materials ferried across and a bit downriver to the Iowa landing. Thus the ferry traveled a triangular course. The ferry was attached to ropes anchored at the starting and stopping points.

A short distance south of the west end of the **South Omaha Bridge** (which carries U.S. 275 across the river) is where the north dugway was located, from which the ferry departed for the Iowa side. The embankment then was steep and difficult, which required wagons and people to descend down the dugway to the loading spot.

The south dugway, where the ferry arrived from Iowa, was not quite 1 mile farther downstream. To find that site, travelers should start from near the west side of the South Omaha Bridge and go south on S. 13th Street not quite a mile, almost to Y Street. Turn left (east) into the **Mt. Vernon Gardens.** Park the car facing east towards the river, or south, and then walk on the cinder path. It goes southeast, then south, and then west until you are overlooking a deep ravine. That is where the south dugway was. There you will see why teams with loaded wagons coming up from the river often were pulled over to the side to rest during the long, steep pull up to the top of the hill. From there they moved west for 4 miles on easier terrain to Cold Spring Camp.

Soon after the first wave of Latter-day Saints from Nauvoo reached the Missouri River in mid-June 1846, **Brigham Young** asked millwright **Frederick Kesler Jr.** to superintend and help construct a ferryboat. It was completed on June 29, 1846. Kesler said:

> I kept at work day and night, ferrying the hosts of Israel with their wagons and all their belongings to a place of safety. We ferried hundreds of wagons across, and at last I had to rest; I was completely tired out. I had worked for weeks, day and night, without money and without price (UHQ 56:58; DN May 29, 1897).

This ferry, a flat boat big enough to transport 3 or 4 fully loaded wagons, operated from July 1 into September 1846, linking the LDS camps on the east side of the Missouri with the Cold Spring Camp (see below), the Saints' first camp on the west side. In September 1846 the ferry was moved north to Winter Quarters (see site 2 above) (MoM 48).

■ **27. Cold Spring Camp.** The location is in Omaha, one block northwest of 60th and L Streets on hills overlooking a huge spring (MoM

263). Today, commercial and residential developments dominate the site. A **historical marker** at the northwest corner of 60th and L Streets tells about this first Mormon camp west of the Missouri River.

This was the first LDS camp and staging point in Nebraska where the 1846 pioneers gathered to organize wagon trains headed for Grand Island or the mountains. They occupied this camp, which was near Little Papillion Creek, on July 1, 1846, and abandoned it on Aug. 6, 1846, when the Quorum of the Twelve, concerned about stragglers in eastern Iowa and western Illinois, decided that Saints west of the Missouri River should find a camp for the winter. They chose a site 9 miles north, which became **Cutler's Park** (discussed above).

In 1846 Pennsylvanian **Thomas L. Kane** resided at the Cold Spring Camp for two months. Four years later he described the camp to the Pennsylvania Historical Society:

> It was situated near the Petit Papillon, or Little Butterfly River, and upon some finely rounded hills that encircle a favorite cool spring. On each of these a square was marked out; and the wagons as they arrived took their positions along its four sides in double rows, so as to leave a roomy street or passageway between them. The tents were disposed also in rows, at intervals between the wagons. The cattle were folded in high-fenced yards outside. The quadrangle inside was left vacant for the sake of ventilation, and the streets, covered in with leafy arbor work and kept scrupulously clean, formed a shaded cloister walk. (MOR 35)

Kane became sick there for weeks and was cared for by the Saints. He received a patriarchal blessing from John Smith on Sept. 7, 1846 (CHC 3:132–33; EnM 2:779; BiE 1:184).

Later, Cold Spring water was piped in an underground culvert to Little Papillion Creek, and hills to the west were leveled to make way for homes (HMS).

● **28. Boys Town.** This large complex is at 136th and West Dodge Road, in Omaha. It is reached by taking I-680 north from I-80 to the Dodge Street exit. There, travel west on Dodge Street to the Boys Town exit.

Boys Town was founded in 1917 by **Father Edward Joseph Flanagan** (1886–1948), an Irish-born Catholic priest. It moved to larger quarters west of Omaha in 1918, and in 1922 the farm became the incorporated village of **Boys Town, Nebraska.** Boys Town has a long history of helping abused, abandoned, neglected, handicapped, or otherwise troubled children. It was made famous by the academy award-winning **1938 movie "Boys Town,"** which starred Spencer Tracy as Father Flanagan.

Boys Town has grown into a small city within Omaha and has branch organizations across the U.S. The first girls enrolled in the 1970s and now make up half the population of what is still called Boys Town, though Girls and Boys Town has become the name of its far-reaching national organization. Boys Town has a middle school and high school, two churches, a park and post office, police and fire stations, athletic facility and fields, and the well-known statue of one boy shouldering the weight of another. As a national historic landmark, Boys Town annually hosts thousands of visitors from around the world.

Historic and Other Sites South of Omaha

■ Bellevue

Bellevue, 8 miles south of Omaha on U.S. 73/75, is Nebraska's oldest continuous settlement. It was started in 1823 as a replacement trading post of the Missouri Fur Company's deteriorated Ft. Lisa, about 30 miles north of Bellevue. Later the new Bellevue post was acquired by the American Fur Company. Bellevue shares its northern border with Omaha and its southern edge with Offutt Air Force Base.

The **Bellevue Log Cabin,** the city's oldest building, is at 805 Hancock Street. It was built about 1835 in the Missouri River flood plains but was soon moved to the upper plateau. In about 1850 it was moved to this location, where it was used as a residence until 1954. This building stood when several mid-19th century LDS emigrant groups passed through that area.

The **Fontenelle Bank,** built in 1856, is at 2212 Main Street. It became the Sarpy County courthouse in 1857 and once was the Bellevue City Hall. It is one of the few surviving buildings that stood when Mormon emigrant companies passed through Nebraska.

Housed in the Sarpy County Historical museum in Bellevue, at 2402 Clay Street, is an excellent collection of mid-19th century farm, carpentry and fur-trade tools. Also displayed there are the journals of 1833–1840 Baptist missionaries Moses and Eliza Merrill, who worked with the Oto-Missouri Indians at Bellevue.

Bellevue's **Old Presbyterian Church,** at 2002 Franklin Street, is the oldest church building in Nebraska. It still contains 19th century oak pews, old stained-glass windows, and summer gardens. Built in 1856, it, too, was standing when LDS emigrants passed through this area after that date.

Offutt Air Force Base is at Bellevue's south edge and is 10 miles south of Omaha. It served as headquarters for the Strategic Air Command and was at the center of much of the Cold War. SAC was responsible for the nation's entire fleet of nuclear bombers, and then Intercontinental Ballistic Missiles, until SAC was deactivated in 1992. Offutt is still a major command base, as the headquarters of U.S.STRATCOM (United States Strategic Command), the replacement for SAC. The Strategic Air Command Museum, once part of the base, moved in 1998 to Ashland, Nebraska.

The **Fontenelle Forest Nature Center,** a 1,300-acre preserve of original wildlife habitat, is located in Bellevue's east edge at 1111 N. Bellevue Boulevard. It contains 15 miles of foot trails through woods and wetlands and provides natural science education programs. Many significant historic sites are located in Fontenelle Forest, including part of Pointe aux Poules, which was a French residential town for Native American wives and children of fur trappers and traders.

Mormon Hollow, a .5-mile-long deep ravine, is also located in Fontenelle Forest. Many pioneering Mormons crossed the Missouri River just north of Bellevue. The ferry was located on the Iowa side just north of the county line between Pottawattamie and Mills Counties (NEB-S: 38). Some Mormons allegedly spent the winter of 1846–47 in Mormon Hollow, although no hard evidence supports this belief. In the hollow itself, which can be reached from Wakonda Boy Scout Camp, is a wooden sign reading "Mormon Hollow." The extreme eastern end of the hollow can be reached by walking .4 mile south along the railroad tracks, south of Childes

Road. A marker, sometimes hard to find in undergrowth, marks the hollow, and says "Many Mormons reached the Elkhorn by following a trail west from this place" (HSM 72).

■ South Mormon Ferry at Plattsmouth

This ferry, once located where U.S. 34 now crosses the Missouri River at Plattsmouth, Nebraska (20 miles south of Omaha), was opened in the spring of 1850. Early in 1849 some 10,000 California gold rushers heavily taxed the wood, water, and good grazing along the Mormon Trail north of the Platte River. Many Latter-day Saints decided to travel south of the Platte in 1850 to avoid the gold rush traffic, at least until they encountered the Old Gold Rush Trail cutting up through south central Nebraska from northeastern Kansas. This trail south of the Platte became a good alternate route for the Saints (HMS) as it also avoided crossing both the Elkhorn and Loup Rivers. A town, **Bethlehem** (no longer in existence), developed just north of Plattsmouth to accommodate the emigrants (NEB-S 149–52).

■ *Wyoming, Nebraska—LDS Emigrant Outfitting Place 1864–1866

Wyoming, Nebraska, also known as "Old Wyoming," is located in Otoe County below where the mouth of Weeping Water Creek joined the Missouri River and near where it is said the **Lewis and Clark Expedition** camped July 20, 1804, under a high bluff a little above the mouth of the Weeping Water Creek (NHM 79). Wyoming is 44 miles south of Omaha and 7 miles north of Nebraska City. To reach the site, take U.S. 75 south from Omaha or north from Nebraska City. Wyoming is 17 miles south of where U.S. 34 turns east to Plattsmouth, 3.6 miles

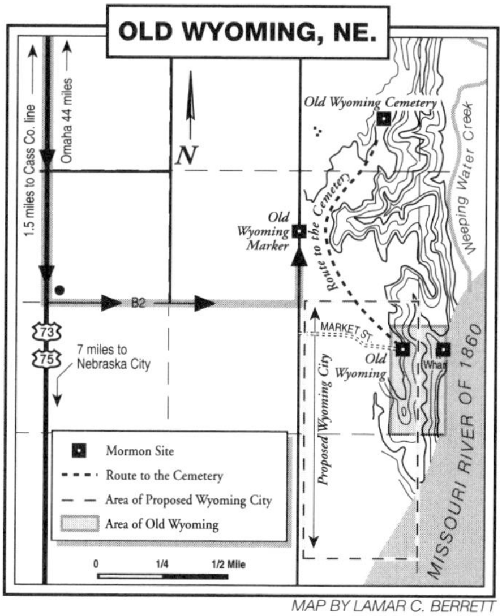

MAP BY LAMAR C. BERRETT

south from where U.S. 34 turns west to Union, and 1.5 miles south of the Otoe and Cass County line in eastern Nebraska. Turn east on County Road B2 (see Old Wyoming map). Take this road 1 mile to a Y in the road. Turn left (north) at the Y and go .25 mile to the home on the east side of the road.

An Old Wyoming **historical marker** can be seen on the southwest corner of the lot. Start your visit of Wyoming at this marker (see Old Wyoming map), which was placed there in October 1998 by the John Watts Berrett Family Genealogical Organization and others, in memory of Old Wyoming and faithful Saints who died there, as they were following counsel to gather to Zion in the Rocky Mountains (AAC 22).[1] Among those who died were **Ann Marie Chatters Hookway** and her **daughter Mary Ann.** In 1936 Helen Roberta Williams of Nebraska City wrote, "A movement was set on foot in 1926 to erect some kind of monument in memory of the Mormon emigrants who died at Wyoming" (NHM 127). Seventy-two years later, a **historic marker** was finally erected.

From this marker, visitors can see in the distance the site of the **Wyoming cemetery** and also look in the direction of the **Wyoming town center.**

Wyoming, Nebraska, named after Wyoming, Pennsylvania, the former home of this Wyoming's founder, **Jacob Dawson,** was a town platted in 1856 with the intention of developing it and selling lots. The proprietors were organized as the Wyoming Town Company, with Dawson as general land agent, attorney, civil engineer, and surveyor. The town grew very slowly over the next eight years, even though it was a mail and stage stop as well as a steamboat stop and was even large enough to support Dawson's weekly newspaper, the ***Wyoming Telescope,*** which was published for two years. Real estate agents, preachers, doctors, lawyers, storekeepers, teachers, freighters, Mormon pioneer emigrants, businessmen, and farmers

---

1. Series editor LaMar C. Berrett and volume coauthor A. Gary Anderson greatly appreciated all who helped make the Wyoming Historical Marker possible. Jim and Mary Johnson and Jim's parents, Harold and Mary, shared with Drs. Berrett and Anderson their love for and knowledge of Wyoming history. The Johnsons, owners of the Wyoming site, provided a place for the marker and have been its caretakers. Also helpful were members of the Nebraska City LDS Ward; Sheila and Barry Woods, Carl H. Jones, and Wally Pohlman; the Nebraska State Historical Society; and researcher and author Helen Roberta Williams. The John Watts Berrett Family Genealogical Organization sponsored and funded the marker, with guidance from president Vere G. Berrett, marker coordinator Laura Berrett Pead, and LaMar C. Berrett, researcher and writer of the marker narrative.

made this an important town on the Missouri River. Speculators felt they would get rich by selling town lots; but it was not until Wyoming became an **LDS emigrant outfitting center (1864–66)** that the town prospered. After the Mormons moved their outfitting site to North Platte, Nebraska, in 1867, Wyoming diminished and became a ghost town.

During the time Wyoming was the outfitting center for Mormon emigrants (1864–66), Saints from European countries landed in **New York City** and traveled by train to **St. Joseph,** Missouri, and from there by steamboat up the Missouri River to **Wyoming, Nebraska.** Close to 7,000 Saints emigrated to Utah by way of this place, traveling in 25 wagon trains (NHM 115). Church **"down-and-back" wagon trains** transported most of them.

In 1864 some 170 wagons, 1,717 oxen, and 277 men were sent to Wyoming to provide transportation for the poor (ChCh 70–71). **Joseph W. Young,** a nephew of Brigham Young and supervising emigration agent in 1864 (BiE 4:546), described Wyoming in April or May 1864, the first year it was an LDS emigration center:

> Wyoming is a new starting point for our emigration, forty-five miles below Florence, and six miles above Nebraska City. It is not much of a town, but so much the better; there are but about a dozen houses in the place, but it is beautifully situated on the banks of the Missouri river, and is very well adapted for camping and outfitting purposes. We have two large warehouses of three stories each, storehouse, office and dwelling-house, and are well situated for doing business. I have charge of the warehouse and store. We are now receiving a very large amount of provisions, as follows—2,500 sacks of flour, 70,000 pounds of bacon, 80 sacks of beans, 50 sacks of dried apples, a stock of dry goods and groceries, stoves, etc. (NHM 114; DBL 1:66)

Among emigrants who outfitted at Wyoming in 1864 were Scandinavians in a company of 973 Saints who crossed the Atlantic on the *Monarch of the Sea,* led by **Church Patriarch John Smith,** son of Hyrum Smith. In 1864 the freight carried by the **William B. Preston company** included **new type fonts** for the Deseret News office (ChCh 71). In 1866 wagons of the **Daniel Thompson company,** the sixth Church train of 1866, carried **Tabernacle organ**

Company of Mormon emigrants camped at Wyoming, NE, 1866. (Courtesy of LDSCA)

materials. Freight in the **Horton David Haight company** that year included 500 miles of **wire** for the **Deseret Telegraph line** in Utah.

Wyoming is important to people whose LDS ancestors began their treks west from there or who died there. In fact, sites in the town of Wyoming are known with more specificity than are sites in other LDS outfitting centers between 1846 and 1868. Today, visitors can walk where the Wyoming wharf, or levee, along the Missouri River once was, where steamboats landed to unload Mormon emigrants and cargo. Research has identified the approximate site of the Mormon warehouses where goods were stored; where the public square was and a public park was planned to be; where the Mormon emigrants lived in their "tent city"; and where Mormon emigrants are buried in the Old Wyoming Cemetery. Visitors can walk down the very road (Market Street) that the Mormon emigrants once walked. Two localities are especially important to historians and to descendants of ancestors who once were in Wyoming:

A. The Old Wyoming Cemetery site is located on the top of a hill 1 mile north of the center of Wyoming. It is now farmland. From the **Old Wyoming historical marker,** the site is .6 mile northeast (25.5 degrees east of magnetic north). To see the site, stand by the marker and look to a distant hill just to the right of the southeast side of the Johnson home. The elevation of the cemetery site is about the same as the home site. More than 60 headstones once stood there, but none remain (DBL 2:67). A few remnants, preserved by the Johnson family, are near the Wyoming marker, but none of the names have been linked to LDS people. Mormon records show that a number of Mormons died at Wyoming, and there is evidence that at least some of them were buried in the Wyoming cemetery. **Lars Petersen,** a philanthropic Danish Mormon emigrant, accidentally drowned in Weeping Water Creek in June 1865, "and a large concourse of Danish Saints followed him to the grave, who feel to mourn his loss" (NHM 122–23; ChCh 73).

Nine-month-old **Sidney Biddle** died June 16, 1865, and was buried at Wyoming. Three-year-old **Samuel A. Shaw** died at Wyoming of measles on June 17, 1865. Others at Wyoming died of scarlet fever and cholera (NHM 122–23).

In 1865 some 636 Mormons emigrated from England aboard the *Belle Wood,* most of whom arrived at Old Wyoming on June 15 (ChCh 72). While encamped, **Ann Marie Chatters Hookway,** a 72-year-old widow, died on June 28 and her **daughter Mary Ann** (age 27) died on Aug. 7. Both were buried, another daughter noted, "at a small burial place of L.D.S. both placed in one grave," perhaps the Old Wyoming Cemetery (DBL 2:63–68). That daughter, Eliza (age 28), reached Utah, married John Watts Berrett and raised five sons, one of whom, Heber, is the grandfather of the general editor of the *Sacred Places* series.

The last 1866 company of Saints from Europe was composed of 201 Scandinavians who came via Hamburg, Germany, to America on the sailing vessel *Cavour* under the leadership of **Niels Nielsen.** They arrived in New York City Aug. 11, went by train to St. Joseph, and from there journeyed by steamboat to Wyoming, Nebraska. Of their death-plagued journey, one in their group, Elder **Elnathan Eldredge,** wrote:

> In travels through the States we stopped at St. Joseph, Missouri, two nights and two days, our company being attacked by cholera. During these two days and two nights we buried thirty-three of the emigrants in the St. Joseph cemetery, after which we continued the journey up the Missouri River to Wyoming, the landing place of the Saints that year. At that place we buried eight more of the emigrants and nearly fifty died on the journey across the Plains. (NHM 126–27)

These **91 deaths** (plus others that might have occurred on the sea) in this company of 201 emigrants mean that 45 to 50 percent of the members of the company died before the group reached the Salt Lake Valley. The famous Willie and Martin handcart companies in 1856 lost approximately 25 percent (HCZ 193; NHM 126–27).

B. Wyoming town center is located .6 miles southeast (127.5 degrees clockwise from magnetic north) of the **Old Wyoming historical marker** and cannot be seen from the marker. To reach the town center from the Old Wyoming historical marker, travel back south on the dirt road you came on, continue south past the "Y" in the road for .125 mile, and turn left (east) on a dirt road (Market Street). Points of interest in the Wyoming town center include the following (see Old Wyoming map):

1. Market Street is the road you will be following through the center of Wyoming. It runs from west to east and ends at a point where the Missouri River used to be, at the site of the 1860s wharfs along the bottom of the bluffs. **Market Street** is the **main street** of Wyoming. Go east .4 mile, passing the **city park** on the right (south).

This Market Street must have been very busy when Mormon wagon trains lined up on it, and excitement probably filled the emigrants' hearts when they began their trek by driving west on Market Street and out of town. After leaving Wyoming, they soon joined a trail known as the **Nebraska City Road.**

2. Top of the bluffs in the center of Wyoming is marked by a large carved and **painted pole sign** with the word "Wyoming." In the 1860s the Missouri River flowed at the bottom of these bluffs, but by 2005 the river was about .5 mile farther east.

3. The public square was on the north side of Market Street, just west of the top of the bluffs.

4. LDS emigration agents built two **three-story limestone warehouses** on the bluff in the vicinity of Market Street. After 1866 local residents used one of the storehouses as a church, schoolhouse, and community center.

5. The road to the Wyoming cemetery started on the top of the bluffs in the vicinity of the public square on the north side of Market Street. It followed a natural level route north. It is easy to imagine a funeral cortege going along the top of the hills to the cemetery, such as that of Lars Peterson, on June 26, 1865: "Today he was buried, and a large concourse of Danish Saints followed him to the grave, who feel to mourn his loss, as he was greatly respected by them" (NHM 122–23).

6. Each emigration season's **Mormon tent city,** where most lived while waiting to head west, was located mostly on the hillside or sloping bluffs on both sides of Market Street and between the top of the bluffs and the levee along the Missouri River (NHM 85).

7. The wharf levee, or landing, on the Missouri River is still visible at the bottom of the bluff at the foot of Market Street.

Steamboats traveling up and down the Missouri River stopped at the Wyoming Levee at the foot of Market Street, south of where Weeping Water Creek emptied into the Missouri River. The river has moved about .5 mile to the east, but the old levee site is still there and is used by summer vacationers who have placed their house trailers on the levee. This hill was a difficult pull for man and beast going from the landing to the town (NHM 86). Joseph Young reported that "Elder John T. Gerber organized a company of nineteen brethren (reserve teamsters) to load and unload freight on steamers at Wyoming. The brethren thus selected . . . pitched a tent for their own use and a cook was appointed for the company" (NHM July 6, 1864, 116).

Several LDS emigrants who passed through Wyoming, Nebraska, on their way to Utah, later became well known. One was **George Reynolds,** who left Wyoming, Nebraska, in 1866. He became a member of the First Council of the Seventy and wrote several books about the Book of Mormon. When his plural marriage test case went to the U.S. Supreme Court, he was found guilty and sentenced to two years in prison. Reynolds began his prison term in Lincoln, Nebraska, but in just under a month, he was transferred to the Utah Territorial Prison for the remainder of his term. Another was **Brigham H. Roberts,** who became a member of the First Council of the Seventy and one of Mormonism's great historians. He was 10 years old when he passed through Wyoming in 1866. That same year, 15-year-old **Andrew Jenson,** who later became an assistant Church Historian, also left Old Wyoming (BiE 1:261–63).

The Ox-Bow Trail/Old Ft. Kearny Road/ Nebraska City Road

Mormon emigrants who crossed the Missouri River below the mouth of the Platte used trail routes from Plattsmouth and Nebraska City that looped northwest to meet the Platte River's south side about 15 miles east of present-day Columbus, Nebraska. From there they followed the Platte River's southwesterly bend to where, east of Ft. Kearny, their route intersected the Oregon-California trail coming from Independence and St. Joseph.

The Ox-Bow Trail connected the ferry at the old Ft. Kearny site on the Missouri with the **new Ft. Kearny** 210 miles away.

In the town of **Ashland,** on U.S. 6 just northeast of where Silver Creek Street intersects that highway, is **"The Ox-Bow Trail" historical marker.** It is near the waterworks operation. Its text begins: "This marker sits astride the Ox-Bow Trail, also known as the Old Ft. Kearny or Nebraska City Road" and tells about "thousands of emigrants and millions of pounds of freight" taking that route. "Many travelers were Mormons bound for the Great Salt Lake Valley," it notes. Part of the trail came down the hill behind the marker.

A major site on Ox-Bow Trail is the **Saline Ford,** where travelers crossed **Salt Creek.** This location is just west of present-day Ashland, slightly north of I-80. There, still-visible limestone ledges formed a natural low-water ford. Thousands of emigrants bound for Oregon, California, and Utah, as well as military men and freighters, used this ford.

An **NPS/NMTA Mormon Trail interpretive panel,** "A Fork in the Road," is located on a dike overlooking the Saline Ford on Salt Creek. The panel tells about the Ox-Bow Trail and the two rock ledges in the streambed at Ashland that provided the shallow crossing. To reach the panel, drive east on U.S. 6 to Silver Street, go under the railroad bridge, cross Salt Creek, and see a small park on the south beyond the levee. From the sign there is a footpath back to the bridge, from which you can see, in low water, the ripples caused by the rock reef of the crossing, one above and one below the bridge.

From Ashland the trail followed the high ridges westward and northwest, crossed present-day U.S. 77 just south of Swedeburg, passed through where Brainard now is, then went north of today's David City, and entered the Platte Valley west of present-day Bellwood. Today's U.S. 30 crossed the trail route 1 to 2 miles north of the junction with State 64. A few miles west of there the trail met the Platte River and followed it west. Travelers on I-80 will again cross the Ox-Bow route at the Grand Island eastbound rest area.

In 1849 Mormon **Howard Egan** led a freight wagon train with some passengers from St. Joseph, Missouri, to Utah. Because of gold rush traffic, they could not cross the Missouri at St. Joseph, so they went upriver and crossed on **a ferry at the Old Ft. Kearny site,** at present-day Nebraska City. There they organized the company, which included 57 people, 22 wagons, and 91 oxen, and then followed the newly opened Ox-Bow Trail (PHJ). On May 21 Egan's journal notes that his company journeyed "to Saline or Salt Creek, had to let wagons down by ropes, banks so steep and high." Ten days later his train passed the junction where the **St. Joseph and Independence Road** intersected his route. He was then caught in gold rush forty-niner traffic: "There is one continual string of wagons as far as the eye can extend, both before and behind us." Egan expected that "if the Platte River is low enough I think I shall cross over to the north side when I get above the head of Grand Island, in order to get out of the crowd, that I may have more sea room. This evening there is twenty-nine camps in sight, numbering from fifteen to forty wagons in a company" (HEJ).

■ Nebraska City

Nebraska City is located beside the Missouri River where State 2 and U.S. 75 meet, 50 miles south of Omaha and 7 miles south of Wyoming, Nebraska.

Lewis and Clark believed that the tableland where the city now is was an ideal site for a future city. In 1838, Col. Stephen Kearny recommended that a fort be built there. That happened eight years later, in 1846, when a blockhouse was built where Fifth Street is now, just south of Main Street. But this **early Ft. Kearny** was operational for only two years because it was not in the mainstream of travel. A **new Ft. Kearny** opened near present-day Kearney, and a trail connecting the old site with the new one became a route that Mormon emigrants used (see **Ox-Bow Trail**). In 1848 a ferry was established, and although the fort was vacated that year, the boat service functioned for many years. Hundreds of gold rush forty-niners crossed the Missouri River there.

When Nebraska Territory opened to settlement in 1854, the fort's old buildings provided a start for a town. First called Table Creek, the town in 1855 was renamed Nebraska City. It became an important steamboat port on the Missouri River. In 1858 the freighting firm of Russell, Majors, and Waddell selected it as an outfitting point for its wagon trains (see **"Utah War"**). They erected large warehouses and in time employed some 1,100 men, 700 wagons and nearly 6,000 yoke of oxen (AHN).

Nebraska City is the **birthplace of Arbor Day,** now an international holiday. Nebraska City newspaper editor **J. Sterling**

Morton gained state approval in 1872 for a day to be set aside for the planting of trees, something barren Nebraska needed. On Apr. 10 that year the state celebrated its first Arbor Day, and estimates say more than 1 million trees were planted in Nebraska that day. Since then the concept of Arbor Day has spread around the entire world. "Other holidays repose upon the past," Morton once said. "Arbor Day proposes for the future." He served as secretary of agriculture in President Grover Cleveland's second administration. Morton's **Arbor Lodge** mansion is now part of **Arbor Lodge State Historical Park.** The **National Arbor Day Foundation** is headquartered in Nebraska City and promotes tree planting, rural land conservation, forest stewardship, and rain forest preservation (ADW).

Nebraska City and the "Utah War." In 1857 **wagon trains loaded with supplies for the U.S. Army** (already traveling toward Utah), left Ft. Leavenworth, the "outfitting place" on the Missouri River. Beginning in 1858, however, the well-known **Russell, Majors, and Waddell Freighting Company,** who held the government freighting contract to carry supplies to 2,500 U.S. troops in Utah, moved their "outfitting place" from Ft. Leavenworth to Nebraska City, which was about 140 miles higher up the Missouri River. Though other "outfitting places" dealt in military trade, most goods bound for U.S. troops in the "Utah War" came by riverboat from St. Louis to Nebraska City (MiSL 55–78).

The enormous responsibility of sending 800 to 1,000 large freight wagons from the new depot caused Alexander Majors himself to move to Nebraska City. He was the most important man in the city. He had high standards and lived what he taught: abstinence from liquor and tobacco, reliance on the Bible, and observance of the Sabbath. He tried in vain to have his teamsters live by his standards (SY).

The army constructed warehouses, and Nebraska City became a teaming hive of about 4,000 inhabitants plus those "passing through." After two years the military business was said to have made Nebraska City the foremost place in Nebraska.

The 1864 Mormon outfitting place named Wyoming was located just 7 miles north of Nebraska City. While an English convert, **John Nicholson,** was in Wyoming helping Saints make preparations to move to the Rocky Mountains in 1866, he became a party to a lawsuit involving William E. McLellin, a former LDS apostle who had been excommunicated in 1838. The lawsuit concerned a Mr. McIntosh and property in Kirtland. McIntosh hired McLellin and five lawyers to represent him. They did manage to get an attachment on property being shipped to Brigham Young and Heber C. Kimball, which included wire for the Deseret Telegraph. The hearing for the lawsuit was held in **Nebraska City.** McLellin shouted in a loud voice during the hearing and grossly misrepresented the Saints' testimonies. The twelve-man jury ruled in favor of Nicholson and Kimball (JWEMc 349–52).

• Lincoln, the Nebraska State Capital

Lincoln is 60 miles southwest of Omaha on I-80. It is the capital city of Nebraska and the state's second largest city, with approximately a quarter of a million residents. It is one of the few large cities of Nebraska not located along either the Platte or the Missouri Rivers.

Lincoln started out in 1856 as the village of Lancaster. Omaha had been the territorial capital since the creation of Nebraska Territory in 1854, but the legislature wanted a capital south of the Platte, where most Nebraskans lived, and as far west as possible. Thus, they chose Lancaster. To derail such a move, however, Omaha interests had the name of the village changed to Lincoln, certain that the legislature, which had been sympathetic towards the Confederacy, would not allow a place named Lincoln to be the capital city. The plan failed, and when Nebraska became a state in 1867, Lincoln was its capital.

Lincoln is home to the flagship campus of the four-campus **University of Nebraska** system. The Lincoln campus has approximately 22,000 students. Lincoln is also home to the **Nebraska State Historical Society,** whose manuscript and book holdings contain much historical information about Mormon involvements with early Nebraska history and the trail routes and sites the Mormon emigrants used.

The **William Jennings Bryan House,** "Fairview," is at 4900 Sumner Street. Born in Illinois in 1860, Bryan moved to Nebraska in 1890 and practiced law. Termed "the Boy Orator of the Platte," he served two terms in Congress. He was the Democratic Party candidate for president in 1896, 1900, and 1908, running as "The Great Commoner" and advocating the monetization of silver. He served as President Woodrow Wilson's secretary of state. Bryan was a prosecuting attorney in the 1925 famous "Monkey Trial" in

Tennessee in which schoolteacher John Scopes was tried for teaching evolution. Scopes was acquitted. Bryan died shortly thereafter. His house in Lincoln is a museum containing mementos of his era and his party. A statue of Bryan stands in front of the home.

Homestead National Monument at Beatrice

About 45 miles south of Lincoln is the **Homestead National Monument,** dedicated to the people who settled lands under the Homestead Act of 1862. The monument is on the site of what might be the first land claimed under that act. The park is reached from I-80 on Lincoln's west side by taking Exit 397 to the Homestead Expressway southbound (U.S. 77) to **Beatrice.** In Beatrice, turn west on Market Street (U.S. 136) for 1.5 miles to State 4 and then turn north and follow that highway as it bends westerly. At 4.5 miles from Beatrice is the park entrance.

The **Homestead Act of 1862** has been called one the most important pieces of legislation in the history of the United States. President Lincoln signed it into law after the secession of southern states, and it went into effect on Jan. 1, 1863. It remained in effect until 1976, when it was repealed by the Federal Land Policy and Management Act (though a ten-year extension through 1986 was authorized in Alaska). It provided that loyal citizens or prospective citizens who were 21 years old or the head of a family could claim 160 acres by paying a $14 filing fee. If they stayed on the claim for five years, built a house, and cultivated 10 acres, they could pay an additional $6 and the land was theirs. During the 124-year history of the Homestead Act, more than 2 million people filed for 160-acre parcels of the public domain. Of these claimants, about 783,000 (approximately 40 percent) were successful in filling the requirements and earning the title to their property. In total, some 270 million acres, or 10 percent of the area of the United States, was claimed and settled under this act. Most of the land claimed was marginal, and most was homesteaded by people who already owned farms. Homesteading took place in every state and territory west of the Mississippi, except Texas, and many east of the Mississippi (USGHA).

One of the first people to file a claim under the Homestead Act of 1862 was **Daniel Freeman.** The government purchased the land from his heirs and created the **Homestead National Monument.** Displays in the **park's visitors center and museum** tell part of the story of the settlement of federal lands in the West. Outside, some 2.5 miles of trails wind through restored tall-grass prairie.

Many **LDS homesteaders in Utah** had once crossed Nebraska by wagon train, handcart, or railroad.

The 1846 Ponca Encampment

■ Bishop George Miller's 1846 Advance Company

In May 1846 at Mt. Pisgah, Iowa, Brigham Young and the Twelve felt frustrated that the cumbersome Camp of Israel was moving so slowly. Plans to reach the Rocky Mountains that year had begun to look unworkable. They decided to send a smaller company ahead, composed of Saints who had equipment and supplies adequate for such a long trek. On June 12, three days before the Camp of Israel reached the Missouri River, Brigham Young sent Bishop George Miller with a small company across the river to push for the Rockies. Meanwhile, 114 miles west of the river, Sioux raiders attacked a **Pawnee village and Presbyterian mission** located by the **Loup Fork** of the Platte River (see **Genoa**). With Brigham Young's approval, the missionaries hired Bishop Miller's company to go to the mission and retrieve the victims' possessions.

■ Loup Fork Temporary Camp

The Miller company of 32 wagons crossed the Missouri on July 6 and headed west. They were joined by a group of Mormons with 20 wagons. They had been in the **James Emmett company** in Iowa. They stopped at the **Pawnee mission** on the Loup Fork. Bishop Miller sent seven wagons back on July 22, carrying the retrieved cargo, but the rest of Miller's company stayed there, expecting to continue west.

Meanwhile, Brigham Young spent early July recruiting men for the Mormon Battalion. On July 16 he announced that more should be sent to join the Miller company, others should make a temporary settlement at Grand Island, and most Saints would have to stop that season by the Missouri River. He sent **two large companies** ahead, one he had recruited with 68 wagons, and one Heber C. Kimball had recruited with about 73 wagons. They crossed the **Elkhorn River** beginning on July 23.

These two companies joined the Miller company at the **Pawnee**

Mission by the **Loup Fork.** By then they had received new instructions from Brigham Young, telling them to winter at the Pawnee village area and to be governed by a 12-man high council (whom he named) with **George Miller** as president. He told the leaders to use their own judgment regarding how to prepare for winter. The combined company contained about 200 wagons and 600 people, involving about 150 families (SBMSJ).

Visiting **Ponca Indians** warned these Mormons that they were in a war zone involving Pawnee and Sioux and should not winter there. The high council accepted their invitation to **winter among the Poncas.** "This decision was not, as some historians say, an act of rebellion against Church leadership. Nor was it an action Miller took to 'run wild' with his authority. Rather, it was a reasoned decision by the high council" (SBMSJ).

After leaving 14 families behind to cultivate goodwill among the Pawnees, the company headed almost due north. They made their **own road** across much of present-day Nebraska. Along the way they encountered immense herds of buffalo. On Aug. 23 they arrived at the **Ponca village** near the mouth of the **Niobrara River** (or Running Water River) where it empties into the Missouri River in northern Nebraska. Native Americans flocked around the newcomers, Newel Knight said, "eager to see our Cattle, sheep, Hens, Pigs, and in fact almost everything we had was entirely new to them" (SBMSJ 417).

By late September, when Mormon leadership was establishing Winter Quarters about 150 miles downriver, Miller's company was building cabins whose backs created a rectangular fort, the back walls having portholes through which the whites could shoot at any attackers. By winter, the outer walls of **Ft. Ponca** included at least 110 cabins as well as 2 large gates that were locked at night. These Ft. Ponca Saints have earned modest fame in Nebraska history for being the first white people to settle in upper Nebraska.

In early October the Poncas packed up their lodges, kettles, and possessions and migrated westward to winter hunting grounds in present-day Wyoming to hunt buffalo, elk, and deer. **William C. Staines** and five other Mormons went with them to hunt and learn Indian skills. Mormon traders from Ft. Ponca kept in contact with them.

As weather permitted, Saints gathered in the center of the fort for outdoor Sunday worship meetings. With the approach of winter, they experienced a power struggle between Bishop Miller and the high council. Bishop Miller and James Emmett insisted that the people form a united economic order, pooling their individual resources and drawing rations equally. Bishop Miller tried to disregard the high council, but they insisted his decisions needed their approval. That winter, too, the Saints suffered from a shortage of food. Ponca Camp stayed in contact with **Winter Quarters,** mostly through trade and buying missions. At least eighteen wagons went from Ponca to Missouri that winter on trading errands.

On Dec. 26 a terrifying **prairie fire** swept by the fort, which was saved by bucket brigades and because the green cabin logs did not burn easily. Some haystacks and wagons were consumed.

On Feb. 6, 1847, apostle **Ezra Taft Benson** and **Erastus Snow** arrived at Ft. Ponca. The camp then numbered 396 Saints, including 98 men (JH Jan. 27–30, Feb. 8 and 15, 1847). The two visitors brought and read the recent revelation to Brigham Young, **"The Word and Will of the Lord"** (D&C 136), regarding how the trek west should be directed by the Twelve. Bishop Miller, who had been in Winter Quarters when the revelation was first presented, disagreed with it and with Brigham Young's decisions. Elders Benson and Snow reorganized the Ponca Camp, replaced Bishop Miller as president, and took him with them to Winter Quarters.

During the winter of 1846–47, the same one in which so many Mormons died at Winter Quarters, at least 23 Ponca Saints also died, including **Newel Knight** (probably of pneumonia). Scurvy caused some of the deaths. A **burial ground** was established on bluffs two miles west of the fort, but searches in recent years have failed to find the site.

As instructed by the Twelve, the Ponca Saints left for Winter Quarters on Apr. 10, 1847. The fort, cabins, stables, and stockyards were all left vacant. Saints believed the fort would serve the Poncas well when the group returned from buffalo hunting. But while camped that evening about 3 miles from the fort, the Saints saw smoke and flames rising from the fort's direction. Sioux warriors had torched the fort to keep the Poncas from using it (TAMF 169–80).

The Ponca company moved south 30 miles along the Bazile Valley (passing where the main business street in **Creighton** now is), rolled southeast to the **Logan River Valley,** and followed it southward. They moved southeast along the east side of the **Elkhorn**

River. At **Winter Quarters** the Ponca company was dissolved. About ten families settled together near Winter Quarters in what was named, appropriately, Ponca Camp, but its location is not known.

By mid-1847 **Bishop Miller** disassociated himself from the Church. He headed south to Texas and joined with disaffected apostle **Lyman Wight** (excommunicated 1848) and then with others who had left the faith. He died in 1856 (CHC 3:157–59).

Ponca Site and Newel Knight Memorial

The general site of Ft. Ponca is reached by driving west from the town of Niobrara 2 miles on State 12 (across the Niobrara River and Mormon Canal). At a point .25 mile west of Mormon Canal, turn south on a gravel road and go about .25 mile. A **monument honoring Newel Knight** and others is on the left (east) side of the road. The Ponca Winter Camp was located west of the monument, but the exact site is undetermined. In 1908 Newel and Lydia's son, Utah millionaire **Jesse Knight,** who was two when Newel died, erected the 16-foot-tall, solid marble monument to memorialize his parents and the other Latter-day Saints who had wintered at Ponca. It bears the names of Newel and ten others who were buried there that winter of 1846–47 (ETN 83–87; TAMF 169–80; MBK 209–29).

The Ponca tribe signed several treaties with the federal government from 1817 to 1865. Like many other tribes in Nebraska, they were forced to witness the shrinking of their homelands until most were moved to the Indian Territory in the present-day state of Oklahoma. When **Chief Standing Bear** tried to return with other Poncas to these Nebraska lands to bury his son, they were arrested. White friends filed writs of habeas corpus to release them. These actions led to a **landmark civil rights decision** in United States District Court in Omaha in 1879 by Judge Elmer Dundy that Native Americans are "persons within the meaning of the law" and have the rights of

Marble monument at Ponca Winter Camp, Niobrara, NE, memorializing all the Latter-day Saints who spent the winter of 1846–47 at Ponca. (Courtesy of RLDSLA)

citizenship. The government appealed Dundy's decision, but on June 5, 1880, the Supreme Court of the United States, in ***Standing Bear v. Crook,*** dismissed the appeal, which decision determined that a Native American is a person within the meaning of the law (PTHM).

In 1966 the United States government terminated recognition of the Ponca tribe of Nebraska, but in 1990 recognition of the Ponca tribe was restored under federal law.

Chief Standing Bear, or Ma-chu-nah-zah, was born on Niobrara reservation lands about 1829 or 1834 (accounts differ). He was elected to the Nebraska Hall of Fame in 1977.

Niobrara is a tiny community on the northeast border of Nebraska, located where the Niobrara River flows into the Missouri River. Native Americans gave the river and town the name which means "running water." At Niobrara, the **Chief Standing Bear Memorial Bridge** links Nebraska State 12 to South Dakota State 37.

Niobrara is the **headquarters of the Ponca tribe of Nebraska,** which numbers only a few hundred. The Ponca Agency's buildings and grounds in Niobrara include a community center building, powwow grounds, cemetery, and bison reserve. In town, next to the Niobrara Museum, a **Ponca Tribal Museum** contains artifacts from the tribe's history, a photo archives, artwork, and a gift shop. Among its displays is a black-etched dark **wood plaque** that tells about the Mormons among the Ponca in 1846 and 1847.

In September 1946 the town of Niobrara celebrated the **centennial of the Mormon settlement at Ft. Ponca.**

Beautiful **Niobrara State Park,** 2 miles west of Niobrara, overlooks the confluence of the Niobrara and Missouri Rivers. It is a recreational park of 1,260 acres, featuring miles of hiking and biking trails, three Missouri River boat accesses, and several campgrounds. At the park's eastern tip, the **J. Alan Cramer Interpretive Center,** an outdoor, covered pavilion, provides an exceptional view of the two rivers' confluence. It features metal **historical marker plaques** that highlight the people and places that played key roles in the history of the area, including the story of the Lewis and Clark Expedition, the Ponca Indians, and the **Mormon encampment.**

The Trek of the 1847 Mormon Pioneers

Assembly Grounds at the Elkhorn River

Three principal Missouri River crossings in the Council Bluffs vicinity meant there were three trails on the Nebraska side that had to merge before there could be a main road west. They converged by the **Elkhorn River** in the vicinity of present-day **Fremont, Nebraska.** All traces of early trails from the Missouri River to that point have vanished under the spreading Omaha metropolis. They followed ridges where possible so the routes were nearly level but not direct. In order to reach the Platte River, routes had to cross the Big Papillion and the Elkhorn, which share a common flood plain.

From the **North Mormon Ferry** at the Winter Quarters site there were two options. One trail went north to the vicinity of the "original" Council Bluffs (present-day **Ft. Calhoun**) to get around the headwaters of the Papillion and then veered westward. The second trail went up the bluffs and then southwest over the upland.

From the **Middle Ferry** one primary road went through what is now downtown Omaha. Near the present-day Douglas County Courthouse the trail went northwest to a point beyond Central High School, where there was a divergence, the main emigrant road swinging west to the vicinity of Boys Town and then northwest. The other, which later became a military road via Ft. Omaha, veered to the northwest to join the Lower Mormon Road near Omaha's Benson Shopping Center.

The **South Ferry, or Trader's Pt.–Bellevue Ferry** led to the Bellevue trading post and mission and the Mormon settlement called **Mormon Hollow.** From this neighborhood there were **three routes westward.** One very circuitously followed the north bank of the Platte River. A second went up Papillion Creek as far as today's town of Papillion and then went west via present-day Millard to join the Bellevue–Platte Valley Road on the Elkhorn bottoms. A third route from Bellevue went northwest to join the Omaha Road at Boys Town. A Lower Bellevue Road went north up the Elkhorn River.

The recombined Omaha Military–Lower Mormon–Upper Bellevue Road went west through present-day Irvington. The north Mormon Road meandered west along the Washington-Douglas county line to the north of present-day Bennington.

Route, Landmarks, and Campsites

Beginning with the **Elkhorn River Crossing,** where the several routes came together, the **names of camps, landmarks, or places** below are marked * to identify those considered important or ** to identify those considered very important. The **dates** when the main group of the original 1847 pioneers camped at a particular place and the number of **miles they traveled** for the day are noted, as is the **nearest current town or city.** Most campsites were not named by the pioneers, so the **authors named some of the sites,** based on geographical landmarks, events, people's names, town names, or other features.[2]

■ ****Elkhorn River Crossing • Brigham Young • Sat.–Sun. Apr. 10–11 • Waterloo**

On Apr. 5, 1847, apostle Heber C. Kimball and a few others started for the Rocky Mountains. Six wagons, variously called the Advance Company or Discovery Company or Pioneer Band, departed Winter Quarters. The group camped for two nights north of **Winter Quarters** (see **The Mormons' First Camp Marker,** Winter Quarters site 14).

The 1847 Brigham Young company's **first appointed staging area** was on the **Elkhorn River** ("The Horn"), which was 27 miles from Winter Quarters and 1,004 miles from the Great Salt Lake.

---

2. An excellent book for travelers to use when following the trail in Nebraska, Wyoming, and Utah is *111 Days to Zion,* by Hal Knight and Stanley B. Kimball. It quotes 1847 pioneer journals day by day. See also the published William Clayton, Thomas Bullock, and Lewis Barney 1847 diaries.

Elkhorn River Crossing, NE. (Steel engraving by Frederick Piercy, 1853)

There, on Apr. 10, 1847, they camped on both sides of the river while **ferrying their wagons** on Apr. 10 and 11.

Experts question the location of the **Elkhorn Crossing site.** Orson Pratt, in the Brigham Young company, recorded latitude readings putting it near today's town of Waterloo. Based on those, some previous pinpointings have said the pioneers crossed about where State 64 (W. Maple Road) crosses the Elkhorn River today, on Waterloo's north edge. This "Waterloo Crossing" is the **traditionally accepted site.**

Near the southeast corner of King Lake, however, is **another possible site.** This is 2 miles above the railroad bridge that crosses the river .5 mile southeast of the center of the town of Waterloo (JWW; JNJ). Earliest Government Land Office maps place the "Old Mormon Road" to Utah at **a more northern crossing,** and there is no doubt this northern site was used by many Mormon emigrants. Designating this more northerly crossing is a small **concrete marker** that tells about the 1847 pioneer ferry and later government bridge across the Elkhorn River. The marker is east of the Elkhorn River, on the south side of State 36 where 140th Street dead-ends at that highway.

There is an **NPS/NMTA Mormon Trail interpretive panel,** "Ferrying the Elkhorn," in the Elkhorn Crossing Recreation Area on the west side of the river, south of State 36, west of Elk City. It tells about how companies ferried wagons across and that Mormons operated a ferry there for several years, collecting tolls from California and Oregon Trail emigrants.

Other Mormon emigrant groups at various times used other ferry sites to cross the Elkhorn (HSM 70).

In 1847 the **Elkhorn River** was 160 feet wide and 4 feet deep at the crossing, and a raft made of dry cottonwood logs carried the wagons across the river. The Mormon-constructed raft was controlled by cattle pulling guide ropes on both sides of the river. Only wagons, cargo, and people were ferried across; horses and cattle had to swim. By 4:00 P.M. of Sunday, Apr. 11, a total of 72 wagons plus a cannon and a leather boat (both on wheels) were ferried to the west bank of the Elkhorn (PCS 119; EmG 41).

■ **ELKHORN RIVER CAMP • BRIGHAM YOUNG • SUN. APR. 11 • 2 MILES • ELKHORN**

With all the **Brigham Young company's wagons** on the west side of the Elkhorn, the pioneers moved to a grove of trees a little southwest of the crossing, on the bank of Rawhide Creek. Shade and firewood were needed. Local Mormon Trail expert Carl Jones (2005) places the **Elkhorn River Camp** about 2 miles north of Waterloo, on Rawhide Creek before it flows into the Elkhorn—at a point within 2 miles south of where State 36 crosses Rawhide Creek (JWW; JAL; DN Apr. 10, 1947; CJ,c).

Elder **Heber C. Kimball** reminded the company that even though they had ferried wagons on Sunday, they were to remember it was the **Sabbath** and not hunt or fish or pursue trivial amusements. This set the precedent for the Mormon pioneers to observe the Sabbath Day during their trek. Of the fifteen Sabbaths spent on the trail by the original 1847 pioneers, meetings were held on eleven of them, and only on four Sabbaths did the camp travel along the trail (usually necessitated by lack of feed for their animals). Of this campground **Horace Kimball Whitney** said, "The country in the vicinity of the **Elk Horn** is one of the most beautiful that I ever saw" (JHKW).

Eight apostles were in this camp: Brigham Young, Heber C. Kimball, Willard Richards, Orson Pratt, Wilford Woodruff, George A. Smith, Amasa Lyman, and Ezra T. Benson. On Apr. 12, they returned to Winter Quarters to meet John Taylor, who had just returned from his mission to England.

Elkhorn Indian Skirmish, 1848. In 1847 and later, other Mormon companies crossed the Elkhorn in this general vicinity. In June 1848, for example, the huge **Heber C. Kimball company** from Winter Quarters was organizing by the Elkhorn for the trek west. On June 6, Indians raided their cattle grazing by the Elkhorn's west shore. Mormon horsemen and footmen rushed to the scene. Both sides fired shots. Several Native Americans were killed, and **Thomas Ricks** and **Howard Egan** were seriously wounded. That evening the 220 wagons of the Kimball company formed into a tight corral. Extra guards were posted. Apparently searchers found and brought back some of the stolen cattle (MHS Spring 1999, 37–60).

Elkhorn Crossing, 1861. During 1861 a large Mormon emigration left in thirteen wagon trains from Florence (see **"down and back" trains,** Winter Quarters site 10). On July 10 the Joseph Horne company reached the Elk Horn crossing. "Here, in this campers' paradise," diarist Thomas C. Griggs wrote, "we remained until Saturday morning, gathering wild grapes, shooting wild ducks, bathing in the river, washing our clothes, having an abundance of wood, water, grass and shade, and being visited by a number of friendly Pawnee Indians" (DBWT 26).

■ ****LIBERTY POLE CAMP • BRIGHAM YOUNG • MON.–THURS. APR. 12–15 • 12 MILES • FREMONT**

Brigham Young's company traveled 12 miles from the Elkhorn River Camp and halted near the **Platte River** in a cottonwood grove. One opinion is that the Liberty Pole site is about 3 miles southeast of the present-day city of Fremont, or .75 mile southwest of U.S. 275 at a point where U.S. 275 crosses the Douglas and Dodge county line (JWC Apr. 15, 1847; JNJ). An alternate site, according to local research, is southwest of Fremont and less than .25 mile southeast of the east entrance toll booth at **Fremont Lakes State Recreation Area.** At this point there were more than 1,000 acres of level grassland between the Platte River and Rawhide Creek (CJ,c).

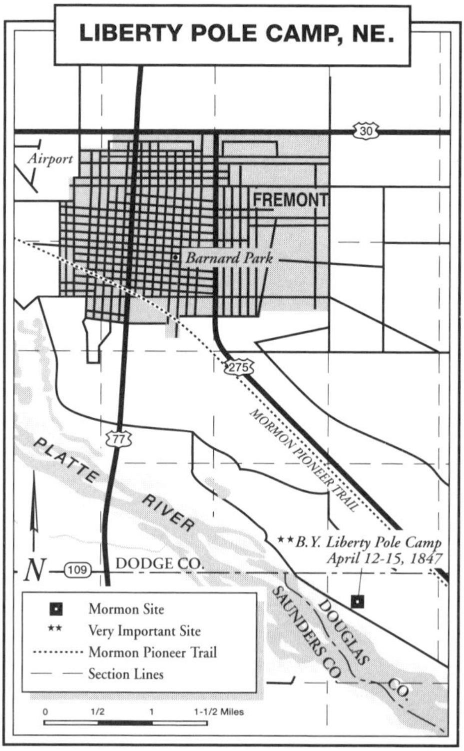

Liberty Pole Camp (given that name two months later) was a staging area where the Brigham Young company gathered to regroup. They camped three days while waiting for their leader, Brigham Young, and the members of the Twelve to return from Winter Quarters. While waiting, they repaired and cleaned wagons, visited with the Indians, and caught fish to eat. For the evening meal of Apr. 14, some of the brethren brought two dozen fish into camp and Wilford Woodruff recorded, "We had a splendid supper composed of fried Cat fish, pork beans, short Cake, Honey Comb, coffee, milk, &c. We all eat vary Harty" (JWW 148).

Brigham Young, prophet and leader of the Mormon pioneers. (Steel engraving by Frederick Piercy, 1853)

On Apr. 15 **members of the Twelve returned** from Winter Quarters with two barometers, two sextants, two artificial horizons, one circle of reflection, and one telescope, which John Taylor had brought from England. **Jesse C. Little** visited the camp to report his mission in the Eastern States, and he brought presents for the Twelve from **Thomas L. Kane,** the Church's friend in the East. Wilford Woodruff's present was a patent life preserver and stop compass.

In the evening of Apr. 15 **Brigham Young** gave instruction that included **nine rules to govern the company:**

1. A bugle will blow each day at 5 A.M. and every man is expected to arise and pray, then attend to his team, get breakfast and be prepared to travel at 7 A.M.

2. Each man is to walk at the side of his team with his gun loaded and within reach.

3. The camp will halt about noon to rest the animals. People must already have their dinner cooked so as not to delay camp by fixing meals.

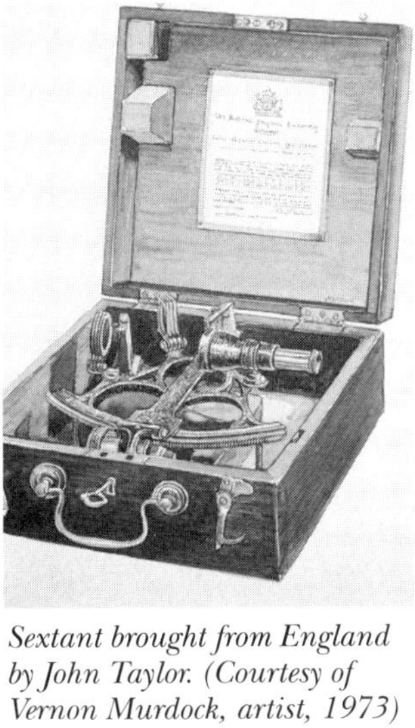

Sextant brought from England by John Taylor. (Courtesy of Vernon Murdock, artist, 1973)

4. At night the wagons are to be drawn into a circle and animals placed inside the circle when possible.

5. The bugle will blow at 8:30 P.M. when every man must return to his wagon and pray, except the night guard. Fires must be out and people in bed by 9 P.M.

6. The camp will travel in close order, and no man is to get farther than 20 rods away (about 330 feet) without permission from his captain of 10.

7. Every man is to help take care of his brother's cattle. No man will be indulged in idleness.

8. Every man is to have his rifle and pistol in perfect working order. A piece of leather should be kept over the firing mechanism to protect it from moisture.

9. All persons will start together and keep together. A company guard will attend the cannon in the rear and see that nothing is left behind at each stopping place. (HEJ)

On Apr. 16 at 8 A.M., the company held an **organizing meeting** (JWC 74; JAL; JWW; JNJ). Brigham Young issued a stern admonition to the group, saying that "if any do not like to obey the necessary rules, without murmuring, they should 'turn back now'" (MVB 104). **Stephen Markham** and **Albert P. Rockwood** were appointed captains of 100s, and five captains of 50s and fourteen captains of 10s were chosen. (In these cases, the number refers to individuals; in other LDS wagon companies, the numbers usually referred to wagons.) The men would camp and cook together in groups of 10.

As originally planned, the company was to be only men, and **144 men** gathered at this campsite. Their mission was to go to the Great Basin in the West, select a workable route to get there, and choose the final site for the future home of the Mormons. Three women and two children joined the company. The women were **Harriet Decker Young,** wife of Lorenzo Dow Young; Harriet's daughter **Clara Decker Young,** who was a wife of Brigham Young; and **Ellen Sanders Kimball,** a wife of Heber C. Kimball. The children were Harriet's sons **Isaac Perry Decker** (by a former husband) and **Lorenzo Sobriski Young** (by Lorenzo Dow Young) (CHC 3:163–64). The company started out with about 72 wagons, 93 horses, 52 mules, 66 oxen, 19 cows, 17 dogs, and some chickens (JWC 76).

Two months later, on June 14, a "Big Company" of Saints set out to follow the Young company, led by apostles Parley P. Pratt and John Taylor. This company erected a 40-foot **cottonwood pole** flying a white flag, giving this camp its name. The so-called **Liberty Pole,** year by year, gradually became covered with names as far up as emigrants could reach. The pole was still in place at least as late as 1857 (HSM 55).

First Utah pioneer women 1847. (L to R) Ellen Sanders Kimball, Harriet Decker Young, and Clara Decker Young. (Courtesy of LDSCA)

In 1848, when Brigham Young was leading another large company of Saints west, little **Charley Beer,** stepson of John Neff, drowned in the Elkhorn River. After a coffin was made from a large log, he was buried near the Liberty Pole, on May 27, 1848 (JDL 129).

From this camp the 1847 original pioneer company reached the **Platte River,** which then became their companion, guide, and source of sustenance for the next 600 miles.

■ FREMONT CAMP • BRIGHAM YOUNG • FRI. APR. 16 • 3 MILES • FREMONT

With the camp organized and ready, the trek began in earnest on Apr. 16, 1847. Norton Jacob recorded: "After being numbered and formed into two lines in a circle around the wagon carrying the leather boat, all kneeled down when Bro. Brigham addressed the Lord by prayer and dedicated the mission and all we had to the Lord God of Israel" (JNJ 48; JWC). That afternoon the camp moved 3 miles up the Platte (JWC). Their campsite was 3 miles west of

The North Platte River, shown in this photo near Scottsbluff, NE, is a mile wide and six inches deep. Occasionally willows take root on sandbars to form little islands. (Courtesy of George L. Strebel, 1935)

Fremont, near where Military Road ends and State 18 goes north to U.S. 30 (CJ,c).

Fremont, population 25,198 in 2003, was founded in 1856 and named after John C. Fremont, famous explorer of the West, whose journals the 1847 pioneers had with them. In 1856, Fremont became the newborn Republican Party's candidate for president, running on a campaign opposed to slavery and to Mormon polygamy.

The Utah Pioneer Trails and Landmarks Association placed a **Liberty Pole Marker** in Fremont's **Barnard Park,** located between Irving and Clarkson Streets on Military Avenue. It tells about the encampment nearby and the military-type organization the pioneers formed (MPNHT 84).

An NPS/NMTA Mormon Trail interpretive panel, "Rally around the Flag," is on Fremont's southwest side near the river, in the **Fremont Lakes State Recreation Area.** To reach it, drive on U.S. 275 (north-south) which bypasses Fremont on the east and then on the north. While on Fremont's east side, turn west on East Military Road (Co. 43) and drive west through Fremont. That road becomes West Military Road. At the west edge of Fremont, turn left (south) on Ridge Road and then turn right at the first road after crossing the railroad tracks, onto State Lakes Road. Go through the East Entrance gate into Fremont Lakes State Recreation Area. The Liberty Pole panel is about 1,000 feet beyond the gate, on the right. The marker explains that the Liberty Pole marked the staging grounds for dividing wagon parties into organized divisions. "The pole and its flag reminded the Mormon Pioneers that they were marching west to freedom."

Utah's sixth governor, **George Henry Dern,** was born 12 miles north of Fremont, in Hooper, Nebraska. Dern was Utah's governor between 1924 and 1932. His campaign slogan was "We want a Dern good governor, and we don't mean Maybey" (Mabey was the incumbent). When President Franklin Roosevelt named Dern as secretary of war, he became the first Utahn to fill a position in a president's cabinet. Although Dern was not a Mormon, his funeral was held in the Tabernacle in Salt Lake City in 1936 (UTG 16–17).

A **branch of the LDS Church** in **Fremont** was organized by missionaries Ferdinand F. Hintze and Anders Frandsen in Apr. 1877 (EnH 566).

Gutzon Borglum, Mt. Rushmore sculptor. Gutzon Borglum was born near Bear Lake, Idaho, to parents who were Danish converts to Mormonism and emigrated to Utah. In 1864 his father and a first wife outfitted in **Wyoming, Nebraska,** and passed through Nebraska on their way to Utah in the **William B. Preston wagon train.** Jens Borglum married his wife's sister, becoming a polygamist. The family lived near Bear Lake, Idaho, where Gutzon was born to the second wife on Mar. 25, 1867. They also lived in Ogden, Utah. When Gutzon was four, his father, a frontier doctor, left the LDS Church. In 1874 the family moved from Idaho to **Fremont, Nebraska.** Gutzon was then seven years old. He was educated in Fremont and Omaha.

In 1884 the family moved to California. Gutzon became a nationally recognized sculptor whose best-known work is the **Mt. Rushmore National Memorial.** The carving of Mt. Rushmore began on Aug. 10, 1927, and spanned 14 years—about six to seven years carving and the rest of the time trying to raise funds. The cost of the project was $900,000. The 60-foot-high granite faces of four American presidents—George Washington, Thomas Jefferson, Abraham Lincoln, and Theodore Roosevelt—are scaled to men who would stand 465 feet tall. In 1941, with the project almost completed, Gutzon suffered a heart attack and died. His son Lincoln finished the project later that year, just before America's entry into World War II. The **Mt. Rushmore National Memorial** is 23 miles southwest of Rapid City, South Dakota (about 60 miles north of the Nebraska panhandle) (IHN; BOL).

■ SABBATH CAMP • BRIGHAM YOUNG • SAT.–SUN. APR. 17–18 • 7 MILES • AMES

Between Fremont and Columbus, U.S. 30 follows rather closely the route of the 1847 Brigham Young company.

On Saturday, Apr. 17, the pioneers awoke to find ice an inch thick in the water buckets (JTB). Bothered by a disagreeable wind, the company moved between the river on their left and sand bluffs on the right. They traveled 7 miles and then camped at the edge of a grove of cottonwoods to spend the Sabbath (JWC; JNJ; JTB). The campsite was .5 mile from the Platte River, perhaps near where the Ames post office is now. Eighty yards north of the trail, at a point 3.25 miles west of State 79 in North Bend, the pioneers passed a large pile of earth—a **grave,** perhaps Pawnee.

William Clayton, general clerk of the 1846 Camp of Israel. (Courtesy of LDSCA)

Near the camp, the brethren felled hundreds of cottonwood trees to feed their teams on the leaves, bark, and small branches, so they could save feed corn for later. At 5 P.M. on Apr. 17th, the camps were called together and **organized in military order** with Brigham Young, lieutenant general (the same rank that Joseph Smith held in the Nauvoo Legion); Stephen Markham, colonel; John Pack and Shadrack Roundy, majors. Thomas Bullock was appointed clerk of the camp and Thomas Tanner captain of the cannon. Brigham Young reminded the pioneers of the camp rules and about keeping guns loaded at all times in case of Indian troubles. A large Pawnee village was not far away (JWC).

While crossing Iowa the previous year, **William Clayton** had served as the "General Clerk" of the "Camp of Israel." But for this 1847 pioneer journey, Clayton was appointed to assist the "Official Camp Scribe," **Thomas Bullock.** Both men kept excellent journals during the long trip to the Salt Lake Valley (TOD 222, 228).[3] That night (Apr. 17), "Ellis Eames and Hans C. Hansen played violins" until the camp bugle sounded at 9:00 P.M. (JWC). Apr. 18 was **Sunday,** and Howard Egan recorded, "Today being set apart by Almighty God for his people to rest, we do not intend to travel" (HEJ; DTZ 32). **Wilford Woodruff** noted that day that the Platte River was "like walking on the edge of a smooth sea Beach. . . . A man or horse will suddenly sink into quick sand & the more He struggles to get out the more he will sink & will soon perish if assistance is not near" (JWW Apr. 18, 1847).

Thomas Bullock, camp scribe in the 1847 Brigham Young pioneer company. (Courtesy of LDSCA)

3. William Clayton, *William Clayton's Journal: A Daily Record of the Original Company of Mormon Pioneers from Nauvoo, Illinois, to the Valley of the Great Salt Lake* (Salt Lake City: Clayton Family Associates, 1921); Will Bagley, ed., *The Pioneer Camp of the Saints: The 1846 and 1847 Mormon Trail Journals of Thomas Bullock* (Spokane, Wash.: Arthur H. Clark Company, 1997). Company member Norton Jacob kept a fine diary that has been published; see Ronald O. Barney, ed., *The Mormon Vanguard Brigade of 1847: Norton Jacob's Record* (Logan: Utah State University Press, 2005).

Ellis Eames announced he was returning to Winter Quarters on account of poor health. He was spitting blood, and the weather was severely cold. He left, carrying company mail to Winter Quarters. His departure reduced the number of men in the company to 143. Later he emigrated to Utah and became a mayor of Provo (DTZ 31).

■ Shell Creek Camp • Brigham Young • Mon. Apr. 19 • 20 miles • Rogers

This camp is located by the Platte, south of the small town of Rogers and .5 mile south of U.S. 30, 3 miles east of where Shell Creek empties into the river.

On Monday, Apr. 19, the wagons moved in double file with about .25 mile between the columns. After 8 miles they arrived at a number of small lakes, saw many ducks, and killed several. (Possibly Legge Lake, which is by the Platte, south of U.S. 30 about .25 mile on Co. 11). After traveling 12 to 15 miles they stopped for their midday meal on the bank of the Platte. "We are now at the North bend of the Platte," Norton Jacob recorded (MVB 108). This bend is the most northern bend of the Platte River. The town of **North Bend,** appropriately named, is located in that general vicinity. They moved on another 5 to 8 miles and camped in a semicircle beside the Platte (JWC; JTB).

While walking on the trail during the afternoon, **William Clayton** and **Orson Pratt** discussed the possibility of fixing a set of wooden cogwheels to the hub of a wagon wheel, in such order as to tell the exact number of miles traveled each day. Orson agreed that it could be easily done with little expense (JWC 83). Clayton had been counting revolutions of a wheel with a red flannel cloth attached to a spoke, but he had apparently heard of an ancient method of keeping track of mileage through the use of an **odometer.** The idea, then a seed, soon would sprout.

Orrin Porter Rockwell, Jackson Redding, Thomas Brown, and Jesse C. Little brought mail from Winter Quarters and more presents from Thomas L. Kane. "I received A stop Box Marriners compass small enough to carry in the pocket," Wilford Woodruff said; "It was A splendid present. May the blessings of God be upon the head of Col Kane for his good feelings towards the servants of God" (JWW).

■ **Fish Camp • Brigham Young • Tues. Apr. 20 • 18–20 miles • Columbus**

Fish Camp was located somewhere within the 2-mile stretch of Loup Fork shoreline (north side) between where U.S. 81 crosses that river in Columbus and where the Loup Fork empties into the Platte 2 miles southeast. Columbus was founded in 1856. On its south edge is Pawnee Park, on the east side of U.S. 81. An **NPS/NMTA generic Mormon Trail panel** is located there, as is Ferry Rock, marking the site of the first Loup River Ferry built to serve Columbus.

During that day's travels **Brigham Young's company** moved 3 miles and crossed **Shell Creek** on a rather poor bridge, possibly built by early traders with the Pawnee villages (JWW 153). They passed through the area where the future city of **Schuyler** was established in 1869 and named after Schuyler Colfax, vice president of the United States. At the city's south side, the trail route crosses State 15 south of U.S. 30 through the community park and campground. An **NPS/NMTA generic Mormon Trail panel** is on the west of State 15 in the community park (CJ,c).

Five miles from the Shell Creek crossing brought them to a small lake or slough with water only in the spring, where they stopped for lunch. That day Wilford Woodruff noted that they could see in the distance "3 Islands in the Platt coverd with timber the largest about 10 acres. Their continues a chain of Islands for miles on the river & some timber on the south side of the Platt" (JWW). After traveling a total of 18–20 miles, they camped in a circle on the banks of the mile-wide **Platte River.** William Clayton suffered pain from a toothache, and Luke Johnson, the camp's doctor, tried to pull the tooth out but only got part of it (JWC).

Near Fish Camp the company cut down cottonwood trees for feed. The horses gnawed "the bark from brouse limbs & sticks 10 inches through as readily as they ate corn. . . . We give each horse also about 3 quarts of corn per day" (JWW).

On the way to this camp, some of the brethren had stopped at a lake (later called Lake McAllister) and caught 213 fish (buffalo and carp) which were divided in the camp. The buffalo fish weighed about 10 pounds and the carp two pounds. It was a good fish supper for everyone in the camp, hence the name Fish Camp. The brethren caught the fish using nets and the leather boat (***Revenue Cutter***) that had been provided by **Father Alanson**

Eldridge. The boat was carried across the plains on a wagon carriage by former apostle Luke Johnson. He used the boat as a wagon box (JWC; JWW).

In Columbus, U.S. 81 goes north and then, at 23rd Street, turns left. Several blocks later it intersects with Howard Boulevard. From that intersection, continue west on 23rd Street for about .6 mile to where it bends northwest and becomes Shady Lake Road. That road is on the original 1847 Mormon Trail for about 3.25 miles. When it ends at a T, drive north 1 mile on the gravel road to its intersection with State 22, turn left, and follow State 22 west into **Genoa** to see LDS sites.

■ LOOKING GLASS CREEK CAMP • BRIGHAM YOUNG • WED. APR. 21 • 15.5 MILES • MONROE

Looking Glass Creek Camp was located 8 miles east of **Genoa** and .75 mile southeast of **Monroe,** near where Looking Glass Creek emptied into the Loup Fork River. The mouth of the creek is now 5 miles west of where it was in 1847 (JWC; JWW; JTB).

On the morning of Apr. 21, the **Brigham Young company** left the Platte River, which bent southwesterly. They traveled 15.5 miles westward along the north side of the **Loup Fork** of the Platte, trying to find a place to cross. They camped on the banks of the Loup Fork at the mouth of **Looking Glass Creek,** so named by Heber C. Kimball because of the clarity of the water (DTZ 40).

A Pawnee on the Loup Fork of the Platte River in Nebraska is greeted by members of the 1847 pioneer company of Brigham Young, Apr. 21, 1847. (Courtesy of Vernon Murdock, artist, 1973)

The center of the **Pawnee nation** was along the Loup River. In 1820 there were three villages along the north bank. In 1844 there was but one, at the mouth of Cedar Creek. This village is the one the Sioux burned in 1846, after which the Pawnees relocated south of the Loup, to the west of present-day Columbus. This "new" Pawnee village is the one that the 1847 Mormon companies saw. On Apr. 21 the pioneers passed a **Pawnee village** of about 100 lodges. Among the Indians was **trader Peter Sarpy,** who was trading for buffalo skins. About 75 Pawnee came to camp, wanting presents. The chief, who rode a mule, bore the name **Sisketuk.** The Saints gave them gifts: salt, powder, fishhooks, lead, tobacco, and flour, but the visitors apparently thought they should have more gifts. Two horse bridles and a copper wash pan were missing from camp after the Pawnees' visit (JWC; MVB 109).

Norton Jacob said the "squaws dug for roots while the men walked with air of great overlords, being perfectly listless and idle" (MVB 110). That night the emigrants readied the cannon for use and had 100 guards (including the Twelve) instead of the usual 50 (JWC). While two guards slept on duty, some of the brethren removed the sleepers' guns as a joke (JWC).

In subsequent years other Mormons used this campsite. On June 6, 1857, for example, 70 eastbound missionaries from Utah pulling 26 handcarts camped at this place after leaving Genoa, where they had participated in a banquet (see **Handcart Companies)** (JJWY). Likewise, in 1860, the Warren Walling wagon train company camped here on June 4 (JTS).

■ **GENOA (1847) • BRIGHAM YOUNG • APR. 22 • GENOA

Genoa, Nance County, Nebraska, is a settlement founded and named by Latter-day Saints in the spring of 1857. It has continued in existence since then, and in 2003 had a population of 1,080. It is located on State 22, 14 miles northeast of Fullerton and 19 miles west of Columbus. It is designated as the "Pawnee Capital of Nebraska."

By early 1856 Church leaders in St. Louis called missionary **Andrew Cunningham** (who had been a bishop in Great Salt Lake City) to establish a Mormon settlement near the Loup Fork River. This was to be a rest and resupply stop for annual LDS emigrating companies. That fall Cunningham and seven others claimed land by Beaver Creek. Early in 1857 the Church obtained a four-year mail contract from the federal government to carry mail between Independence, Missouri, and Great Salt Lake City. The Brigham Young Express and Carrying Company (the YX Company) sent hundreds of men that spring to establish settlements in Wyoming while others developed Genoa to be one of the main stations on the mail line (GBK 161–68).

Genoa was located on a slight eminence .75 of a mile north of the Beaver Creek ford and laid out in blocks of ten acres with eight lots 18 x 9 rods to the block. The streets, four rods wide, crossed each other at right angles (GBK 168).

On Apr. 26, 1857, Cunningham arrived from Florence with 17 men, four wagons, some plows, and seeds. The group established Genoa's townsite near where the Beaver River entered the Loup Fork. The next day they laid out a farm, plowed, and planted wheat and other seeds. Additional men and families from St. Louis and Alton, Illinois, brought Genoa's population to about 100 settlers. Within three weeks they cooperatively fenced about 1,000 acres, plowed and planted about 600 acres, and had cattle in a common herd. They erected a meetinghouse of cottonwood logs. During the short time the settlement was a Mormon town, meetings were held regularly on Sundays and Thursday nights, and the settlement boasted a good choir (GBK 161–68; OPH 1:10–11; EnH 277).

On June 6, 1857, a hard-pressed handcart brigade of 70 outbound missionaries from Utah arrived, weary and famished after a 45-day trek. Elder Martindale met some of them with provisions and wagons for the last miles into Genoa, where they rested and were fed (JH June 10, 1875).

The outbreak of the **Utah War** ended the mail contract in June 1857 and caused Mormons at Genoa to leave for Utah in July to help defend the Mormons against the federal army being sent there. When Genoa was vacated, it was on the verge of becoming a flourishing farm village:

> Two farms, of 750 and 100 acres respectively, were bound with sod fences, and planted to corn, potatoes, buckwheat, and garden greens. A saw mill was set in operation and a quantity of housing lumber was prepared. A brick yard was also operating "full blast." The number of available hands led company officers to boast that they would "build a city not a whit behind any other in Nebraska." The city itself was 400 acres in size with the Mormon village plan of settlement. Like a miniature Salt Lake City, the blocks were ten acres in size, with eight lots in a block, and the wide streets ran due east-west and north-south. By July 1, the colony numbered 162 persons, largely men, and a great variety of livestock, including 42 yoke of oxen. (GBK 168)

On July 18, meanwhile, the first of some **2,500 U.S. soldiers** left Ft. Leavenworth to march to Utah. The rest of the army pulled out for Utah in September.

That same year, when the **Christiansen handcart company** passed Genoa on its way to Utah, **Christian and Inger Hansen** dropped out for health reasons. They traded their place in the company to a man for his 160-acre farm. They survived on the farm's potatoes and picked grapes, berries, and plums that grew in abundance in the area. The next spring they planted corn, potatoes, and a vegetable garden, and Christian built a log cabin to replace the dugout they had lived in. Threats from Native Americans forced them to leave and move to Council Bluffs. They finally went to Utah in 1861 (BZ 180–83).

In 1860 the LDS **Warren Walling company** camped here. Their journal-keeper Thomas Sleight noted on June 5: "Crossed the Loupe Fork on ferry boat at Genoa and camped." He also penned some reflections about Genoa:

> Leaving Genoa was like leaving home. Three years ago I with three or four hundred people reached this place and commenced to plow and fence. . . . We lived here until August 1859, when a government Indian agent ordered us to vacate. . . . He said we were on Indian soil. (JTS)

On June 22, 1860, the **Daniel Robinson handcart company** arrived at Genoa, where they enjoyed an evening of music and dancing (HCZ 182).

The **Genoa Historical Museum,** located in the old Genoa Bank at 402 Willard Avenue, contains a large collection of Pawnee weapons, tools, relics, and artifacts. Displays tell the story of **the Mormons at Genoa.** Of special value are **two diaries by Henry Hudson,** one of Genoa's Mormon founders, which are part of the Mormon exhibit.

An NPS/NMTA Mormon Trail interpretive panel, "An Unexpected Windfall," is southwest of Genoa 7.5 miles on the north side of State 22 near where it crosses Council Creek. The panel faces the river and a Pawnee mission site and tells about the 1847 Mormon pioneers coming upon an abandoned Presbyterian mission to the Pawnee, located where Council Creek (referred to as Plum Creek by Mormon diarists) empties into the

Loup Fork River. The mission site is located on private property west of the sign, in the woods along Council Creek. A **historical marker,** "Genoa: 1857–1859," telling about Mormons in Genoa, is in the **Genoa Park** near the edge of town.

Wagon wheel ruts near Genoa are still visible 1 mile east and 1.2 miles south of the junction of Highways 22 and 39.

In the fall of 1859, the Mormon colony was told to abandon Genoa when the settlement became part of the small, newly created Pawnee Reservation. Genoa served as the **Pawnee Indian Agency** until 1876, when the Pawnee were removed to the Indian Territory and the reservation lands offered for sale. When Mormons were forced to leave Genoa in the fall of 1859, some moved their cabins east near **Looking Glass Creek,** and their community was known as **Zig-Zag.** Others went to Columbus, where **Henry Hudson** was the long-time leader of the branch (CJ,c).

The **Genoa U.S. Indian School** operated in Genoa from 1884 to 1934. Genoa was selected as the site because the federal government already owned the Pawnee reservation property there. The school's purpose was to educate Native American children and teach them Christianity. Students from 10 states and 20 tribes attended there, and in time the school grew from the original 74 students to nearly 600 and encompassed more than 30 buildings and 640 acres. The school's **Manual Training Building** survives, was recently restored, and is now **a museum** containing exhibits about life at the school.

In 1990 and 1995 the remains of almost 1,000 Pawnee and their relatives were reinterred in Genoa after having been held in museums and other locations. A **stone marker for the Pawnee graves** is located at the east end of the Valley View Cemetery south of Genoa on the former campsite of the Pawnee.

■ ***PAWNEE MISSIONARY STATION CAMP • BRIGHAM YOUNG • THUR. APR. 22 • 17 MILES • FULLERTON**

The Pawnee Missionary Station Camp was located 4.5 miles northeast of the center of **Fullerton.** It was on Plum Creek, .25 mile south of Highway 22, and is identified as Merchiston on some maps (JES; JAL).

On Apr. 22, 1847, **Brigham Young's company** traveled 2 miles, crossed Looking Glass Creek, traveled another 15 miles, and camped at the **Pawnee Missionary Station on Plum Creek.** This is where **Bishop George Miller's blended company in 1846** stopped and then went north to winter among the Ponca on the Niobrara River (see **The 1846 Ponca Encampment**). Amasa Lyman said the campsite in 1847 was "beautifully located" and that Plum Creek was lined with "cotton wood, elm, coffee nut, burr oak, ash willow" (JAL).

While on the way to Plum Creek, the 1847 Brigham Young company stopped at Beaver Creek, near the future Mormon town of Genoa. When they arrived at the **Pawnee Missionary Station,** they found Plum Creek running through several log buildings that had been deserted in the fall of 1846. The station, established in 1838, had been run by Rev. J. Dunbar. Cattle feed, scrap iron, and plows at the station were useful to the Saints. A government station .25 mile south had been burned by the Sioux, but not the missionary station. Brother **A. James Case,** in the 1847 company, had worked as a farmer at the government station for seven years and converted to Mormonism while there (MVB 111–12).

■ ****LOUP RIVER FORD AND CAMP • BRIGHAM YOUNG • FRI. APR. 23 • 4.25 MILES • FULLERTON**

Loup River Ford and Camp was 1 mile southeast of the current hospital in the center of Fullerton on the banks of Loup Fork of the Platte River (JWC; JES; JWW).

The more famous **Loup Ford and Ferry** was later established 4 miles downriver, northeast of this camp and ford, and 1 mile directly south of the Pawnee Missionary Station. Over the years, the Mormons used many fording sites above and below the fording site used by the 1847 pioneer company. The "Big Company" that followed the 1847 Brigham Young company, for example, crossed the Loup about 13 or 14 miles west of today's Fullerton, north of present-day Palmer, near an earlier Pawnee village (CJ,c).

Loup Fork Ferry .5 mile south of the Pawnee Missionary Station, NE, was used after the 1847 pioneers passed this way. (Steel engraving by Frederick Piercy, 1853)

The 1847 pioneers traveled only 4.25 miles from their previous camp at the Pawnee Missionary Station on Plum Creek before they camped at their ferry crossing of Loup Fork. (They had crossed Cedar Creek 2 miles earlier.) They managed to get four wagons across the Loup Fork, but quicksand, deep waters, and swift current almost caused a disaster, so they decided to move upstream .25 mile. At that point they camped, ready to cross the next day.

On July 26, 1856, the **Ellsworth handcart company,** the Church's first handcart company, was detained at Loup Fork, where they were caught in "a most terrific storm of thunder and lightning." In open prairie without tents, "two brothers and two sisters were knocked down by lightning," the camp journal says. "Brother Henry Walker from Carlisle was killed. Age fifty-eight." They buried him the next morning 4 miles west of the Loup Fork Ferry "on a sandy rise, right hand side of the road" (HCZ 204).

■ ****PONCA WINTER CAMP • NIOBRARA**

The general site of Ft. Ponca is reached by driving west from the town of Niobrara 2 miles on State 12 (across Niobrara River and Mormon Canal). At a point .25 mile west of Mormon Canal, turn south on a gravel road and go about .25 mile. A **monument honoring Newel Knight** and others is on the left (east) side of the road. The Ponca Winter Camp was located west of the monument, but the exact site is undetermined. (See **Ponca Site and Newel Knight Memorial,** above.)

■ **LOUP SABBATH CAMP • BRIGHAM YOUNG • SAT.–SUN. APR. 24–25 • 4 MILES • FULLERTON**

The Loup Sabbath Camp was located on the south side of Loup Fork River, 4 miles southwest of Loup Ford, or 4.5 miles southwest of the center of today's Fullerton (JWW; JTB; MVB 112; JWC).

Loup Fork was about 400 yards wide and very shallow—three feet at the deepest point—with a bottom that was mostly quicksand.

Fording Loup Fork of the Platte River. (Courtesy of Vernon Murdock, artist, 1973)

Brigham Young's company built 2 rafts the

morning of Apr. 24 and began crossing their greatest obstacle to date—the Loup Fork of the Platte River. The *Revenue Cutter* boat was used to carry goods so the wagons would be lighter. **Tarlton Lewis** and **Thomas Woolsey** superintended the building of two log rafts, but at a place just above where the ferry was operating, some of the brethren hitched two teams onto the loaded wagons and with more horsepower dragged the wagons across. Most crossed this way, and by 3 P.M. all were on the south side of the river without mishap.

After safely crossing "the Loup," the company traveled west for 4 miles along the south side of Loup Fork and then camped by a small lake along the river. They readied the cannon, because during the previous night they had had to fire guns to scare off a handful of Indians who were creeping in the darkness to steal their horses.

Apr. 25 was a **Sunday,** and to honor the Sabbath the company remained in camp for the day. Wilford Woodruff said that "the order of the Camp is that there be no fishing, Hunting or labour of any kind on Sunday except such as is actually necessary" (JWW 159). Thomas Bullock said they observed the Sabbath

> as a day of rest, for meditation, prayer & praise. All was harmony, peace, & love, and an holy stillness prevailed throughout the day—the principal sounds heard, were the tinkling of the cow Belles, & the screams of Wild Geese as they flew past our camp—the Sky was beautiful with a South Wind. about 5 P.M. The brethren were called together to worship the Supreme, when Prest. Young called on the Choir to sing "This land was once a garden place" followed by H.C. Kimball making prayer to our Heavenly Father; several of the brethren then spoke their feelings, & while G.A. Smith was relating the Prophet Joseph's instructions, not to kill any of the animals or birds, or anything created by Almighty God that had life, for the sake of destroying it. (JTB 132)

William Clayton recorded:

> Afternoon **Elijah Newman** was baptized by Tarlton Lewis in the lake for the benefit of his health. Brother Newman has been afflicted with the black scurvy in his legs and has not been able to walk without sticks, but after being baptized and hands

> laid on him he returned to his wagon without any kind of help seemingly much better. (JWC 103; emphasis added)

Amasa Lyman said that he and two others "took good wash and swim in the Loup." Another man rode his horse into the river and sank in sand, losing his rifle worth 10 or 12 dollars (JAL).

During the day the brethren saw their first antelope and elk.

A **Mormon Pioneer Camp marker** is located 2.5 miles southwest of the center of Fullerton, across the Loup River and west of State 14 in a roadside parking area. It tells about the 1847 Brigham Young company and says that other Mormon companies followed, "many of them camping at or near this spot."

Travelers today who follow the Mormon Trail route going west will probably want to take State 14 south from Fullerton to U.S. 30 and I-80 to continue west. The Mormon Trail itself headed south from the Loup Fork toward the Platte.

■ Small Creek Camp • Brigham Young • Mon. Apr. 26 • 14 miles • Palmer

At 3 A.M. on Apr. 26, while at the Loup Sabbath Camp, James Craig sounded the bugle as Indians tried to sneak into camp. The guards fired and scared them off as all the men prepared their arms for protection. The Indians later returned to Small Creek Camp and ran off with two horses. Some of the brethren went in pursuit of the horses, without success (JWC; JAL). This day the company traveled 14 miles and encamped on the east side of a small creek with a gravel bottom, probably Elk Creek. The camp was about 3.5 miles east-northeast of the center of Palmer (CJ,c). Thomas Bullock said they were "making **an entire new road,**" instead of using the existing roads they had been following (JTB 133).

■ *Prairie Creek Crossing & Camp • Brigham Young • Tue. Apr 27 • 15 miles • Chapman

On Apr. 27, the company left the Loup Fork River and turned directly south towards the Platte. The prairie was dry and dusty. They saw rattlesnakes, Native Americans, and antelope. On this day they killed their first antelope. As they moved south they made a new road. During the day four brethren were shot at as they were looking for their stolen horses. In the evening they camped on the north side of **Prairie Creek** after a hot, dusty 15 miles (JWC; MVB 118; JTB). This location was about 6 miles northwest of Chapman.

Ten years later, it was at Prairie Creek on Aug. 25, 1856, that **Almon W. Babbitt's** advance wagon train was attacked by Cheyenne. He was secretary of the Utah Territory and was returning to Utah with four wagons loaded with territorial supplies. A. Nichols and another man were killed; Orrin Parrish and another man, who was wounded, escaped. A mother, Mrs. Wilson, was wounded and carried away captive and her child was found with its skull crushed. Col. Babbitt was not with the train at the time but later (Sept. 7) was attacked and killed by the same band of Cheyenne near **Ash Hollow,** Nebraska (CHC 4:213–14; OPH 11:553–54; HOUW 1:553–54).

On Sept. 11, 1856, the **Martin handcart company** passed the graves of the two men and a child who had been in Babbitt's wagon train. Handcart member **John Jacques** said the site was 8 or 9 miles before they reached the Wood River (EJWM 108–9).

■ Mormon Trail Wayside Park and Marker • Central City

At the junction of U.S. 30 and State 92, which is 6 miles northeast of Central City is the **Mormon Trail Wayside Park and marker** on the south side of U.S. 30. This marker is located approximately where a later trail from Columbus intersects the 1847 Brigham Young route from Genoa. In the small park is a **historical marker,** "The Mormon Trail." It says that the Mormon pioneers traveled the trail about 1 mile to the south, and explains why they chose to follow the north side of the Platte. It notes that "the trail became one of the great roadways to the west, used by Mormons, military expeditions, gold seekers and settlers," and that the Union Pacific 1869 route and then the Lincoln Highway (Highway 30) in the early 20th century followed that roadway, too (HSM 74–75).

● Lone Tree Marker • Central City

The trail of the **1847 Brigham Young company** led across the quicksand of the Loup River and a few miles west of the **Lone Tree,** a giant, solitary cottonwood that stood on the north side of the Platte River some 2.5 miles southwest of present-day Central City. The **Lone Tree historical marker** is 10 miles west of the Mormon

Trail Wayside Park and is located at the western end of Central City.

The massive tree was a noted Platte River landmark as early as 1833. Ten to twelve feet in circumference, the tree's total height was about fifty feet; its lowest branches were about twenty feet above the ground. Because the prairie lacked trees, this one was visible to travelers 20 miles away. Although it stood only 80 rods away from the smaller trees and brush on the Platte River, from a distance it seemed alone in a treeless region. The **Mormon Trail** passed by Lone Tree, as did the Omaha–Ft. Kearny stage route.

The tree also gave its name to a stage station and a town, later renamed Central City. Lone Tree Ranch was established in 1858 at a little distance from the tree. Later the post office there and the Union Pacific station 3 miles away each bore its name.

Passing travelers often camped beneath Lone Tree and carved their initials on its trunk. This probably hastened its end, for the tree was dead by 1863. A severe storm in 1865 brought it down. Part of its trunk was taken to Lone Tree station, now called Central City. Here it stood on the depot platform until it was nearly all carried away in fragments by tourists.

In 1911 residents of Merrick County erected a 10-foot-tall granite monument in the likeness of a cottonwood stump on the site once occupied by the tree (HSN). From the Lone Tree historical marker on U.S. 30 in Central City, the **stone tree-trunk monument** is 2 miles south and .5 mile southwest. It is reached by going due south 2 miles on the dirt road by the historical marker (Lone Tree Road, also called 15th Road or Co. 29). The monument is on the left just beyond where that dirt road turns to the right. It is inscribed, "On this spot stood the original Lone Tree on the old California Trail" (HSM 75–76).

In 1856, **John Jacques,** in the Martin handcart company, mentioned being near Lone Tree on Sept. 11 (EJWM 11). A 15-year-old girl, **Lucy Canfield,** said in her diary entry for Aug. 10 that her company (her father, Isaac Canfield, was the captain) "camped at Lone Tree, pleasant place" (OPH 6:27–30).

■ **Grand Island Camp • Brigham Young • Wed. Apr. 28 • 15 miles • Grand Island

On Apr. 28, 1847, **Brigham Young's company** spent an hour making a road to cross Prairie Creek and then traveled south about

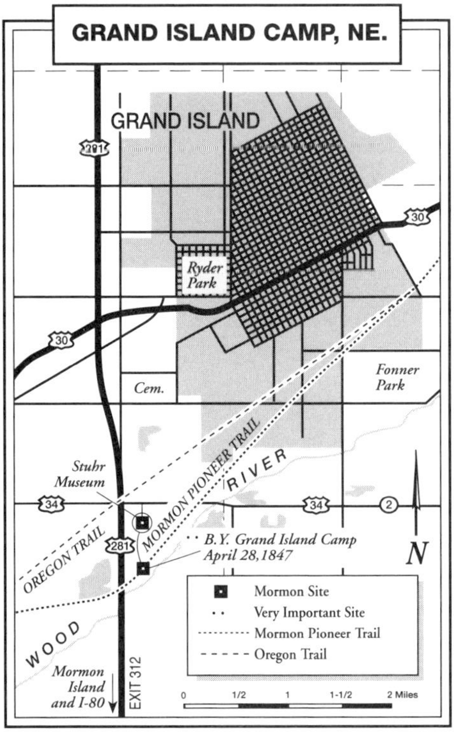

7 miles from the Prairie Creek Camp to a point northeast of Grand Island, where they had lunch. Then they traveled southwest along the Wood and Platte Rivers another 8 miles for a total of 15 miles for the day. The pioneers camped on Wood River near the present-day city of **Grand Island** (settled in 1856). The camp was located on Wood River, 4 miles north of the I-80 Grand Island-Hastings exit 312, south of Grand Island, which exit is located on "Mormon Island." The camp was .25 mile south of the main building of **Stuhr Museum** (see Grand Island Camp, NE, map) (JWC; JWW).

During the day **Luke Johnson** shot a rattlesnake 4 feet long and used oil from the snake to rub on Zebedee Coltrin's blackleg, which oil did a great deal of good (JTB).

The **Platte River,** being broad and shallow, creates numerous islands. One of the largest was **Grand Island.** It was located just south of the city of Grand Island and was about 45 miles long and 2 miles wide. It extended upriver (westerly) from today's Grand Island more than halfway to today's city of Kearney, and downriver 12 miles. **Ft. Kearny** was located near the head of the island. Two channels of the Platte River created the island. No topographical maps were made during the trail era showing the island's length and breadth. "Whatever is left of Grand Island today has been fragmented by new channeling" (GPRR 194).

Mormon Island Recreation Area is located on **Mormon Island,** about 7 miles south of the center of Grand Island City on the northeast side of the I-80 Grand Island-Hastings turnoff, Exit 312. It is a landscaped park with camping, swimming, and fishing on a lake. **A marker** on Mormon Island notes that several Mormon families stayed here briefly in the 1880s during their journey to Utah because of available wood and water.

■ Stuhr Museum of the Prairie Pioneer • Grand Island

The Stuhr Museum complex at Grand Island is reached from I-80 by taking Exit 312 and going north 4.5 miles on U.S. 281 to the junction of U.S. 34 and U.S. 281. The Grand Island Camp was barely south of this museum complex, or perhaps within the museum grounds.

The main building is the Stuhr Building, which has many indoor exhibits of period rooms, tools, and household articles and furnishings to introduce visitors to Nebraska's history from 1860 to 1920. The Fonner Rotunda houses noted collections of Native American and Old West memorabilia that present the contrasting cultures of the Plains Indians and the early western settlers. A complex of eight structures, the 1860s Log Cabin Settlement interprets the 1850s-60s "road ranches" that were built along the pioneer trails and served travelers heading west. There were once eleven road ranches in Hall County. They were located along the emigrant roads of the Platte Valley and were places where travelers could pause to buy provisions and make repairs on equipment.

Other outdoor exhibits include a reconstructed Pawnee earth lodge and teepees, buffalo grazing on the prairie, and Railroad Town, an 1890s re-created prairie community that tells the story of Nebraska town development in the late 19th century. In it are 60 old shops, homes, and outbuildings moved to the site and restored. One is the Grand Island house where actor Henry Fonda (1905–82) was born. Railroad Town has been the location for several films, including *My Antonia, Adventures of the Old West,* and *Sarah, Plain and Tall.*

A **historical marker,** "The Mormon Trail," is located on the museum grounds. Erected by the Hall County Historical Society and the Nebraska State Historical Society, it gives readers a good summary of the Mormon emigration story as it related to the Platte River Valley:

> Religious freedom, an American ideal, has on occasion been denied certain sects because of prejudice. Mormons were

once persecuted and forced from their homes. The north bank of the Platte River served as the exodus route for thousands of members of the Church of Jesus Christ of Latter-day Saints (Mormons). Driven from Nauvoo, Illinois, Mormon leader Brigham Young led the first migration up this valley in 1847 to found the proposed state of Deseret, now Utah.

During the following two decades, thousands more gathered at Winter Quarters on the west bank of the Missouri River near present-day Florence, Nebraska, before beginning the trek across the plains and mountains to their land of Milk and Honey. The journey called for strength and courage, as well as faith, for tragedy often stalked their wagons and handcarts, turning this valley into a Mormon "trail of tears." Hundreds of pioneers lie buried along this trail, most in unmarked graves.

After 1860 the overland trail along the south bank of the river was lined with road ranches and stage stations, but the Mormon Trail had few such conveniences, and the pioneer settlements here in Hall County were almost the last vestiges of civilization until the travelers reached Utah.

• Aurora

Aurora is approximately 18 miles east-southeast of Grand Island. It is on U.S. 34 and is reached from I-80 by way of Exit 332 and going north 3.5 miles on State 14.

Established in 1871, Aurora sits where the **Nebraska City Cut-off** once passed, along which freight wagons hauled tons of freight from Nebraska City to the Ft. Kearny area. The cut-off replaced the Ox-Bow route, starting about 1860. **Mormon wagon trains** that outfitted at **Wyoming, Nebraska,** in 1864–1866 followed this cut-off.

The **Plainsman Museum,** at 210 16th Street in Aurora, gives attention to the Nebraska City Cut-off. Inside the museum's impressive rotunda are eight heroic-sized murals illustrating key events in the region's history. One mural depicts the Deepwell Ranch, which was a popular stopping place for freighters and travelers on the trail because of its deep well that never failed in its supply of pure water. Mormon companies probably watered there.

• Nebraska City–Ft. Kearny Cut-off Marker • York

About 20 miles east from Aurora on I-80 is the York I-80 rest area. Both the east and west rest areas have markers entitled

"Nebraska City–Ft. Kearny Cut-Off," which tells about the heavy freight traffic on that route, including supplies for the Utah War ("Mormon War") "which passed near this point."

● **WILLA CATHER HOME AND MEMORIAL • RED CLOUD**

The Willa Cather Pioneer Memorial is in Red Cloud, directly south of Grand Island. Red Cloud is reached from I-80 by taking the Grand Island/Hastings exit (Exit 312) and driving south 60 miles on U.S. 281. Red Cloud is 6 miles north of the Kansas border and 18 miles from the geographic center of the continental United States. The Cather Memorial is located at 413 N. Webster, Red Cloud's main north-south street (U.S. 281). A Pulitzer Prize-winning author, **Willa Sibert Cather** (1873–1947) spent her formative years in Red Cloud. Her best-known novels are *My Antonia* and *Death Comes to the Archbishop.* Many of the scenes and characters in her writings are based on the people, streets, and landscapes she encountered in Red Cloud in her youth. Visitors can see eight period structures that influenced her writing, including her childhood home and the Pavelka Farmstead, home of Annie Pavelka, the basis for the title character in *My Antonia.*

■ ***WOOD RIVER CROSSING • ALDA**

On Apr. 29, 1847, the **1847 Mormon pioneers** traveled southwest parallel to Grand Island and the Platte River. The **pioneers crossed the Wood River** 5 miles from the Grand Island Camp and 8 miles southwest of the center of Grand Island City. This crossing was identified by an 1846 Mitchell's Map the company carried. Erastus Snow described the river as "a beautiful stream with a gravel bottom, slightly scattered with timber as far as we have followed its course today, parallel with Grand Island, which is said to extend seventy-five miles" (JES). Amasa Lyman said the trees along the Wood River were "cottonwood, elm, white ash, willow, Plum trees, &c., the latter in blossom" (JAL).

Wood River Crossing became a noted camping spot for later pioneers and a supply depot for emigrants.

In June 1862 five wagon loads of flour were taken from Florence, Nebraska, to Wood River Crossing for the use of emigrants who were traveling west over the trail (AJB June 12, 1862). A town on U.S. 30 located 7 miles southwest of the Crossing is named Wood River.

■ **MURDOCK-MORMON TRAIL RUTS • ALDA

Three-quarters of a mile southwest of Wood River Crossing, is a prominent wide and shallow trail swale (indentation) made on the Mormon Trail (Military Road) when travelers were funneled onto a narrow ridge that separated the winding Wood River from the wetlands of the Platte River. It is located 1.5 miles south of State 30 at Alda, and 3.3 miles north of I-80 at Exit 305 on Link 40C. From Exit 305, go north 1 mile, east 1 mile, and then north 2 miles to where Guenther Road, a gravel road, intersects with Link 40C. The site is on the northwest corner of that intersection, on 2.5 acres of public land (Sec. 23 T59N R27W). It is 1 mile southwest of the Wood River Crossing.

A **granite marker** is located on the trail at the east end of the 2.5 acre site. The marker, placed there in 1923 by the Hall County Historical Society, specifies the trail swale as "The Old California Overland Trail." On the top of this marker is an arrow pointing down the path of the swale. The swale is from decades of wagon wheels, plodding livestock, and pioneers on foot. They have survived because the small patch of ground between the modern road and the Wood River was too small to cultivate. The site was bought and saved by the Hall County Historical Society in 1996.

An NPS/NMTA Mormon Trail interpretive panel, "Decades of Wagon Wheels," is located on the south side of the property at the pedestrian entrance. It tells about visible swales, or depressions, seen ahead of the panel, worn by wagon wheels, livestock, and pioneers on foot from the 1840s through 1860s. After the Mormon pioneers passed here in 1847, hundreds of wagon trains did too, bound for Utah, California, and Oregon. A row of small white wooden telegraph poles runs along the ruts.

■ WOOD RIVER CAMP • BRIGHAM YOUNG • THURS. APR. 29 • 19 MILES • SHELTON

Wood River Camp of the Mormon pioneers. (Steel engraving by Frederick Piercy, 1853)

Brigham Young's company left their Grand Island Camp on Apr. 29, crossed at the **Wood River Crossing,** and continued on, traveling a total of 19 miles before they camped on the banks of the

Platte River, 2 miles southeast of the town of Shelton (MVB 120; JWC; JTB).

■ Wood River Center (Shelton) • Mormon Settlement Site

During the overland trail period, **Wood River Center** was where the small town of Shelton now is, 25 miles west of Grand Island on U.S. 30 and about 4 miles north of I-80.

One of the first settlers was **Joseph Ellis Johnson,** a Mormon who had earlier published a newspaper in Council Bluffs. In 1858 he settled on a bend of the Wood River. He was soon surrounded by several others. These men established ranches and raised vegetables and other crops, for which trail traffic and Ft. Kearny, 15 miles to the west, provided a market. Johnson said that he "imported and planted many varieties of fruit trees, vegetables, grain and seeds, surveyed a level farm of 1,000 acres" and "commenced to fence and open fields." There, he "prepared for a career of horticultural labor and experiment." Buffalo County histories credit Johnson for being the first to demonstrate the adaptability of the local soil to crop-raising purposes. He also helped establish a post office at Wood River Center (HTW 10:198) and published the ***Huntsman's Echo*** **newspaper** for two years. In 1860 he was elected to the Nebraska Legislature. In August 1861 he and his family left for Utah. Once the Union Pacific tracks came through the county, the trading and stage ranches gave way to farming and stock-raising.

The ***Huntsman's Echo*** was undoubtedly the first newspaper published west of the Missouri River towns. Johnson was a fluent writer and pointed out in glowing terms the beauties and advantages of this country, and his reports doubtless did much toward the settlement of the country in after years. The paper's motto was "Independent in Everything—Neutral in Nothing." The *Echo* carried articles about the revelations of Joseph Smith, including the Civil War prophecy, and frequent notices concerning people traveling to and from Utah. The last issue was published Aug. 1, 1861.

A state **historical marker** honoring "Joseph E. Johnson and the *Huntsman's Echo*" is in Shelton's Railroad Park, where Main Street and U.S. 30 intersect. The marker tells about Johnson's newspaper but also notes that his "ranche" was an important supply point "serving Mormons and other travelers on the Council Bluffs Road (Mormon Trail)." It included "a general store, blacksmith shop, post office, mill and a farm that grew crops and vegetables." **An**

NPS/NMTA generic Mormon Trail panel is also located in this park.

In Shelton, the area that was Johnson's Gardens straddles U.S. 30, within a nearly rectangular area bounded by North B Street (west side) and North C Street (east side) and by West 1st Street (north) and the Union Pacific Railroad tracks (south) (MTN 20).

A Nebraska historical marker, "Original Townsite of Wood River," is located 4 miles east of today's Wood River on U.S. 30. It says that "between 1844 and 1866 thousands of emigrants, gold seekers, and Mormons moved west through the Platte Valley" and notes that "the first settlers along Wood River 1858–60" included "Mormon, Joseph E. Johnson." They operated road ranches to serve travelers. Johnson's "Ranche," it says, was known then as "Wood River Center" and was where Shelton now is. The text then explains the founding by 1866 of what is still the town of Wood River.

Wood River Center as Mormon Emigration Station. Between 1858 and 1863, Wood River Center became a general stopping and resting place for Mormon emigrants heading west. In the **1857 Christiansen handcart company, Anna Marie Sorensen** gave birth in July at Wood River. "I remember a certain sister who came up one morning when the tents were being packed up, with something in her apron," a sub-captain wrote; "Upon inspection it proved to be a little person who had come into the world the previous evening. The mother had walked with her handcart all day the previous day" (BZ 186). Wood River Center was the fourth and last **flour storage station** where the 1861 **LDS "down and back" companies** (eastbound) deposited flour to be picked up and used during the return trip. According to **1861 LDS emigrant Bartlett Tripp,** Wood River Center was "a large ranch . . . at which considerable is done—printing office, blacksmith shop, store, etc., a number of settlers in the vicinity—houses all in backwoodsman style but cheering to the traveller" (DBWT 27). Another LDS traveler that year, F. W. Blake, said that "Wood River Centre" was also known as "Johnson's Ranch" (FWBJ July 22, 1861).

The Oliver Family. Local histories say that in 1860 a broken front axle of the wagon owned by the **Edward Oliver Sr. family** caused the family, converts heading for Utah, to stop at Wood River Center for repairs. The family included seven children, one of whom was married. Dropping out of their wagon company, they hauled the broken wagon to the Joseph E. Johnson ranch, which did blacksmithing.

Repaired with green wood, the wagon soon broke down again, so the Oliver family returned to Wood River Center. They decided to stay for the winter and built a log hut with a sod and dirt roof at a point about 1 mile west of Wood River Center, on the banks of Wood River. The father, Edward Oliver Sr., continued to Salt Lake City in the spring, but his wife and children declined to go with him. He kept in contact with them and encouraged his wife to join him in Utah. He had a second wife in Utah and a large family there. (His letters to Sarah, the first wife, are in the Buffalo County Historical Society in Kearney.) Meanwhile, **Sarah Oliver** took care of the family in Nebraska and proved to be a woman of energy. The family raised corn and vegetables and sold them to the emigrants on the trail and to Ft. Kearny, 15 to 20 miles to the west. She helped many travelers. One of her sons became the first sheriff of Buffalo County, another the first assessor, and a third a member of the first board of county commissioners and later county treasurer. Sarah Oliver died in 1871. Many of her descendants still live in the vicinity of Shelton (OFS).

● Harold Warp's Pioneer Village • Minden

The **Pioneer Village** museum is located at Minden on U.S. 6, 12.5 miles south of I-80. At 34 miles west of Grand Island, take Exit 279 onto State 10 and travel south. The complex contains 28 buildings on 20 acres, housing over 50,000 historical objects. Around a circular green are 12 historic buildings that include a frontier fort, Pony Express station, and sod home. A general store and toy store contain goods from yesteryear. More than 500 antique vehicles are displayed. ($)

■ City of Kearney

Kearney is located exactly halfway between Boston and San Francisco. It is less than 1 mile north of I-80 via Exit 272 and 186 miles west-southwest of Omaha. Its population in 2003 was 28,211. Kearney derives its name from nearby **Ft. Kearny,** 9 miles to the southeast, but due to a postal error, an "e" was inadvertently added and then never changed. Settlement began in Kearney the summer of 1871, the year Ft. Kearny was abandoned.

A Mormon historical marker is located in Kearney at the Centennial Park on Eleventh Street.

● GREAT PLATTE RIVER ROAD ARCHWAY MONUMENT • KEARNEY

Midway across southern Nebraska, the structurally unique **Great Platte River Road Archway Monument** museum is housed in a large arch that spans I-80. It is located at 3060 East 1st Street in Kearney and reached by taking Exit 272 north from I-80 (State 44, or 2nd Ave.), turning east on Talmage Road to Central Avenue, turning right (south) to Arches Parkway, and then left to the Monument. This "interactive experience" pays tribute to the pioneers who passed through this region of Nebraska on their way west by covered wagon, handcart, and train. It showcases Native American tribes; trappers and traders making their way to annual rendezvous; the Oregon, California, and **Mormon Trail;** stagecoach drivers and their passengers; Pony Express riders; the telegraph; and homesteaders. It presents the transportation story up to the Lincoln Highway, the interstate highways, and even fiber-optic networks linking the nation. The archway's promotional literature bills it as "a state-of-the-art immersive experience over two levels of the 11-story-high, football-field-long Archway spanning I-80."

An **NPS/NMTA Mormon Trail interpretive panel,** "Buffalo—At Last," is scheduled (2005) to be installed in the Archway complex. The panel notes that on May 1, the 1847 pioneers sighted buffalo,

Aerial view of the Great Platte River Road Archway Monument in Kearney, NE. Photo by J. Nabb. Courtesy GPRRAM.

through telescopes, on bluffs west of present-day Kearney. Hunters brought fresh meat to camp, and the company by then was relying on "buffalo chips" for fuel (see **Buffalo Hunt Camp**).

■ *FT. KEARNY CAMP • BRIGHAM YOUNG • FRI. APR. 30 • 17 MILES • KEARNEY

Ft. Kearny Camp was about 4 miles east of the center of present-day Kearney. It was about 4 miles north of the future New Ft. Kearny, which would be built in 1848.

On Apr. 30, 1847, **Brigham Young, Heber C. Kimball** and **Amasa Lyman** rode ahead of the pioneer company to check on the best route along the "Old Trail." The rest followed them for 17 miles along the Platte River and camped under a bluff without wood or water, a good mile from the river (JAL; JWW; JES; JOP). They dug three four-foot-deep wells and procured dark-colored

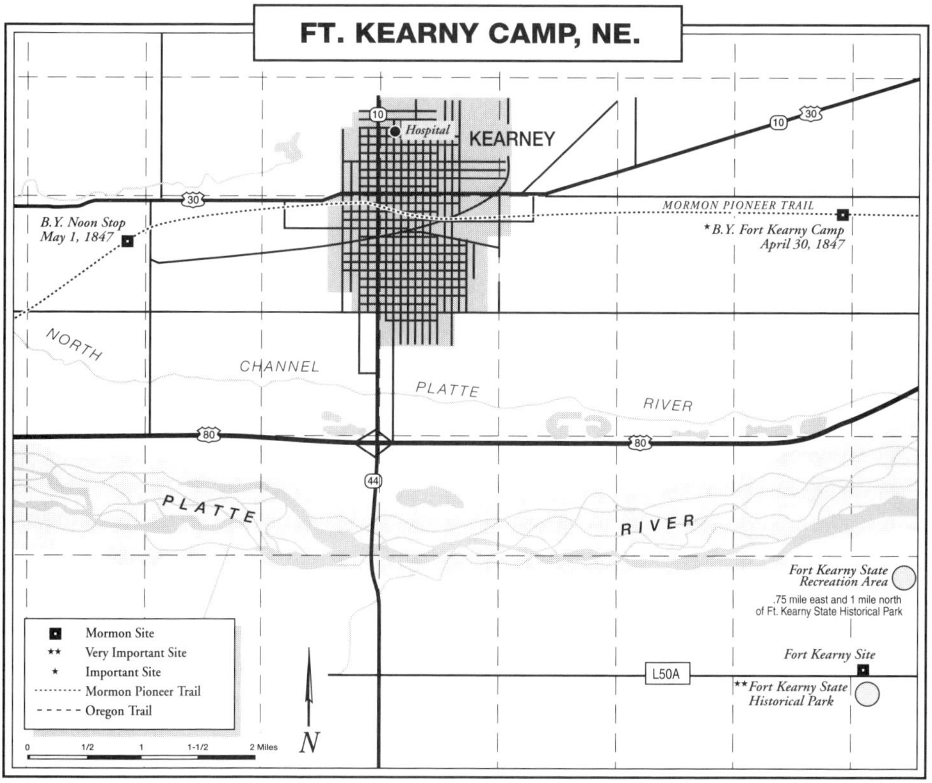

water for the cattle. Thomas Bullock recorded that "Prest. Young gave liberty for the brethren to have a dance & enjoy themselves, as they had neither wood to warm, nor good water to drink" (JTB 137). Orson Pratt recorded the temperature at 41 degrees. Amasa Lyman wrote, "My fingers are so cold I can hardly write" (JAL).

For the first time, the company used **buffalo dung (buffalo chips) for fuel.** They experimented with ways to burn the buffalo chips in pits or holes. **Luke Johnson** "used a buffalo skull for a chimney on his fire, creating some amusement in camp at the sight of smoke puffing out the horns" (DTZ 59). LDS teenager Sarah Southworth, in the 1852 John B. Walker company, recalled that

> we gathered dried dung and buffalo chips to make a fire to cook our food, dug a hole in the ground, put the skillet in the hole with a tight lid on it, put the buffalo chip on the lid, and set it afire. It baked the bread fine. That was the way we did our baking until we got where there was wood again. (SBR 28)

In 1850, as **Wilford Woodruff's company** of 1850 passed opposite Ft. Kearny north of the Platte River on July 15, **William Ridge** was struck by lightning and instantly killed. Three of his cattle were killed at the same time, and one of his children slightly injured (JSG; JWW).

■ **Ft. Kearny State Historical Park • Kearney

Ft. Kearny State Historical Park is located 4 miles south of the center of Kearney on State 44 and then 4 miles east on L50A. It is the actual site of the **New Ft. Kearny** of the overland trails period. That post was established in 1848 and functioned until 1871. It was one of the most important military posts in the West.

Gen. Stephen Watts Kearny founded the first Ft. Kearny **(Old Ft. Kearny)** in 1846 by the Missouri River where **Nebraska City** now is. In June 1847 the War Department directed that a better location be found near Grand Island, 197 miles to the west. A site was selected near the head of Grand Island, upriver from where the Oregon Trail routes across Kansas reached the Platte. A request for money, materials, and labor advocated the employment of Mormons located by the Missouri River, but such did not happen (HFK). The fort was built in 1848. Kearny died that October, and the War Department named the new fort in his honor.

Mormons had a direct connection with Gen. Kearny. The **Mormon Battalion** in the Mexican War, commanded by Lt. Col. Philip St. George Cooke, was attached to **Gen. Kearny's Army of the West** for its California campaign. When Gen. Kearny returned from that campaign, he chose 15 men of the Mormon Battalion to be his bodyguards from California to Ft. Leavenworth, and 13 finished the trip with him. He and they escorted **Lt. Col. John C. Fremont** to face a court-martial. The group's route included Ft. Sutter in California, Ft. Hall in Idaho, Fort Laramie in Wyoming, and the Oregon Trail in Nebraska and Kansas. They arrived at **Ft. Leavenworth, Kansas,** on Aug. 22, 1847 (MBN 225–52; MRB-R 167). Interestingly, Nebraska has places named for both Fremont and Kearny, both of whom had Mormon bodyguards who accompanied them across half of America.

Gold rush traffic in 1849 subsequently made the fort a center of activity on the Oregon-California Trail. It was the first and only post the government established along that trail solely to protect emigrants. Jim Bridger's fort (in Wyoming) was built for emigrants, but for his profit, not their protection. Ft. Kearny marked the first important station for people who started out on the Oregon Trail. There the emigrants could receive their first news from home. The fort had a hospital, so it was a medical oasis. During most of its lifetime, the fort did not have a stockade fence, except a small one in the mid-1860s, and it lacked trees and grass.

The fort was strategically located where trails from Missouri River points such as Independence, St. Joseph, Nebraska City, and Omaha converged to form a single major route westward to Ft. Laramie, Wyoming. Its troops guarded emigrants, the Pony Express, the telegraph, and railroads in the Platte Valley. Ft. Kearny also served as an assembly and outfitting point for numerous **military expeditions** during the Indian wars of 1864–65. In 1871, two years after completion of the transcontinental railroad, the fort was discontinued as a military post.

In 1849 **Howard Egan's LDS freight company** of 27 wagons and 57 people took the Ox-Bow route from Old Ft. Kearny. Approaching New Ft. Kearny, his train passed the junction where the "St. Joseph and Independence Road" intersected its route. He noted on May 31 that "there is one continual string of wagons as far as the eye can extend, both before and behind us." Egan expected that "if the Platte River is low enough I think I shall cross over to the north side when I get above the head of Grand Island, in order to get out of the crowd, that I may have more sea room." That evening, he noted, "there is twenty-nine camps in sight, numbering from fifteen to forty wagons in a company." The Egan train stopped at Ft. Kearny at noon on June 1. That day Egan recorded facts he was learning at the fort about the heavy forty-niner traffic on the trail:

> I ascertained that there had 4131 wagons passed here up to the last of May, and there is probably about two thousand behind. It is reported that there is 2000 wagons [ahead] at the crossing of the South Fork of the Platte, waiting as the river is so high that they cannot cross. There is some of the companies selling their wagons, and packing [on horses or mules] from this place. (HEJ June 1, 1849)

During 1855 the preferred LDS emigration outfitting place on the Missouri River was **Mormon Grove, Kansas,** 4 miles west of Atchison. Between June 7 and Aug. 4, 1855, eight companies—totaling about 2,500 people and 337 wagons—left for Utah from Mormon Grove, and one company did the same in 1856. From Mormon Grove the first wagon route was the Independence–St. Joe Road across northeast Kansas to Ft. Kearny. There they crossed the Platte River to travel on the north side, on the Mormon Trail.

Between 1846 and 1866 some 41 organized LDS companies traveled on the **Ox-Bow Trail** and the **"Nebraska Cutoff"** from **Wyoming, Nebraska,** to Ft. Kearny. Ft. Kearny was a camping place and supply station for the estimated 14,448 Mormon emigrants in those companies. At Ft. Kearny the LDS companies from Wyoming, Nebraska, crossed the Platte River to join the Mormon Trail on the north side (DMT 39–41; EnH 256).

Ft. Kearny is one of the bases from which **Gen. Albert Sidney Johnston's Utah Expedition** moved against Utahns during the brief "Mormon War" in 1857 (TUD 32–34). The first installments of his forces were at Ft. Kearny in late July 1857. In the 1860s Ft. Kearny was also the site of a **Pony Express station** and a telegraph station. One of the fort's final functions was protecting workers building the Union Pacific Railroad. In 1871 Ft. Kearny was discontinued as a military post, its buildings were torn down, and the property opened for homesteading.

In 1960 the state of Nebraska began developing the site as a historical park. Visitors to the **Ft. Kearny State Historical Park** can see a split-log stockade, sod blacksmith-carpenter shop, and powder magazine. The original fort had sod and adobe buildings and two two-story blockhouses made of heavy timbers. The park's interpretive center has authentic relics from the Oregon Trail era.

■ **Ft. Kearny State Recreation Area • Kearney**

This 152-acre recreation area is .75 mile east and 1 mile north of Ft. Kearny State Historical Park. It has exceptional camping and is the site of the annual spring migration of the sandhill cranes, the world's largest gathering of the species.

● **Buffalo Skulls and Mail • Odessa**

An **NPS/NMTA Mormon Trail interpretive panel,** "Frontier Mail Carriers," is located in an I-80 rest stop for eastbound traffic on the south side of I-80 about 5 miles east of Exit 263 for Odessa. That place is about 4 miles west of the I-80 exit (272) for Kearney, but drivers going westbound on I-80 need to turn off at the Odessa exit and turn around to head eastbound to the rest stop. The panel is located west of the rest rooms. It says that about 8 miles west of that location, on May 4th, **Brigham Young's 1847 company** gave eastbound fur trader Charles Beaumont letters to carry to the Winter Quarters area. The sign says traders recommended the south side of the Platte as the better route but that Church leaders favored the north side "for the sake of those who would follow." Farther west, the panel says, pioneers wrote messages on scraps of paper for travelers who would come later and stuck them to trees, posts, and the bleached skulls of buffalo. Buffalo skulls were considered the "Bulletin of the Plains."

Referring to these skulls, **Mary Lois Walker** (Morris) of the **Joseph W. Young company** in 1853 said: "We often passed a post-office which was the skull of an ox or a buffalo white by exposure, upon which was written [messages]. . . . The news cheered us and we were glad to know that our friends were well and progressing on their journey." Her captain, Joseph W. Young, added a message (TPH 3:40).

■ **Dripping Springs on the Little Blue River • Fairbury**

Dripping Springs, a southern Nebraska site on the Oregon Trail segment running from Independence, Missouri, to Ft.

Kearny, Nebraska, is located about 160 miles southeast of the city of **Kearney.** To go there, leave I-80 at Exit 379 and drive 40 miles south on State 10 to State 136 at Franklin. Turn east on State 136 and go about 95 miles to Fairbury, and inquire for directions. Dripping Springs can also be reached by driving due south from **Schuyler** on State 15 for 79 miles.

In 1855 Mormon emigrants from Europe who had sailed to New Orleans and then to St. Louis outfitted for crossing the plains at **Mormon Grove, Kansas** (4 miles west of Atchison, Kansas). Between June 7 and Aug. 4, 1855, eight companies—totaling about 2,500 people and 337 wagons—left Mormon Grove and joined the Independence Road part of the **Oregon Trail.** They traveled northwest 240 miles to **Ft. Kearny,** where they joined the well-traveled Mormon Trail to Utah (DMT 130).

According to Fairbury local history, about 50 Mormons died of cholera on their way from Mormon Grove to Ft. Kearney and were buried in unmarked graves at Dripping Springs on Whitney Run near the Little Blue River (HJC 62). To honor these pioneers, a **historical marker** has been erected at an historic schoolhouse, which is about 8.5 miles northwest of the actual gravesite at Dripping Springs. This marker can be reached from Fairbury by going west on State 136 for 5 miles from the viaduct, turning north on 562nd Avenue for 5 miles, turning west just before the railroad track, and driving to the schoolhouse on the north side of the road. The marker was erected in 1976 due to the tireless efforts of descendants of **Jacob Foust Secrist,** who was captain of one of the wagon train companies (ENS July 1989, 20–22). Thirteen names of pioneers who died of cholera in the Secrist company, along with the death dates on the marker, are in the footnote below.[4]

---

4. 13 Jun 1855 Daniel Horrocks, a native of England.
20 Jun 1855 Thomas Morgan, age 12; born Alton, Illinois.
23 Jun 1855 Jens Poulson, age 70; Danish division.
26 Jun 1855 Mothe Marie Clemenson Christiansen, age 3.
27 Jun 1855 John Falkner, age 2; Nova Scotia.
28 Jun 1855 Johana Mauritzens; Danish division.
29 Jun 1855 Stephen Walsh; Nova Scotia.
2 Jul 1855 Jacob Foutz Secrist, age 34; captain of company.
4 Jul 1855 Martin Poulsen, age 1; Danish division.
5 Jul 1855 Mary Ann Falkner, age 37; Nova Scotia.
7 Jul 1855 Stephen Falkner, age 14; Nova Scotia.
9 Jul 1855 Burke Falkner, age 4; Novia Scotia.
10 Jul 1855 Mary or Nancy Welsh, age 50; Nova Scotia.

The actual **Dripping Springs site** itself is 3 miles northeast of Fairbury and is difficult to find without directions from local residents.

● **ROCK CREEK STATION STATE HISTORICAL PARK • FAIRBURY**

Rock Creek Station State Historical Park is 6 miles east of Fairbury. From Fairbury take the PWF Road east 4.5 miles to 573 Avenue, go 1 mile south on 573 Avenue, and turn east on 710 Road for 1.25 miles. The park visitors' center overlooks some 350 acres of prairie hilltops, timber-studded creek bottoms, rugged ravines, and deep trail ruts. These ruts, carved by many wagons that traveled the Oregon-California and Pony Express Trails, are plainly visible.

S. C. Glenn established the station in 1857. This road ranch catered to stages, freight lines, and emigrant traffic on the Oregon Trail. In 1860 Russell, Majors, and Waddell, owners of the Overland Stage Company and founders of the Pony Express, rented the east ranch and used it as a stage station as well as a Pony Express station. **James Butler (Wild Bill) Hickok,** a hired stable hand, in 1861 killed David McCanles and so began his gun-fighting career. Rock Creek Station continued as a stage station until 1867 and was developed as a Nebraska State Historical Park in 1980.

■ **BUFFALO HUNT CAMP • BRIGHAM YOUNG • SAT. MAY 1 • 16.5 MILES • ELM CREEK**

On May 1, 1847, the **original company of Mormon pioneers** traveled 16.5 miles from Ft. Kearny Camp and stopped for the night near a small lake about 1 mile above where the head of Grand Island was located. The site is in present-day Buffalo County about 3.5 miles southeast of the town of Elm Creek (JWC; JWW; JAL).

During the day the pioneers observed the **first buffalo** of the trek, nearly 200 of them, near the bluffs to the north and opposite the head of Grand Island. Most had never seen a buffalo, so they were very excited as they participated in their

Buffalo hunt in Nebraska. (Steel engraving by Frederick Piercy, 1853)

first buffalo hunt. They killed twelve, had a feast on buffalo meat, and said the meat was sweet, tender as veal, and better than beef (JWC). Each group of 10 pioneers received a quarter of a buffalo for sustenance. "Brigham Young issued an ultimatum that 'there should be no more game killed until such time as it should be needed, for it was a sin to waste life and flesh.' He was to repeat this injunction time and again warning that 'if we do slay when we do not need, we will need when we cannot slay'" (BYAM 137).

In 1851, near this location, **Jean Rio Baker** in the John Brown wagon train said on June 30 they were "much bothered with Buffalo, which are very numerous. Stragglers are apt to run in among our cattle, terrifying them very much, and it has been all the horsemen could do to prevent their doing mischief on encamping for the night" (DJRB).

■ Elm Creek Camp • Brigham Young • Sun.–Mon. May 2–3 • 2 miles • Elm Creek

The company "traveled 2 miles & camped at the mouth of a small creek [Elm Creek] as it empties into the Platte River" (JTB; JWC; JES). The camp was 2 miles southeast of the present-day small town of **Elm Creek** on U.S. 30. The pioneers remained here two days to rest their teams. They were not to hunt on the Sabbath, May 2, but all hands were employed putting up racks in order to dry the meat of buffalo they had previously killed. Thomas Bullock said:

> The Meat was cut up in strips & part dried over the fire to preserve it for future use. The hides were cut up into ropes & thongs & stretched between Stakes. The hair on the Bull's head was about a foot long & the hide about 1 inch thick. (JTB 143)

The original pioneers hunted and blacksmithed on Monday, May 3, and an exploring party was sent out to find a future camp. Norton Jacob observed that "Indians had set fires to destroy grass and drive buffalo so we could not subsist—Prairie was burned over as far as the eye can see" (MVB 124).Thomas Bullock noted that "the wind blew the ashes of the burnt grass in all directions which caused us to look like [chimney] sweeps. However, by washing, after our halt, we were enabled to discern each other again" (JTB May 5, 1847; capitalization standardized).

During the day the company's exploring party saw a war party of about 200 to 300 Native Americans. The hunters were called back to camp, and the cannon was fired about nine o'clock to give warning that the camp was prepared.

Two years later, on Aug. 5, 1849, the **Silas Richards company** of Saints camped on Elm Creek. It being the Sabbath, they held a religious meeting (JSRi).

■ *BUFFALO CREEK CAMP • BRIGHAM YOUNG • TUES. MAY 4 • 7 MILES • OVERTON

On Tuesday, May 4, **Brigham Young's company** traveled four or five abreast for protection in case of attack. After going 7 miles, they camped on a gravel-bottom creek that Heber C. Kimball named **Buffalo Creek.** The name has remained to this day. The camp was 3.75 miles southeast of present-day **Overton** (JWC; JES; JWW).

During the day the pioneers saw traders on the south side of the Platte traveling east from Ft. Laramie, Wyoming, to Council Bluffs, Iowa. French trader **Charles Beaumont** waded the 2-mile-wide river to get provisions from the Saints. Beaumont volunteered to be a mail carrier, so the pioneers sent 54 letters with him to deliver to Winter Quarters. The traders recommended the pioneers cross the Platte and travel on the south side where the Indians had not burned the grass. They said the road was better on that side and the Mormons could cross at that point because the river was only two feet deep and had a solid bottom. But, knowing they were blazing the trail for future companies of Saints, they voted. Apostle **Wilford Woodruff** noted that the consensus was to let the river separate Mormons from other emigrants to avoid quarrels over wood, grass, and water. By the time the next company came along, they believed, the grass would be improved on the north side (JWW). **Willard Richards** wrote instructions on a board for the next camp.

In 1855 the **Richard Ballantyne company** held a celebration at that site on July 24, honoring **Pioneer Day.** In the morning, before leaving their previous camp, they had given three hearty cheers for Brigham Young. Then, with flags of all sizes and shapes on poles, floral wreaths adorning their wagons, and flowers adorning the oxen, they traveled to this campsite on Buffalo Creek. Here they painted a flag on a 14-by-6-foot canvas with a star, eagle, beehive, and mottos: "O God, save Israel," "We'll never give up the ship," and "Glory to God and Brigham Young." The flag waved in the breeze on a tall pole.

They used trunks and boxes to make a table 60 or 70 yards long in the center of the wagon circle, and they covered the tables with white tablecloths. The pioneers put on their best clothes and feasted on venison, roasted and boiled buffalo, puddings, tarts, tea, and coffee, which were served to each company of ten. Elder **William Pitt** played the violin as they continued their celebration with dancing. Speeches by **Capt. Ballantyne** (future father of the Utah LDS Sunday Schools) and others, along with appropriate prayers, made this a special 24th of July celebration while in the Nebraska wilds (LDC).

■ Willie Handcart Company Cattle Loss • Overton

On Sept. 3, 1856, the **Willie handcart company** had crossed **Buffalo Creek,** about 2 miles east of Overton, and the next day they camped by a small lake (either Willow Lake, 20 miles from Buffalo Creek, or Ptah Lake, both on the south side of the road used by the 1847 Brigham Young company; neither now exists; see EmG 50–51). According to the Willie company journal, they were 265 miles from Florence. On the morning of Sept. 4, they discovered that some 30 cattle were gone, having strayed or stampeded during the night. "President Willie dispatched all the able-bodied men to search for them, and after several hours search, the brethren returned with reports of failure." Other searches were made, but the cattle were gone. So, badly hurt by the loss of dray animals, the handcart brigade resumed their trek on Sept. 8. This loss of cattle contributed to their disaster in the Wyoming snows six weeks later (EJWM 24–26).

■ Island Camp • Brigham Young • Wed. May 5 • 14 miles • Lexington

The **Brigham Young 1847 company** traveled 15 miles from the Buffalo Creek Camp and then retreated 1 mile when prairie fires, set by the Indians, threatened. The pioneers camped on an island in the Platte River, which provided wood, grass, and protection from the fires (JWC; JES; JWW). **Island Camp** was close to where State 283 goes north from I-80 to Lexington. The camp was about .5 mile southeast of the exit and 3 miles southeast of the center of

Lexington. According to clerk William Clayton, "We soon after came to a very bad slough and had to bear off to the north to find a place to cross it." He noted that "the prairie is all burned bare and the black ashes fly bad, making the brethren look more like Indians than white folks" (JWC 131–32; JOP; JES; JAL).

Heber C. Kimball and Orrin Porter Rockwell captured alive a fine buffalo bull calf, which they wanted to take to the mountains, but the calf died during the night.

About 3 miles northwest of where the pioneers camped, the town of **Lexington** later developed. It started in 1860 as a trading post named Plum Creek, 12 miles southeast of present-day Lexington, located on the south side of the Platte River on the Oregon Trail. "It was an infamous rendezvous for gamblers, thieves and hold-up men" (DTZ 71). In 1864 the **Plum Creek Massacre** took place on bluffs near the town. The massacre involved a small wagon train that Native Americans attacked on Aug. 7, 1864. They killed all eleven in the company, plundered the wagons, and then set fire to them. The Plum Creek telegraph station was destroyed. This marked the beginning of a war against the Sioux and Cheyenne that lasted for several years. Because of the railroad, Plum Creek was restarted north of the Platte River and renamed Lexington in 1889.

■ ***SPY GLASS CAMP • BRIGHAM YOUNG • THURS. MAY 6 • 15 MILES • COZAD**

Brigham Young's company traveled about 15 miles on May 6 and camped on the bank of the Platte River near some islands (JWC). This camp was about where the I-80 turnoff for Cozad, Exit 222, is now. That day **William Clayton** wrote in his journal about innumerable buffalo:

> One part of the horsemen's business today has been to drive the buffalo out of our track, judging it unsafe to risk them between the wagons and the river. . . . We have never been out of sight of herds of buffalo today, and from where we are camped, I am satisfied we can see over five thousand with the glass. The largest herd, we have yet seen is still ahead of us. The prairie looks black with them, both on this and the other side of the river. Some think we have passed fifty and some even a hundred thousand during the day, or have seen them. It is truly

> a sight wonderful to behold, and can scarcely be credited by those who have not actually seen them. (JWC 134–35)

That day Brigham Young lost a **spyglass** worth $40 while riding to drive buffalo from the wagons, but it was found the next day (JWC; JES).

Cozad and the 100th Meridian

Cozad is a small town in central Nebraska, population just over 4,000. It is 200 miles west of Omaha and 33 miles west of Kearney on U.S. 30, and less than 1 mile north of I-80 via the Cozad exit. It is close by the Platte River. Cozad lies on the 100th meridian. Government explorer Stephen H. Long, based on his western expedition in 1820, produced a map on which the semiarid area from the 100th meridian west to the Rocky Mountains is labeled the **Great American Desert,** a name it retained until after the Civil War. Today the area is called the **Great Plains.** The 100th meridian is considered the boundary between the tall grass prairie to the east and the short grass prairie to the west. Beginning in 1862 ranchers and farmers moved into the region to stake land claims. The region today is thinly settled but is one of the largest producers of beef and wheat in the world.

Soon after the transcontinental railroad reached the 100th meridian in 1866, **Robert Cozad** thought that was an ideal place for a town, built a hotel, and promoted settlement. At the 100th meridian the Platte River widened to several miles.

A historical marker terming the 100th meridian the place "Where the humid east meets the arid west" is located in Cozad one block south of the business district, along the railroad tracks. The town of Cozad has a north-south street named **Meridian Street.**

The 100th Meridian Museum in Cozad is at 206 East 8th Street. Its displays tell the story of Cozad's pioneer history and the westbound emigration that passed there, including the Mormons.

Cozad Possible Pony Express Station. A restored cabin, believed by some (doubted by others) to have been an original **Pony Express station,** once located at Willow Island west of Cozad, is now on the grounds of the **Robert Henri Museum and Historical Walkway,** 218 East 8th Street. Built in 1848 as a trading post, it was used later, some say, as a stagecoach and Pony Express station. The building was moved to this site in 1938 and is a tourist center providing informative displays about the Pony Express.

Legendary in American history, the **Pony Express** operated only from Apr. 1860 to Oct. 1861. In short, fast relays, riders carried small saddlebags *(mochila)* of mail (about 20 pounds) between Sacramento and St. Joseph, Missouri—1,966 miles—in an average of 10 days. Mail at first was $5 per ounce and later $1. Founded by the freighting firm of **Russell, Majors, and Waddell,** the company name was the **Central Overland California and Pike's Peak Express company** (C.O.C. & P.P.). The Pony Express employed between 80 and 100 riders at a time, going both directions, and used about 400 horses. Riders ranged in age from 11 to the mid-40s and had to weigh less than 125 pounds. Riders changed horses every 10 to 15 miles, and the riders changed every 75 to 100 miles. Their average speed was 10 miles per hour. Estimates are that the company had between 150 and 190 Pony Express stations located 5 to 20 miles apart. Every fifth station was a home station where riders changed. The Pony Express phased out once the transcontinental telegraph was completed on Oct. 24, 1861. Financially the Pony Express was a failure (PEx).

■ WILLOW ISLAND CAMP • BRIGHAM YOUNG • FRI. MAY 7 • 7 MILES • GOTHENBURG

On May 7, **Brigham Young's company** traveled 7 miles and camped on the bank of the Platte River near several small islands. This campsite is about .25 mile south of U.S. 30, near present-day Willow Island, and about 4 miles southeast of today's Gothenburg. **Thousands of buffalo** were seen by the pioneers, and wolves followed the buffalo to eat those who died from wounds, accident, or disease. The pioneers did not travel far this day because they spent time searching for and finding Brigham Young's spyglass (JES; JWC; MVB 130; JTB).

President Young instructed the camp to take better care of the cows: "Yesterday there was no one with the cows & they started twice to go to the Buffalo & I had to run my horse twice to bring them back, in doing which I lost a good telescope" (PCS). He "chastized" Erastus Snow, who had been in charge of the cows. Porter Rockwell and two others rode back and searched fo the valued spy glass, and found it (JWC).

■ Gothenburg Pony Express Station • Gothenburg

Gothenburg is located on U.S. 30 where it crosses State 47. It is about 1 mile north of the Platte River, about in the middle of the length of the state. Its promotion literature labels it the "Pony Express Capital of Nebraska."

A reconstructed Pony Express station has been moved (1934) to Ehmen Park at 15th Street and Lake Avenue. Possibly this was the **Machette Stage Station** that was located 4 miles east of Ft. McPherson. Built about 1859, it served as a trading post and a Pony Express and overland stage station. In Ehmen Park there is an **NPS/NMTA generic Mormon Trail panel** by the station.

■ *Bluff Camp • Brigham Young • Sat. May 8 • 11.25 miles • Brady

Brigham Young's company traveled 11.25 miles from Willow Island Camp and camped for the night of May 8, 1847, on the bank of the Platte just below where the bluff cuts off the bottoms for a short distance (JAL; JWC; JWW). This site is about 7.5 miles northwest of the center of Gothenburg, or 4.75 miles southeast of Brady between U.S. 30 and I-80.

Again the pioneers saw buffalo. In their journals they described the **buffalo herds.** Both Thomas Bullock and William Clayton referred to the buffalo as "the Lord's cattle" (JTB May 7, 1847; JWC May 8, 1847, 137). Pioneers said "the Mormon pioneer wagons are like ships adrift in a sea of buffalo"; Wilford Woodruff said it looked as though "the face of the earth was alive and moving like the waves of the sea" (JWW 3:171).

William Clayton expressed frustration over his task of recording mileage for each day's travel. He wrote in his journal on May 8:

> I have counted the revolutions of a wagon wheel to tell the exact distance we have traveled. The reason why I have taken this method which is somewhat tedious, is because there is generally a difference of two and sometimes four miles in a day's travel between my estimation and that of some others, and they have thought I underrated it. This morning I determined to take pains to know for a certainty how far we travel today. Accordingly I measured the circumference of the nigh hind wheel of one of Brother Kimball's wagons being the one I sleep in, in charge of Philo Johnson. I found the wheel 14 feet 8 inches in

circumference, not varying one eighth of an inch. I then calculated how many revolutions it would require for one mile and found it precisely 360 not varying one fraction which somewhat astonished me. I have counted the whole revolutions during the day's travel and I find it to be a little over eleven and a quarter miles,—twenty revolutions over . . . I have repeatedly suggested a plan of fixing machinery to a wagon wheel to tell the exact distance we travel in a day, and many begin to be sanguine for carrying it into effect, and I hope it will be done. (JWC 136–37)

The machinery, **an odometer,** would soon be in place, but even without it, William Clayton started a practice on this day that he continued for the whole pioneer trek. He put a small cedar post in the ground and wrote on it in pencil, "From Winter Quarters, two-hundred and ninety-five miles, May 8, '47 Camp all well. Wm. Clayton" (JWC 137).

Wilford Woodruff recorded how the pioneers improvised soap by using the Spanish soap root that Mexicans used for washing. The top of the root resembled a pineapple (JWW 172).

During the day the pioneers passed by the site of the future city of Gothenburg.

■ Brady Island Camp • Brigham Young • Sun. May 9 • 3.75 miles • Brady

The site of this camp is either on the east edge of today's small town of **Brady** or about .7 mile southeast of Brady (CJ,c). Brady is on U.S. 30 about 24 miles southeast of North Platte City.

The **Brigham Young company** traveled only about 3.75 miles on May 9, 1847. It was the Sabbath Day. They went around some of the bluffs and turned down a low, sandy bottom. They camped on a bend of the Platte River near a small island .75 mile from the main stream of the Platte (JWC; JAL; JWW; JTB). They took horses onto the island and cut down cottonwood trees for them to browse on.

The pioneers used the Sabbath Day as a day for bathing, washing, writing, and reflection. They also held a meeting. The bugle sounded and the Saints assembled around the ***Revenue Cutter*** (a portable boat), which served as "the stand." Wilford Woodruff recorded: "We had a meeting & a good one. The spirit of God rules over the camp. Peace, quietness & contentment seems to pervade almost every breast" (JWW 3:172; spelling standardized).

■ **BRADY ISLAND WEST CAMP • BRIGHAM YOUNG • MON. MAY 10 • 10 MILES • MAXWELL**

Brigham Young's company traveled 2 miles and crossed a small creek that Heber C. Kimball named **Skunk Creek (Pawnee Creek).** It was easily forded, though the ground was soft on the west side. They traveled a total of 10 miles and camped adjacent to Brady's Island. The camp was 1 mile northeast of the present-day town of Maxwell and U.S. 30. "The Bluffs on the South side are getting sharp and rugged in appearance," clerk Thomas Bullock noted, "& destitute of vegetation" (JTB 152). Bullock further recorded that he "made out a copy of the Epitome also the **laws regulating the pioneer camp,** for the benefit & comfort of the Saints who follow after. Read same to Prest. Young, who said, 'That's scripture'" (JTB 151).

William Clayton noted a lack of buffalo: "The grass evidently springs later the farther west we travel, and nature seems to have taught the wild cattle this lesson, hence their eastward progress" (JWC 142).

On this day Brigham Young asked **Orson Pratt** to give the mileage-counting apparatus serious attention. In the afternoon Pratt proposed the method of using a "double endless screw" (JOP 35) to measure distance. This "mile machine" became known as an **odometer.** One of Heber C. Kimball's wagons, driven by Philo Johnson, had rear wheels with a circumference such that 360 revolutions equaled 1 mile. Pratt suggested that a device be placed on Kimball's wagon so it could be activated by the moving of the wheel. Six rotations of the wheel would cause a screw to make one revolution. The screw then turned a wooden wheel with sixty cogs, or teeth. This wheel turned one revolution per mile. It rotated another screw that acted upon a wheel with thirty cogs, and each cog represented 1 mile. With the cogs numbered, the mileage would be determined to the accuracy of .10 mile (JOP; see also OJ Fall 1995:14–24; BYUS 37:1, 1997–98: 82–115).

Using Pratt's suggestions as a guide, **William Clayton** and **Appleton Harmon,** a mechanic, constructed the machine to measure mileage, and it was used two days later on May 12. The "mile machine" proved to be very accurate and helpful (JOP; JWW; JTB).

Before the original pioneers left this camp, they found four wolf pups in their den .25 mile from camp. They were the size of rabbits. After bringing them to camp alive, they killed them and made hats with their fur.

• Ft. McPherson National Cemetery • Maxwell

Ft. McPherson National Cemetery is located in Lincoln County, Nebraska, about 4 miles south of Maxwell on State 56A, or 2 miles south of I-80 via Exit 190. It is Nebraska's only national cemetery and one of America's most beautiful.

Built in 1863, **Ft. McPherson** once guarded the Oregon-Mormon Trail. Troops were stationed there to provide military protection during construction of the transcontinental railroad, and to protect trail emigrants. A cemetery for troops at the post was established southeast of the post and then moved southwest of it. After completion of the railroad and when trail travel decreased, the army abandoned many military posts, leaving isolated cemeteries neglected. Establishment of the 107-acre **Ft. McPherson National Cemetery** in 1873 accommodated the removal and reinterment of remains from at least 23 cemeteries at abandoned posts in Kansas, Colorado, Wyoming, Idaho, and Nebraska. This cemetery is also the final resting place for service men and women who were in various wars up to the present.

About 1 mile southeast of the cemetery is a monument marking the site of the flagstaff of the old military post. In the cemetery itself is a monument memorializing Lt. John Lawrence Grattan and 28 of his men who were killed in the **Grattan Massacre.**

The Grattan Massacre. A **Mormon emigrant's lost cow** led to the Grattan Massacre. On Aug. 17, 1854, a cow from the Hans Peter Olson company strayed and was taken into a camp of Sioux, along the North Platte east of Ft. Laramie, Wyoming. As many as 4,000 Brule and Oglala Sioux were waiting for their annual issue of government beef and goods, promised them by treaty in 1851. They killed the stray cow. The owner complained to the military at Ft. Laramie, Wyoming, demanding the cow be replaced and the offenders punished. Brevet Sec. Lt. John. L. Grattan with 28 men rode into the Sioux camp near **Ash Hollow** to arrest the man who killed the cow. Lt. Grattan misunderstood what was being said, panicked, and ordered his men to open fire. They killed Chief Conquering Bull, whereupon the Sioux swarmed over the soldiers and killed all but one. The Sioux called this **"The War of the Mormon Cow."** The massacre site, with a historic marker, is just west of Lingle, Wyoming. The massacre was the start of more than 35 years of intermittent hostility between the army and the Sioux, which culminated in the infamous **Wounded Knee Massacre** in December 1890 (HSN; Grattan Massacre Websites).

■ **JUNCTION-ODOMETER CAMP • BRIGHAM YOUNG • TUES. MAY 11 • 8.5 MILES • NORTH PLATTE

Brigham Young's 1847 company traveled 8.5 miles on this day and camped in what today are the outskirts of North Platte. They camped near today's U.S. 30, 4.5 miles east of the intersection of U.S. 30 and U.S. 83. The camp was .75 mile north of the **junction of the North Platte and South Platte** Rivers (MVB 133; JAL), near present-day Whitehorse Creek, and 1 mile east of the east runway of the Lee Bird Airport (JWC; JWW).

The nearby creek provided grass for the cattle but poor drinking water, so the pioneers dug **two wells** four feet deep. They

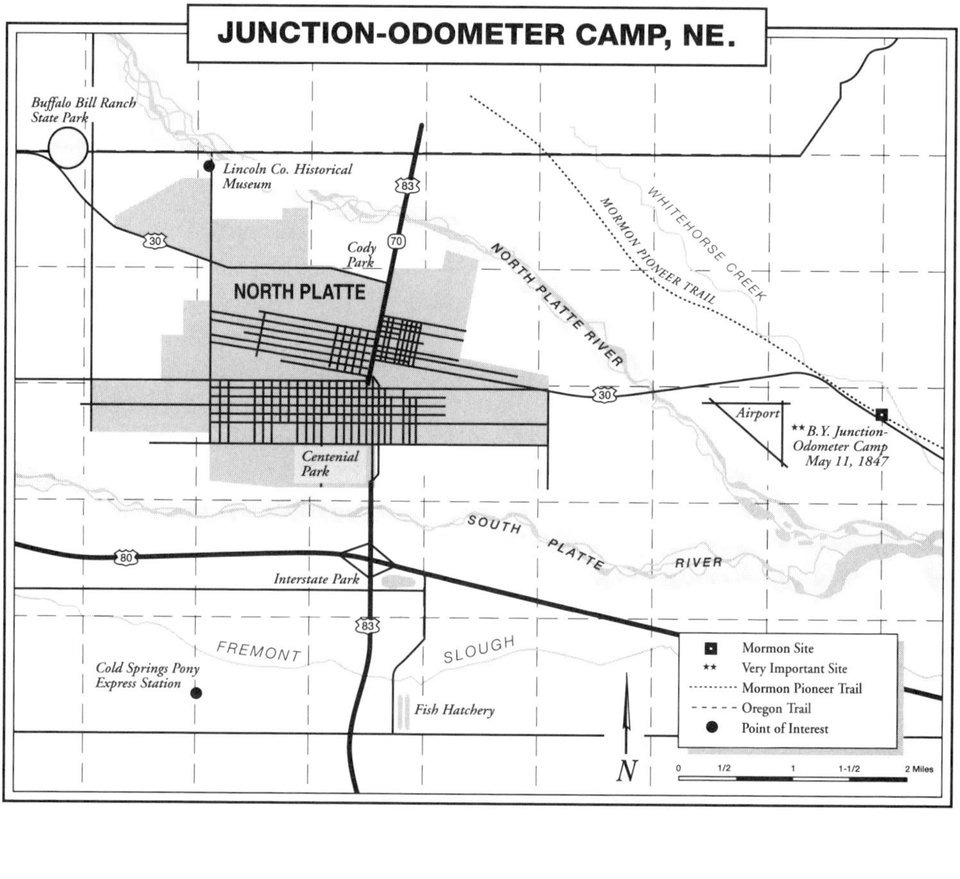

Mormon pioneer odometer. (Courtesy of LDSCA)

were able to collect a pailful every minute from one of the wells.

At this camp on the morning of May 12, an **odometer** was attached to Heber C. Kimball's wagon, driven by **Philo Johnson** (JTB). William Clayton was relieved that the difficult task of counting the revolutions of a wheel was over. Now a very accurate account of mileage traveled was recorded.

An NPS/NMTA Mormon Trail interpretive panel, "How Far Is a Mile?" is located near the North Platte Airport by the flagpole in the airport parking lot. The airport is .5 mile east of where U.S. 30 enters North Platte from the east. The panel tells about the designing and building of the **odometer.**

- **North Platte**

The county seat of Lincoln County, North Platte is located at the southeast corner of the Nebraska sandhills and is nestled between the North and South Platte Rivers that connect just east of the city. (The North Platte flows out of Wyoming and the South Platte out of Colorado.) Its population (2003) was estimated at 23,924. The **Mormon Trail** is located about 2.5 miles north of the center of the city, and from that point gradually begins to turn northwesterly, which means the route gradually separates from today's more westerly I-80.

North Platte in its entire history has been closely associated with **railroading and ranching.** With the construction project came close to 3,000 workers and others, with no governing authority, making the place lively and unruly. Construction of the road was resumed by July 1867, and the camp moved west. North Platte was organized as a city on Dec. 28, 1873. During its first decade, North Platte was also the end of the Texas cattle trail and a wild and rowdy place to be. An early resident was the honorable Col. William F. ("Buffalo Bill") Cody, who resided in North Platte for more than thirty years.

In 1921 North Platte opened the **first lighted airfield** in the

Mormon pioneer historical marker, moved from east side of State 70 beside the Platte River to Lincoln County Historical Museum grounds, North Platte, NE.

United States. Asked by the post office to provide a night landing field for pilots carrying mail, residents leveled a hay meadow, built wooden hangars, and lined the strip with kerosene lamps hung on stakes in the ground.

During World War II, the city gained fame for its **North Platte Canteen,** where townspeople established a tradition of welcoming every train of soldiers passing through the town. Hundreds of clubs and organizations used a huge unused dining room in the Union Pacific depot to greet an estimated 6 million members of the armed forces, providing them with food, magazines, and dances with local women. The canteen was open day and night for 51 months, frequently serving as many as 23 trains—up to 8,000 servicemen—in 24 hours (information obtained from various Websites).

In November 1866 the Union Pacific's tracks reached North Platte, which terminus served the next year as the **outfitting city and departure point** for at least one company of LDS emigrants. Some 500 emigrants and 50–60 wagons started across the plains with Leonard G. Rice as captain (OPH 11:42–49). Theirs was an independent company that used their own teams, rather than Utah down-and-back teams.

Brigham Young Jr. was among the outfitting Saints at North Platte. He said that train tickets from New York to Omaha were "$25 greenbacks" and from Omaha to North Platte, $10 per adult (JH Dec. 4, 1867). Ruth May, age 13, was in the company. Later, (married name **Ruth May Fox**) she served as the third general president of the LDS Young Ladies' Mutual Improvement Association (1929–37). She said her group spent nine days by train going from the East Coast to North Platte. There, they waited a month for their teams. "The full quota of wagons had not yet been purchased and the housing of men, women, and children was a real problem." Finally the Union Pacific let them use "a great barn of a building" where they set up "some kind of housekeeping" until departure time. They left in mid-August and arrived in Salt Lake City on Oct. 5 (RMF).

Bertha Marie Jensen, also in the company, was 10 years old. She recalled that the railroad equipment was "very poor," noting that "we sat on benches without backs. The cars, having no springs, rattled and jolted us over the newly built railroad." **James M. Christensen,** also in that company, said that during their weeks in North Platte, "there was much sickness" and that "fifteen died and were buried there." Their burial site has not been identified. "Before we left," he added, "the men were given guns and taught how to use them, but were instructed never to shoot unless some dire situation arose" (OPH 11:50).

Buffalo Bill Ranch State Historical Park is located northwest of North Platte on U.S. 30, about 3.5 miles from U.S. 83, at 2921 Scouts Rest Ranch Road. This was one of the homes of **William Frederick ("Buffalo Bill") Cody.** He acquired his nickname by supplying buffalo meat to workers on the Kansas railroad. With legendary marksmanship and riding skills, in 1883 he formed an immensely popular Wild West Show that toured America and Europe for 30 years. His "Old Glory Blowout" is the forerunner of the modern rodeo. This ranch is where he came to rest and entertain world-renowned figures between stints of the Wild West Show. The historical park includes Cody's elegant Victorian house, built in 1886, and a huge barn on what Cody called the "Scouts Rest Ranch." The barn, built in 1886, features Wild West Show memorabilia, original posters, and a movie made of period film clips taken while the show was touring.

Lincoln County Historical Museum, 2404 N. Buffalo Bill Ave., has a World War II Canteen display and, outside, period buildings and a **Mormon pioneer historical marker** noting William Clayton's "measuring device."

■ NORTH PLATTE CAMP • BRIGHAM YOUNG • WED. MAY 12 • 12 MILES • NORTH PLATTE

Brigham Young's company traveled 12 odometer-measured miles on this day, following for the first time the North Platte River and camping near the mouth of a wide clear stream 8 miles northwest of the center of what is now the city of North Platte. The trail was 2.5 miles north of the city center. William Clayton indicated

North Platte River, NE. (1975)

that they made a **new road** this day (JWC).

Thomas Bullock described the valley through which they passed that day as the "**valley of dry bones**" because of the immense number of bleached buffalo bones found in it (JTB 154). Wilford Woodruff recorded that this was a **Native American hunting ground** where 500–1,000 Sioux had preceded them by eight to ten days and where 400 lodges were located (JWW).

■ **NORTH BLUFF FORK CAMP • BRIGHAM YOUNG • THURS. MAY 13 • 10.75 MILES • SUTHERLAND**

On May 13, 1847, the **Brigham Young company** traveled west along the north bank of the North Platte River 10.75 miles and camped on the west side of the largest river they had crossed since the Wood River. Brigham Young called the 200-foot-wide river **North Bluff Fork.** Their camp was located 100 yards from where the North Bluff Fork emptied into the North Platte River. It is now called Birdwood Creek and is about 2 miles east of the **Sand Hill Ruts** and 5 miles northeast of Sutherland (JWW; JTB).

The morning was cold enough for overcoats and buffalo robes. During the day President Young and Elder Heber C. Kimball saw what the latter said was the largest rattlesnake he had ever seen.

In 1853, as the **Daniel A. Miller and John W. Cooley company** passed through the general area of the North Bluff Fork Camp, on July 9, 11-month-old **Samuel William Cooley** died. He was the son of John W. Cooley and Susan Jane Hunt. Elijah Mayhew, camp clerk, wrote,

> This child was buried on a ridge extending down from the Bluffs a few rods, west of Shepherd's Creek, and about five rods north of the road—supposed to be about two miles east of east foot of Sandy Bluffs No. 3—and about 336 miles from Old Winter Quarters. A board with the following inscription was placed at the head of the grave—"S. W. Cooley, aged 11

> months, son of Isaac [John William] W. Cooley, died July 9, 1853." A grove of timber supposed to be on an island in the Platte may be seen from this point about two or three miles to the southwest, opposite the east of Sandy Bluffs, Sheperds Creek is not named in Clayton's Guide, but is laid down in Horns [*Horn's Overland Guide,* by Hosea B. Horn, New York City, 1853]—Came six miles and camped on Petite Creek. (JEM in JH Sept. 9, 1853, 16; JJAL in JH Aug. 9, 1853, 12, 90)

It's possible that Samuel William Cooley was the infant whose grave was dedicated May 20, 1997, by Kearney Stake president Brian Hill when the sesquicentennial wagon train paused at an infant's grave near Sutherland, Nebraska. The grave is now well marked with a white fence and plaque. To reach it, take the dirt road at the foot of the bluffs east for 2 miles to where the road turns. There the gravesite is nearly straight ahead (CJ,c; DN May 24, 1997).

In 1856 the **Willie and Martin handcart companies** crossed the Platte and traveled on its **south side** through western Nebraska (the Martin company crossed back to the north side near Ash Hollow). On Sept. 12 the **Willie handcart company** was at North Bluff Creek and then forded the Platte to the south side and camped immediately after crossing. They then traveled on **the Oregon Trail** through the rest of present-day Nebraska (EJWM 31).

■ **SAND HILLS HISTORIC AREA RUTS • SUTHERLAND

Some of the best preserved **Mormon Trail wagon ruts** in Nebraska are near Sutherland. These Sutherland **Sand Hills ruts** are on the north side of the North Platte River and can be reached from I-80 by taking the Sutherland exit and going north 1 mile on State 25 to Sutherland. There, turn east on U.S. 30 and go to the eastern edge of town. At North Prairie Trace Road, turn and go north approximately 3 miles. After crossing the North Platte River, cross a dirt road; just beyond it is an **NPS/NMTA Mormon Trail interpretive panel,** "Where There's a Will," on the east side of the road. The panel tells about the formidable barrier the great sand bluffs were for travelers, causing them to double team to make the hard pull up through the loose, deep sand. It tells about the braided ruts that can be seen there, caused by later wagon trains. The ruts are on top of the sand hills, about 100 yards east of the north end of the Sutherland Bridge over the North Platte River and about 1.75 miles west of the North Bluff Fork Pioneer Camp (HSM 64–65).

On May 14, **Brigham Young's 1847 company** passed through this general area, probably in the south edge of the next valley to the north (CJ,c) before camping that night.

Oregon Trail Ruts on the south side of the South Platte River can also be seen at **O'Fallon's Bluff,** a noted landmark of the mountain men. The bluff is located 2 miles southeast of Sutherland. The ruts are 400 feet behind the rest stop that is by the eastbound lanes of I-80 (1.6 miles east of the Sutherland exit, or mile marker 159.6) and can be seen for 1,000 feet along the big bluff.

■ SAND HILLS CAMP • BRIGHAM YOUNG • FRI. MAY 14 • 8.75 MILES • SUTHERLAND

On Friday, May 14, 1847, the **Brigham Young company** took a circuitous route through the sand hills and bluffs because the bluffs were steep at the edge of the North Platte River. The wagons traveled 8.75 miles (about 5.5 miles in a straight line) and camped .5 mile from the river at a point 3.5 miles northwest of Sutherland from the junction of State 25 and U.S. 30. Amasa Lyman said the hills "look like billows on the ocean in a high storm" (JAL 26). During the night Indians lurked around the camp, and one was fired upon (JOP). Many footprints were seen in the area, but no one saw Native Americans during the day.

William Clayton noted, "We are satisfied the Lord hears the prayers of his servants and sends them [the Indians] out of the way before we come up to them" (JWC 148).

In the 1851 John Brown company, **Jean Rio Baker,** traveling in these sand hills on Aug. 4, said they had "a very heavy days travelling we had to cross a great many sand hills, saw thousands of lizards, snakes and grasshoppers" (DJRB).

There is no modern road between this camp and the next.

■ *ADMONITION CAMP • BRIGHAM YOUNG • SAT.–SUN. MAY 15–16 • 7 MILES • PAXTON

To reach this site, take the paved road (Road East T N) north out of **Paxton,** turn east on the first dirt road after crossing the North Platte river, and continue for about 4 miles.

On May 15 the **Brigham Young company** traveled over sand hills during the day. The hills extended to the banks of the North Platte River, so it became necessary to cross them. Pulling wagons in sand was very hard on teams (JTB; DTZ 94). The company managed to travel only 7 miles and camped where there was good feed for the animals (JWC). They remained there two days and honored the Sabbath Day by not traveling.

William Clayton felt that the weather was more like January than May. Their camp being .5 mile from the river, the pioneers dug wells three to four feet deep rather than haul river water. **Amasa Lyman** said the well water tasted of iron rust (JTB; JAL). Very little timber was nearby, so the pioneers used buffalo chips and driftwood for fuel (JWC).

Eric Glines, age 25, upset leaders when he shot an antelope and buffalo on Sunday. According to **Thomas Bullock,** the buffalo weighed 700 to 800 pounds, and the shaggy hair on his forehead was about a foot long (JTB). A meeting at 3 P.M. Sunday focused on obeying counsel. Both Elders **Heber C. Kimball** and **Willard Richards** addressed the inappropriateness of hunting on the Sabbath. Other admonitions were given but also some deserved praise. Bullock recorded:

> Elder Kimball got into the boat [*Revenue Cutter*] and testified that he had travelled in many Companies; that he was in the Zion's Camp that went up to Missouri in 1834, but he never was in a Camp or company that behaved themselves better than this Camp. These Pioneers were like clay in the hands of the Potter. (JTB 156)

Nine Zion's Camp veterans were in the company. After Elder Kimball finished praising the pioneers, Bullock read to the congregation the laws to regulate the camp (JTB 156; JAL). **Norton Jacob** also recorded the words of Heber C. Kimball:

> Bro. Heber said that the Lord had prospered us continually on this journey. That his Guardian angels were with us on our right hand and on our left, our front and our rear, only they were not visible to the natural eye but the angels of God were nevertheless with the camp of the Pioneers . . . if the camp walked according to the commandments and covenants of the

> Lord, no one of them would fall into the earth on this journey. (MVB 138–39; emphasis added)

William Clayton said that **Appleton Harmon** refined the odometer by "adding a wheel to revolve once in ten miles, showing each mile and also each quarter mile we travel, and then casing the whole over so as to secure it from the weather" (JWC 152). The odometer was about 18 inches long, 15 inches high, and 3 inches thick (JWC).

Clayton was especially grateful that day for half of a sweet- and rich-smelling candle made of buffalo tallow that **Edson Whipple** had given him. By its light that evening, he wrote in his journal (JWC).

■ **CEDAR BLUFFS CAMP • BRIGHAM YOUNG • MON. MAY 17 • 12.75 MILES • KEYSTONE**

This site is about 3 miles east of **Keystone** on paved County Road 49.

On May 17 the company traveled 12.75 miles and camped 3 miles east of **Cedar Bluffs.** The bluffs are close to the river and were thinly covered with small cedars. The camp was 4 miles east of **White Tail Creek,** 11 miles northeast of **Ogallala,** and 2.5 miles east of **Keystone.** The pioneers crossed a dozen springs coming from the bluffs, and during the day they found five springs bubbling up several inches (JWC; HEJ).

At 7:00 the next morning, May 18, **Brigham Young** "called the captains of tens to his wagons and gave them a pretty severe lecture. . . . [He said] God has given us a commandment that we should not waste meat, nor take life unless it is needful" (JWC 156). He also expressed displeasure at "horsemen for their indifference in picking out the road" (JWW 178; spelling and punctuation standardized). The captains in turn admonished their hunters.

● **CALIFORNIA HILL TRAIL RUTS • BRULE**

When today's travelers follow the Mormon Trail in the area of **Lake McConaughy,** they could take time to see the dramatic **California Hill Trail Ruts.** To do that, take U.S. 26 south from Ash Hollow State Historical Park toward Ogallala. Turn off U.S. 26 onto a gravel road that goes directly south to U.S. 30. About 4.5 miles west of the town of Brule is **California Hill,** on the north side of

U.S. 30. **A trail marker** in front of a farmhouse describes California Hill, where the trail ascends the plateau between the two Platte rivers. The **Oregon Trail** went past where the marker is, through a feedlot, and up California Hill, then northwest about 17 miles to **Ash Hollow,** where it turns west to follow the south side of the North Platte (the Mormon Trail continues on the north side). The ruts of California Hill are .5 mile west and .8 mile north of the marker. The hill is owned by the Oregon and California Trails Association.

The **Lower Crossing of the South Platte River** is 12 miles west of **Ogallala,** or 4 miles west of **Brule,** and 2 miles southeast of **California Hill.** From I-80, take the Brule turnoff (Exit 117) and go west on U.S. 30 for 4.5 miles. This crossing was used by the most of the Oregon Trail emigrants, including **Mormons** who traveled on the south side of the Platte until 1859, when the **Upper California Crossing** (near today's **Sidney, Nebraska)** became most used. California Hill is so named because it was popularized by the gold rush hopefuls bound for California.

To travel from California Hill to **Ash Hollow,** return to U.S. 30, go west 5 miles, turn north 10 miles to U.S. 26, and turn left to the hollow.

● LAKE MCCONAUGHY STATE RECREATION AREA • OGALALLA

This lake, Nebraska's largest, is 8 miles northeast of Ogalalla. It backs up the North Platte River behind the **Kingsley Dam,** which was completed in 1941. When full the lake is 22 miles long, 4 miles wide, and 142 feet deep at the dam; it has a 100-mile-long shoreline. The **Mormon Trail and sites are submerged** beneath the lake. **Ash Hollow State Historical Park** lies near the upper end of the lake. Along the north shore are several beaches and campgrounds and some creeks flowing into the lake. **Lemoyne,** an unincorporated village on the north shore, is 7 miles west of the dam. Highways along both sides of the lake—U.S. 26 on the south side and State 92 on the north side—are each designated as a **Western Trails Scenic and Historic Byway.**

■ EAGLE CREEK CAMP • BRIGHAM YOUNG • TUES. MAY 18 • 15.75 MILES • LEMOYNE

The **Eagle Creek Camp** site is now 1 to 2 miles out in Lake McConaughy, where Eagle Creek (evidently today's Lonergan

Creek) once flowed into the North Platte River near present-day Lemoyne on the north shore of the lake (CJ,c). Lonergan Creek flows into the lake .25 mile northwest of Lemoyne.

On May 18, 1847, at 8:15 A.M., after **Brigham Young** rebuked the hunters at Cedar Bluffs Camp, the company broke camp. They traveled 15.75 miles and camped on the west bank of **Eagle Creek,** where it ran parallel to the North Platte. They were .5 mile above the outlet of Eagle Creek into the North Platte (JAL).

■ Sand Hill Bluff Camp • Brigham Young • Wed. May 19 • 8 miles • Ruthton

This campsite lies beneath the waters of Lake McConaughy, out from the shore that is now between Cedar Vue and Omaha Beach campgrounds. That site is about 2.5 miles southeast of a railroad area called Ruthton, at the northwest edge of the lake. Cedar Vue, 15 miles west of the dam, is west of Otter Creek, which flows out of the sand hills on the lake's north side.

To reach this campsite, the **Brigham Young company** traveled 8 miles in sand nearly to the wheel hubs, making it a "most uncomfortable day," according to **William Clayton:**

> Traveled six miles today over the worst road we have had from Winter Quarters, rendered worse, doubtless, by the heavy rains. . . . this has been the most uncomfortable day we have had and the hardest on our teams. The brethren, however, feel well and cheerful. The ox teams are improving in their condition, but the horses do not stand it as well. (JWC 162)

Elder Kimball went ahead and saw several wolves, one of them nearly as large as a two-year-old steer (JWC 162–63).

■ **Ash Hollow State Historical Park and Windlass Hill • Lewellen

The **Ash Hollow State Historical Park, visitors' center, cave, Pioneer Springs, and cemetery** are best reached from Lewellen by driving .5 mile east and 3 miles south on U.S. 26.

Ash Hollow, named for its ash trees, was the site of the principal entryway to the North Platte Valley for travelers on the **Oregon Trail.** From the Lower Crossing of the South Platte 4.5 miles west of present-day **Brule**, the Oregon Trail headed northwest toward the North Platte River. Travelers on that segment went from the South Platte over **California Hill** and then, nearing the North Platte, descended **Windlass Hill** on a very steep grade and reached **Ash Hollow** beside the North Platte.

Sweet spring water and large shady trees (the first that emigrants had seen for nearly 100 miles) made Ash Hollow an **important stopping place** on the Oregon Trail. The **Ash Hollow State Historical Park** contains more than 1,000 acres that include a visitors' center on the bluff overlooking the mouth of the canyon, a hiking trail from that center down to the spring at the bottom of the canyon, a restored schoolhouse, a trading post site, a cemetery with graves of some trail emigrants, and picnic areas and rest rooms.

Windlass Hill and Oregon Trail Ruts are in a separate part of the park, 2.25 miles south of the park's main center visitor center, on U.S. 26. Visitors are provided an interpretive shelter, informal signs, and a walkway to the crest of the hill to view deep ruts carved by wagon traffic (and significant erosion) on the **Oregon Trail. Windlass Hill** was named from a legend that wagons had to be winched down its 25-degree-steep slope for about 300 feet—a vertical drop of 150 feet; however, the name Windlass Hill is contemporary, and there is no evidence to support the legend. Wagon wheels were "rough-locked" for the descent and this left visible tracks. In 1852, government surveyor **Howard Stansbury** let his wagons down the hill with ropes. Many others did the same (HiS 79–88).

■ ****ASH HOLLOW CAMP • BRIGHAM YOUNG • THURS. MAY 20 • 15.75 MILES • OSHKOSH**

May 20 was a very important and exciting day for the **Brigham Young company** as they traveled west 15.25 miles to Ash Hollow Camp. They stopped for lunch on the north side of the North Platte River, 7.75 miles from Sand Hill Bluff Camp and across the North Platte from **Ash Hollow,** one of the best known sites on the Oregon Trail in Nebraska. The lunch stop site was 1 mile southeast of today's **Lewellen** near the north end of the bridge (U.S. 26) that crosses the North Platte River. Across the river they saw a large ravine that led into the river from the south. **John Brown,** who had traveled west along the Oregon Trail as the leader of the Mississippi Saints in 1846, recognized the ravine as **Ash Hollow.** Fremont's map

Ash Hollow aerial photo looking south across the North Platte River. Note the river bridge in the foreground, the Mississippi Saints 1846 campground in the mouth of the hollow, the visitors' center on the left bluff near the center of the photo, and Windlass Hill at the very top center. The Brigham Young company of 1847 stopped for lunch opposite the Hollow, May 20, 1847. (1978)

called it Ash Creek. Here the **Oregon Trail,** coming from the east along the south side of the Platte and then across the South Platte, struck the North Platte River and followed it along the south side. The name Ash Hollow was used as early as 1832.

While the Mormon pioneer camp was stopped for lunch, **Orson Pratt, Amasa Lyman, Luke Johnson,** and **John Brown** crossed the river in the ***Revenue Cutter*** and determined that the ravine was definitely **Ash Hollow** (JTB). On that side, John Brown found the grave of an Oregon emigrant he had helped bury the previous season while leading the **Mississippi Saints** west. These Saints had camped in the 15- to 20-acre area at the mouth of Ash Hollow on the banks of the river, a major camping area for Oregon Trail travelers, in 1846.

On May 20, 1847, after their lunch stop opposite Ash Hollow, **Brigham Young's company** passed by about 5 miles of bluffs located on the south side of the North Platte River. They were called **Castle Bluffs,** because, the pioneers said, they resembled castles of England and Scotland. **Thomas Bullock** said that one of the bluffs was "like Solomon's temple and are named 'Castle Bluffs'" (JTB 161). Today's names for two of those bluffs are Signal Butte and

Windlass Hill, showing the Pioneer Trail coming off the top center. (1997)

Barn Butte (CJ,c). At a point 8 miles west of their lunch stop the pioneers camped .5 mile from the river on two small streams. That location is 5 miles southeast of the center of **Oshkosh** and .25 mile south of U.S. 26, or 7 miles west of Lewellen (JAL; JWC).

Regarding **Ash Hollow,** in 1853, Mormon artist **Frederick Piercy** noted on July 18 that his Miller-Cooley company "passed Ash Hollow, which is on the south side of the Platte, where we could see an immense herd of buffalo, which good judges said could not number less than 10,000" (RFL 117–18).

In 1856 the **Willie handcart company,** then following the Oregon Trail, descended into Ash Hollow. The company journal says that on Sept. 16 the Saints "struggled over a deep winding ravine, over a very heavy, sandy road. Since noon yesterday we have been traveling over a long range of bluffs which have opened at noon today, on the Platte bottom." They passed through Ash Hollow to the Platte River bottoms and camped (EJWM 31).

A **Sister Stewart** in the Willie handcart company became lost during the day's travel. A search party found her footprints going up Ash Hollow. The next day, Sept. 17, Capt. Willie and others searched for her while those in camp repaired handcarts. A third search party went out, and while they were gone, she came into camp. She had heard the lowing of cattle and the sound of axes and went to where she found some of the men in **Ash Hollow** cutting wood to make axles. Exhausted and barely able to speak, she had spent the night alone on the bluffs in open prairie and was followed by wolves. One came within two yards of her, but she stared it down and scared it off (EJWM 36).

On Sept. 7, 1856, on the north side of the North Platte not far beyond **Ash Hollow, Almon W. Babbitt,** secretary of the Utah Territory, along with two companions, was killed by Cheyenne on his journey back to Utah from Washington, D.C. Babbitt had gone to Washington to purchase supplies for the new statehouse in Salt Lake City. The Mormons at Council Bluffs and an officer at

Ft. Kearny counseled him to wait for a larger wagon train or a military escort, but he did not. Four of Babbitt's wagons traveling without him had also been attacked on Aug. 25 near Prairie Creek, east of Ft. Kearny (HOUW 553–54).

On Sept. 22, 1856, the **Martin handcart company,** apparently near Ash Hollow, crossed the North Platte River and resumed travel on the trail on the north side. The next day they came upon the **Babbitt murder site.** They were 6 miles east of **Bluff Creek.** About 70 yards to the left of the road they saw a little harness, two wagon wheels, and the springs of a burned carriage or buggy, among other items, which they felt were relics of Babbitt's outfit. The next day about noon they "saw the blood stained garments of Thomas Margetts's wife and child, who had been murdered by the Indians. At the site were a quantity of feathers strewn about, a blood stained shirt, and a child's skull" (EJWM 112).

When the **U.S. Army's Utah Expedition** came down Ash Hollow on Aug. 27, 1857, on their way to what is termed the "Utah War," there was a stampede of military horses. Soldier **Charles Scott** described it:

> Horses dashing furiously with the pieces down the hills and precipices. the noise, dust and confusion, the men shouting hallooing, and women screaming, made an impression on my memory, never to be effaced; two horses were killed and seven disabled and unfit for service, in all about $25,000 damage done. (DCAS in UHQ 28 no. 2: 163; spelling standardized)

In 1861 Mormon Trail teamster **Zebulon Jacobs** said that when his wagon company was approaching Ash Hollow, he and another man "crossed the river and found plenty of chokecherries and currants." They ate till satisfied, then "we filled our hats and pockets with berries, which we took to camp and distributed them." While recrossing the river "we got ducked several times, but hung on to the fruit." The company moved 2.5 miles that day and "camped opposite Ash Hollow," where they found the mosquitoes "rather friendly" (DTD 10).

● *The Harney Massacre Site • Lewellen

Blue Creek flows south into the North Platte about 1.25 miles west of Lewellen. Along that creek on Sept. 3, 1855, **Col. William S.**

Harney's force of 600 men attacked and destroyed a Lakota village. The Americans were avenging the annihilation of Lt. John Grattan's command in 1854 (see **Grattan Massacre**). The infantry killed 86 Sioux, captured 70 women and children, and looted and burned their village. This slaughter became known as the **Battle of Blue Water,** the **Battle of Ash Hollow,** or the **Harney Massacre.** The campaign against the Lakota Sioux kept open the emigrant trail routes and postponed until 1863–64 more serious warfare. **A historic marker,** "The Battle of Blue Water," which tells about the battle, is located on U.S. 26 at a point 1.5 miles west of Lewellen.

Gen. Harney was in command of the **Utah Expedition** when it left Ft. Leavenworth on July 18, 1857, to march against the Mormons in Utah. In Wyoming, Gen. Harney was replaced by **Gen. Albert Sidney Johnston** on Aug. 28, 1857.

■ Mammoth Bone Camp • Brigham Young • Fri. May 21 • 15.5 miles • Oshkosh

Brigham Young's company traveled 15.5 miles on this day and periodically had to leave the river bottoms to cross over bluffs because the river shore was so narrow. They returned to the river bottom and camped a mile from the river. The site is by U.S. 26 and 10.5 miles northwest of Oshkosh, 5.25 miles southeast of Lisco, and immediately north of U.S. 26. They dug wells for water (JWC).

They found a large **petrified leg bone of a mammoth** during the afternoon. It weighed 27 pounds and measured 17.5 inches from the knee downwards, and at the greatest width was 11 inches. Two friendly Native Americans visited the camp in the evening (JOP; JWC; JTB).

Brigham Young named some bluffs near the Mammoth Bone Camp **Bluff Ruins,** but most trail accounts call them **Ancient Bluff Ruins** (JTB; JWC). These are on the north side of the Platte, unlike the landmark rock formations they would soon pass that were on the south side: Courthouse Rock, Jailhouse Rock, Chimney Rock, and Scotts Bluff.

■ *Frog's Head Bluff Indian Lookout Pt. • May 22 • 15.5 miles • Lisco

Leaving the Mammoth Bone Camp, the company crossed a stream near present-day **Lisco.** They called the stream **"Crab Creek"** because they saw a large crab in it.

Frog's Head Bluff is what William Clayton called a "200 foot high prominent bluff" located on the north side of today's U.S. 26, 2 miles west of Lisco. As Clayton gazed at the bluff, a little distance from its base he saw "a large rock projecting from one corner which very much resembled a frog's head of immense size with its mouth part open." The consensus was that the bluffs ought to be named and the choice was **Frog's Head Bluffs** (JWC 171–72). Locally the bluff today is known as **Indian Lookout Pt.** (EmG 57).

While the pioneers were stopped for their noon rest directly south of the bluff, **Porter Rockwell** climbed to the top and was the first of the group to see in the distance **Chimney Rock,** a famous trail landmark. Although 41.5 miles to the west, it could be seen with the naked eye, and many of the pioneers climbed up the bluff for the view. William Clayton wrote his name with red chalk on a large rock on the top of the bluff (JWC). That afternoon, as the pioneers traveled over the tops of some of the bluffs, they could see Chimney Rock from their wagons (JTB).

■ ****ANCIENT BLUFF RUINS AND CAMP • BRIGHAM YOUNG • MAY 22–23 • 15.5 MILES • BROADWATER**

West of Lisco 6.5 miles, on the north side of U.S. 26, is an **NPS/NMTA Mormon Trail interpretive panel,** "The Rapture of Spring." It explains that Brigham Young's 1847 company camped just west of the sign and that on May 22 and 23, "the rapture of spring" and being in camp gave rise to exploring, reflection, and amusements, including a dance. Some in the company explored the bluffs.

At this site there is also a Nebraska State Historical Society **historical marker commemorating Narcissa Whitman and Eliza Spalding,** the first white women to cross the Rocky Mountains. Following the north side of the Platte on horseback, they were a part of the Oregon Protestant Mission that passed this point in June 1836. Eleven years later, in November 1847, Narcissa, her husband Marcus, and eleven others were massacred by Cayuse at their Walla Walla Mission, now a national historic site in Washington State.

From these markers the **1847 Brigham Young route** drops down into the bottoms, where U.S. 26 basically follows it where it approached **Ancient Bluff Ruins.** On May 22, Brigham Young's company traveled 15.5 miles and camped with their wagons circled between the North Platte River (.25 to .5 miles to the south) and the 235-foot-high Ancient Bluff Ruins 1 mile north of their camp. Their **Ancient Bluff Ruins Camp site** was 3.5 miles southeast of the present-day town of **Broadwater** on U.S. 26.

William Clayton said words could not describe the "romantic beauty" surrounding their campsite (JWC 175). "The bluffs on our route today have presented the most singular natural scenery that I ever beheld in my travels on the earth," said Wilford Woodruff (JWW 181; spelling standardized). The sandstone and limestone bluffs had been formed by wind and water into cones, pyramids, pillars, and various shapes that reminded the pioneers of castles with towers, walls, and openings in the walls. The shapes caused them to think of ancient cities in ruins (EmG 58).

Trail ruts are visible .75 mile west of the campsite. They are .3 mile east of a ranch road leading into the bluff area on the north side of U.S. 26.

During their May 22 travels, the pioneers saw many petrified bones. That evening was spent **dancing** and having a **mock trial of James Davenport,** who jokingly was prosecuted for blockading the highway and turning ladies out of their course.

On Sunday, May 23, the company did not travel. **William Clayton** gratefully accepted an offer by **Howard Egan** to wash his dirty clothes. **Nathaniel Fairbanks** hiked into the bluffs and was bitten by a rattlesnake, which made him very sick. The brethren applied tobacco juice, turpentine, and leaves and gave him a dose of lobelia, alcohol, and water. He was also administered to, and he recovered. Over **a dozen rattlesnakes** had been seen in the area, and six or seven were killed (JWC; JTB).

At the camp's noon Sabbath meeting, President Young admonished the brethren to seek after knowledge and be faithful to acknowledge God in all things but never take his name in vain. He was satisfied that the Lord was leading the camp, and he had never seen a company of people more united. He said that "not one had refused to obey his counsel on the road." Norton Jacob recorded that Brigham Young said:

> Some expressed fears that we would not be able to get in crops. Well, suppose we do not, we have done all we could and traveled as fast as our teams are able to go. When we have done all we can we should feel just as well satisfied as if we had a

thousand acres planted with grain. The Lord would do the rest. (MVB 145)

Many in the company hiked to the top of the **Ancient Bluff Ruins.** Members of the **Quorum of the Twelve** were on one of the high, detached bluffs when they found a **buffalo skull.** On it, **Wilford Woodruff** wrote the names of all the members of the Twelve present and then set it on the southwest corner of the bluff. **John Brown** also wrote his name on it (JWW).

In 1853 the **Joseph W. Young company** camped after passing the **Bluff Ruins. Hannah T. King** (later a leading poetess in Utah) in that company termed them "very beautiful." In their camp that night, she complained in her diary that "the Mosquitoes dreadful! . . . We have had the Platte river by us for the past week it is very pretty—full of little islands—Oh! I can write no more the mosquitoes drive me mad! Oh for an end to this Journey!" (CWW 6:210).

■ ***COURTHOUSE ROCK CAMP • BRIGHAM YOUNG • MON. MAY 24 • 16.5 MILES • BRIDGEPORT**

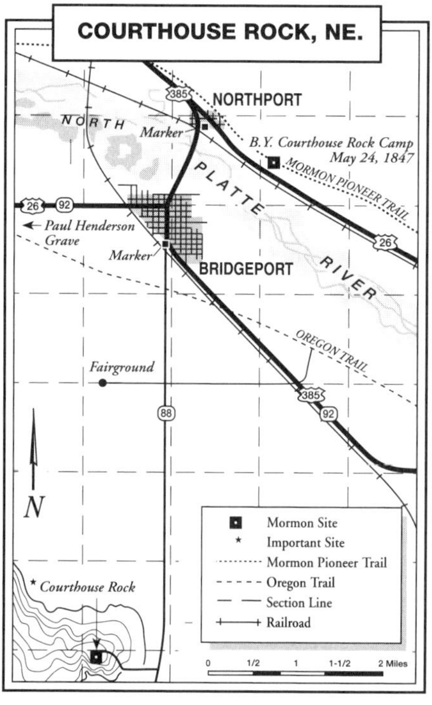

Usually the 1847 **Mormon route** paralleled the North Platte River about 1 mile to the north. On this day the company traveled 16.5 miles and camped .25 mile from the river. Their camp was 6 miles north-east of **Courthouse Rock** (**Castle Rock**), 1.5 miles northeast of the center of present-day Bridgeport and just east of the junction of U.S. 26 and State 92/U.S. 385 near Northport.

Thirty-five **Sioux** crossed from the south side of the river to visit the pioneers' camp. According to Erastus Snow,

> They were all dressed in their richest costumes. Some had fur caps and cloth coats, and others had cloth pants and shirts, and the rest were neatly dressed in skins ornamented with beads, feathers, paint, etc., and they were by all odds the cleanest and best appearing Indians we have seen west of the Missouri River. (JES 1101)

Although the visitors were well armed with muskets, when they had been fed a meal the pioneers prepared, they stayed near the camp and were no threat to the Mormons (JTB).

■ *COURTHOUSE ROCK AND JAILHOUSE ROCK • BRIDGEPORT

Courthouse Rock is 4 miles south of the Oregon Trail, on the south side of the North Platte River. A massive outcropping of Brule clay and Gering sandstone, it was mentioned as a prominent landmark years before the Brigham Young company passed by it. It was also called by other names, such as Castle Rock, McFarlan's Castle, or Parker's Castle. It rises 340 feet above the level of the valley, and upon its summit is a small tableland. "Grand and massive in form," it is visible for 50 miles (HSN). William Clayton said it was "a very large rock very much resembling a castle of four stories high, but in a state of ruin" (JWC 181). Many names have been carved into the walls of Courthouse Rock, dating from the 1850s. A smaller outcrop nearby is called **Jail** or **Jailhouse Rock.** Both of these landmarks can be visited by going south of U.S. 26 in Bridgeport 5.2 miles on State 92/U.S. 385 and State 88.

Two Mormon Pioneer Trail markers are in Bridgeport. A stone pillar, with a plaque that tells about this campsite, has been moved several times but currently (2005) is located in a little park west of U.S. 26 on the river bottoms on Bridgeport's north edge (CJ,c). The other is located near the railroad station in the

Courthouse Rock on the right and Jailhouse Rock on the left. These famous landmarks are near Bridgeport, NE, and the Mormon Trail but nearer the Oregon Trail, which is on the south side of the North Platte River. (1975)

south part of Bridgeport at the junction of State 88 and State 92/U.S. 385.

● **MUD SPRINGS • DALTON**

A Pony Express and stagecoach station was at Mud Springs. The site, about 12 miles southeast of Bridgeport, is located near U.S. 385 where it is midway between U.S. 26/State 92 and I-80. To reach the turnoff from the north, drive south on U.S 385 for 8.2 miles; from the south, drive north on U.S. 385 to 5.3 miles north of Dalton. At that spot, drive west 1.5 miles on a dirt road. The site is .25 mile beyond the bend in the road, across a generally dry creek bed. The spring feeds a nearby pond.

Mud Springs Station was constructed in 1859 as a stagecoach station on a cut-off road between the North Platte and the main Oregon Trail. Famous world-traveler **Sir Richard F. Burton,** on his way by stagecoach to Utah in 1860, found a **Mormon family in charge** of the station (CoS). It was later used as a Pony Express home station, providing meals, lodging, and fresh horses. After the Pony Express ceased operations, the facility served as a stagecoach and telegraph station. In February 1865, soldiers from Ft. Laramie, Wyoming, clashed with Sioux and Cheyenne in the Battle of Mud Springs. A **Mud Springs Station stone historical marker** is at the site.

■ ***CHIMNEY ROCK CAMP • BRIGHAM YOUNG • TUES. MAY 25 • 12 MILES • BAYARD**

On May 25, Brigham Young's company traveled 12 miles and camped 3.5 miles northeast of **Chimney Rock** (JWC; JES; JAL; JTB). Their campsite is 3 miles southeast of the center of present-day Bayard. It was almost 2 miles east of where U.S. 26 goes south out of Bayard and 1.5 miles directly north of State 92 and U.S. 26 (south of Bayard). **Chimney Rock** was considered the halfway landmark on the trail west from the Missouri River to the Salt Lake Valley.

For supper that night, **Brigham Young** dined on some bread baked by his wife in Nauvoo nearly a year and a half earlier. "It was still very good," Thomas Bullock wrote (JTB 168). **Lorenzo and Harriet Young** found some pigweed on the prairie and picked a mess of greens. The evening was very pleasant, except for mosquitoes, and the brethren passed their time dancing until after nine o'clock (JWC).

**CHIMNEY ROCK NATIONAL HISTORIC SITE • BAYARD

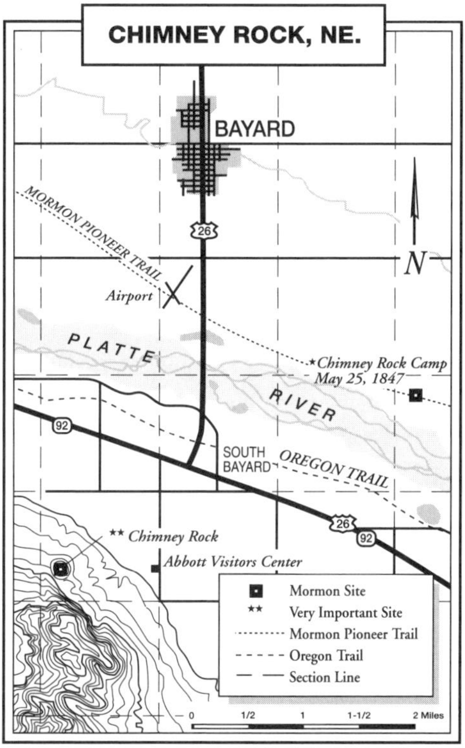

Chimney Rock is the **most famous landmark** on the Oregon, Mormon, California, and Pony Express trails. It is a prominent column of clay and sandstone that resembles a factory chimney. It is south of the North Platte River, 4 miles south-southwest of the center of the town of Bayard and 1.25 miles south of State 92. It is 325 feet from the top to bottom of this funnel-shaped column. It was higher when the pioneers first saw it, but it has worn down. The 120-foot-tall sandstone shaft is 22 feet in diameter at the bottom and 17 feet in diameter at the top. The 205-foot-high base is Brule clay. A county road goes south .6 mile from State 92 at a point 1.25 miles west of the intersection of U.S. 26 with State 92. The road takes the visitor to within .5 mile of the monument. Hiking is permitted from there to the monument. Hikers to Chimney Rock from the nearby Chimney Rock Cemetery (directions available at the visitors' center) can go there without crossing any fences, but they should be on the lookout for rattlesnakes.

Chimney Rock, near Bayard, NE; aerial view to the southwest. (1975)

Chimney Rock, near Bayard, NE. (1975)

The **Abbott Visitors' Center,** operated by the Nebraska State Historical Society, was completed in the fall of 1994 and is located 1 mile south of State 92 from a point .25 mile west of its intersection with U.S. 26. The first known written record using the name "Chimney Rock" is a journal entry by Joshua Pilcher in 1827, although it was well-known to travelers before that time (OTR 210). Native Americans called it the **Teepee.** It was and is an outstanding curiosity. World-traveler **Sir Richard Burton** called it the "Pharos of the prairie-sea," alluding to the lighthouse on the island of Pharos, one of the seven wonders of the ancient world (CoS 83).

Chimney Rock served as a guide to early travelers making the overland journey. They could see it for three to four days before passing by it. It is mentioned in hundreds of pioneer diaries. Thousands of names were inscribed on it. When Mormon Trail emigrants saw Chimney Rock, they knew they had reached the **halfway point** between the Missouri River and Salt Lake Valley. The landmark also signaled that the **Great American Desert** would soon give way to the more difficult mountainous part of the journey. Travelers on the Oregon Trail found a good spring and camping place near Chimney Rock, and that spot became the site for Pony Express, telegraph, and stagecoach stations. The Mormon pioneers' trail was located 3 miles north of Chimney Rock.

A dragoon in the **Utah Expedition** in 1857 said he climbed to the very top of the Chimney Rock pinnacle in August 1857. He said he did this almost impossible feat "by the aid of my spurs, which I strapped on my toes and the pin of my Lariat rope." His descent was made "faster than convenient" by a fall and roll to the plain, with no serious injury (TUD 47).

An NPS/NMTA Mormon Trail interpretive panel, "Halfway to Zion," is located approximately 1 mile south of Bayard on U.S. 26 on the west side of the road near a crossroad. The panel tells how the 1847 Brigham Young company was delighted to reach a point opposite Chimney Rock on May 26, because it marked the halfway point on their trek to Utah.

■ ***Terrace Bluffs Camp • Brigham Young • Wed. May 26 • 12.5 miles • Minatare**

On May 26, after traveling about 4.5 miles from Chimney Rock Camp, the pioneers passed about 3 miles north of Chimney Rock—nearly 42 miles from where they had first seen it. That day they traveled near the North Platte River, 12.5 miles total, and camped 10.5 miles northwest of Chimney Rock. Their camp was on the banks of the North Platte River, and they parked their wagons in a circle. The campsite is now 1 mile southwest of the railroad and the central street in the town of Minatare and .5 mile east of the gauging station on the North Platte River.

William Clayton recorded in his journal entry for that day that he had written in **Heber C. Kimball's journal** (by assignment) until he retired at 10:30 P.M. (JWC 186). At this camp the next morning, May 27, Clayton noted: "We have seen a number of romantic spots on our journey, but I consider our view this morning More Sublime than any other. Chimney Rock lies southeast. . . . To the southwest, Scott's Bluffs look majestic and sublime. . . . The scenery is truly delightful beyond imagination" (JWC 186). Amasa Lyman wrote that they camped nearly opposite **Terrace Bluffs** (JAL). These formations are currently called Castle Rock, Steamboat Rock, Coyote Rock, and Roundtop, among other names.

■ ****The Rebecca Winters Grave • Scottsbluff**

Iron wagon tire with Rebecca Winters's name chiseled in it, near Scottsbluff, NE.

The **Rebecca Winters Grave** (1852) is a very important historic site for the overland trails. Hers is one of the few known graves of any of the several thousand Mormons who died while crossing the plains (COF 158–60). It is 2 miles east of **Scottsbluff** on the southeast side of Scottsbluff by way of U.S. 26. It is reached from U.S. 26 or by starting from the Frank Park Pioneer Park on 27th Street and Broadway in Scottsbluff, going south from the park 1.5 miles to Beltline Highway (truck

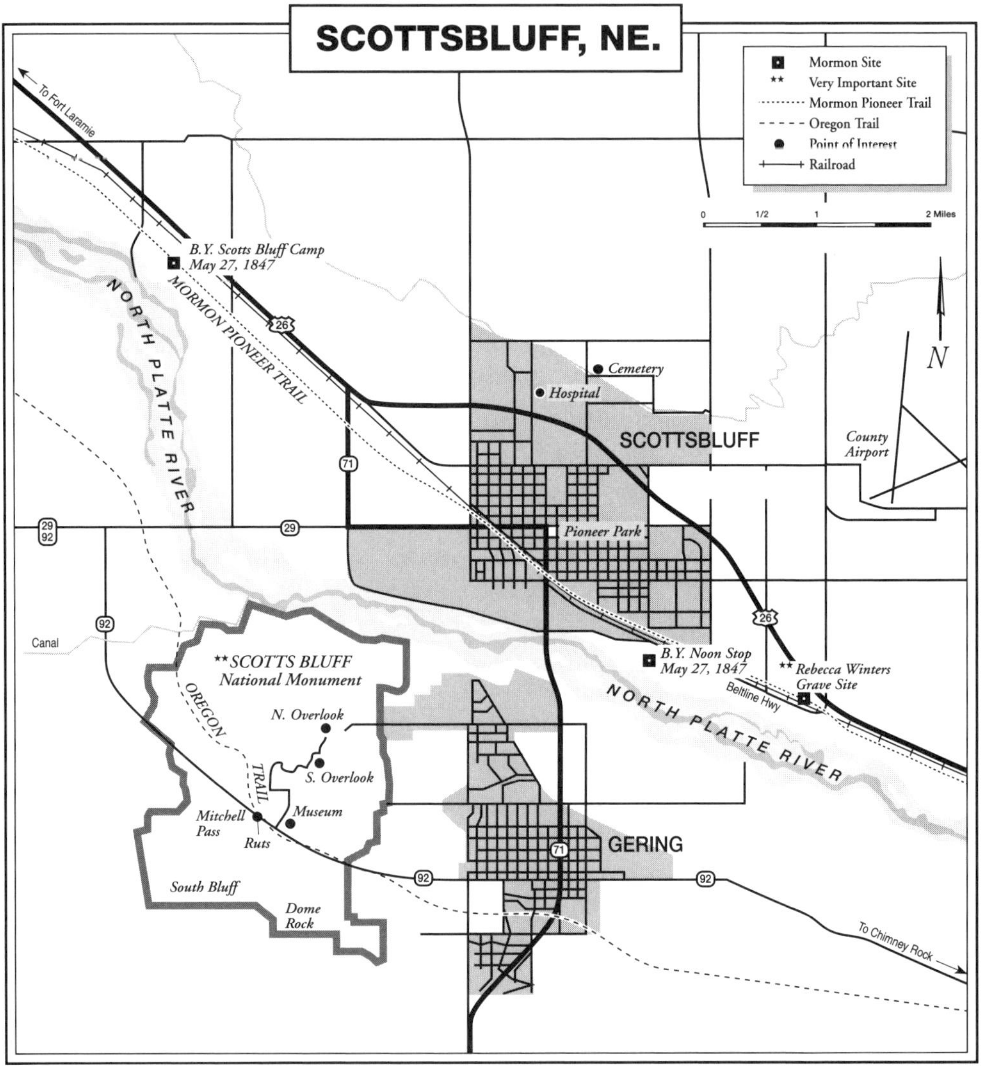
SCOTTSBLUFF, NE.
Mormon Site
Very Important Site
Mormon Pioneer Trail
Oregon Trail
Point of Interest
Railroad
0
1/2
1
2 Miles
N
To Fort Laramie
B.Y. Scotts Bluff Camp
May 27, 1847
MORMON PIONEER TRAIL
NORTH PLATTE RIVER
26
71
29
92
Cemetery
Hospital
SCOTTSBLUFF
County
Airport
Pioneer Park
Canal
B.Y. Noon Stop
May 27, 1847
Rebecca Winters
Grave Site
Beltline Hwy
SCOTTS BLUFF
National Monument
OREGON
TRAIL
N. Overlook
S. Overlook
Museum
Mitchell
Pass
Ruts
South Bluff
Dome
Rock
GERING
To Chimney Rock

Rebecca Winters's name in the iron wagon tire. Near Scottsbluff, NE. (1975)

bypass route), and then east-southeast on Beltline Highway 2.8 miles to its intersection with U.S. 26. The marker (now .2 mile east of the original gravesite) is on the southeast side of that intersection, between the railroad tracks and U.S. 26. She was buried 1.25 miles east of the Brigham Young company's May 27, 1847 noon stop.

Rebecca Winters, born Dec. 16, 1802, died of cholera on Aug. 15, 1852, while crossing the plains in the **James C. Snow company. Asa S. Hawley,** in the company, recalled:

> The cholera broke out in our camp, and many died. The most sorrowful to me was the death of Sister [Rebecca Burdick] Winters, one of God's noble and courageous women. We buried her on the Platte River opposite Scott's Bluffs. Great was our sorrow in having to leave her there. (ASH)

Her body was wrapped in blankets and placed between two levels of wooden planks. To mark her grave, family friend **William Fletcher Reynolds** obtained a steel wheel rim found on the trail and spent the night chiseling "Rebecca Winters–Aug 1852–Age 50" on the rim. His young daughter, Ellis Reynolds, held a candle to give him light. **Hiram Winters** was Rebecca's husband (ERA Feb. 1945: 71, 109–10).

LDS Church president and prophet George Albert Smith at Rebecca Winters's grave by the railroad tracks near Scottsbluff, NE.

In 1886 **Lorenzo DeMott** homesteaded the land where the grave is, and for years his family cared for the grave. The site became a local landmark, and the community gave the Winters name to a

Rebecca Winters's grave by the railroad tracks and Scotts Bluff National Monument, NE, in the distance. (1975)

creek, a voting district, and a boulevard. When DeMott sold the **Chicago, Burlington & Quincy Railroad** a right of way through his land, he made provision that the grave not be disturbed. An 1899 survey placed the rail line directly over the grave, so De Mott fought the railroad in the courts, forcing it to survey a route that avoided the grave.

In 1902, the centennial year of Rebecca's birth, family members placed a **granite headstone** to the west of the iron rim. It reads: "She died a faithful Latter-day Saint Aug. 15, 1852, aged 50 years, while making that memorable journey across the plains with her people to find a new home in the far distant Salt Lake Valley. She gave her life for her faith. Her reward will be according to her works." The railroad erected a fence around the grave area.

In 1921 the **Daughters of the American Revolution** (DAR) began maintaining the gravesite, and in 1929 they placed **a DAR "Real Daughter" marker** at the site, which says "Daughter of a soldier of the Revolution." (Her father, Gideon Burdick, was a drummer boy in Gen. Washington's army.) That marker was stolen during World War II, but several years later the DAR chapter replaced it with the one seen today (BFN).

Increased railroad traffic made it too dangerous for people to visit the original gravesite, because they had to cross the tracks to reach it. So, in 1994, **Burlington Northern** officials **relocated the grave.** With descendants' permission, the body of Rebecca Winters was exhumed on Sept. 5, 1995, and moved to a new and safer site

Rebecca Winters's reburial site, .2 mile east of the original grave site, near Scottsbluff, NE.

shortly thereafter. The new gravesite was dedicated on June 22, 1996. It looks identical to the old one, with the original wagon wheel iron and the two monuments. The original grave was near the north side of the railroad tracks, .2 mile west of the new grave. (The Scottsbluff map shows where the original gravesite was located; CN Sept. 16, 1995: 6). Railroad workers in Scottsbluff maintain the grave, headstone, and fence, and water the grass daily in the summertime (BFN). On the site is a **Nebraska State historical marker,** "Rebecca Winters."

A granddaughter of Rebecca Winters, **Augusta Winters,** became the **wife of LDS Church President Heber J. Grant** (CN Sept. 16, 1995: 6).

● SCOTTSBLUFF

Twenty miles from the Wyoming border and 452 miles from Omaha, **Scottsbluff** is the largest city in the western Nebraska panhandle, with just under 15,000 residents. Laid out in 1899, it is located on the north side of the **North Platte River** 6 miles northeast of the **Scotts Bluff National Monument.** The city's name, Scottsbluff, is one word, but the name of the rock formation and the national monument name is two words: Scotts Bluff.

■ **SCOTTS BLUFF NATIONAL MONUMENT • GERING

Scotts Bluff National Monument is located 3 miles west of Gering, Nebraska, on State 92. To reach the monument from Scottsbluff, take State 71 south to Gering and then State 92 west into the monument. Or, from I-80, exit at Kimball and drive 40 miles north to Gering.

Included in the 3,000-acre national monument are Scotts Bluff, Mitchell Pass, and adjacent prairie lands, set aside to preserve sites and memorialize history of the Oregon, California, and Mormon trails.

Scotts Bluff National Monument, NE, a pioneer landmark. (Courtesy of George L. Strebel, 1935)

Scotts Bluff is a massive set of bluffs rising 750 feet above the prairie lands just south of the North Platte River. It was the last famous landmark along the Great Platte River Road in Nebraska. These bluffs were named during the fur trade days for **Hiram Scott** (a clerk with a fur-trading company), who died nearby. Legends surround his death, one being that because he was ailing, his colleagues left him some 60 miles away. The next year his bones were found near these bluffs, which meant he had crawled that distance before dying. The bluffs became named for him. At first the name was applied only to the northernmost peak, but in time it became attached to the range of rocky bluffs.

This immense sandstone and clay formation blocked wagon travel along the south bank of the North Platte River, so the trail made a wide detour south of the present-day monument, up the Gering Valley, and over **Robidoux Pass,** then northwest to regain the Platte near the mouth of Horse Creek. A natural gateway, Robidoux Pass is located 8 miles west of the monument headquarters. To drive through the pass, in Gering go .3 mile south on State 71, turn west on Robidoux Road, and within 8 miles the road is in the pass and at Robidoux Ranch. From there a dirt road can be taken west to a paved road that takes you north to Morrill on U.S. 26.

Robidoux Pass was the **first Scotts Bluff pass,** used by fur traders, emigrants to Oregon, Francis Parkman (author of the classic Oregon Trail account), soldiers, and forty-niners. **Westbound Mormon emigrants** using the Oregon Trail on the south side of the North Platte also went over that pass.

In 1850 a shorter Oregon Trail route was opened through what later was named **Mitchell Pass,** which stayed closer to the river and eliminated the eight-mile veer to the south to Robidoux Pass. State 92 uses Mitchell Pass inside today's Scotts Bluff National Monument. Starting in 1851, virtually all wagons used it instead of Robidoux Pass. More than 50,000 wagons moved over this pass in 1852 alone, so ruts became well-worn, and are now several feet deep. Stagecoaches, the Pony Express, and the overland telegraph went through this pass. From Mitchell Pass the trail headed down towards the North Platte and Horse Creek. Mitchell Pass was named for **Gen. Robert B. Mitchell,** who ordered construction of military stations to protect overland communications in 1864. Also named for him was short-lived **Ft. Mitchell,** an outpost of Ft. Laramie, Wyoming which westbound travelers encountered almost immediately after leaving the bluffs through the pass now named after him. The fort remained in place for perhaps 3 or 4 years. Its site was located off State 92 in today's Scotts Bluff National Monument (RHN).

The **Scotts Bluff National Monument Oregon Trail Museum** contains exhibits about the human and natural history of the area and also holds a unique collection of watercolor paintings by the frontier photographer and artist **William Henry Jackson.** There is also a **Mormon Trail exhibit** with a full-sized handcart.

A short section of deep and eroded **Oregon Trail Ruts** in Mitchell Pass is now a walking and interpretive trail immediately west of the museum and visitors' center. Visitors can walk on the trail and ruts for about 1.5 miles.

By taking a paved road to the top of the bluffs, visitors can have a **panoramic view** of the countryside, including the route of the Oregon and Mormon trails. On clear days, Laramie Peak can be seen, almost 60 miles away to the west.

■ Scotts Bluff Camp • Brigham Young • Thurs. May 27 • 13.75 miles • Scottsbluff

The **1847 Brigham Young company** traveled on the north side of the North Platte. With Chimney Rock and Scotts Bluff in sight on the morning of May 27, 1847, William Clayton wrote, "I consider our view this morning more sublime than any other." He said, "Scott's Bluffs look majestic and sublime," adding that "the scenery is truly delightful beyond imagination" (JWC May 27, 1847, 186).

That day the company **stopped for noon** 1.5 miles southeast of where the city of Scottsbluff's Pioneer Park is today (see Scottsbluff, NE, map), which is 1.25 miles west of the **Rebecca Winters Grave.** In total they traveled 13.75 miles and camped 4.25 miles north and west of today's city of Scottsbluff, and their circled wagons were near the banks of the North Platte River (JWC; JOP; JTB). Elder Wilford Woodruff, who spent much of the day scouting the trail, said of the company that day: "It should be understood that we are piloting a road for the house of Israel to travel in for many years to come. Therefore it requires the greater care" (JWW 185).

Of that evening's dancing at this camp, Elder **Erastus Snow** said: "While I write I hear the sound of music and dancing on the other side of the circle. This is a very common recreation in camp, though we have to dispense with the ladies, a very great desideratum" (JES in ERA).

Although this 1847 company continued from this point to stay north of the Platte River until they reached Ft. Laramie, Wyoming, many later LDS companies crossed the North Platte near Scotts Bluff to the south side and followed the **Oregon Trail** to Ft. Laramie, Wyoming.

During the morning of May 28, rain was falling at Scotts Bluff Camp, so the brethren were called together to see if they wanted to move in the rain. All agreed to stay until fairer weather. This was a typical demonstration of the **spirit of democracy** that prevailed in Brigham Young's company.

Six years later, on July 18, 1853, LDS artist **Frederick Piercy,** in the Miller-Cooley company, sketched the bluffs. He included the drawing in his ***Route from Liverpool to Great Salt Lake Valley,*** published in England in 1855. In his diary entry that day he wrote:

> Scott's Bluffs were in view all day. They were certainly the most remarkable sight I had seen since I left England. Viewed from the distance at which I sketched them the shadows were an intense blue, while the rock illuminated by the setting sun partook of its gold, making a beautiful harmony of color. They present a very singular appearance, resembling ruined palaces, castellated towers, temples and monuments. (RFL 118–19)

■ *COVENANT CAMP • BRIGHAM YOUNG • FRI. MAY 28 • 11.5 MILES • MORRILL

On Friday, May 28, Brigham Young's company left the Scotts Bluff Camp about 11 A.M. and traveled 11.5 miles. They parked their wagons in a circle on the bank of the North Platte River near a creek that originated from a spring. This camp's location was 1.75 miles south of today's U.S. 26 and the east edge of **Morrill.** During that travel day they passed a creek that had beaver dams and fish. Elder Woodruff, an avid fisherman, observed that "this is the first stream I have met with containing trout since I left the New England States. Therefore I name it trout creek" (JWW 186). He also recorded President Brigham Young's concerns about some misbehavior in camp:

> During the evening [of May 28] President Young called at my fire & seeing several of the brethren playing dominoes in a wagon nearby began to teach by saying that the devil was getting power over the camp. That for several days past nearly the whole camp had sank into a spirit of card, checker, & domino playing & dancing & the spirit of folly & if they did not speedily repent their works, labors, & journey would be in vain. (JWW 186; spelling and capitalization standardized)

President Young warned about the profane language uttered by some. "I felt the force of his remarks," Elder Woodruff said, "& thought them necessary." Brigham Young stated that "he had rather travel with 10 righteous men who would keep the Commandments of God than the whole camp while in a careless manner & forgetting God" (JWW 186; capitalization standardized).

Brigham Young addressing the original 1847 Mormon pioneer company at Covenant Camp, 13 miles west-northwest of Scotts Bluff. Scotts Bluff National Monument, NE, is in the distance. Brigham Young's "stand" was a leather boat mounted on wheels and called the Revenue Cutter. *(Courtesy of Vernon Murdock, artist, 1973)*

The next morning, Saturday, May 29, a **covenanting meeting** took place. Brigham Young called the camp together at 10:30 A.M., and and after a roll call to see if all were present, he stood in the *Revenue Cutter* and addressed them: "Unless there is a change and a different course of conduct, a different spirit to what is now in this camp, I go no farther" (JWC 191). He

> addressed them severely on their levity, dancing, checkers, cards, Swearing, & When the Priesthood was called into ranks, of the Twelve 8, High Priests 19, Seventies 78, Elders 8 who severally covenanted with the uplifted hand, to serve the Lord, humble themselves, repent of their sins, cleave unto the Lord & renew their former Covenants. It was a very solemn & impressive meeting. (JTB May 29, 1847, 171)

All the members made covenants to keep the commandments of God and raised their hands to the square, as a witness to all, of their commitments. Many were in tears, and all were humbled. Elders Heber C. Kimball, Orson Pratt and Wilford Woodruff also preached. Elder Kimball remarked that "not one of us or one of our families would die till our return, if we would abide counsel as given" (JAL May 29, 1847, 37). His prophecy was fulfilled.

■ ****SACRED PRAYER CAMP • BRIGHAM YOUNG • SAT.–SUN. MAY 29–30 • 8.5 MILES • HENRY**

The site of the company's **last camp in Nebraska,** given the name of **Sacred Prayer Camp,** was in the northwest corner of Scotts Bluff County, Nebraska, between the North Platte River and U.S. 26 at a point about .4 mile east of the Wyoming-Nebraska border and southeast of the present-day town of **Henry.**

After the May 29 chastisement and covenanting meeting ended, the company broke camp by 1:30 P.M. and resumed its journey in peace. **George A. Smith** and **Wilford Woodruff** left ahead of the pioneer company to pilot out the road, and they mentioned the fact that one of the bluffs they passed looked like a steamboat. Wilford called it "Stone Steamboat Bluff," and Orson Pratt called it "Boat Rock" (JWW 190; JOP; spelling and capitalization standardized). After the wagon train traveled 8.5 miles, it halted on the banks of the North Platte River, 200 yards from a creek of clear water to the south.

Although they camped in a downpour of rain, they were grateful for the events of the day. **Amasa Lyman** recorded: "We all felt well & thankful for the sudden change for the better, since our covenant" (JAL May 30, 1847, 38). Of their afternoon travels and the actions of the camp members, **William Clayton** wrote:

> No loud laughter was heard, no swearing, no quarreling, no profane language, no hard speeches to man or beast, and it truly seemed as though the cloud had burst and we had emerged into a new element, a new atmosphere, and a new society. (JWC 201)

Erastus Snow journalized that day that "we are the pioneers for the whole camp of Israel going, like Abraham, by faith, knowing not whither we go, to seek a home for the Saints where the Lord

Sacred "Prayer Circle Bluffs," looking west-northwest with the town of Henry, NE, in the distance. (1994)

has promised to locate a stake of Zion" (JES in ERA 15:53–57).

The next day, Sunday, was not a travel day but a day of fasting, prayer, and four special meetings. At 9:00 A.M. a prayer meeting took place a little south of the camp. **Bishop Tarlton Lewis** began the meeting by singing "The Spirit of God like a Fire Is Burning," then many of the brethren prayed, spoke, and sang in this testimony-prayer meeting. An 11:00 A.M. meeting followed. A special, sacred, prayer meeting took place at 12:30 P.M. in the bluffs to the north, east, or northeast of the camp, hidden from the eyes of the world.[5] **William Clayton** described what took place:

> All the members of the council of the K.[ingdom] of G.[od] in the camp, except Brother Thomas Bullock, went onto the bluffs and selecting a small, circular, level spot surrounded by bluffs and out of sight, we clothed ourselves in the priestly garments and offered up prayer to God for ourselves, this camp and all pertaining to it, the brethren in the army, our families and all the Saints, President Young being mouth. We all felt well and glad for this privilege. The members of the above council are Brigham Young, Heber C. Kimball, Willard Richards, Orson Pratt, George A. Smith, Wilford Woodruff, Amasa Lyman, Ezra T. Benson, Phineas H. Young, John Pack, Charles Shumway, Shadrack Roundy, Albert P. Rockwood, Erastus Snow, myself, Albert Carrington and Porter Rockwell. The two latter, having no clothing with them, stood guard at a little distance from us to prevent interruption. (JWC 202–3)

---

5. Amasa Lyman called this spot "a basin in the hills" (JAL 37; spelling standardized).

Although a black cloud threatened rain, it held off until the special prayer was held, and then it "rained considerably" (JWC 203).

Mormon Trail expert **Dr. Stanley B. Kimball** indicated that the bluffs where the prayer circle took place were the sandy low bluffs about 1 mile east of Henry. "They may be reached off U.S. 26 by following a service road along the Ramshorn Canal," he directed, "but the road is very sandy. The bluffs are also visible from the highway [U.S. 26]" (HSM 69). The bluffs are in Section 3 (T23N R58W).

William Clayton said of the Sabbath Day's effect on the pioneer company: "I never noticed the brethren so still and sober on a Sunday since we started as today. There is no jesting nor laughing, nor nonsense" (JWC 203).

Then, when the rain stopped just before 5 P.M., **President Young** and a few others hiked about 3 miles to a high point among the bluffs (DTZ 129). They closed the sacred day by expressing gratitude to God. High bluffs located 2–3 miles to the northwest may have been the site of the meeting of evening prayer. Erastus Snow said they were on the "highest point within our reach . . . the highest ground we have stood upon" (JES). As the sun set, the brethren bowed their heads in prayer before returning to camp, "satisfied with the proceedings of the day" (JES in ERA 15:54; JWW).

About 2 miles east of Henry on U.S. 26 is a pull-off on the north side of the road. In it are three Nebraska State historical society signs, as well as the farthest west **NPS/NMTA Mormon Trail panel.**

The next morning, May 31, the company moved on, traveling between the North Platte on the left and sand bluffs on the right, and entered present-day Wyoming, thus **completing their 491-mile crossing of Nebraska** from Winter Quarters (EmG 56).

Within two days they would reach Ft. Laramie, Wyoming (27 miles from the Nebraska border), and enter the Oregon Trail, which would take them across most of today's Wyoming.

■ ALTERNATE: THE OVERLAND TRAIL

In the 1860s a new trail route came into use that was more direct to Ft. Bridger from the Nebraska panhandle, avoiding the Oregon and Mormon and California Trails' long northerly curve deep into Wyoming. This Overland Trail extended from present-day **Sidney** west to present-day **Cheyenne** and on west to **Ft. Bridger.**

Because of Indian problems along the North Platte, this Overland Trail route became used for overland stage and mail coach travel after 1862 and by wagon trains. This was the heaviest used westward trail of the 1860s. The **transcontinental railroad** basically followed this route, as does today's Interstate 80. In Nebraska this trail extended 60 miles from where Sidney is today to the Colorado border. I-80 and U.S. 30 approximately follow that route (ARZ).

This more direct route proved useful for LDS emigrants who outfitted at Nebraska City in 1865 and 1866, which positioned them on the south side of the Platte. When the transcontinental railroad terminus moved west beyond North Platte in 1867 to Benton, Wyoming and Laramie City, Wyoming, in 1868, and then to Utah in 1869, Mormon emigrants rode trains that traveled along this same Nebraska route.

On July 23, 1867, **Brigham Willard Kimball,** 22-year-old son of President Heber C. Kimball, died near Lodgepole Creek approximately where **Kimball, Nebraska** (not named for him), is today (ARZ).

LDS Handcart Companies in Nebraska

Between 1856 and 1860, ten LDS handcart companies crossed present-day Nebraska, bound for Utah Territory. In addition, in 1857, one missionary company went from Utah eastbound to the Missouri River pulling handcarts. During these years of handcart travel, LDS wagon trains continued to use the trail also (HCZ).

In 1856 six handcart companies outfitted in **Iowa City, Iowa.** These companies represented about three-quarters of that year's total LDS emigration. They pulled across Iowa and then stopped briefly at **Florence, Nebraska,** to rest, repair, and resupply. Two companies combined into one, making five handcart companies for the push west. After that, departing separately, they trekked across Nebraska during summer and early fall.

The first three handcart units in 1856—the **Edmund Ellsworth, Daniel D. McArthur, and Edward Bunker companies**—reached Utah in reasonably good time and condition. But the last two, the **James G. Willie and Edward Martin companies,** due to a late start, larger size, and various travel difficulties, suffered tragedy when caught in Wyoming blizzards. With them in that disaster were the **John A. Hunt and William B. Hodgetts wagon trains.**

To demonstrate faith in the handcart system despite the Willie and Martin companies' sufferings, Church leaders in 1857 had missionaries heading east from Utah pull handcarts instead of going by wagon train. That year, in addition to the eastbound **missionary handcart company,** the westbound **Israel Evans and Christian Christiansen handcart companies** made the journey from Iowa City to Utah, transporting 40 percent of the year's LDS emigrants (HCZ, BZ).

A year later, 1858, the LDS emigration flow essentially dried up because of the **Utah War** situation, but it resumed in 1859. That year, **Florence** replaced Iowa City as the starting point for the handcarts, and it served as outfitting site for LDS emigrating companies from that year until 1864. In 1859 the **George Rowley handcart company** outfitted at Florence (with about 17 percent of that year's LDS emigration), as did, the next year, the **Daniel Robinson and Oscar O. Stoddard handcart companies** (with about 20 percent of the 1860 LDS emigrants). After 1860 the brief era of handcart usage ended (HCZ).

In total, the 10 westbound handcart companies started with nearly 3,000 people from Iowa City or Florence, but scores dropped out along the way, and dozens died during the normal course of travel. Perpetual Emigrating Fund records show that in the Willie and Martin 1856 handcart companies 191 died between Iowa City and Utah, including those caught in the Wyoming blizzards (HCZ; DS,p).

To cross Nebraska the handcart companies followed rather closely the **Brigham Young company's 1847 route** along the north side of the Platte River, except two 1856 companies who crossed to the south side for part of the way. However, the companies sometimes deviated to travel on stretches of newer, better trail and to avoid natural and seasonal impediments. It needs noting that no handcart group blazed any new trail variants of major consequence; they used existing roads and trails.

The 1856 Handcart Companies

During the historic first year of handcart travel, 1856, the Ellsworth, McArthur, and Bunker companies followed the **Brigham Young 1847 company's route.** The Willie and Martin companies, when in western Nebraska, crossed to the south side of the Platte River and traveled briefly along the **Oregon Trail** (EJWM). The tragedies of the Willie and Martin companies in Wyoming have given their journeys prominence in overland trail history and among Latter-day Saints. And they have become the symbols of all handcart travel if not for the entire Mormon Trail experience.

As was the case during the Iowa crossing, wagons accompanied each handcart company to haul food, tents, and equipment. In addition, the **John A. Hunt and William B. Hodgetts wagon trains** traveled near the Willie and Martin handcart companies, and the

Hodgetts wagon company had frequent contact with the Martin company.

The departure dates from Florence were as follows:

Aug. 16	Willie Handcart Company
Aug. 25	Martin Handcart Company
Aug. 25	Hodgetts Wagon Company
Aug. 31	Hunt Wagon Company

A company of elders that included **LDS emigration official Daniel Spencer** left Florence on Sept. 3 and within a week had passed, in order, the Hunt, Hodgetts, Martin, and Willie companies. The Willie handcart company was five days ahead of the Martin handcart and Hodgetts wagon companies and seven days ahead of the Hunt wagon company. Elder Spencer noted the numbers of people, wagons, and handcarts in each, as follows (LDS,c):

COMPANY	PEOPLE	WAGONS	HANDCARTS
Willie Handcart Company	404	6	87[6]
Martin Handcart Company	576	7	146[7]
Hodgetts Wagon Train	150	33	
Hunt Wagon Train	240	54	

The Willie handcart company required 43 days to cross Nebraska; the Martin handcart company, 41 days. During the Nebraska part of the journey, 7 people in the Willie company died and 24 in the Martin company.

These last four companies left Florence at a time when the Cheyenne were on a rampage. Both the army and the Cheyenne were to blame for troubles that broke out along the Platte during the travel season of 1856. The Native Americans,

6. This number does not include the four private wagons and occupants that accompanied them.

7. If 146 carts, then the ratio of people per cart would be 3.94, a figure unreasonably low. With 5 persons per handcart, the company would have had 116 carts. Another tally, by diarist Samuel Openshaw, put the Martin total at 132 carts.

responding to the wrongful killing of one of their men, in June killed an emigrant below Ft. Kearny and then rode into the fort itself. In August they attacked a mail coach, causing the army to attack the Cheyenne on the Platte above the fort and kill 10. As a result, all along the route, the Cheyenne struck back and within a month killed, wounded, or captured about a dozen travelers (FIB 20–121). During the Willie and Martin companies' Nebraska travels, Native Americans murdered three different parties at locations the handcart people passed or saw. Two involved Utah Territory secretary Almon G. Babbitt's small company of four wagons (he was not in that group) and subsequently himself and others traveling in his carriage.

Midway across Nebraska the Willie company's cattle stampeded one night, and 30 were never found or replaced. Their loss meant that loads on the now-teamless wagons had to be apportioned out to the handcarts, which extra weight caused hardship to carts and to their pullers.

The James G. Willie Handcart Company, Aug. 16—Sept. 28, 1856

■ Florence Reoutfitting Camp • Aug. 11–15

The Willie handcart company spent Aug. 11–15 in Florence, resting from their long trek across Iowa and preparing for the rest of the journey. They occupied "the campground near the old sawmill" (SLT Nov. 30, 1913, 11). On Aug. 13 LDS Church officials settled up accounts and found out who were stopping and who would continue on. An Aug. 14 report said the company was delayed in Florence because of "their carts being unfit for their journey across the Plains; some requiring new axles, and the whole of them having to have a piece of iron screwed on to prevent the wheel from wearing away the wood" (HCZ 94).

Levi Savage later recalled that he warned the travelers of hardships they would probably face, especially deep snow and lack of proper clothing. He "spoke warmly" about the lateness of the season and urged that they halt and winter there. Capt. Willie countered that God would help them, and Elder Millen Atwood suggested all pray to know for themselves, whether to go or stay. A proposal to stop did not meet with general approval (HCZ 96).

If a few score had voted to stop and stay in the region until the next April (8 months), the Saints probably could have found some kind of housing and work. But upwards of 1,200 in the two handcart and two wagon companies could not have been provided for in Florence, Council Bluffs, or Omaha City combined. Unlike 1846, when Saints had government permission to establish Winter Quarters on Indian lands for two years, in 1856 land and timber for a large temporary settlement were not available. Nor did LDS emigration agents have funds to provide food and supplies or transportation downriver to St. Joseph or St. Louis. Even if these Saints had been able to establish some kind of makeshift winter village, that winter of 1856–57 was one of the worst in Nebraska's history in terms of long-lasting subzero cold, deep snow, and loss of livestock. If Saints had wintered there in inadequate housing and with meager food, there could have been a catastrophe from exposure and illness worse than what the Saints at Winter Quarters had experienced in 1846–47.

The Willie company spent the next two days fixing the handcarts. Carpentering and iron work were done in earnest. Just before departure time, the emigrants heard exhortations to go forward from Brothers James McGaw, William H. Kimball, George D. Grant, and Almon Babbitt (HCZ 96; EJWM 19–20).

■ Route: Little Papillion to Loup Fork Ferry • Aug. 16–23

On Aug. 16, some 87 handcarts pulled out, led by Capt. Willie and accompanied by several wagons. They camped that night at the Little Papillion. (The Martin handcart company followed them nine days later.) The 400-plus people were divided into five subcompanies of roughly 100, captained by Millen Atwood, Levi Savage, William Woodward, John Chislett, and J. A. Ahmanson. Andrew Siler was captain of the **independent wagon company.** Niel Lars Christiansen served as interpreter and counselor for the Danish Saints. That evening **Col. Almon Babbitt** and four wagons camped with them.

After resting on Sunday, they moved on to camp at the **Big Papillion,** 9 miles from Florence. Their campsite is on the far northwest edge of Omaha, where Big Papillion Creek crosses Military Road, just east of N. 126th Street. They camped within the triangle of land northeast of the intersection of those two roads and the southeast-flowing Big Papillion.

Between Aug. 19 and 22 they ferried across the **Elkhorn River,** reached the **Platte River,** and crossed **Shell Creek.** On Aug. 23 they ferried across the **Loup Fork River** while their cattle forded it.

■ Route: Loup Fork to Wood River • Aug. 24–30

From the Loup Fork crossing site, the Willie handcart company traveled along the **south side of the Loup Fork** for about 30 to 40 miles, Aug. 24–26. On Aug. 28 they crossed **Prairie Creek** and arrived at **Wood River** after dark. Next day, they received news that on Aug. 25 Col. Babbitt's wagons had been attacked by **Cheyenne,** who killed two of his men and a child and took a Mrs. Wilson captive; two men escaped. That day Willie company officers visited a large encampment of **Omaha** .5 mile from camp. They were numerous and had a great quantity of horses. They bartered buffalo meat for Mormon articles.

On Aug. 30, perhaps 20 miles from **Wood River,** the company came upon the **graves of the two men and a child,** onto which they shoveled more earth to protect them. They again crossed the **Wood River** and camped 4 miles up from where they crossed before. There, Col. Babbitt and a man and a woman arrived in camp with five mules and a carriage and camped with them. The woman, a Sister Stewart, joined the Hunt wagon company that was also camped there. At that point the Willie handcart company was approximately 200 miles from Florence.

■ Loss of 30 Cattle • Sept. 4, 1856 • 265 miles from Florence

On Aug. 31 Babbitt went to Ft. Kearny. On Sept. 1 the handcart company crossed **Elm Creek** and on Sept. 2 crossed **Buffalo Creek.** Next day they traveled and camped by a small lake. There, on Sept. 4, they suffered a major loss when their cattle stampeded in the evening. Men went in pursuit, but a count in the morning showed that **30 cattle were missing.** John Chislett, years later, described the crisis this loss caused:

> We hunted for them three days in every direction, but did not find them. We at last reluctantly gave up the search, and prepared to travel without them as best we could. We had only about enough oxen to put one yoke to each wagon; but as they were each loaded with about three thousand pounds of flour,

> the teams could not of course move them. We then yoked up our beef cattle, milch cows, and, in fact, everything that could bear a yoke—even two year-old heifers . . . we were unable with all our stock, to move our loads. As a last resort, we again loaded a sack of flour on each cart. (HCZ 100)

The company, severely handicapped by that loss and delayed three days' travel time because of it, moved on 4 or 5 miles and camped in the bend of a "fine creek near the Platte." That day **Col. Babbitt** came to their camp from Ft. Kearny, after having talked to the two men who had escaped the attack on his wagons.

While camped the next day, Sept. 7, a Sunday, leaders **met concerning the cattle crisis.** Because of the loss of pulling teams and beef for food, they called on the emigrants to reform in conduct and to obey company officers. They spent the morning of Sept. 8 "fixing up of our remodeled teams, and the changing of freight from one wagon to another." That morning a rider, Henry Bauichter, came among them with **news about murders by Indians** up ahead. He said that Thomas Margetts, a couple named Cowdry, and a child were killed and Mrs. Margetts was missing. The tragedy site, he estimated, was 70 miles to the west, on North Bluff Creek. That night the Willie handcart company traveled along the Platte bottom, some of it very swampy and sandy, for 10 or 12 miles and camped close to the river. They collected firewood from an island in the river and moved on, camping late Sept. 9 near where **Skunk Creek** empties into the Platte (EJWM 26–30).

■ Route: North Bluff Fork and Crossing the Platte • Sept. 12, 1856

On Sept. 12, 302 miles from Florence, the Willie handcart company crossed the **North Bluff Fork** and camped by it. That day **important LDS visitors** visited their camp. These leaders and returning missionaries included Franklin D. Richards, William H. Kimball, George D. Grant, Joseph A. Young, Chauncey G. Webb, Nathaniel H. Felt, William C. Dunbar, and others. At that point, the company journal says, the Willie company had **404 people, 87 handcarts, 6 wagons,** 6 yoke of oxen, and 32 cows and mules, and notes that they were considerably weakened by the loss of so many cattle.

■ ROUTE: SOUTH SIDE ON OREGON TRAIL • SEPT. 13–28, 1856

Based on Elder Richards's counsel, on Sept. 13 they **forded the North Platte** at a place he had found and then camped on the south shore. The route now was on the Oregon Trail. They moved along the North Platte and then over bluffs. On Sept. 18 they entered **Ash Hollow** and camped near its mouth by the North Platte River. There, they lost two days while repairing handcarts and looking for a missing sister.

Resuming the trek, they closely followed the North Platte River and camped by it. On Sept. 24 they passed **Chimney Rock.** On Sept. 26 they left the river, approached **Scotts Bluff,** and camped near it.

The next day they crossed **Horseshoe Creek,** and on Sept. 28 were probably in present-day Wyoming. That day they learned about the **murder of Almon Babbitt** and the two men with him.

The Edward Martin Handcart Company, Aug. 25–Oct. 6/7, 1856

■ FLORENCE RE-OUTFITTING CAMP, AUG. 22–25

On Aug. 22 the Martin company crossed from Iowa on ferryboats to Florence. They rested one day and had meetings the next. Apparently the company lacked sufficient wagons, so some handcarts had to carry 100 pounds of flour—"a heavier load than ever before"—and big tents were loaded on some carts. (That flour would be eaten first, so the number of extra pounds would be reduced daily and would be gone by the time the handcarts reached Ash Hollow.) The company had provisions for 60 days, allowing for a ration of 1 pound of flour per adult and half a pound per child (LHWJJ 123, 129).

■ ROUTE: CUTLER'S PARK TO THE PLATTE RIVER • AUG. 25–30

The Martin handcart company left Florence on Aug. 25, nine days behind the **Willie handcart company,** and moved 2.5 miles to the area of **Cutler's Park** (see also **Winter Quarters**). Next day, the men of the company went back to Florence to start the cattle west. While they were there, **Almon G. Babbitt,** Utah's territorial secretary, called on them. He was "dressed in corduroy pants, woolen overshirt and felt hat" and "seemed in high glee." He was heading for Salt Lake Valley in one carriage, offered to carry mail for anyone, had "a considerable amount of money," and expected to make the long trip within 15 days. His carriage had room, so a Sister Stewart opted to go with him (EJWM 106).

That day the **Hodgetts wagon train** also moved from Florence to the Cutler's Park area.

On Aug. 27 the Martin company moved 6 miles and camped on **Little Papillion Creek.** The next day they covered 15 miles, crossing the **Big Papillion** about noon and camping by the **Elkhorn River.** At that point they had 132 handcarts, 8 wagons, and 280 head of cattle. The next day, Aug. 29, they ferried across the **Elkhorn River,** finishing about noon. They camped by **Rawhide Creek** 3 miles farther on . On Aug. 30 they reached the banks of the **Platte,** and rested there the next day, Sunday (EJWM 106).

■ Route: Platte River to Opposite Ft. Kearny • Sept. 1–13

Monday, Sept. 1, the Martin company traveled from 7 A.M. to 7 P.M., with an hour lunch break at **Shell Creek.** They camped on the prairie, short of the river and, lacking wood to cook with, went to bed without supper. The next day they moved 4 miles to the Platte River, had breakfast there, and then moved to and **ferried across the Loup Fork River** that day and the next, Sept. 3, until sunset. Because the handcart company occupied the ferry, the **Hodgetts wagon company** had to wait until the next day to cross. On Sept. 4 the Martin company moved 14 miles, and the next day rains reduced their travel time to only 2.5 hours. That night they camped by the Platte, put up tents, and it rained again.

On Sept. 6 they "met a **large party of Indians,** men, women and children, with their horses and mules, all loaded with skins," Samuel Openshaw recorded, "going to Missouri to trade with the Whites. They are the first Indians that we have seen" (EJWM 107). On Sunday, Sept. 7, the small westbound company of leaders, including Franklin D. Richards, and returning missionaries, reached them. After covering 24 miles on Sept. 8, they came late at night to **Prairie Creek,** "which is very good water," Samuel Openshaw said (EJWM 108). For the next two days they followed and camped by **Prairie Creek.** On Sept. 11, about 8 or 9 miles before the Wood River, the company passed the **graves of two men and a child.** They had been in **Almon Babbitt's four-wagon train** and were killed on Aug. 25 by Cheyenne. Two of Babbitt's teamsters had escaped, but Mrs. Wilson was taken captive and never heard of again.

On Sept. 12 they came to the **Wood River,** crossed on a small bridge, and continued down the side of that river. During morning travels the next day, they passed opposite **Ft. Kearny.** Mid-morning, a strange incident happened. While two bachelors, traveling together, were pulling their cart, the weaker one said he couldn't go on, they argued, and he died. Josiah Rogerson put his body into a less-heavily loaded cart, covered him with a quilt, and pulled him for 5 or 6 miles to the noon camp. They buried him "a short distance west of Fort Kearney" on the north side of the Platte (EJWM 109–10). That afternoon they caught up to and passed the **Hodgetts wagon train,** who had waited for them so both companies could travel together on account of the danger of attack.

■ ROUTE: BUFFALO CREEK TO NORTH PLATTE CROSSING • SEPT. 15–30

By midday on Sept. 15 the Martin handcart company, with the Hodgetts wagon company close by, reached and followed **Buffalo Creek.** That day they saw "several droves of **buffalo**" (EJWM 110). On Sept. 16 the wagon train had to wait for the handcart company to cross **Buffalo Creek.** By then, the **Hunt wagon train** was less than 2 days behind the Martin and Hodgetts companies.

On Sept. 17 the Martin and Hodgetts companies camped near each other, and some of the Hodgetts cattle bothered the handcart Saints. The next day the handcart people left first; the wagon train caught up with them by 5 P.M. Sept. 19 they encountered sandy bluffs, which meant very hard pulling. In the afternoon they traveled along the Platte and camped by the river.

During the next three days the wagon and handcart companies traveled near each other, passing **Skunk Creek** and **Carron Creek.** Rain fell on Sunday, Sept. 21, and as wet buffalo chips would not burn, they did no cooking (EJWM 111).

On Sept. 22 the companies came to and crossed **North Bluff Fork,** which was 10 rods wide and 2 feet deep. Sept. 23 was for the Martin handcart company "the hardest day we have had," because of sandy bluffs and roads and deep sand (EJWM 112). They covered only 11.75 miles. For the next four days they continued to struggle through the **region of sandy bluffs.**

On Sept. 23 the Martin company came upon the **site of the Babbitt killing.** They were then 6 miles east of **Bluff Creek.** About

70 yards to the left of the road, John Jacques said, they saw a little harness, two wagon wheels, and the springs of a burned carriage or buggy, among other items, which they felt were relics of Babbitt's outfit (EJWM 112).

The next day about noon they came upon "the blood stained garments of Thomas Margetts wife and child, who had been murdered by the Indians. At the site were a quantity of feathers strewn about, from a feather bed, a blood stained shirt, and a child's skull" (EJWM 112). That night they camped at **Duckwood Creek.**

On Sept. 30 the Hodgetts company and then the Martin company **crossed the North Platte River** to its south side. Two days later the **Hunt wagon company** crossed the North Platte, too, a little above **Ash Hollow.**

■ Route: On the Oregon Trail to Present-day Wyoming • Oct. 1–6

The Martin and Hodgetts companies followed along the North Platte, using the **Oregon Trail.** On Oct. 4 the Martin company passed **Chimney Rock** and then **Scotts Bluff.** The **Hunt wagon train** also passed Chimney Rock that day, so by then they were less than a day behind the Martin and Hodgetts companies.

Sometime during the next two days the Martin company entered present-day Wyoming, and on Oct. 8 they reached Ft. Laramie some 20 miles inside present-day Wyoming. The Hodgetts and Hunt wagon trains left present-day Nebraska on Oct. 7 or 8; the former reached Ft. Laramie on Oct. 8 and the latter on Oct. 9 (EJWM 180, 199).

The Transcontinental Railroad

Construction of the Railroad

In 1862 President Abraham Lincoln signed the **Pacific Railroad Act** that had earlier been passed by Congress, allowing for construction of the transcontinental railroad. Two companies were chosen to complete specific tasks. The **Central Pacific Railroad of California** was to build eastward from Sacramento. The **Union Pacific Company** was to build westward up the Platte River Valley from Omaha, Nebraska.

Building the transcontinental railroad is one of the greatest construction projects in United States history. In **Nebraska,** little construction took place until 1865. Then, with the Civil War over and thousands of demobilized soldiers needing work, the railroad hired large construction crews, supplemented the next year by Irishmen hired in eastern cities.

After Grenville Dodge was appointed chief construction engineer, Union Pacific track-laying proceeded in earnest. The pick and shovel men, teamsters, blacksmiths, mechanics, carpenters, masons, and track layers were mostly Irish immigrants or Civil War veterans. They worked 12- to 16-hour days, including weekends, and earned on average a dollar a day. With experience, Union Pacific crews were laying 1 mile or more of track per day (UPK).

Across Nebraska the tracks followed the **north side of the Platte River Valley.** As the tracks and their trains moved continually westward, so did the annual outfitting locations for emigrant wagon trains.

A newspaper reporter present at the construction in mid-Nebraska in 1866 described the "science" of track laying that he witnessed:

> A light car, drawn by a single horse, gallops up to the front with its load of rails. Two men seize the end of a rail and start forward, the rest of the gang taking hold by twos, until it is clear of the car. They come forward at a run. At the word of command the rail is dropped in its place, right side up with care, while the same process goes on at the other side of the car. Less than thirty seconds to a rail, and so four rails go down to the minute. The moment the car is empty it is tipped over on the side of the track to let the next loaded car pass it, and then it is tipped back again, and it is a sight to see it go flying back for another load, propelled by a horse at full gallop at the end of sixty or eighty feet of rope. Close behind the first gang come the gaugers, spikers and bolters, and a lively time they make of it. It is a grand "Anvil Chorus" that those sturdy sledges are playing across the plains. It is in triple time, three strokes to the spike . . . ten spikes to a rail, four hundred rails to a mile. (UPH)

Two problems hampered the project: Nebraska's lack of trees to be used for railroad ties, and Native American tribes who opposed the project. By July 1866 crews had completed but 60 miles of track west from Omaha. In October they passed the 100th meridian, and in November the rail line reached what became the city of North Platte. Nonetheless, in 1867, **LDS emigrants** were able to cross the United States by train to the Mississippi River, ferry across it, and board a Union Pacific train to ride to their **North Platte outfitting grounds** to join a wagon train there.

The Union Pacific route crossed the North Platte River to the south side and then followed a course across the southern edge of present-day Wyoming, close to the route of today's I-80, instead of making the big swing northward that the Oregon and Mormon Trails made. In Utah Territory, hundreds of **Mormon workmen** helped grade and lay track. On May 10, 1869, the Union Pacific and Central Pacific railroads' tracks met and joined with the driving of the **golden spike** at Promontory Summit in Utah Territory. The new tracks spanned 2,000 miles from the West Coast to Omaha, Nebraska. Another 1,500 miles of track reached from there to New York, giving the nation a transcontinental railway system. Trains could move passengers from Omaha to California in six days instead of the four to six months required for travel by wagon (UPK).

Omaha had a grand celebration on **May 10, 1869,** when news came by **telegraph from Utah** of the junction of the Union Pacific and Central Pacific. Citizens draped private homes and public buildings with bunting, flags, banners, and mottoes. Bells rang. One hundred guns boomed in rapid succession—a salute to the good news. An anonymous poem conveys some of the joy that Omahans felt that day:

> Ring out, oh bells! Let cannons roar
> In loudest tones of thunder,
> The iron bars from shore to shore
> Are laid, and nations wonder.

Mormon Railroad Travel across Nebraska

The effect of having trains cover the 3,000 miles between the east and west coasts in ten days' time was monumental. When the line opened in 1869, it effectively **ended the era of Mormon Trail wagon trains** and opened a **new era of rail travel to Utah.** Nevertheless, until March 1872, when a railroad bridge opened across the Missouri River, train travelers had to disembark from one train, cross the river by ferry boat, and then board another train. Omaha was a busy transfer terminal.

In July 1869 Elder **Henry G. Boyle** led a group of converts from the Southern States to Utah by train. They left New York City on July 12. One in the group said regarding the train ride from **Omaha** to Utah: "The cars in which the passengers rode were very primitive; seats were either placed along the sides of the car with space in the middle for the luggage, eating baskets, personal belongings, or seats were placed crosswise with an aisle down the middle." They reached Ogden about July 21 (OPH 8:371–74).

In late July 1869 a ship carrying a company of **750 European Saints** docked in New York, where the emigrants boarded trains for **Omaha. Jacob I. Jacobson**, a Swede in that company, described their primitive travel circumstances during their train trip from Omaha to Utah:

Our next stop was Omaha, where we were obliged to stop several days, waiting for the trains of the Union Pacific Railroad. While there we stayed in a four-story frame hotel, one of the best in Omaha at that time, but due to our rooms being infested with bedbugs, which we had never seen before, we had to light the lamps and sit up through the night. Finally the maiden trip of the U.P. was ready, and we climbed aboard some old battered passenger coaches that had been used in the Civil War. Two engines were used—one pushing and one pulling. Much precaution was taken on account of the new road construction, making it a slow and tiresome trip. We were forced to wait at the Platte River while men relined the railroad lines, and ballasted the gravel. The ties and rails had been laid over the buffalo grass on the plains. (OPH 8:392–93)

In October 1869 **Sarah E. Hutchings** and a group of **English LDS converts** arrived in New York Harbor. She said they traveled by rail to the Missouri River, ferried across to **Omaha,** "and waited two days for the train to come back" from the West. "We were put in freight cars to sleep, as none knew anything about camping out, and we had nothing to camp with anyway." Their trip from New York to Ogden took 11 days (OPH 8:382).

About the General Editor

Dr. LaMar C. Berrett, the general editor of the six-volume work *Sacred Places,* is a professor emeritus of Church history and doctrine at Brigham Young University. He was born and reared in Riverton, Utah, and served as a rifleman and platoon runner in the Second Infantry Division of the United States Army during World War II. While serving, he spent 110 "combat days" in Belgium, Germany, and Czechoslovakia during the Battle of the Bulge. He later served a mission in the Southern States, where he served as a counselor to the mission president. He has since served in many positions in the Church, including stake clerk, high councilor, bishop's counselor, and bishop. He was a member of the Church Historical Arts and Sites subcommittee for three years and president of his family genealogical organization for 25 years.

Dr. Berrett received a bachelor's degree in business from the University of Utah. He went on to earn a master's degree in Church history and philosophy and a doctorate in educational administration from BYU. Following nine years as a seminary teacher, he joined the BYU faculty, teaching at the university for 29 years and serving as the chair of the Church History Department for nine years before retiring in 1991.

He has researched, written, and directed many TV and video productions for use in the classroom. He is the author of several books, including the much-acclaimed *Discovering the World of the Bible,* and coauthor with Blair G. Van Dyke of *Holy Lands: A History of the Latter-day Saints in the Near East.* He conducted a comprehensive aerial photography project in 1978, which involved infrared photography of significant Church history sites from New Hampshire to Salt Lake City. He has also conducted numerous Church history travel tours and has hosted more than 150 tours worldwide.

Dr. Berrett has written more than 50 percent of the text of the *Sacred Places* series, and with the help of other contributing authors, he created all of the exact-scale, never-before-published maps appearing in the series. In addition, he took all photographs unless otherwise noted. A lifetime of researching the history of The Church of Jesus Christ of Latter-day Saints has been to him a "soul-satisfying labor of love."

Dr. Berrett and his wife, the former Darlene Hamilton, reside in Orem, Utah. They are the parents of nine children.

About the Authors

William G. Hartley is an associate professor of history at Brigham Young University. He received B. A. and M. A. degrees in history at BYU and completed doctoral course work in history at Washington State University. In 1972 he became a research historian and oral history project director on the staff of LDS Church historian Leonard Arrington. In 1981 he joined the BYU faculty as part of the Joseph Fielding Smith Institute for Church History. He directed BYU's Family and Genealogy Research Services for six years, was founding president of the Mormon Trails Association, helped start the Iowa Mormon Trails Association, has been a member of the editorial boards of the *Journal of Mormon History* and *Mormon Historical Studies,* served as president of the Mormon History Association, and is an editor on the Joseph Smith Papers project for the Department of Family and Church History of The Church of Jesus Christ of Latter-day Saints. He has published in professional journals and in LDS periodicals more than 100 articles on LDS history and family biography and is the author or coauthor of 14 books, including the award-winning *Stand by My Servant Joseph: The Story of the Joseph Knight Family and the Restoration* (Deseret Book, 2003). He grew up in Butte, Montana, and San Lorenzo, California. He served as a missionary in the Eastern States/Cumorah Missions and later as a bishop in Sandy, Utah. He is married to the former Linda Perry. They live in Murray, Utah, and are the parents of six children.

A. Gary Anderson was an associate professor of Church history and doctrine at Brigham Young University. He received his bachelor's degree in business administration from the University of Utah and his master's and doctorate in educational administration from BYU. He served as director of the institute of religion at Dixie College in St. George, Utah, for nine years before joining the faculty at BYU in 1971. He researched and wrote the text used for some years for the course Teachings of the Living Prophets taught in the Church Educational System and at BYU. Born and raised in Ephraim, Utah, he was elected student body president at Snow College in Ephraim. After serving a mission to Denmark, he married Annette Dean, and they became the parents of nine children. Dr. Anderson and his son Ronald D. Anderson assisted editor LaMar C. Berrett as they traveled dusty roads on foot or in four-wheel-drive vehicles across sagebrush fields and streams and plotted significant finds on U.S. Geological Survey topographical maps. They spent several weeks on this project, after completing extensive research in numerous books and journals. Dr. Anderson was not well during these excursions and passed away soon afterward, in January 1995.

Abbreviations Used in Photo Captions

LDSCA	LDS Church Archives, Family and Church History Department, The Church of Jesus Christ of Latter-day Saints, Salt Lake City, Utah.
RLDSLA	Library Archives and Museum, Reorganized Church of Jesus Christ of Latter Day Saints (The Community of Christ), Independence, Missouri.
GPRRAM	Great Platte River Road Archway Monument, Kearney, Nebraska.

Bibliography

AAC Call, Anson. Autobiography. Typescript. L. Tom Perry Special Collections, Harold B. Library, Brigham Young University, Provo, Utah.

ABM Van Wagoner, Richard S., and Steven C. Van Wagoner. *A Book of Mormons.* Salt Lake City: Signature Books, 1986.

ACJ Alfred Cordon Journal. LDS Church Archives, Salt Lake City, Utah.

ADW Arbor Day Website: www.arborday.org

AEDG Gibbs, Eliza Dana. "Autobiography of Eliza Dana Gibbs." *Autobiographies of Mormon Pioneer Women.* Salt Lake City: Pioneer Press, 1994.

AF Ancestral File. Computerized Genealogy Database. Salt Lake City: The Church of Jesus Christ of Latter-day Saints Family History Library, 1999.

AGW "Life [Autobiography] of George Whitaker: A Utah Pioneer." Typescript. LDS Church Archives, Salt Lake City, Utah.

AHAI Andreas, A. T. *Illustrated Historical Atlas of the State of Iowa, 1875.* Chicago: Andreas Atlas Co., 1875.

AHMW Whitney, Helen Mar Kimball. Autobiography. LDS Church Archives, Salt Lake City, Utah. Appears in numerous issues of *Women's Exponent.*

AHMW,h Whitney, Helen Mar Kimball. *A Woman's View: Helen Mar Kimball Whitney's Reminiscences of Early Church History.* Edited by Jeni B. Holzapfel and Richard N. Holzapfel. Provo, Utah: Brigham Young University Religious Studies Center, 1997.

AHN *History of the State of Nebraska.* Chicago: Western Historical Co., 1882. www.kancoll.org/books

AJB Brown, John. "Autobiography of John Brown 1820–1896." Edited by John Zimmerman Brown. Salt Lake City: privately published, 1941.

AJH Holbrook, Joseph. Autobiography. ("The Life of Joseph Holbrook, 1806–1871.") Typescript. L. Tom Perry Special Collections, Harold B. Library, Brigham Young University, Provo, Utah.

ALB Barney, Lewis. "Autobiography and Diary." Typescript. Copy in possession of Ron Barney, Salt Lake City, Utah.

ALFH *Amasa Mason Lyman Family History.* Vol. 2. Compiled by Melvin A. Lyman. Delta, Utah, 1969.

AMBS Biographical Sketch of Albert Merrill. Typescript, 11 pp. Copy in possession of William G. Hartley.

AnI *The Annals of Iowa.* Published quarterly. Des Moines, Iowa: Iowa State Historical Dept., Division of Historical Museum and Archives, 1863–.

AOS Nixon, Loretta D., and L. Douglas Smoot. *Abraham Owen Smoot: A Testament of His Life.* Provo, Utah: Brigham Young University Press, 1994.

APPP Pratt, Parley P. *Autobiography of Parley Parker Pratt.* 3d and 4th ed. Salt Lake City: Deseret Book, 1938, 1985.

ARC Crookston, Robert, Sr. Autobiography. LDS Church Archives, Salt Lake City, Utah.

ARZ Kimball, Stanley B. "Another Route to Zion: Rediscovering the Overland Trail." *Ensign* (June 1984), 340–45.

ASH Hawley, Asa S. Autobiography. On LDS Church website: lds.org/churchhistory/library/pioneer company sources

ATI Mott, David C. *Abandoned Towns, Villages and Post Offices of Iowa.* Council Bluffs, Iowa: N.p., 1973.

AWF Foote, Warren. Autobiography. LDS Church Archives, Salt Lake City, Utah.

BFN Mueller, Frank. "Rebecca Burdick Winters and the Mormons." Burdick Family Newsletter, April 2005, www.burdickfamily.org/

BiE *Latter-day Saint Biographical Encyclopedia.* Compiled by Andrew Jenson. 4 vols. Salt Lake City: Andrew Jenson History Co., 1901–36. Reprint, Salt Lake City, Utah: Western Epics, 1971.

BJI Johnson, Brigham. *Iowa: Its History and Its Foremost Citizens.* Vol. 1. Chicago, Ill.: S. J. Clarke Publishing, 1918.

BLI *Blockton, Iowa: A Town for All Generations, 1888–1988.* Blockton, Iowa: Blockton Centennial Committee, 1988.

BOL www.Borglumonline

BYAM Arrington, Leonard J. *Brigham Young: American Moses.* New York: Alfred A. Knopf, 1985.

BYUS *Brigham Young University Studies.* Published quarterly at Brigham Young University, Provo, Utah.

BZ Christensen, Allen C. *Before Zion: An Account of the 7th Handcart Company.* Springville, Utah: Council Press, 2004.

CEBDC *Come Explore Beautiful Davis County, Iowa.* Travel brochure. Bloomfield, Iowa: Davis Co. Tourism Corporation, 1993.

CFFC Hartman, Patrice. "Mormon Pioneers in Iowa: The Connyers Families at Four Corners, Lost Camp, and Little Sioux." Typescript, Dec. 23, 1996. 7 pp.

CHC Roberts, B. H. *A Comprehensive History of The Church of Jesus Christ of Latter-day Saints.* 6 vols. Salt Lake City: The Church of Jesus Christ of Latter-day Saints, 1930.

ChCh Jenson, Andrew. *Church Chronology.* Salt Lake City: Deseret News Press, 1899.

CHMB Tyler, Daniel. *A Concise History of the Mormon Battalion in the Mexican War, 1846–1847.* Salt Lake City, Utah: Daniel A. Tyler, 1881. Reprint, Glorieta, N. Mex.: Rio Grande Press, 1969.

CJ,c Carl Jones to William G. Hartley, Jan. 10, 2005. Copy in author's files.

CN *Church News.* Salt Lake City: The Church of Jesus Christ of Latter-day Saints, 1936–.

COF Kenison, David T. *Chronicles of Faith.* Orem, Utah: LDS Gems Press, 1997.

CoS Burton, Richard F. *The City of the Saints.* Edited by Fawn M. Brodie. New York: Alfred A. Knopf, 1963.

CSI Jorgensen, Danny L. "The Cutlerites of Southwestern Iowa." *Annals of Iowa* 58 (Spring 1999): 131–61.

CWW *Covered Wagon Women: Diaries and Letters from the Western Trails, 1840–1890.* Compiled and edited by Kenneth L. Holmes. 11 vols. Glendale, Calif.: Arthur H. Clark Co., 1983–91.

DBD Jenson, Andrew. *Day by Day with the Utah Pioneers.* St. George, Utah: American Graphics Printing, 1994.

DBL Berrett, LaMar C. *Down Berrett Lane.* 2 vols. Orem, Utah: J. Watts Family Genealogical Organization, 1980.

DBWT Hartley, William G. "Down-and-Back Wagon Trains: Travelers on the Mormon Trail in 1861." *Overland Journal* 11, no. 4 (1993): 23–34.

DCAS Scott, Charles A. "Diary of Charles A. Scott." *Utah Historical Quarterly* 28, no. 2, 154–76; 28, no. 4, 386–402.

DFA Allen, Franklin. Diary July 1846 to July 1848. Microfilm. LDS Church Archives, Salt Lake City, Utah.

DGMK Keysor, Guy Messiah. "Diaries and Reminiscences, 1846–1857."

Microfilm of holograph. LDS Church Archives, Salt Lake City, Utah.

DHOC *Witness of the Second Elder: Documentary History of Oliver Cowdery.* Edited by Richard Lloyd Anderson and Scott H. Faulring. 4:489–90. Provo, Utah: Foundation for Ancient Research and Mormon Studies (FARMS), 1999.

DHS Stout, Hosea. *Diary of Hosea Stout.* Vols. 1 and 2. Edited by Juanita Brooks. Salt Lake City: University of Utah Press, 1964.

DIA *Dialogue: A Journal of Mormon Thought.* Dialogue Foundation, Salt Lake City, Utah.

DJC Cummings, James Willard. Diary (1842–79). LDS Church Archives, Salt Lake City, Utah.

DJDL *A Mormon Chronicle: Diaries of John D. Lee, 1846–1876.* Edited by Robert Glass Cleland and Juanita Brooks. 2 vols. San Marino, Calif.: Huntington Library, 1955. Reprint, Salt Lake City: University of Utah Press, 1983.

DJO Oakley, John. Diary, 1856. LDS Church Archives, Salt Lake City, Utah.

DJRB Baker, Jean Rio Griffiths. Diary. In *Covered Wagon Women: Diaries and Letters from the Western Trails, 1840–1890.* Compiled and edited by Kenneth L. Holmes. 11 vols. 3:203–81. Glendale, Calif.: Arthur H. Clarke Co., 1983–91.

DJS John Smith. Diary, 1846–1854. Holograph. LDS Church Archives, Salt Lake City, Utah. See also JJoS and JJS.

DLDY Young, Lorenzo Dow. "Diary of Lorenzo Dow Young." *Utah Historical Quarterly* 14 (1946): 133–71.

DLHH Hatch, Lorenzo Hill. Diary of Lorenzo Hill Hatch. LDS Church Archives, Salt Lake City, Utah.

DMHPR Mary Haskin Parker Richards. Diary (1846–48). LDS Church Archives, Salt Lake City, Utah. Or see *Winter Quarters: The 1846–1848 Life Writings of Mary Haskins Parker Richards.* Edited by Maurine Carr Ward. Logan, Utah: Utah State University Press, 1996.

DMT Kimball, Stanley. *Discovering Mormon Trails: New York to California, 1831–1868.* Salt Lake City: Deseret Book, 1979.

DN *Salt Lake City Deseret News,* 1850–.

DNCA *Deseret News Church Almanac.* Salt Lake City: *Deseret News* in cooperation with the LDS Historical Department, 1974–.

DPM Madsen, Peter. Diary, 1856. Holograph. LDS Church Archives, Salt Lake City, Utah. Translation in possession of Don H. Smith, Pullman, Washington.

DSL Smith, Don H., to LaMar C. Berrett. Pullman, Washington, Apr. 26, 1994.

DSL-H Smith, Don H., to William G. Hartley. Pullman, Washington, July 10, 1995.

DSP Smith, Don. Willie Company Task Paper, unpublished.

DS,p Proofreading corrections by Don Smith, Willie handcart company expert, on this book's manuscript, Aug. 22, 2005.

DTD Hartley, William G. "Diary of a Teenage Driver [Zebulon Jacobs]." *New Era* (July 1984), 8–11.

DTZ Knight, Hal, and Stanley B. Kimball. *111 Days to Zion.* Salt Lake City: Deseret News, 1978.

EBTJ Enoch B. Tripp Journal. L. Tom Perry Special Collections, Harold B. Library, Brigham Young University, Provo, Utah.

EDCB Babbitt, Charles H. *Early Days at Council Bluffs.* Washington, D.C.: Bryon S. Adams, 1916.

EJWM Turner, Lynne S. *Emigrating Journals of the Willie and Martin Handcart Companies and the Hunt and Hodgett Wagon Trains.* Lynne Slater Turner, 1996.

EMCMT "Explore Mills County: Find the Mormon Traces." Brochure. 8 pp. Mills County Tourism Group, 1997.

EmG Clayton, William. *The Latter-Day Saints' Emigrants' Guide.* Edited by Stanley B. Kimball. Gerald, Mo.: Patrice Press, 1983.

EnH Jenson, Andrew. *Encyclopedic History of The Church of Jesus Christ of Latter-day Saints.* Salt Lake City: Deseret News Publishing, 1941.

EnM *Encyclopedia of Mormonism.* Edited by Daniel H. Ludlow. 5 vols. New York: Macmillan, 1992.

ENS *Ensign.* Published monthly by The Church of Jesus Christ of Latter-day Saints, Salt Lake City, Utah. 1971–.

ERA *Improvement Era.* The Church of Jesus Christ of Latter-day Saints, 1897–1970.

ETN Rich, Russell R. *Ensign to the Nations.* Provo, Utah: Brigham Young University Publications, 1972.

FAN "Fort Atkinson, Nebraska," NEBRASKAland Magazine, 1987, posted on various "Fort Atkinson" websites, 2005, including http://www.fortatkinsononline.org/

FG *Frontier Guardian.* Published in Kanesville (Council Bluffs), Iowa, 1849–52.

FIB Utley, Robert M. *Frontiersmen in Blue: The United States Army and the Indian, 1848–1865.* Lincoln, Nebr.: University of Nebraska Press, 1967.

FWBJ F. W. Blake Journal. Holograph. LDS Church Archives, Salt Lake City, Utah.

GBK Arrington, Leonard J. *Great Basin Kingdom.* Cambridge, Mass.: Harvard University Press, 1958.

GFF Hartley, William G. "The Great Florence Fitout of 1861." *BYU Studies* 24 (Summer 1984): 341–71.

GGH Holmes, Gail George. "Narrative Tour of Historical Sites of the Church of Jesus Christ of Latter-day Saints in the Omaha and Council Bluffs Area." Typescript. Copy in possession of William G. Hartley.

GLO Government Land Office Map. National Archives, Washington, D.C.

GPRR Mattes, Merrill J. *The Great Platte River Road.* Lincoln, Nebr.: University of Nebraska Press, 1987.

GS *Gospel Standards: Selections from the Sermons and Writings of Heber J. Grant.* Compiled by G. Homer Durham. Salt Lake City: Improvement Era, 1942.

GTMC Wortman, Allen. *Ghost Towns of Mills County, Iowa.* Malvern, Iowa: Allen Wortman, 1975.

HAM Brown, S. Kent, Donald Q. Cannon, and Richard H. Jackson. *Historical Atlas of Mormonism.* New York: Simon and Schuster, 1994.

HC Smith, Joseph. *History of The Church of Jesus Christ of Latter-day Saints.* Edited by B. H. Roberts. 2d rev. ed. 7 vols. Salt Lake City: The Church of Jesus Christ of Latter-day Saints, 1932–51.

HCCI *History of Cass County, Iowa.* Springfield, Ill.: Continental Historical Co., 1884.

HCKM Kimball, Stanley B. *Heber C. Kimball: Mormon Patriarch and Pioneer.* Urbana, Ill.: University of Illinois Press, 1981.

HCMP High Council Minutes, Pottawattamie County, Iowa. LDS Church Archives, Salt Lake City, Utah.

HCVG *Harrison County Visitor's Guide.* 24 pp. Logan, Iowa, ca. 2001.

HCZ Hafen, LeRoy Reuben, and Ann W. Hafen. *Handcarts to Zion.* Glendale, Calif.: Arthur H. Clark Co., 1960.

HDHC Waterman, G. F. *History and Description of Harrison County, Iowa.* Magnolia, Iowa: Western Star Book and Job Office, 1868.

HEJ Howard Egan Journal. Beinecke Library, Yale University, New Haven, Connecticut.

HFG Hyde, Myrtle Stevens. "Orson Hyde and *The Frontier Guardian,*" *Nauvoo Journal* 8 (Fall 1996): 62–70.

HFK "History of Fort Kearny," website: www2.sandi.net/kearny/history/swk/fk.html

HHCI Hunt, Charles W. *History of Harrison County, Iowa.* Indianapolis, Ind.: B. F. Bowen and Co., 1915.

HiR *The Historical Record.* Periodical published monthly in Salt Lake City by Andrew Jenson, assistant Church historian and editor, 1882–90. Book 1. Salt Lake City: Andrew Jenson, 1889.

HiS Haines, Aubrey L. *Historic Sites along the Oregon Trail.* Gerald, Mo.: Patrice Press, 1981.

HJC Dawson, Charles. "The Mormons." In *Pioneer Tales of the Oregon Trail and of Jefferson County.* Vol. 1. Topeka: Crane and Co., 1912, 61–68.

HLDS *Hymns of The Church of Jesus Christ of Latter-day Saints.* Salt Lake City: The Church of Jesus Christ of Latter-day Saints, 1985.

HMC Iowa Historical Company. *History of Mills County, Iowa.* Des Moines, Iowa: State Historical Co., 1881.

HMCI *The History of Monroe County, Iowa.* Chicago, Ill.: Western Historical Co., 1878.

HMEK Weber, Alois J. *History of the Mormon Encampment at Keokuk in 1853.* Keokuk, Iowa: Lee County Historical Society Publication No. 7, 1963.

HMOMc McCandless, Perry. *A History of Missouri, Vol. II, 1820–1860.* Columbia, Mo.: University of Missouri Press, 1971.

HMS Holmes, Gail. "Historic Mormon Sites to Visit in Greater Omaha–Council Bluffs." Pamphlet, n.d.

HmTZ Mulder, William. *Homeward to Zion: The Mormon Migration from Scandinavia.* Minneapolis, Minn.: University of Minnesota Press, 1957.

HoLC *History of Lucas County, Iowa.* Des Moines, Iowa: State Historical Co., 1881.

HON Olsen, James C. *History of Nebraska.* Lincoln, Nebr.: University of Nebraska Press, 1955.

HOUW Whitney, Orson F. *History of Utah.* Vol. 1. Salt Lake City: George Q. Cannon and Sons, March 1892.

HPC *History of Pottawattamie County Iowa.* Chicago: O. L. Baskin and Co., 1883.

HPCF Field, Homer H., and Joseph R. Reed. *History of Pottawattamie County.* Vol. 1. Chicago, Ill., 1907.

HRSMT Kimball, Stanley B. *Historic Resource Study: Mormon Pioneer National Historic Trail.* Denver, Colo.: U.S. Department of Interior/National Park Service, 1991.

HSM Kimball, Stanley B. *Historic Sites and Markers along the Mormon and Other Great Western Trails.* Urbana, Ill.: University of Illinois Press, 1988.

HSN Sheldon, Addison Erwin. *Histories and Stories of Nebraska.* Chicago, Ill., and Lincoln, Nebr.: University Publishing Co., 1914. Website: www.olden-times.com/OldtimeNebraska

HTC *History of Taylor County, Iowa.* Des Moines, Iowa: State Historical Co., 1881.

HTW *Heart Throbs of the West.* Compiled by Kate B. Carter. 12 vols. Salt Lake City: Daughters of the Utah Pioneers, 1947.

IHN www.Idahohistory.net

IMT *The Iowa Mormon Trail: Legacy of Faith and* Courage. Edited by Susan Easton Black and William G. Hartley. Orem, Utah: Helix Publishing, 1997.

IOW-W Webb, Lynn Robert. "The Contributions of the Temporary Settlements Garden Grove, Mount Pisgah, and Kanesville, Iowa, to Mormon Emigration, 1846–1852." Master's thesis, Brigham Young University, 1954.

IPLD Lokken, Roscoe L. *Iowa Public Land Disposal.* Iowa City: State Historical Society of Iowa, 1942.

IWZ Madsen, Susan Arrington. *I Walked to Zion.* Salt Lake City: Deseret Book, 1994.

JAL Lyman, Amasa. Journal. LDS Church Archives, Salt Lake City, Utah.

JCEB Bolton, Curtis Edwin. Journal. *Curtis Edwin Baldwin, Pioneer Missionary.* Compiled by Cleo H. Evans. Fairfax, Va.: Evans, 1968. Or see Curtis Edwin Bolton. Journal. LDS Church Archives, Salt Lake City, Utah.

JD *Journal of Discourses.* 26 vols. Liverpool: Latter-day Saints' Book Depot, 1853–86.

JDL Brooks, Juanita. *John Doyle Lee, Zealot, Pioneer-Builder, Scapegoat.* Glendale, Calif.: Arthur H. Clark Co., 1961.

JEFJ John Erick Forsgren Journal. Typescript. LDS Church Archives, Salt Lake City, Utah.

JEM Mayhew, Elijah. Journal. In Journal History, Sept. 9, 1853. LDS Church Archives, Salt Lake City, Utah. See also JH.

JEPL Lyman, Eliza Partridge. "Life and Journal of Eliza Maria Partridge Lyman." L. Tom Perry Special Collections, Harold B. Library, Brigham Young University, Provo, Utah. Or see Eliza Maria Partridge Lyman, Journal. In *Amasa Mason Lyman Family History.* Compiled by Melvin A. Lyman. Provo, Utah, 1969. See also ALFH.

JERS Snow, Eliza R. "Pioneer Diary of Eliza R. Snow." *Improvement Era* 47, no. 2 (Feb. 1944): 88–89, 113–18. See also PWERS.

JES Snow, Erastus. Journal. LDS Church Archives, Salt Lake City, Utah.

JH Journal History of The Church of Jesus Christ of Latter-day Saints. Manuscript. LDS Church Archives, Salt Lake City, Utah.

JHB Ballard, Henry. Journal. Typescript. LDS Church Archives, Salt Lake City, Utah.

JHE Egan, Howard. *Pioneering the West, 1846–1878: Major Howard Egan's Diary.* Edited by William M. Egan. Richmond, Utah: Howard R. Egan Estate, 1917. See also HEJ.

JHKW Whitney, Horace Kimball. Journal [Diary]. LDS Church Archives, Salt Lake City, Utah.

JHP Pugh, Henry. Journal. Journal History, Oct. 10, 1853. LDS Church Archives, Salt Lake City, Utah. See also JH.

JHTK King, Hannah Tapfield. "My Journal." Excerpt in *Covered Wagon Women: Diaries and Letters from the Western Trails, 1840–1890.* Compiled and edited by Kenneth L. Holmes. 11 vols. 6:191–97. Glendale, Calif.: Arthur H. Clark Co., 1986.

JI *Juvenile Instructor.* Predecessor of *The Instructor.* See ThI.

JJAL James A. Linforth, Journal, in Journal History, Aug. 9, 1853, 1–20.

JJD Dunn, James. Journal (Diary). LDS Church Archives, Salt Lake City, Utah.

JJFC "A Pioneer Journal, Forsgren Company, Containing the Story of the First Danish Company to Emigrate to Utah." In *Heart Throbs of the West* 6 (1945): 16–20. See also HTW.

JJGW Willie, James G. Journal. LDS Church Archives, Salt Lake City, Utah.

JJN Settle, William A. Jr. *Jesse James Was His Name; or, Fact and Fiction Concerning the Careers of the Notorious James Brothers of Missouri.* Lincoln, Nebr.: University of Nebraska Press, 1977.

JJoS Smith, John. Journal. Holograph (v. 1) and typescript. LDS Church Archives, Salt Lake City, Utah.

JJS Journal of John Smith. Journal no. 2, 1846–54. Holograph. LDS Church Archives, Salt Lake City, Utah.

JJSB Black, Joseph Smith. Journal. In *Our Pioneer Heritage.* Compiled by Kate B. Carter. 10:261–97. Salt Lake City: Daughters of the Utah Pioneers, 1967.

JJW Weibye, Jens C. A. Journal [Diary]. LDS Church Archives, Salt Lake City, Utah.

JJWY Young, Joseph W. Journal. LDS Church Archives, Salt Lake City, Utah.

JLAS *Journal of Luman Andros Shurtliff, 1807–1884.* N.p., n.d.

JLNS Scovil, Lucius N. Journal (Diary). LDS Church Archives, Salt Lake City, Utah.

JLS *Levi Savage Jr. Journal.* Edited by Lynn M. Hilton. N.p.: John Savage Family Organization, 1966.

JLSN Snow, Lorenzo. Journal. LDS Church Archives, Salt Lake City, Utah.

JMGA Atwood, Minor G. "Journal of Minor G. Atwood." Typescript. In Journal History, 10 June 1857. LDS Church Archives, Salt Lake City, Utah. See also JH.

JMJ Newell, Linda King, and Valeen Tippetts Avery. "Jane Manning James: Black Saint, 1847 Pioneer." ENS, Aug. 1979, 26–29.

JNJ Jacob, Norton. Journal. LDS Church Archives, Salt Lake City, Utah. See also MVB.

JNK Knight, Newel. Journal. LDS Church Archives, Salt Lake City, Utah.

JNM Nealon, John S. "Macedonia Transplanted—A History of the Latter-day Saints in Macedonia, Iowa." Paper presented at Mormon History Association Convention, May 23, 1997. Typescript in possession of William G. Hartley.

JOP Pratt, Orson. Journal. LDS Church Archives, Salt Lake City, Utah. Published version by N. B. Lundwall, *Exodus of Modern Israel.* Salt Lake City: N.B. Lundwall, n.d.

JPS Sessions, Patty. Journal. LDS Church Archives, Salt Lake City, Utah. Or see *Mormon Midwife: The 1846–1888 Diaries of Patty Bartlett Sessions.* Edited by Donna Toland Smart. Logan: Utah State University Press, 1997.

JPTB Bermingham, Patrick Twiss. Journal. In Journal History, Sept. 26, 1856. LDS Church Archives, Salt Lake City, Utah. See also JH.

JRLC Campbell, Robert L. Journal. Harold B. Lee Library, Brigham Young University, Provo, Utah.

JRMi Miller, Reuben. Diary, 1848–1849. LDS Church Archives, Salt Lake City, Utah.

JSG Goodridge, Sophia Lois. Journal. In *Our Pioneer Heritage,* 15:262. See also OPH.

JSRi Richards, Silas. "Silas Richards Journal." Typescript. L. Tom Perry Special Collections, Harold B. Library, Brigham Young University, Provo, Utah.

JTB Thomas Bullock Journal. Handwritten. LDS Church Archives, Salt Lake City, Utah. Or see *The Pioneer Camp of the Saints: The 1846 and 1847 Mormon Trail Journals of Thomas Bullock.* Edited by Will Bagley. Spokane, Wash.: Arthur H. Clark Co., 1997. See also Thomas Bullock, "Journal of Thomas Bullock." In *BYU Studies* 31, no. 1 (Winter 1991): 15–75. See also PCS.

JTS Sleight, Thomas. Journal. Merrill Library, Utah State University, Logan, Utah.

JWC Clayton, William. Journal. L. Tom Perry Special Collections, Harold B. Library, Brigham Young University, Provo, Utah. Or see *An Intimate Chronicle: The Journals of William Clayton.* Edited by George D. Smith. Salt Lake City: Signature Books and Smith Research Associates, 1995.

JWEMc McLellin, William E. *The Journals of William E. McLellin 1831–1836.* Edited by Jan Shipps and John W. Welch. Provo, Utah: Brigham Young University Studies; Urbana, Ill.: University of Illinois Press, 1994.

JWHu Huntington, William. Journal. L. Tom Perry Special Collections, Harold B. Library, Brigham Young University, Provo, Utah.

JWR Richards, Willard. Journal. LDS Church Archives, Salt Lake City, Utah.

JWW Woodruff, Wilford. *Wilford Woodruff's Journal, 1833–1898.* Edited by Scott G. Kenney. 9 vols. Midvale, Utah: Signature Books, 1983.

JWYCJ Joseph W. Young Company Journal. Kept by Henry Pugh. In Journal History, Oct. 10, 1853. LDS Church Archives, Salt Lake City, Utah.

JWYJ Joseph W. Young Journal. In Journal History, June 1857. LDS Church Archives, Salt Lake City, Utah.

KG,c Gunzenhauser, Karla, to William G. Hartley, Nov. 6, 1993; copy in possession of William G. Hartley. Letter to LaMar C. Berrett, Aug. 31, 1995; copy in possession of William G. Hartley.

KR,c Risser, Kay. E-mail correspondence with William G. Hartley. June 8 and 9, 1999.

KSLL Little, James A. *From Kirtland to Salt Lake City.* Salt Lake City: James A. Little, 1890.

LCS Godfrey, Kenneth W. *Charles Shumway, A Pioneer's Life.* Provo, Utah: J. Grant Stevenson, 1974.

LDC — Caveen, Daniel. Letter to Editor of *Deseret News,* Aug.13, 1855. In Journal History, July 24, 1855. LDS Church Archives, Salt Lake City, Utah. See also JH.

LDS,c — Spencer, Daniel, and Franklin D. Richards. Letter to Brigham Young, in *Deseret News,* Oct. 22, 1856, 258.

LFH,c — Harlow, LeRoy F. Letter to William G. Hartley, June 14, 1992.

LGW — Whitaker, George. "Life [Autobiography] of George Whitaker, A Utah Pioneer (1820–1907)." Typescript. N.p. LDS Church Archives, Salt Lake City, Utah.

LHWJJ — Bell, Stella Jaques. *Life History and Writings of John Jaques, Including a Diary of the Martin Handcart Company.* Rexburg, Idaho: Ricks College Press, 1978.

LJCB — Smith, Andrew F. *The Saintly Scoundrel: The Life and Times of Dr. John Cook Bennett.* Urbana and Chicago, Ill.: University of Illinois Press, 1997.

LJL — Anderson, Oliver Lowry. "Life Sketch of John Lowry." Typescript in possession of William G. Hartley.

LLP — Bates, Irene M., and E. Gary Smith. *Lost Legacy: The Mormon Office of Presiding Patriarch.* Urbana and Chicago, Ill.: University of Illinois Press, 1996.

LRF,c — Farrer, Roger. Letter to William Farrer, Dec.15, 1846. In "Roger Farrer Letters." LDS Church Archives, Salt Lake City, Utah.

LRTB — Seegmiller, Janet Burton. *Be Kind to the Poor: The Life Story of Robert Taylor Burton.* N.p.: Robert Taylor Burton Family Organization, 1988.

LSHA — Badger, Louisa Adeline Ashby Noble. "A Life Sketch of Susan Hammond Ashley Noble." LDS Church Archives, Salt Lake City, Utah.

LTLB — Barney, Ronald O. *One Side by Himself: The Life and Times of Lewis Barney, 1808–1894.* Logan, Utah: Utah State University Press, 2001.

MBK — Hartley, William G. *My Best for the Kingdom: History and Autobiography of John Lowe Butler, a Mormon Frontiersman.* Salt Lake City: Aspen Books, 1993.

MBN — *Army of Israel: Mormon Battalion Narratives.* Edited by David L. Bigler and Will Bagley. Logan, Utah: Utah State University Press, 2000.

MCI — Solomon, D.H. *History of Mills County, Iowa.* Glenwood, Iowa: Mills County Historical Book Committee, 1985.

MFP — *Messages of the First Presidency of The Church of Jesus Christ of Latter-day Saints.* Compiled by James R. Clark. 6 vols. Salt Lake City: Bookcraft, 1965–75.

MHBY — Young, Brigham. *Manuscript History of Brigham Young, 1801–1844.* Edited by Eldon Jay Watson. Salt Lake City: Smith Secretarial Services, 1968. Vol. *1846–1847,* Salt Lake City: E. J. Watson, 1971.

MHGI Daugherty, Ruth. "The History of the Mormons at Harris Grove, Iowa." Typescript. 8 pp.

MHI Iowa, Manuscript History. LDS Church Archives, Salt Lake City, Utah.

MHPR Ward, Maurine Carr. *Winter Quarters: The 1846–1848 Life Writings of Mary Haskin Parker Richards*. Logan, Utah: State University Press, 1996.

MHS Spring Hartley, William G. "Howard Egan, the Elkhorn Skirmish, and Mormon Trail Emigration in 1848." *Mormon Historical Studies* 1 (Spring 1999): 37–60.

MiSL Lass, William E. *From the Missouri to the Great Salt Lake: An Account of Overland Freighting*. Lincoln, Nebr.: Nebraska State Historical Society, 1972.

MoM Bennett, Richard E. *Mormons at the Missouri, 1846–1852: "And Should We Die—."* Norman, Okla.: University of Oklahoma Press, 1987.

MoP McGavin, Elmer Cecil. *The Mormon Pioneers*. Salt Lake City: Stevens & Wallis, 1947.

MOR Kane, Thomas L. *The Mormons: A Discourse Delivered Before the Historical Society of Pennsylvania, March 26, 1850*. 2d ed. Philadelphia Pa.: King and Baird, Printers, 1850.

MPNHT Kimball, Stanley B. *Historic Resource Study: Mormon Pioneer Historic Trail*. National Park Service, 1991. Or see Cass County Mormon Trails Association, *Mormon Pioneer National Historic Trail, Cass County, Iowa*. Travel brochure, 1966.

MPTDC *The Mormon Pioneer Trail in Davis County, Iowa*. Travel brochure. N.p.: Iowa Mormon Trail Association, 1995.

MRB-R Ricketts, Norma Baldwin. *The Mormon Battalion: U.S. Army of the West, 1846–1848*. Logan, Utah: Utah State University Press, 1996.

MRB-Y Yurtinus, John F. "A Ram in the Thicket: A History of the Mormon Battalion in the Mexican War." Ph.D. diss., Brigham Young University, 1975.

MTAAC *Mormon Trails across Appanoose County, Iowa*. Edited by Willis M. Heusinkveld. Centerville, Iowa: Appanoose County Mormon Trail Association, 1995.

MTB "Mary Turpin Bennion." In Hardin Bennion, *The Bennion Family of Utah*. Vol. 1. Salt Lake City: Bennion Family Association, 1931.

MTN Jones, Carl Hugh, and Andy Grow. *Mormon Trails in Nebraska: Prepared for the Nebraska Mormon Trails Association Sesquicentennial Celebration, 1847–1997* (Apr. 17, 1997).

MUB Beecher, Maureen Ursenbach. "The Iowa Journal of Lorenzo Snow." *BYU Studies* 24 (Summer 1984): 261–73.

MVB Barney, Ronald O. *The Mormon Vanguard Brigade of 1847: Norton Jacob's Record*. Logan, Utah: Utah State University Press, 2005.

NEB-S Steele, Olga Sharp. "The Geography of the Mormon Trail across Nebraska." Master's thesis. University of Nebraska, Lincoln, Nebraska, 1933.

NHM Williams, Helen Roberta. "Old Wyoming." *Nebraska Historical Magazine* 17, no. 2 (April–June 1936).

NJ *The Nauvoo Journal*. Edited by Maurine Ward Carr. Published semiannually in Hyrum, Utah, 1989–.

OFS Oliver, Grace. "The Mormon Trail: The Oliver Family of Shelton." In *Buffalo Tales,* published by the Buffalo County Historical Society, 1 (Feb. 1978), posted at bchs.kearney.net/BTales (1995).

OHH Hyde, Myrtle Stevens. *Orson Hyde: The Olive Branch of Israel*. Salt Lake City: Agreka Books, 2000.

OJ *Overland Journal*. Published quarterly in Gerald, Mo., by The Oregon–California Trails Association, 1983–.

OPH *Our Pioneer Heritage*. Compiled by Kate B. Carter. 20 vols. Salt Lake City: Daughters of the Utah Pioneers, 1958–77.

OPHC Omaha's Prospect Hill Cemetery walking tour website: www.ops.org/ooe/prospect/pdfs/walking_tour

OrH Barron, Howard H. *Orson Hyde: Missionary, Apostle, Colonizer.* Bountiful, Utah: Horizon Publishers, 1977.

OTR Franzwa, Gregory M. *The Oregon Trail Revisited*. St. Louis, Mo.: Patrice Press, 1988.

PCS *The Pioneer Camp of the Saints: The 1846 and 1847 Mormon Trail Journals of Thomas Bullock*. Edited by Will Bagley. Spokane, Wash.: Arthur H. Clark Co., 1997. See also JTB.

PEx Ponyexpress.org/history. Or see Richard E. Fike and John W. Headley, *Pony Express Report*. Bureau of Land Management Cultural Resources Series Monograph 2. Washington, D.C.: U.S. Government Printing Office, 1979.

PH,c Hartman, Patrice. Letter to William G. Hartley. June 5, 1977.

PHJ Peter O. Hansen. Journal. Typescript in Journal History, Aug. 7, 1849.

PITH "The Mormon Trail through Pella." *Pella, Iowa: A Touch of Holland*. Pella Chamber of Commerce, 1988.

PP Clifton, James A. *The Prairie People: Continuity and Change in Potawatomi Indian Culture, 1665–1965*. Lawrence, Kans.: Regents Press, 1977.

PTHM Ponca Tribe Historical Marker, near entrance to Niobrara State Park, Niobrara, Nebraska.

PWERS Snow, Eliza Roxcy. *The Personal Writings of Eliza Roxcy Snow*. Edited by Maureen Ursenbach Beecher. Salt Lake City: University of Utah Press, 1995. See also JERS.

RA Arnold, Ralph. Telephone conversation with William G. Hartley, Dec. 6, 1995.

RB,c Brown, Randy. Letter to LaMar C. Berrett. Douglas, Wyoming, 29 May, 1995.

RFL Piercy, Frederick. *Route from Liverpool to the Great Salt Lake Valley: Illustrated with Steel Engravings and Wood Cuts from Sketches Made by*

Frederick Piercy. Edited by James A. Linforth. London: Latter-Day Saints' Book Depot, 1855.

RHG Goodson, Robert H. "Among the Poorest of Saints: Mormon Migration to and Through Burlington, Iowa, 1846–1887." *Mormon Historical Studies* 4 (Fall 2003): 97–112.

RHN Moulton, Candy. *Roadside History of Nebraska.* Missoula, Mont.: Mountain Press Publishing, 1997.

RMF Fox, Ruth May. "From England to Salt Lake Valley in 1867." *Improvement Era,* July 1935, 408–09, 450.

ROC Faulring, Scott H. "The Return of Oliver Cowdery." In *The Disciples as Witness: Essays on Latter-day Saint History and Doctrine in Honor of Richard Lloyd Anderson.* Edited by Stephen D. Ricks et al. Provo, Utah: Foundation for Ancient Research and Mormon Studies (FARMS), 2000.

RRH,c Roenfeld, Ryan. Letter to William G. Hartley, Aug. 10, 1998. Copy in possession of William G. Hartley.

RWCS "Reminiscences of William C. Staines." *Contributor* 12 (June 1891): 315–17. Edited by Junius F. Wells. Published monthly in Salt Lake City, 1879–96.

SBMSJ Hartley, William G. *Stand by My Servant Joseph: The Story of the Joseph Knight Family and the Restoration.* Salt Lake City: Deseret Book, 2003.

SBR "Sarah Burbank Reminiscences." In *Voices from the Past: Diaries, Journals, and Autobiographies.* Provo, Utah: Brigham Young University Division of Continuing Education, 1980.

SJJ Statement of Jane Johnston. Located in front of Diary of Joseph Smith Black. Typescript. L. Tom Perry Special Collections, Harold B. Library, Brigham Young University, Provo, Utah.

SLT Rogerson, Josiah. "The Story of Trials of the Handcart Pioneers." *Salt Lake Tribune,* Nov. 30, 1913, 11.

SPP "A Sketch of the Life of Patience Delila Pierce Palmer." Typescript. LDS Church Archives, Salt Lake City, Utah.

SQ Vinton, Merri Allen. *Summer Quarters.* Brochure. Washington County, Nebraska, Historical Association, 1997. Posted on website info@newashcohist.org 2005.

SWIH *Southwest Iowa's Heritage: A History of Page and Fremont Counties.* Compiled by R. E. Cunningham. Shenandoah, Iowa: World Publishing, 1973.

SY Majors, Alexander. *Seventy Years on the Frontier.* Lincoln, Nebr.: University of Nebraska Press, 1989. Reprint of 1893 original.

T&S *Nauvoo (Illinois) Times and Seasons.* Published monthly, 1839–46.

TAMF Hartley, William G. *They Are My Friends: A History of the Joseph Knight Family, 1825–1850.* Provo, Utah: Grandin Book, 1986.

TF Hartley, William G. "Where's Arthur?" *Friend.* Salt Lake City: The Church of Jesus Christ of Latter-day Saints, May 2004, 4–7.

ThI *The Instructor.* Published bi-weekly, monthly. Salt Lake City:

Deseret Sunday School Union, January 1866–1929. Predecessor called *Juvenile Instructor;* see also JI.

ThM *The Mormon*. Published weekly in New York, February 17, 1855–September 19, 1857.

TOD Allen, James B. *Trials of Discipleship: The Story of William Clayton, a Mormon*. Urbana and Chicago, Ill.: University of Illinois Press, 1987.

TPH *Treasures of Pioneer History*. Compiled by Kate B. Carter. 6 vols. Salt Lake City: Daughters of Utah Pioneers, 1952–57.

TUD *To Utah with the Dragoons*. Edited by Harold D. Langley. Salt Lake City, Utah: University of Utah Press, 1974.

UGHM *Utah Genealogical and Historical Magazine*. Salt Lake City: Utah Genealogical and Historical Society, Jan. 1910–Oct. 1940.

UHQ *Utah Historical Quarterly*. Published in Salt Lake City by the Board of Control, Utah Historical Society, Jan. 1928–.

UPH Union Pacific History website: http://www.uprr.com/aboutup/history/

UPK Klein, Maury. *Union Pacific: The Birth of a Railroad 1862–1893*. New York: n.p., 1978.

USGHA U.S. Government website regarding the Homestead Act: /www.nps.gov/home/homestead_act.html

UTC,p Utah Travel Council website regarding Swedes in Utah: www.utahtravelcenter.com/stateinformation/peopleinutah/swedish.htm

UTG "Utah's Governors." *Beehive History* 18 (1992): 16–17.

VBCG *Van Buren County Business Directory & Visitors Guide* (2003).

VBCI "Van Buren County, Iowa, Inventory of Historical Places." Typescript. Farmington, Iowa, Library.

WGH Hartley, William G. "LDS Emigration in 1853: The Keokuk Encampment and Outfitting Ten Wagon Trains for Utah." *Mormon Historical Studies* 4 (Fall 2003): 43–76.

WiQ Bryson, Conrey. *Winter Quarters*. Salt Lake City: Deseret Book, 1986.

WMHC *Emigrating Journals of the Willie and Martin Handcart Companies and the Hunt and Hodgett Wagon Trains*. Compiled by Lynne A. Turner. N.p.: Lynne Slater Turner, 1996.

WW Woodruff, Wilford. *Wilford Woodruff, Fourth President of The Church of Jesus Christ of Latter-day Saints*. Compiled and edited by Mathias F. Cowley. Salt Lake City: Bookcraft, 1964.

WYW Chatterley, L. Matthew. *Wend Your Way: A Guide to Sites along the Iowa Mormon Trail*. Ames, Iowa: Iowa State University Press, 2000.

ZJD Zebulon Jacobs Diary. LDS Church Archives, Salt Lake City, Utah.

Index

A

Abbott Visitors' Center, Chimney Rock, Nebraska, 322
Adair County Historical Museum, 98
Adams County, Iowa, 154
Adell, Iowa, 179
Admonition Camp, Nebraska, 306–7
Advance Company (Kimball, 1847): leaves Winter Quarters, 251; includes apostles, 253; rules governing, 255–56; is organized into military order, 260
Advance Party (Miller, 1846), 245–48
Afton, Iowa, 83, 96
Ahmanson, Johan August, 227, 340
Albia, Iowa, 95
Alda, Nebraska, 278
Alexander, Grover Cleveland, 197
Allen, Franklin, 145
Allen, James, Capt., 86, 119–20, 137, 148
Allen, Orville M., 32, 92
Allerton, Iowa, 68–70
Allred, Isaac, 76
Allred, James, 74
Allred, Reuben F., 142
Amana Colonies, 172–73
Ambrosia, Iowa, 15
American Fur Company, Bellevue, Nebraska, 146
American Gothic House, 46
Ames Stake, 11
Amish, 52, 163–64
Anabaptists, 164
Ancient Bluff Ruins, 315; Camp, 317–18
Anita, Iowa, 179, 180–81
Apple Grove, Iowa, 177
Apple Grove Inn, Mitchellville, Iowa, 176
Arbor Day, 241
Arbor Lodge State Historical Park, Nebraska, 242
Argyle, Iowa, 34
Army barracks, Montrose, Iowa, 13–14
Army of the West, 285
Ashby, Nathaniel, 42
Ashby, Susan Hammond, 42
Ash Hollow, Nebraska, 272, 308, 310–12; State Historical Park, 309, 310–11; Camp, 311–14; battle of, 315
Ashland, Nebraska, 240
Astaire, Fred, 197
Atlantic, Iowa, 104, 180, 181–82
Atwood, Milan, 109, 339, 340
Augusta, Iowa, 21–22
Auntie Green Museum, Bonaparte, Iowa, 43
Aurora, Nebraska, 276
Austin, Iowa, 152
Averett, Elisha, 57, 59

B

Babbitt, Almon G.: edits Kanesville newspaper, 129; is attacked by Indians, 272, 341; death of, 313, 339, 342; encourages Willie company, 340; in Florence, 343–44

Baer, Max, 197
Baker, Jean Rio: on Mt. Pisgah, 88; uses Mormon Trail Variant B, 95; on camping at Macedonia, 111–12; on Kanesville, 124; on buffalo, 290; on sand hills, 306
Baker family, 152
Ballantyne, Richard, company, 291–92
Bank of Florence Museum, 219
Bank of Memories, Orient, Iowa, 97
Banks Ferry, 57
Baquejappa, Chief, 100
Barnard Park, Fremont, Nebraska, 258
Barn Butte, 313
Barnes, Mr., 48
Barney, Lewis, 30n, 159
Barney's Grove, Iowa, 159
Bauichter, Henry, 342
Bayard, Nebraska, 321–22
Bayliss Park, Council Bluffs, 131–32
Beatrice, Nebraska, 244–45
Beaumont, Charles, 287, 291
Beeker, Sister, 108
Beer, Charley, 257
Bellevue, Nebraska, 231–32; roads, upper and lower, 251
Belle Wood, 237
Benjamin Leland Cabin, 160
Benner family, 154
Bennett, John C., 178
Bennington, Nebraska, 251
Benson, Ezra T.: captains Camp of Israel company, 56; is made apostle, 145; travels to Ft. Ponca, 247; in 1847 Advance Company, 253; at Sacred Prayer Camp, 333
Benson, Ezra Taft (president of the Church), 78
Benson, George Taft, 78
Bent, Samuel, 56, 75, 76
Benton, Thomas Hart, 43
Bentonsport, Iowa, 43–44
Bermingham, Patrick Twiss, 170
Berrett, Eliza Hookway, 237
Berrett, John Watts, 234, 237
Bertrand, 157, 224; Museum and Excavation Site, 224
Bethlehem, Iowa, 143, 151, 210
Bethlehem, Nebraska, 233
Betty Ford Rose Garden, 226
Bickford, George, 154
Biddle, Sidney, 237
Bigler's Grove, Iowa, 160
Big Papillion, Nebraska, 340–41
Big Sioux River, Iowa, 162
Black, Joseph Smith, 152
Black Angel Statue, Fairview Cemetery, Council Bluffs, 131
Blake, F. W. 280
Blockhouse, Council Bluffs, 128; branch, 126, 128
Blocktown, Iowa, 155
Bloomer, Amelia Jenks, 131
Bloomfield, Iowa, 51–52
Blue Water, battle of, 315
Bluff Camp, Nebraska, 296–97
Bluff Creek, 313
Bob White State Park, Iowa, 70
Bodmer, Karl, 226
Bolton, Caroline, 43
Bolton, Curtis Edwin, 42
Bonaparte, Iowa, 41–43; gristmill, 42, 43
Borglum, Gutzon, 259
Borglum, Jens, 259
Borglum, Lincoln, 259
Boswick children, 69
Bowers, James, 177
Boyer River, Iowa, 162
Boyle, Henry G., 349
Boys Town, Nebraska, 230–31
Bradshaw, Jeremiah, 108
Brady, Nebraska, 297–98
Brady Island Camps, 297–98
Brando, Marlon, 197
Bridgeport, Nebraska, 318–19
Brigham Young University, 226
Broadwater, Nebraska, 316
Broomberry Hill Camp, 98
Brown, James S., 22, 30n
Brown, John, 306, 311–12, 318
Brown, John (abolitionist), 110

Brown, Thomas, 261
Browning, Elizabeth Barrett, xi
Browning, Jonathan, 149
Brule, Nebraska, 308–9
Bryan, William Jennings, 197
Buffalo: sightings of, 204, 293–97, 313; dung of, 283, 284; skulls of, 287; hunting of, 289–90
Buffalo Bill Ranch State Historical Park, 303. *See also* Cody, William Frederick
Buffalo Creek Camp, 291–92
Buffalo Hunt Camp, 289–90
Buffet, Warren, 197
Bullock, Thomas: records Winter Exodus, 28n; visits Poor Saints Camp, 32; on miracle of the quail, 32–33; on homes in Winter Quarters, 214; is clerk of Advance Company, 260; on Loup Sabbath Camp, 270; on forging new roads, 271; at Ft. Kearny Camp, 284; on using buffalo meat, 290; on buffalo, 296; makes copy of camp laws, 298; on North Platte Camp, 304; on Admonition Camp, 307; on Castle Bluffs, 312; at Chimney Rock Camp, 320
Bullock's Grove, Council Bluffs, 139
Bunker, Edward, 76, 152
Bunker, Emily Abbott, 76
Bunker handcart company, Edward: uses Upper Ferry, 156; is third handcart company, 170–71, 202, 336
Bunnell family, 108
Burdick, Gideon, 326
Burlington, Iowa, 9, 22–23
Burlington and Missouri River Railroad, 23
Burton, Maria, 153
Burton, Robert T., 30n, 153
Burton, Sir Richard F., 320, 322
Burton, Theresa Hannah, 153
Butler, Ann Binnall, 159
Butler, John Lowe: leaves for Emmett Expedition, 55; stays at Indian village, 106; and Emmett company, 113, 161–62
Butler, Lorenzo Dow, 159

C

Cahoon, Reynolds, 15
California Hill Trail Ruts, 308–9
Call, Anson, 14, 30n
Camp Creek, 177; Camp, 70
Camp of Israel: Winter Exodus known as, 5, 23–25, 35; is reorganized at Chariton River, 55–56
"Camp of Israel, The," 38–39
Campbell, Anna, 77
Campbell, Joan, 31–32
Campbell, Robert, 31–32
Canfield, Isaac, 273
Canfield, Lucy, 273
Cantonment, Missouri, 223
Carrington, Albert, 333
Carson, Johnny, 197
Carson family, 76
Carter, Jimmy, 5
Carter family, 76
Case, A. James, 268
Casey, Iowa, 179
Castle Bluffs, Nebraska, 312
Castle Rock. *See* Courthouse Rock, Nebraska
Castlerock Farm, 85
Cather, Willa Silbert, 197; home and Pioneer Memorial, 277
Catlin, George, 226
Cavett, Dick, 197
Cavour, 237
Cedar Bluffs Camp, 308
Cedar Creek, 95
Cedar Rapids Stake, 11
Cemeteries and gravesites, Mormon: Iowaville Cemetery, 46; Richardson's Pt. Camp, 49–50; Spencer Cemetery, 50; Tharp Cemetery, 66; Garden Grove Cemetery, 76–77; Mt. Pisgah Cemetery, 89; Last Chance

Cemetery, 95; of Stout and Smith children, 103; Fairview (Kanesville) Cemetery, Council Bluffs, 130–31; Manti Cemetery, 153–54; Honey Creek Mormon Pioneer Cemetery, 157; Woodbine Cemetery, 159; of Job Welling Jr., 175; Dalmanutha Cemetery, 179; Winter Quarters Mormon Pioneer Cemetery, 215–16; Prospect Hills Cemetery, Omaha, 227; Old Wyoming Cemetery, 236–37; Ponca memorial, 248; of Pawnee graves, 267; at Dripping Springs, 288; Ft. McPherson National Cemetery, 299–300; of Samuel Cooley, 304–5; at Ash Hollow, 310; Rebecca Winters grave, 323–24
Centerville, Iowa, 56–57
Central City, Nebraska, 273
Central Overland California and Pike's Peak Express Company, 295
Central Pacific Railroad, 132, 347
Central Route, 12
Chariton, Iowa, 19, 93
Chariton River Camp and Ford, 53, 54–56
Charleston, Iowa, 19, 38, 39
Cheyenne Indians, 338–39
Chicago, Burlington & Quincy Railroad, 326
Chief Standing Bear Memorial Bridge, 249
Chieftain Hotel, Council Bluffs, 150
Chimney Rock, Nebraska, 204, 315, 316; Camp, 320–21; National Historic Site, 321–22
Chislett, George, 109, 340
Chislett, John, 341–42
Christensen, James M., 303
Christiansen, Christian, 22–23
Christiansen, Mothe Marie Clemenson, 288n
Christiansen, Niel Lars, 340
Christiansen handcart company, Christian, 172, 203; passes Genoa, 266; stops at Wood River Center, 280; successful journey of, to Salt Lake, 336
Church of Jesus Christ (Cutlerite), 153
Cincinnati, Iowa, 56–57
Clapper family, 154
Clark, James, 166
Clark County Historical Museum, Osceola, Iowa, 81–82
Clawson, Moses, company, 19
Clayton, Commodore, 23
Clayton, Diantha, 64–65
Clayton, William Adriel Moroni, 65–66
Clayton, William: in Winter Exodus group, 24; manages Nauvoo Band, 36; on performing in Keosauqua, Iowa, 44–45; as clerk for Camp of Israel, 56; writes "Come, Come, Ye Saints," 64–65; at the Nodaway River, 102; is assistant camp scribe in Advance Company, 260; and odometer for Advance Company, 261, 296–97, 298, 301, 308; at Fish Camp, 262; on baptism of Elijah Newman, 270; on Indian-set prairie fires, 293; on buffalo, 293–94, 298; on Brady Island camp, 297–98; on North Platte Camp, 303; on Sand Hills Camp, 306; at Admonition Camp, 307; on traveling in sand, 310; names Frog's Head Bluff, 316; on Ancient Bluff Ruins Camp, 317; on Courthouse Rock, 319; on Terrace Bluffs Camp, 323; on Scotts Bluff Camp, 329; at Sacred Prayer Camp, 332, 333, 334
Clyman, Jim, 200
Cody, William Frederick (Buffalo Bill), 10, 197, 301, 303
Coffman, Jacob, 54
Coffman's Settlement Camp, 53–54
Cold Spring, 108

Cold Springs Camp, Nebraska, 208, 220, 229–30
Cold Springs County Park, Lewis, Iowa, 105
Colesburg, Iowa, 164
Colfax, Schuyler, 262
College of St. Mary, Omaha, 225
Coltrin, Zebedee, 274
Columbus, Nebraska, 262–63, 267
"Come, Come, Ye Saints," 64–66
Community of Christ, 11, 78
Community of True Inspiration, 172
Confidence, Iowa, 93
Conquering Bull, Chief, 299
Conyer, George Washington, 23, 80
Conyer, John, 23, 80
Conyer, Mary, 80
Conyer, Rebecca, 23
Conyer, Sarah Bradford, 23, 80
Cooke, Philip St. George, 285
Cooley, John William, company, 304
Cooley, Samuel William, 304–5
Cooley, Sarah Jane Hunt, 304
Coons, Labbeus T., 151–52
Coonsville, Iowa, 151–52
Cooper's Lake, 18
Coralville, Iowa, 167–68
Cordon, Alfred, 22
Corning, Iowa, 154
Corydon, Iowa, 68
Cottonwood Jail, Council Bluffs, 129
Council Bluffs, Iowa: location of, 9; importance of, 118–19, 199, 208; map of, 125; Kanesville renamed, 125; historic sites in, 128–42; Saints cross Missouri River at, 200; as headquarters after 1848, 213, 214
Council Bluffs, Nebraska, 222–23, 250
Council Bluffs Road, 200
Council Bluffs Stake, 11
Council House, Winter Quarters, 212
Council Pt., Council Bluffs, 142
Courthouse Rock, Nebraska, 315, 319; Camp, 318–19
Covenant Camp, Nebraska, 330–31
Covenanting meeting, 331–32
Covered Bridge Festival, Madison County, Iowa, 91
Cowdery, Oliver, 135, 140–41
Cowdry/Cowdery family, 342
Cowley, Matthias, 172
Cox, Brother, 109
Cox family, 152
Coyote Rock, 323
Cozad, Nebraska, 293–95
Cozad, Robert, 294
Crab Creek, Nebraska, 315
Craig, James, 271
Cramer Interpretive Center, Niobrara, Nebraska, 249
Cream Camp, 81
Creighton, Edward and John, 228
Creighton, Nebraska, 247
Creighton University, Omaha, 225, 228
Crescent, Iowa, 150
Creston, 5, 97
Crisman, Charles, 56
Crook, George C., 221; House Museum, 220–21
Crooked River, battle of, 53
Croton, Iowa, 39
Cumberland, Iowa, 101
Cummings, James W.: goes to Emmett Expedition, 55; stays at Indian village, 106; arrives at West Nishnabotna River, 113; reaches Emmett company, 161–62
Cunningham, Andrew, 219, 264–65
Cutler, Alpheus, 152, 153, 155; family of, in Winter Quarters, 214; founds Cutler's Park, 220
Cutler's Camp, Iowa, 152
Cutler's Park, Nebraska, 208, 215, 219–20, 230
Cutlerites, 153, 155

D

Dagger, Madison, 129–30
Dagger's Mill, Council Bluffs, 129–30
Dalmanutha, 179–80

Dalton, Nebraska, 319
Danish Capital of America, 160
Danish Windmill Museum and Welcome Center, Elk Horn, 160
DAR Memorials: in Mt. Pisgah, 89; in Lewis, 105; in Council Bluffs, 132; in Iowa City, 167–68; at gravesite of Rebecca Winters, 326
Davenport, Iowa, 9, 163
Davenport, James, 317
Davenport Stake, 11
Davis County Historical Museum, Bloomfield, Iowa, 51
Dawson, Jacob, 234
Decantur, Iowa, 5
Decker, Isaac Perry, 256
Demick family, 76
DeMott, Lorenzo, 325–26
Dennis, Sandy, 197
Dern, George Henry, 258
Deseret Telegraph Line, 236
Des Moines, Iowa, 9, 175, 177–78
Des Moines–to–Council Bluffs Road, 19
Des Moines Hotel, Keosauqua, Iowa, 44
Des Moines River, 39, 41–42
Des Moines Stake, 11
Desoto Bend National Wildlife Refuge, Iowa, 157
DeSoto National Wildlife Refuge, Nebraska, 224
Dinesen Prairie Wildlife Area, 160
Discovery Company. *See* Advance Company
Dodge, Grenville: as railroad construction engineer, 119, 131, 347; historic home of, 132, 134
Dodge, Ruth Ann, 131
Dog Town, Iowa, 47
Donnellson, Iowa, 38
Douglas County Historical Society Library and Archives, 221
Dover, Iowa, 50
"Down and back" wagon trains, 217–19, 235, 254, 280
Dragoon Trail, 18, 19, 81
Drakesville, Iowa, 19, 52, 92
Drakesville Town Park, 52
Dripping Springs, Nebraska, 287–88
Dubuque, Iowa, 9, 164
Dubuque, Julien, 9
Duel family, 153
Dunbar, Rev. J., 268
Dunbar, William C., 342
Dundy, Elmer, 248–49
Dunham, Jonathan, 100
Dunn, James, 59
Durham Western Heritage Museum, 225–26
Duzette, Edward P., 55
Dyersville, Iowa, 164–65
Dyke family, 154
Dykes, George P., 111

E

Eagle Creek Camp, Nebraska, 309–10
Eames, Ellis, 260, 261
East Nishnabotna River, 105–6, 109
East Plattsmouth, Iowa, 151
Eddyville, Iowa, 19–20, 95
Edwards, William, 77
Egan, Howard: is captain of Camp of Israel company, 56; freight company of (1849), 240–41, 285–86; injured in Elkhorn skirmish, 253; on Sabbath Camp, Advance Company, 260; at Ancient Bluff Ruins, 317
Eisenhower, Mamie Doud, 10
Elbert, John D., 48
Eldon, Iowa, 46
Eldredge, Alanson, 262
Eldredge, Elnathan, 237
Eldredge, Horace S., 172
Elk Horn, Iowa, 160
Elkhorn Indian Skirmish (1848), 253
Elkhorn River, Nebraska, 245, 247, 250, 251; Crossing, 251–54; Camp, 253–54
Ellsworth handcart company, Edmund: uses Upper Ferry, 156;

is first handcart company, 170, 202; death of Welling child in, 175; goes through Anita, 180; camps at Loup Fork, 269; reaches Utah, 336
Elm Creek Camp, Nebraska, 290–91
Ely Ford/Mormon Crossing, 46
Emigrant Landing, 142–43
Emmett, James, 247
Emmett Expedition, James: through Iowa, 10; passes through Fort Madison, 21; at Camp Vermillion, 55, 106; near Council Bluffs, 113; at Council Bluffs, 161–62; assembles in Iowa City, 165; at Marengo, 173; at Mormon Ridge, 174; some of, join Miller advance party, 245
Ettleman family, 154
Evans, J. H., 51n
Evans, Priscilla, 170–71
Evans, W. A., 51n
Evans handcart company, Israel, 172, 203, 336
Evans' Camp, Iowa, 51
Ewell family, 154
Exline, Iowa, 54

F

Fairbanks, Avard, 216
Fairbanks, Nathaniel, 317
Fairbury, 287–89
Fairview Cemetery, Council Bluffs, 130
Falkner family, 288n
Fall Exodus, 11, 25–26
Families Are Forever Court of Memories and Gardens, Council Bluffs, 127–28
Farar family, 76
Farmer's and Traders Bank, Bonaparte, Iowa, 43
Farmington, Iowa, 39, 40–41
Farrer, James, 51
Feller, Bob, 10
Felt, Nathaniel H., 342
Ferrin, James, 108
Ferryville, Iowa, 143, 156, 210
Field of Dreams, 164–65
Fielding, Amos, 25
Findley House, William, Bloomfield, Iowa, 52
"First Camp," Nebraska, 221
First Congregational Church, Farmington, Iowa, 41
First Mormon Ferry, 143–44
First Presidency: want all Saints out west, 124–25; reconstitution of, 126, 141; attend a social at Traders Pt., 147
Fish Camp, Nebraska, 262–63, 336
Fisher family, 152
Fitzpatrick, Thomas, 200
Flanagan, Edward Joseph, 231
Florence, Nebraska: as LDS wagon train outfitting camp, 199, 216–19, 336–37; as North Omaha, 214–15
Florence Park (Mormon Park), Winter Quarters, 212
Follett, Warren, 152
Follett, William A., 152–53
Fonda, Henry, 197, 225, 275
Fontenelle Bank, Bellevue, Nebraska, 231–32
Fontenelle Forest Nature Center, Bellevue, Nebraska, 232
Ford, Gerald Rudolph Jr.: as famous Nebraskan, 197; birth site and gardens, 226–27; commemorative highway, 227
Fordham, Elijah, 13–14
Forney family, 154
Forsgren, John, company: as first Scandinavian company to emigrate to Utah, 17; uses same route as 1846 company, 19; passes through Dog Town, Iowa, 47; passes through Stringtown, 51
Ft. Atkinson, 118, 223; State Historical Park, 222–23
Ft. Calhoun City, Nebraska, 223, 250
Fort Des Moines, 13

Ft. Kearny, Nebraska, 274, 281, 284; Camp, 282–84; State Historical Park, 284–87; State Recreation Area, 287
Ft. Leavenworth, Kansas, 121, 285
Ft. Lisa, 222, 231
Fort Madison, 9, 12, 21
Ft. McPherson National Cemetery, 299–300
Ft. Mitchell, 328–29
Ft. Omaha Historic District, 220–21
Ft. Ponca, 246, 248–49, 269
Four Corners, Iowa, 23, 80
Fox River Camp, Iowa, 52–53
Fox, Ruth May, 302
Frandsen, Anders, 258
Freeman, Daniel, 244
Fremont, John C., 258, 285
Fremont, Nebraska, 250, 258; Camp, 257–59
Fremont County, Iowa, 152–54
Fremont Lakes State Recreation Area, 254, 258
Fremont Township, 80–81
French, Daniel Chester, 131
Frog's Head Bluff/Indian Lookout Pt., 315–16
Frontier Guardian, Council Bluffs: published by Orson Hyde, 123, 124; offices of, 129; Browning's advertisement in, 149
Fullerton, Nebraska, 267
Fullmer, David, 75, 76
Fullmer, Rhoda, 76

G

Galland, Isaac, 16, 160
Galland's Grove, 160
Gallup, George H, 10
Garden Grove Settlement, Iowa, 70, 73–78; Camp, 72–73; Town Park, 78
Gardner, Archibald, 30n
Garrett–Phelps House, Burlington, 23
Gates, Jacob, 228; company, 19
Genoa, Nebraska, 263–67; Historical Museum, 266; U.S. Indian School, 267; Park, 267
George B. Hitchcock House, 109–10
Gerber, John T., 239
Gibbs, William, 40
Gibson, Bob, 197
Giles, John D., 89
Glenn, S. S., 289
Glenwood, Iowa, 149, 151–52
Glines, Eric, 307
Golden Spike Monument, Council Bluffs, 134
Gold rush travelers: outfitted in Kanesville, 124; use Upper Ferry, 210; use South Ferry, 233; on St. Joseph and Independence Road, 241; stop at Ft. Kearny, 285; travel California Hill, 309
Good, Charles, 178
Gothenburg, Nebraska, 295–96
Grace College of the Bible, Omaha, 225
Graceland College, 11, 79
Grandfield, Farmer, 85
Grand Island, Nebraska, 245, 274; Camp, 273–75
Grand River Camp, 96–97
Granite rock, Mt. Pisgah, 85
Grant, George, 340, 342
Grant, Heber J., 198, 216, 327
Grattan, John Lawrence, 299, 315
Grattan Massacre, 299–300, 315
Graybill Creek, 110
Great American Desert. *See* Great Plains
Great Divide of Iowa, 98
Great Plains, 196, 204, 294, 322
Great Platte River Road Archway Monument, Kearney, 282
Greef General Store, Bentonsport, Iowa, 44
Green, Fidelia, 77
Green, John and Mary, 43
Greene, Evan M. and Susan, 131
Greene, John P., 130–31
Greenfield, Iowa, 98
Griffiths, Elizabeth, 90

Griggs, Thomas C., 218, 254
Grove, the, 16–17
Grove Township, 160
Gunzenhauser, Karla and Paul, 67n, 75, 76n
Gurley, child, 77

H

Haight, Horton David, company, 236
Haight, Isaac, 18, 30n
"Hairy Nation," 95–96
Hales family, 76
Halfday, Chief, 147
Hall, William, 48
Hamburg, Iowa, 149, 152, 162
Hancock, Levi W., 148
Hancock, Mosiah, 30n
Hancock, Solomon, 107; company, 81
Hancock House, Bentonsport, Iowa, 44
Handcart companies: history of, 168–72; through Nebraska, 202–3; start journey in Florence, 217–18; camp at Looking Glass Creek Camp, 264; statistics on, 337; trails followed by, 337. *See also* Mormon Handcart Trail
Handcart Family Statue, 178
Handcart song, 171
Handcart Trail. *See* Mormon Handcart Trail
Hansen, Christian and Inger, 266
Hansen, Hans C., 260
Harlan, Iowa, 160
Harmon, Appleton, 298, 308; company, 19
Harney, William S., 314–15
Harney Massacre, 314–15
Harpersville, Iowa, 50
Harris, John, 158
Harris, Martin, 178
Harris Grove, Iowa, 158–59; Creek, 158
Harrison County, Iowa, 157–58; Historical Museum, 158
Harvey, John, 56
Hatch, Lorenzo Hill, 29
Haven, Jesse, handcart company, 171
Haven, John, 153
Hawkes family, 76
Hawley, Asa S., 325
Hawley's Settlement, 15
Haws, Peter, 56
Healings, 13–14
Heartland of America scenic park, Omaha, 225
Helgenberger, Marg, 197
Henry, Nebraska, 332
Hickok, James Butler (Wild Bill), 197, 289
Hickory Grove Camp, 58–61
Hickory Thunder Camp, 79–80
Higbee, John S., 209
Highland Grove, Council Bluffs, 139
Hill, Bill, 127, 128
Hill, Brian, 305
Hinckley, Gordon B., 127, 215, 216
Hinman, Lyman, 161
Hintze, Ferdinand F., 258
Hodgetts, William B.: leads wagon train from Iowa City, 172; accompanies handcart companies, 336, 337–38, 345; statistics on, 338
Hoffheins, Jacob, 172
Holbrook, Joseph, 30n
Homer, Russell K., 172
Homestead Act of 1862, 244–45
Homestead National Monument, 244–45
Honey Creek, Iowa, 157; Mormon Pioneer Cemetery, 157
Hookway, Ann Marie Chatters, 234, 237
Hookway, Mary Ann, 234, 237
Hoover, Herbert, 10; National Historic Site and Presidential Library, 163
Hopkins Building, Bonaparte, Iowa, 43
Horne, Joseph, company, 254

Horrocks, Daniel, 288n
Hudson, Henry, 266, 267
Humeston, Iowa, 93
Hummel Park, Winter Quarters, 222
Hunt, John A.: leads wagon train west from Iowa City, 172; accompanies handcart companies, 336, 337–38, 345; statistics on, 338
Hunter, Alexander, 211
Huntington, William, 79, 86, 87, 88
Huntsman's Echo, Shelton, Nebraska, 279–80
Huston family, 154
Hutchings, Sarah E., 350
Hyde, Orson: dedicates Nauvoo Temple, 25; records Spring Exodus, 30n; presides over church in Kanesville, 123, 124, 140–41; Music Hall, Council Bluffs, 129
Hyde, William, 120–21
Hyde Park, Council Bluffs, 135, 139–41
Hyde Street (now 1st Street), Council Bluffs, 122, 128–29

I

I–80, handcart companies follow route of, 63
Iconium, Iowa, 92, 93
Independence, Missouri, 200
Indian Creek, 106, 121; Camp, 47–48
Indian Lookout Pt., 315–16
Indiantown, Iowa, 19, 105, 108–9
Inn of the Six Toed Cat, Allerton, Iowa, 70
Interpretive panels. *See* Mormon Trail interpretive panels
Iowa: map of Mormon Trail through, 2–4; description of, 9–10
Iowa City, as capital of Iowa, 9; connection of, to Mormon history, 165–67, 202; 1856 handcart companies outfit in, 336
Iowa City Railroad Depot, 166
Iowa Des Moines Mission, 11
Iowa Historic Route 1, 12
Iowa Historic Route 2, 12, 109
Iowa Mormon Trails Association, 12n
Iowa School for the Deaf, 117, 134, 135
Iowa Stake, 14–15
Iowaville Cemetery, 46
Iranistan, Iowa, 108–9
Irvington, Nebraska, 251
Island Camp, Nebraska, 292–93
Iverson, Iver N., 172

J

Jackson, William Henry, 329
Jacob, Norton: on dedicating mission of Advance Company, 257–58; on the Platte River, 261; on Pawnee Indians, 264; on Indian-set prairie fires, 290; on admonitions from leaders, 307–8, 317
Jacobs, Henry B., 55
Jacobs, Henry Chariton, 55
Jacobs, Zebulon, 314
Jacobs, Zina D. Huntington, 55
Jacobson, Jacob I., 349–50
Jailhouse Rock, Nebraska, 315, 319
James, Isaac, 111
James, Jane Manning, 111
James, Silas F., 111
Jannsen, David, 197
Jaques, John: on Silver Creek, 113; on Marengo, 173; on Rising Sun, 177; on Dalmanutha, 180; on gravesites near Prairie Creek, 272; near Lone Tree, 273; on site of Babbitt killing, 346
Jasper County Historical Museum, 176
Jensen, Bertha Marie, 303
Jenson, Andrew, 89, 239

John Pierre Cabannes's Trading Post, 222
Johnson, Aaron, 75, 76
Johnson, Harold and Mary, 234n, 236
Johnson, Jim and Mary, 234n, 236
Johnson, Joel H., 129
Johnson, Joseph Ellis, 129, 279–80
Johnson, Luke: as doctor of Advance Company, 262; brings leather boat across plains, 263; shoots rattlesnake, 274; at Ft. Kearny Camp, 284; at Ash Hollow Camp, 312
Johnson, Philo, 296, 298, 301
Johnson Emporium, Council Bluffs, 129
Johnston, Albert Sidney, 286, 315
Johnston, Jane, 37
Joliet, Louis, 9, 198
Jolley, Bryant, 159
Jones, Carl, 253
Jones, Dan, 172
Joslyn, George and Sarah, 226
Joslyn Art Museum, Omaha, 225, 226
Jubilee (1848), Council Bluffs, 127
Junction–Odometer Camp, 300–301

K

Kalona, Iowa, 163–64
Kane, Iowa, 121. *See also* Kanesville, Iowa
Kane, Thomas L.: on births at Sugar Creek, 37; relationship of, with Saints, 122; on bowery on Redemption Hill, 137–38; records speech of Indian chief, 147–48; on Cold Spring Camp, Nebraska, 230; sends presents to Church leaders, 255, 261
Kanesville, Iowa: importance of, 11, 95, 118, 121–25; Boulevard, 122; Cemetery, 130; Historic Park, 127–28; Log Tabernacle, 126–27, 140. *See also* Council Bluffs, Iowa
Kanesville Restoration, Inc., 127
Kansas–Nebraska Act, 196
Kay, John, 40, 147
Kearney, Nebraska, 281–82
Kearny, Ft. *See* Ft. Kearny, Nebraska
Kearny, Stephen Watts, 18, 120, 241, 284. *See also* Ft. Kearny, Nebraska
Kedron, 34
Keg Creek: Camp, 113–14; Settlement, 151
Keiser, Bob, 127
Keokuk, Chief, 16–17
Keokuk, Iowa: as LDS outfitting camp, 11, 17, 18; historical sites within, 16–18; Dam and Power Plant, 17–18, 28
Keokuk–to–Des Moines Road, 19
Keosauqua, Iowa, 44–45
Kesler, Frederick, 21–22, 116, 144
Kesler, Frederick, Jr., 210, 229
Keysor, Guy M.: erects Redemption Hill bowery, 138; in Mormon Battalion, 145; on Battalion Farewell Ball, 145; on Traders Pt., 146
Keystone, Nebraska, 308
Kilbourne, Florence, 216–17
Kimball, Benjamin Willard, 335
Kimball, David, 49
Kimball, Ellen Sanders, 256
Kimball, Heber C.: in Winter Exodus group, 24; is a president of Camp of Israel companies, 56; camps on Shoal Creek, 57; stays behind at Locust Creek, 67–68; on Cream Camp, 81; meets Indian chiefs, 100; preaches at Ring Camp, 101; at West Nishnabotna River, 113; supervises trading, 116; becomes official counselor in First Presidency, 126, 140; Monument, 221; Farm, 222; is involved in lawsuit, 243; leads Advance Company, 251; names Looking Glass Creek, 263; at Loup Sabbath Camp, 270; at Ft. Kearny Camp, 282–83; names Buffalo

Creek, 291; at Island Camp, 293; wheel of, used for odometer, 296, 298, 301; at North Bluff Fork, 304; praises and admonishes Pioneer camp, 307; at Sand Hill Bluff Camp, 310; journal of, on Terrace Bluffs Camp, 323; on safety of families, 332; at Sacred Prayer Camp, 333

Kimball, Heber C., company: at Pleasant Pt., 70; at Long Creek, 82; at Pleasant Valley Camp, 104; at Graybill Creek, 110–11; at Mosquito Creek Camps, 115, 117; in Winter Quarters, 214; fights Indians at Elkhorn River (1848), 253

Kimball, Helen, 64–65

Kimball, Sarah Ann Whitney, 49

Kimball, Spencer W., 155

Kimball, Stanley B., 12n, 27n, 334

Kimball, William, 50–51, 340, 342

Kimballton, Iowa, 160; City Park, 161

King, Hannah T., 318

Kingsley Dam, 309

Kingston, Thomas and Margaret, 76

Klokkenspel, 21

Knaphus, Torleif, 178

Knight, Jesse, 248

Knight, Joseph Sr., 89

Knight, Lydia, 25

Knight, Newel: in Spring Exodus, 25; records exoduses, 28n, 30n; on leaving Nauvoo, 36; at Soap Creek, 92; on Ponca village, 246; death of, 247; monument to, 248, 269

Knight, Vinson, 16

Korean War Memorial, Des Moines, 178

Krumm, Jacob, Nature Preserve, Iowa, 175

L

Lacey-Keosauqua State Park, 46

Lamb family, 76

Lamoni, Iowa, 11, 78–79

Landers, Ann, 10

Langley, James, 80

Langley, John, 80

Last Camp/Last Chance Camp, Garden Grove, 94–95

LDS Visitors' Center, Council Bluffs, 127

LDS Winter Quarters Memorial, Nebraska, 155

Lebanon, Iowa, 48

Le Clerc (Le Clair), Chief, 147–48

Lee, John D.: in Winter Exodus group, 24; crosses frozen Mississippi, 29; records gravesites at Richardson's Pt., 50; on worship meeting at Locust Creek, 66; at Garden Grove, 74; names Pleasant Prairie Encampment, 104; on Indian village, 106; on Missouri River Camp, 116; is foreman of Summer Quarters, Nebraska, 224

Leigh, William Robinson, 226

Lemoyne, Nebraska, 309

Leon, 82

Lewellen, Nebraska, 311

Lewis, Ellenor Roberts, 156

Lewis, Iowa, 104–5, 109, 182

Lewis, John L., 10

Lewis, Tarlton, 270–71, 333

Lewis and Clark Expedition: on border of Iowa, 9, 115, 118; commemoration of, 146; monument to, 151; along eastern and northern border of Nebraska, 195; near Winter Quarters, 222; in Wyoming, Nebraska, 233

Lewis Central High School, 117

Lexington, Nebraska, 292–93

Liberty Hall Historic Center, Lamoni, Iowa, 78–79

Liberty Pole Camp, Nebraska, 254–58

Libertyville, Iowa, 19

Lick Creek Camp, 39–40

Lied Historical Building, Council Bluffs, 146
Lighthouse Lake, Iowa, 162
Lincoln, Abraham: on Council Bluffs, 119, 143; commissions transcontinental railroad, 132, 347
Lincoln, Nebraska, 196, 243–44
Lincoln County Historical Museum, Nebraska, 303
Lincoln Highway, 159
Lincoln Memorial, Council Bluffs, 131
Linfleu, John D., 146
Linger Longer Park, Montrose, Iowa, 33–34
Lisa, Manuel, 222
Lisco, Nebraska, 315
Little, Edwin S., 49
Little, Jesse C.: is friend of Thomas Kane, 122; works with Pottawattamies, 148; reports on Eastern states mission, 255; brings gifts and mail to Advance Company, 261
Little Blue River, 287–88
"Little Mermaid," fountain, Kimballton, 161
Little Papillion, Nebraska, 340
Little Sioux River, Iowa, 162
Lock and Dam No. 11, Keokuk, Iowa, 18
Locust Creek Camps, Iowa, 60–66
Logan, Iowa, 159
Logan River Valley, Nebraska, 247
Lone Tree marker, Nebraska, 272–73
Long, Stephen H.: on Nebraska, 196; explores north side of Platte, 200, 222; labels 100th Meridian, 294
Long Creek Camp, 82
Long's Landing County Park, Iowa, 115, 143
Looft Continuing Education Center, Iowa Western Community College, 150
Looking Glass Creek Camp, 263–64, 267
Lost Camp, Iowa, 23, 80–81
Lost Fork Bridge, 104
Lott, Cornelius P., 29
Louisiana Purchase, 195
Loup Ford and Ferry, 268
Loup Fork, Nebraska, 245, 263, 269, 270
Loup River Ford and Camp, 268–69
Loup Sabbath Camp, 269–70
Lower Mormon Road, Nebraska, 250–51
Lowry, Elizabeth, 43
Lowry, John, 42–43
Lucas, Robert and Friendly, 167
Lyman, Amasa: at Peter's Bridge Camp, 80; in 1847 Advance Company, 253; on Pawnee Missionary Station, 268; at Loup Sabbath Camp, 271; at Ft. Kearny Camp, 284; on Sand Hills Camp, 306; at Admonition Camp, 307; at Ash Hollow Camp, 312; on Terrace Bluffs, 323; at Sacred Prayer Camp, 332, 333
Lyman, Amasa, company: camps at Pleasant Pt., 69; at Peter's Bridge Camp, 80; at Long Creek Camp, 82; on Wood River, 277
Lyman, Eliza Maria Partridge, 35
Lyman, Iowa, 100, 104
Lytle, Charles, 41
Lytle, Christiana (Mrs. John), 41

M

Macedonia, Iowa, 110, 111–12
Macedonia company, 111
Machette Stage Station, Gothenburg, 296
Madison, Fort. *See* Fort Madison
Madison County, Iowa, 91
Madsen, Carol Cornwall, 30n
Maguire, Dorothy, 197, 225
Majors, Alexander, 242
Malcolm X, 197, 227
Mammoth Bone Camp, 315

Manawa, Lake, State Park, 141–42
Manning, Edwin, 45
Manning, Hotel, Keosauqua, Iowa, 45
Manti, Iowa, 152–55; Cemetery, 153–54; Memorial Park, 153–54
Mantle, Luellen, 48
Marengo, Iowa, 165, 173
Margetts, Thomas, wife and child, 314, 342, 346
Market Street, Wyoming, Nebraska, 238–39
Markham, Stephen: leads advance company, 36; is captain of Camp of Israel company, 56; at Garden Grove, 74; is captain of Advance Company, 256; is colonel in Advance Company, 260
Marquett, Jacques, 9, 198
Marsh, Thomas B., 219
Marshalltown, Iowa, 165, 174
Marsh family, 108
Martin, Jesse B., 172
Martin handcart company, Edward: through Indiantown, 108; camps at Silver Creek, 113; in Council Bluffs, 150; problems of, 171–72, 336; in Des Moines, 178; through Adel, 179; through Dalmanutha, 179–80; travels south side of Platte River, 202–3, 337, 346; passes gravesites at Prairie Creek, 272, 344; passes Lone Tree, 273; crosses the Platte, 305; passes Babbitt murder site, 314; statistics on, 338; re-outfits at Florence, 343; route of, 343–46
Martindale, Elder, 265
Mason House Inn, Bentonsport, Iowa, 44
Massena, Iowa, 99
Mauritzens, Johana, 288n
Maxwell, Nebraska, 297
Mayhew, Elijah, 304–5
Maytag, Fred, 176
McAllister, John D. T., 171
McAllister, Lake, Nebraska, 262
McArthur handcart company, Daniel: is one of first handcart companies, 170, 202, 336; and story of lost boy, 180–81
McBride family, 76
McCanles, David, 289
McClurg, J. J., Mansion, Garden Grove, 78
McConaughy, Lake, 308; State Recreation Area, 309
McFarlan's Castle. *See* Courthouse Rock, Nebraska
McGraw, James, 156–57, 340
McIntosh, John A., Cabin, 160
McIntosh, Mr., 243
McKay, David O., 155, 209
McLellin, William E., 242–43
Mecham family, 76
Meeks, Priddy, 153
Meek's Mills, William, 41–42
Mennonites, 163–64
Merrill, Albert, 94
Merrill, Margaret Ann, 94
Merrill, Moses and Eliza, 232
Merry Brook School Museum, Woodbine, Iowa, 159
Mesquakie Indians, 100
Metropolitan Community College, Omaha, 225
Mexican War, 86, 120
Meyer, Heinrich, 173
Middle Mormon Ferry: near Council Bluffs, 142, 143–44; on Nebraska side, 228–29; Mormon Trail from, 250
Miller, Alfred Jacob, 226
Miller, Daniel A., 121; company (1853), 304
Miller, Emanuel, House, Farmington, Iowa, 41
Miller, George: in Winter Exodus group, 24; is a president of Camp of Israel companies, 56; leads advance party, 104, 105, 245–47, 268; supervises trading, 116; supplies fish for camp, 117; disaffects from Church, 247–48

Miller, George, company: camps at Pleasant Pt., 69; as advance party building bridges, 104, 105, 110; at West Nishnabotna River, 113; at Mosquito Creek Camp, 115
Miller, Glenn, 10
Miller, Henry W.: cofounds Miller's Hollow, 121, 128; oversees construction of Kanesville tabernacle, 126; statue of, 127
Miller, John, 146
Miller, Samuel F., Home, Keokuk, 17
Miller's Hollow, 117–18, 121
Millerton, Iowa, 93
Mills County, Iowa, 151–52
Minatare, Nebraska, 323
Minden, Nebraska, 281
Miner, Albert, 46
Miracle of quail, 26, 32–33
Missionary handcart company, 203, 265, 336
Mississippi River: Lock and Dam No. 19, 18; Winter Exodus crossing of, 29–30, 36; Spring Exodus crossing of 30–31
Mississippi Saints, 312
Missouri, 58; Compromise Act, 9
Missouri River, 198–99; Camp, 115–16, 143
Missouri Valley, Iowa, 157; Welcome Center, 158
Mitchell, Iowa, 19
Mitchell, Robert B., 146–47, 328
Mitchell, Thomas, 176; Park, 176
Mitchell Pass, 328
Mitchellville, Iowa, 176–77
Monarch of the Sea, 235
Monroe, Nebraska, 263
Monroe County, Iowa, 95
Montrose, Iowa, 5, 12–15; Riverfront Park, 12, 28
Moravia, Iowa, 92–93
Morgan, Thomas, 288n
Morley, Isaac, 223–24
Mormon Battalion: enlistment and departure of, from Council Bluffs, 11, 119–21, 148, 245; enlists soldiers from Mt. Pisgah, 86–87; memorial marker for, 134; mustering grounds of, 138–39, 148; headquarters of, near Traders Pt., 144; farewell ball of, 145; path of, through Iowa, 148–49, 152–53; connection of, to General Kearny, 285
Mormon Creek, 92
Mormon Ferry. *See* Upper Ferry, Iowa
Mormon Grove, Kansas, 286, 287
Mormon Handcart Trail: through Iowa, 2–4; through Lewis, 105, 182; merges with Mormon Trail, 109; through Macedonia, 112, 113; past Keg Creek, 114; passes through Council Bluffs, 118, 150–51; over Upper Ferry, 156; follows general route of I–80, 163; begins in Iowa City, 166, 167–68; passes South Amana, 172; passes Marengo, 173; through Newton, 176; through Mitchellville, 176–77; through Rising Sun, 177; through Des Moines, 177–78; through Adel, 179; through Dalmanutha, 179–80; through Anita, 180–81; through Nebraska, 202–3
Mormon Hollow, Bellevue, Nebraska, 232–33, 250
Mormon House, Bentonsport, Iowa, 44
Mormon Island, Grand Island, Nebraska, 274–75
Mormon Island Recreation Area, 274–75
Mormon Lake, Iowa, 98–99
Mormon migration, uncommon aspects of, 202
Mormon Mill, Old, Winter Quarters, 210–11
"Mormon Monument," 154

Mormon Pioneer Cemetery, Winter Quarters, 215–16
Mormon Pioneer Memorial Bridge, 155, 198, 208–9
Mormon Pioneer National Historic Trail: designation of, 5, 25; plaque of, in Keokuk, Iowa, 16; highway of, through Council Bluffs, 142; designation of, through Nebraska, 201
Mormon Ridge, Iowa, 174; Road, 174
Mormon Tabernacle organ, 235
Mormontown, Iowa, 155
Mormon Trail: map of, through Iowa, 2–4; map of, through Nebraska, 184–87; designation of, 200, 201; submerged under Lake McConaughy, 309
Mormon Trail Auto Route: through Iowa, 5; through Nebraska, 189–90
Mormon Trail Center, Historic Winter Quarters, 215
Mormon Trail County Park, Adair County, Iowa, 98–99
Mormon Trail Highway: through Fort Madison, 21; U.S. and State roads designated, 82
Mormon Trail interpretive panels: in Montrose, 12–13, 28; in Keokuk, 16; erected for sesquicentennial, 27–28; in Linger Longer Park, 33–34; in Bonaparte, 42; in Keosauqua, 44; in Bloomfield, 51–52; in Drakesville, 52; at Chariton River Ford, 54; in Tharp Cemetery, 67; in Corydon, 68; at Garden Grove, 75; at Osceola, 82; at Murray, 83; at Mt. Pisgah, 90; by Rathbun Lake, 93; in Chariton area, 93; by Threemile Lake, 96; in Orient, 97; at Mormon Lake, 99; at Lyman, 104; near Lewis, 109; near Hitchcock House, 110; at Macedonia, 112; in Council Bluffs, 135, 139; throughout Nebraska, 204; in Winter Quarters, 212; at Saline Ford, 240; at Elkhorn River Crossing, 252; in Fremont Lakes State Recreation Area, 258; near Fish Camp, 262, in Genoa, 266; near Wood River Crossing, 278; in Shelton, 280; in Kearney, 282; near Odessa, 287; in Gothenburg, 296; at North Platte Airport, 301; at Sand Hills Historic Area, 305–6; at Ancient Bluffs Ruins and Camp, 316; near Bayard, 322; near Henry, 334
Mormon Trail Junior-Senior High School, 78
Mormon Trail School District, Garden Grove, 78
Mormon Trail Variant A, 92–93
Mormon Trail Variant B, 80, 81, 93–95
Mormon Trail Variant in Monroe County, 95
Mormon Trail Visitors' Center, Keosauqua, Iowa, 45
Mormon Trail wagon ruts: near SevenMile Creek Camp, 83; near Mormon Lake, 99; near Genoa, 267; near Wood River Crossing, 278; at Sand Hills Historic Area, 305–6; at Ancient Bluff Ruins, 317
Mormon Trail Wayside Park and marker, Nebraska, 272–73
Mormon Trek Boulevard, University of Iowa, Iowa City, 166
Morrill, Nebraska, 330
Morrison Park, S. T., Iowa City, 167
Morton, J. Sterling, 241–42
Mosquito Creek: Hill Camps, 114–15, 116–17, 134–35; Settlement, 135
Moulton, Iowa, 54
Mt. Moriah Settlement, 90
Mt. Pisgah, Iowa, 19, 66, 86–90;

Camp, 83–86; LDS Cemetery, 88–89; Memorial Park, 89
Mt. Rushmore National Monument, 259
Mt. Sterling, Iowa, 46–47
Mt. Vernon Gardens, Omaha, 229
Mud Springs Station, Nebraska, 320
Muddy Creek Camp, 72
Murdock, James, 32
Murdock family, 152
Murray, Iowa, 82–83
Murray Historical Complex, Murray, Iowa, 83

N

Nashville, Iowa, 15
National Arbor Day Foundation, 242
National Danish Immigrant Museum, Elk Horn, 160
National Farm Toy Museum, Dyersville, Iowa, 165
National Historic Riverfront District: in Bonaparte, Iowa, 43; in Bentonsport, Iowa, 44
National Western Historic Trails Center, 145–46
Native Americans: in Iowa, 9; in Nebraska, 204
Nauvoo, battle of, 25–26
Nauvoo Band: follows advance company, 36; performs in Farmington, 40; performs in Keosauqua, 44–45; is attached to Haws company, 56
Nauvoo Temple, 25
Nebraska: maps of Mormon Trail across, 184–87; introduction to, 195–97; Conference, 198; Association of, 204; State Historical Society, 243
Nebraska City, 241–43, 284; Road, 238; Cut-off, 276–77, 286
Neff, John, 257
Nelson Pioneer Farm and Museum, 20
New Boston, Iowa, 19, 34
Newman, Elijah, 270–71
"New Purchase," 59–60
Newton, Iowa, 175–76
New York Evening Post, 169–70
Nichols, A., 272
Nicholson, John, 242–42
Nielsen, Niels, 237
Niobrara, Nebraska, 249; River, 246, 249; State Park, 249
Nishnabotna Middle Fork Camp, 110–11
Noble, Joseph Bates, 14
Nodaway River, 100, 101
Nolte, Nick, 197
Norris, George, W., 197
North Bend, Nebraska, 261
North Bluff Fork, Nebraska, 304–5
Northern States Mission, 11
North Mormon Ferry, 250
North Platte, 301–304; Canteen, 302; Camp, 303–4
North Raccoon River, 179

O

Oakley, John, 177
Octagonal Home, Willard Richards, 212
Odessa, Nebraska, 287
Odometer: creation of, 261; use of, 296–97, 298; refinements of, 301, 308
O'Fallon's Bluff, Nebraska, 306
Offutt Air Force Base, Bellevue, Nebraska, 232
Ogallala, Nebraska, 308
Old California Overland Trail, 278
Old Capitol Building, University of Iowa, Iowa City, 166–67
Old Des Moines Fort, 13, 177
Old Ft. Kearny Road, 240–41
Old Market District, Omaha, 225
Old Mormon Trail, 52–53, 57–58
Old Order Amish, 164
Old Presbyterian Church, Bellevue, Nebraska, 232
Old Towne Park, Macedonia, Ohio, 112

Old Warehouse District, Omaha, 225
Old WyomingCemetery, 236–37
Oliver, Edward Sr., 280–81
Oliver, Sarah, 281
Olson, Hans Peter, company, 299
Omaha, 218
Omaha, Nebraska, 196, 224–25, 349; Waterworks, 212
Omaha Indians, 220
100th Meridian, Cozad, Nebraska, 294–95; Museum, 294
Openshaw, Samuel, 344
Oregon Trail (south of Platte): is more frequently used, 200, 210; Willie handcart company follows, through Nebraska, 305, 337; wagon ruts of, 305–6, 308–9, 311, 329; follows North Platte River, 311; campsite of, near Chimney Rock, 322
Orient, Iowa, 97–98
Osceola, Iowa, 80–81, 93
Oshkosh, Nebraska, 313
Oskaloosa, Iowa, 19, 20
Osterdock, Iowa, 164
Oto Indians, 220
Ottumwa, Iowa, 19, 46
Overland Trail, 334–35
Overton, Nebraska, 291
Ox, Iowa, 50
Ox-Bow Trail, Nebraska, 239–41, 286

P

Pace, James, 74
Pacific Railroad Act, 347
Pack, John, 260, 333
Page, John E., 145
Palmer, Brother, 40
Paradise Camp, 68–69
Parker, Arthur, 180
Parker, Robert and Ann, 180–81
Parker's Castle. *See* Courthouse Rock, Nebraska
Parkman, Francis, 328
Parrish, Orrin, 272
"Path of Names," 146
Patten family, 152
Pawnee: village and mission, Nebraska, 245; Missionary Station Camp, 267–68; Creek, 298
Pawnee Indians, 263–64; gravesites of, 267; Reservation, 267
Paxton, Nebraska, 306
Pearson, Benjamin Franklin, 45; House, 45
Pearson, Richard, 146
Peart, Jacob, 74
Pella, Iowa, 19, 20–21; Historical Village, 21
Pelzer, Joseph, 109
Perkins, Andrew H., 111
Perpetual Emigrating fund, 217, 337
Perry Place, Old, Farmington, Iowa, 41
Pershing, John J., 197
Peter's Bridge Camp, 80
Petersen, Lars, 236
Pettengill family, 108
Pfister home, Farmington, Iowa, 41
Pidcock, Elbert, 67n
Pidgeon Creek, Iowa, 162; Branch tabernacle, 127
Pied Rioche, Chief, 147–48
Piercy, Frederick: describes Keokuk camp, 17; uses Upper Ferry, 156, 210; on destruction of Winter Quarters, 214; on Ash Hollow, 313; on Scotts Bluff, 330
Pilcher, Joshua, 322
Pioneer Day celebration, 291–92
Pioneer Grand Encampment, 118, 135–36, 208
Pioneer Meetinghouse, Garden Grove, Iowa, 77
Pioneer Memorial Trail pavilion, 34
Pioneer Museum, Farmington, Iowa, 41
Pioneer Park, Council Bluffs, 139
Pioneer Trail Road, 113, 139
Pitt, William, 36, 66, 292. *See also* Nauvoo Band

Plainsman Museum, Aurora, Nebraska, 276
Platte River: Road, Great, 198, 200–201; description of, 199–200; Fish Camp at, 262
Plattsmouth, Nebraska, 151, 233
Pleasant Grove Camp, 71–72
Pleasant Pt. Camp, 69–70
Pleasant Valley: (Pleasant Prairie) Camp, 104; (Walnut Creek) Camp, 110
Plumb Hollow, Iowa, 154
Plum Creek Massacre, Nebraska, 293
Plum Grove Historic Home, Iowa City, 167
Poe Building, Bonaparte, Iowa, 43
Pointe Aux Poules, 146–48
Polk, James K., 86, 119–20
Polk City, Iowa, 178
Ponca Encampment (1846), 245–47, 268, 269; Winter Camp, 269
Ponca Indians, 246, 248–49; Tribal Museum, 249
Ponds, Brother, 65
Pony Express station: in Ft. Kearny, 286; in Cozad, 294–95; in Gothenburg, 296; at Mud Springs, 320
Poor Saints camp: in Mississippi west shore, 26, 31–32; miracle of the quail at, 32–33; births at, 37
Pottawattamie County: Road G66, 113; Jail, Council Bluffs, 132
Pottawattamie Forks Trail, 108
Pottawattamie Indian(s), 101–102, 147; Village, births at, 37, 105–6; Sawmill, 144, 149–50; Agency headquarters, Traders Pt., Iowa, 146
Potter, William, 113
Potter's Park, Harlan, Iowa, 160
Potter's Slough, 31–32
Poulsen, Martin, 288n
Poulson, Jens, 288n
Poweshiek, Chief, 100
Prairie country, 20
Prairie Creek Camp, Nebraska, 271–72
Prairie dog towns, 203–4
Prairie Trails Museum of Wayne County, 68
Pratt, Louisa Barnes, 30n
Pratt, Orson: in Winter Exodus group, 24; records Winter Exodus, 28n; on Sugar Creek camp, 35; on passing through Bonaparte, 42; company, 68–69, 115; at Mt. Pisgah, 85; organizes Saints in Mt. Pisgah and Garden Grove, 94; council meeting held in tent of, 145; on Elkhorn River crossing, 252; in 1847 Advance Company, 253; creates odometer for Advance Company, 261, 298; at Ft. Kearny Camp, 284; at Ash Hollow, 312; speaks at Covenant Camp, 332; at Sacred Prayer Camp, 332, 333
Pratt, Parley P.: relates healing of Elijah Fordham, 13–14; in Winter Exodus group, 24; records Winter Exodus, 28n; is a president of Camp of Israel companies, 56; company, 79, 83–84, 136; on choosing Mt. Pisgah site, 83–84; at Mt. Pisgah, 85; swims Indian Creek, 107; speaks to Saints on Redemption Hill, 138; leads big company of pioneers (1847), 256–57
Preston, William B., company, 235, 259
Promontory Summit, Utah, 132, 348
Prospect Hill Cemetery, Omaha, 227
Pulsipher, John, 204

Q

Quail, miracle of, 26, 32–33

R

Raccoon Barracks, Iowa, 81, 99, 177
Raccoon Forks Trail, 108

Railroad Town, Grand Island, Nebraska, 275
Rand Park, Keokuk, Iowa, 16
Rappleye, Tunis, 159
Rathbun Lake, Iowa, 93
Rattlesnakes, 68
Reasoner, Harry, 10
Red Cloud, Chief, 197
Red Cloud, Nebraska, 277
Redding, Jackson, 261
Redemption Hill, Council Bluffs, 117, 136–37
Redfield, Iowa, 179
Red Rock Treaty, 59
Reed, Donna, 10
Reed's Creek, Iowa, 40–41
Reeves, Christiana, 19
Remington, Frederic, 226
Reno Methodist Cemetery, 101, 102
Reorganized Church of Jesus Christ of Latter-day Saints, 11, 78–79. *See* Community of Christ
Retreat Restaurant, Bonaparte, Iowa, 43
Revenue Cutter, 262, 270; is used as a stand, 297, 307, 331; crosses North Platte River, 311
Reynolds, Ellis, 325
Reynolds, George, 239
Reynolds, William Fletcher, 325
Rice, Leonard G., company, 302–3
Rich, Charles C., 29, 56, 74, 88
Richards, Franklin D., 342–43, 344
Richards, Mary Haskins Parker, 30n, 40, 153
Richards, Samuel W., 30n
Richards, Silas, 128, 291
Richards, Willard: in Winter Exodus group, 24; as historian of Camp of Israel, 56; stays behind at Locust Creek, 67–68; on Muddy Creek Camp, 72; names Hickory Thunder Camp, 79; company, 97; meets Indian chiefs, 100; preaches at Ring Camp, 101; fishes Mosquito Creek, 115; becomes official counselor in First Presidency, 126, 140; sets up post office on Redemption Hill, 137; advises handcart companies, 168; octagonal home of, in Winter Quarters, 212; in 1847 Advance Company, 253; writes note to following camps, 291; praises and admonishes Pioneer Camp, 307; at Sacred Prayer Camp, 333
Richardson, Shadrach and Solomon, 49
Richardson's Point, 19, 45, 48–50
Ricks, Thomas, 253
Ridge, William, 284
Ring (Circled Wagon) Camp, 100–101
Ripley, Alanson, 15
Rising Sun, Iowa, 177
Riverboat Bertrand Museum, 157
River Creek, Iowa, 162
Riverfront Park, Montrose, Iowa, 12
Riverview Park, Fort Madison, Iowa, 21
Robert Henri Museum and Historical Walkway, 294–95
Roberts, Brigham H., 239
Robidoux Pass, 328
Robinson handcart company, Daniel, 203, 266, 337
Rock Creek Station State Historical Park, 289
Rockwell, Orrin Porter: brings gifts and mail to Advance Company, 261; at Island Camp, 293; finds spyglass, 295; sees Chimney Rock, 316; at Sacred Prayer Camp, 333
Rockwood, Albert P.: is captain of Camp of Israel company, 56; at Garden Grove, 74; supervises trading, 116; is captain in Advance Company, 256; at Sacred Prayer Camp, 333
Rocky Mountain prophesy, 14
Rogers, Aurelia Spencer, 48
Rogers, Noah, 89

Rogerson, Josiah, 345
Rolling Prairie Camp, 67–68
Ross Settlement, 43
Round Barn, Allerton, Iowa, 70
Round Lake, Iowa, 162
Roundtop, 323
Roundy, Shadrach, 74, 151, 260, 333
Route from Liverpool to the Great Salt Lake City Valley, 17
Rowley handcart company, George, 203, 337
Rushville, Iowa, 151–52
Russell, Lillian, 10
Russell, Majors, and Waddell Freighting Company, 241, 242, 289, 295
Ruthton, Nebraska, 310

S

Sabbath Camp, Nebraska, 259–61
Sabbath worship, 253
Sacred places, xi
Sacred Prayer Camp, 332–33
Saline Ford, Nebraska, 240
Salt Creek, Nebraska, 240
Sand Hill Bluff Camp, 310
Sand Hills Camp, Nebraska, 306; Historic Area Ruts, 304–6
Sarpy, Peter: trading post of, 115–16, 121, 146–48; ferry of, 148; trades with Indians, 264
Sarpy County Historical museum, 232
Savage, Levi Jr., 109, 150, 339, 340
Scholte, Hendrick Pieter, Home, 20–21
Schuyler, Nebraska, 262, 287
Scott, Charles, 314
Scott, Hiram, 328
Scotts Bluff, 204, 315; National Monument, 327–29; Camp, 329–30; and Oregon Trail Museum, 329
Scottsbluff, Nebraska, 323–27
Scovil, Lucius, 30n, 42
Secrist, Jacob Foutz, 288, 288n
Sedan, Iowa, 54
Selma, Iowa, 45
Sergeant Bluff, Iowa, 162
Sessions, Patty: records Winter Exodus, 28n; on Sugar Creek camp, 35; healing of horse of, 47; assists in birth of Stewart baby, 63; records move to Rolling Prairie Camp, 68; on move to Pleasant Pt., 69; assist birth of Louisa Stout, 70; on Garden Grove, 75; on Spring Exodus catching Camp of Israel, 81; on White Breast Creek and Long Creek camps, 82; keeps part of granite rock, 85; on Platte water camping, 97; on Small Creek Prairie Camp, 99; on the Nodaway River and Circled Wagons Camp, 101; on Pleasant Prairie Camp, 104; assists birth of Silas James, 111
SevenMile Creek, 104; Camp, 83
Seymour, Iowa, 58–61, 63
Sharpsville, Iowa, 151
Shaw, Samuel A., 237
Shelby County, Iowa, 160–61; Historical Settlement, Harlan, 160
Shell Creek Camp, Nebraska, 261
Shelton, Nebraska, 279–81
Shenandoah, 153
Sherwood, Lafayette, 95
Shoal Creek Camp, 56
Shumway, Charles, 28, 333
Shurtliff, Luman, 32, 76
Sidney, Iowa, 152
Sidney, Nebraska, 309
Signal Butte, 312
Siler, Andrew, 340
Silver Creek: Camp, 112–13; Grove, 152; handcart camp, 181
Simon, George, 150
Sioux City Stake, 11
Sioux Indians: raid village and mission, 245, burn Ft. Ponca, 247; and the Plum Creek Massacre, 293; and the Grattan

Massacre, 299–300; hunting grounds of, 304; Lakota, and Harney Massacre, 315; at Courthouse Rock Camp, 318–19
Sisketuk, Chief, 264
Six-Mile Grove, Iowa, 159
Skunk Creek, 298
Sleight, Thomas, 266
Small Creek Camp, Nebraska, 271
Small Creek Prairie Camp, Iowa, 99–100
Smith, Asahel and Elizabeth, 46
Smith, Augusta Bowen, 103
Smith, George A., 80, 253, 270, 332, 333; company, 80, 82
Smith, George Albert, 90
Smith, Isabella, 103
Smith, Jedediah, 200
Smith, John: as president of Zarahemla Stake, 15; records Winter Exodus, 28n; is captain of Camp of Israel company, 56; at Garden Grove, 74; camps at Nodaway River, 103; on Pioneer Grand Encampment, 136; is confirmed as Church Patriarch, 140; blesses Thomas Kane, 230; leads Scandinavian Saints west, 235
Smith, John Lyman, 103
Smith, Joseph, Jr.: heals many in Nauvoo and Montrose, 13–14; gives Rocky Mountain prophecy from Montrose, 14; meets with Iowa Indian chiefs, 16–17; attends church meeting in Augusta, 22; visits Burlington, 23; sends James Emmett Expedition west, 165
Smith, Joseph III, 11, 78–79
Smith, Mary Fielding, 25
Smith, W. Wallace, 79
Smith, William, 42
Smith, William (brother of Joseph Smith), 164
Smoot, Abraham O., 15, 30n, 39
Snake Alley, Burlington, Iowa, 23
Snow, Eliza R.: in Winter Exodus group, 24; records Winter Exodus, 28n; on births at Sugar Creek, 37; on second Sugar Creek camp, 38; writes "The Camp of Israel," 38–39; drinks from Des Moines River, 42; on Chariton River Camp, 55; on Hickory Grove Camp, 59; on Locust Creek Camp No. 3, 63–64; on move to Rolling Prairie Camp, 68; on move to Pleasant Pt., 69; on prairie fires and Pleasant Grove Camp, 71–72; on Mt. Pisgah, 88; on Indian village, 107; on Traders Pt. Settlement, 144
Snow, Erastus: travels to Ft. Ponca, 247; on Wood River, 277; chastisement of, 295; on Sioux at Courthouse Rock Camp, 318; on music and dancing in camp, 329–30; on Sacred Prayer Camp, 332–33
Snow, James C., company, 325
Snow, Leonora, 89
Snow, Lorenzo, 85, 88, 89; family, 35
Soap Creek Camp, 92
Sod homes, 203
Soldier Creek, Iowa, 162
Sorensen, Ann Marie, 280
South Amana, Iowa, 172–73
South Bentonsport, 43
Southern Route, 12
South Mormon Ferry, Plattsmouth, Nebraska, 233, 250
South Omaha Bridge, 143–44, 228–29
Southworth, Sarah, 284
Spaulding, Eliza, 316
Spencer, Catherine, 47–48
Spencer, Claudius V., company, 51
Spencer, Daniel, company: uses same route as 1846 company, 19; at Pleasant Pt., 70; at Garden Grove, 74; at West Nishnabotna

River, 113; at Mosquito Creek Camp, 115; in charge of handcart outfitting, 168; passes Willie and Martin handcart companies, 338
Spencer, Elizabeth, 50
Spencer, Orson, 47–48
Spencer, Samuel, Jr., 50
Spidle, John, 153
Sprague Encampment, 81
Spring Branch Presbyterian Church, Allerton, Iowa, 70
Spring Exodus (1846): through Iowa, 10, 91; uses Dragoon Trail from Keokuk, 18; uses ferry at Eddyville, 19–20; through Pella area, 20–21; description of, 25; recorded accounts of, 30n; uses Sugar Creek as staging area, 36; through Charleston, 39; through Farmington, 40–41; through Bonaparte, 42; catches up with Camp of Israel, 79–80
Spy Glass Camp, 293–94
Squirrel Cage Jail, Council Bluffs, 132
St. Joseph and Independence Road, Nebraska, 241, 285
St. Joseph, Missouri, 200, 210, 235
St. Mary/St. Joseph Catholic Mission, Council Bluffs, 128
Staines, William, 246
Standing Bear, Chief, 197, 248–49
Stansbury, Howard, 311
State Capitol Building, Des Moines, Iowa, 178
State Highway 2, near Fort Madison, 21
State Historical Society Building, Des Moines, 178
State Line House, Farmington, Iowa, 41
Steamboat Gothic architecture, 45
Steamboat Rock, 323
Steamboats, importance of, 199, 239
Stegner, Wallace, 10
Stevens, Elisha, 200
Stewart, Maria Judd, 63
Stewart, Rufus Putman, 63
Stewart, Rufus Putman Jr., 63
Stewart, Sister, 313, 341, 344
Stoddard handcart company, Oscar O., 203, 337
Stout, Hosea: in Winter Exodus group, 24; records Winter Exodus, 28n; on crossing the Mississippi and Sugar Creek encampment, 34–35; on Bonaparte and crossing Des Moines River, 42; on Richardson's Pt. Camp, 50; remembers Old Mormon Trail, 53; on Chariton River Camp, 55; on leaving Missouri, 59; on Locust Creek campsites, 61; on winds at Garden Grove, 74; illness afflicts family of, 77; on recruitment of Mormon Battalion, 87, 120; on Indians at Nodaway River, 102; on death of son, 103; company, 106–7; on Parley P. Pratt swimming Indian Creek, 107; on Thomas Kane, 138; visits Wicks sawmill, 150
Stout, Hyrum, 77
Stout, Louisa (daughter of Hosea and Louisa), 70
Stout, Louisa Taylor, 70
Stout, William Hosea, 103
Strang, James J., 178
Stringtown, Iowa, 19, 50–51
Stringtown Stagecoach House, 51
Study, Leonard C., 154
Stuhr Musuem, Grand Island, Nebraska, 274–76
Sugar Creek Camp No. 1: location of, 15, 34; Camp of Israel assembles at, 24, 35–36; Spring Exodus camps at, 36; babies born at, 37, 107
Sugar Creek Camp No. 2, 38–39
Summer Quarters, Nebraska, 223–24

Sunshine riverboat, 218
Sutherland, Nebraska, 306

T

Tanner, Brother, 63
Tanner, James M., 49
Tanner, Sidney, 49
Tanner, Thomas, 260
Taylor, Allen, 32
Taylor, John: family, 13; is a president of Camp of Israel companies, 56; moves company to Locust Creek Camp No. 2, 63; company, 136; advises handcart companies, 168; returns from mission to England, 253; brings sextants, etc, from England, 255; leads big company of pioneers (1847), 257
Taylor County, 154–55
Teepee. *See* Chimney Rock, Nebraska
Telegraph lines, transcontinental, 228, 236
Tennessee Hollow, Iowa, 158
Terrace Bluffs Camp, Nebraska, 323
Territory of Nebraska, 196
Tharp Cemetery, 66–67
Thayer, Iowa, 83
Thomas, Samuel, 77
Thomas family, 76
Thompson, Daniel, company, 235
Thompson family, 76
Thurman, Iowa, 149, 154
Traders Pt., Iowa, 115–16, 144, 146–48, 162
Trader's Pt.-Bellevue Ferry, 250
"Tragedy of Winter Quarters," 216
Transcontinental railroad: ends wagon train travel to Utah, 219, 349–50; start of, in Omaha, 225; follows Overland Trail, 335; construction of, 347–49
Treynor, Iowa, 112–13
Triangle Park, Keokuk, Iowa, 17
Tripp, Bartlett, 280
Tripp, Enoch and Roxanna, 22
Troy, Iowa, 50
Tulip Festival, Pella, Iowa, 21
Turkey Creek, Iowa, 180
Twelve-Mile Grove, Iowa, 159–60
Twelve-Mile Prairie Camp, 97
Two-Mile Creek, Iowa, 96
Tyler, Daniel, 28n, 120

U

Underground Railroad, 45, 110
Union Hotel site, Council Bluffs, 129
Union Pacific Railroad, 132, 134; Museum, Council Bluffs, 132; headquarters of, in Omaha, 225; workers protected at Ft. Kearny, 286; through North Platte, 302; builds westward, 347
Unionville, Iowa, 19, 92
University of Iowa, 166–67; Mormon Handcart Park and Nature Preserve, 167
University of Nebraska: Lincoln, 243; Omaha, 225
Upper California Crossing, 309
Upper Ferry, Iowa, 155–56, 209–10
Utah Expedition, 286, 315, 322
Utah War: Nebraska City's connection to, 242–43; Genoa, Nebraska's connection to, 265–66; Ft. Kearny's connection to, 286; Ash Hollow's connection to, 314; stops migration, 336

V

Valier family, 76
Valley of David, 49
Van Buren, Abigail, 10
Van Buren County Courthouse, Keosauqua, Iowa, 44
Van Buren family, 76
Vance, Dazzy, 98
Verity, George M., Riverboat Museum, Keokuk, 17
Vermeer Windmill, Pella, Iowa, 21
Vermillion, Camp, 55, 161, 166
Vernon, 43

Veterans Memorial Bridge, near Council Bluffs, 143
Von Seggen Farm House, Farmington, Iowa, 41

W

Wabash Trace, 135
Wagon trains, 201–202
Walker, Henry, 269
Walker, John B., company, 283–84
Walker, Mary Lois, 287
Wallace, Henry A., 98
Walling, Warren, 264, 266
Walnut Creek, 110
Walsh, Stephen, 288n
Walters, Archer, 170, 181
Walton, Harry, 76
War of the Mormon Cow, 299
Warner family, 108
Warnock homestead, Farmington, Iowa, 41
Warp's Pioneer Village, Harold, Minden, Nebraska, 281
Waterloo, Nebraska, 252
Watts, Stan, 127
Waukee, Iowa, 178
Wayne, John, 10
Webb, Chauncey, 168, 342
Weber, Jacob, 211
Weber Mill, Winter Quarters, 210
Welcome Centers, 10
Weldon, Iowa, 80
Welling, Job Jr., 175
Welsh, Mary or Nancy, 288n
Welsh Tabernacle site, near Council Bluffs, 143
West Branch, Iowa, 163
Western Engineer, 222
Western Skies Scenic Byway, 159
Western Trails Scenic and Historic Byway, 309
Western Weekly Bugle, Council Bluffs, 129
West Fork Nishnabotna (Silver Creek) Camp, 112–13
West Grove, Iowa, 53
Wheelock, Cyrus, company, 19, 20
Whipple, Edson, 308
Whitaker, George, 39–40
White Breast Creek Camp, 82
White Catfish Camp, 115
White Tail Creek, Nebraska, 308
Whiting family, 152
Whitman, Marcus, 316
Whitman, Narcissa, 316
Whitney, Helen Mar Kimball: records Winter Exodus, 28n; on Sugar Creek camp, 36; on second Sugar Creek camp, 38; on men working through Iowa, 42; on rattlesnakes at Rolling Prairie Camp, 68
Whitney, Horace K.: records Winter Exodus, 28n; crosses frozen Mississippi, 29; in Stringtown, 50–51; on Hickory Grove Camp, 58; on Pleasant Pt., 70; on Pleasant Grove Camp, 72; on Pottawattamie Indians, 101, 106; on seeing Missouri River, 115; supervises trading, 116; on Missouri Camp, 116; on Thomas L. Kane, 122; on ferry over the Missouri, 144; on Elkhorn River, 253
Whitney, Newel K., 24, 49
Wicks, S. E., 144, 149–50
Wicks family, 108
Wight, Lyman, 15, 21, 160, 248
William Fordney House, Burlington, Iowa, 23
William Jennings Byran House, 243–44
Williams, Andy, 10
Williams, Helen Roberta, 234
Williams County School, Allerton, Iowa, 70
Willie, James G., 176–77
Willie handcart company, James G.: in Indiantown, 109; in Council Bluffs, 150; uses Upper Ferry, 156–57; problems of, 171–72, 336; in Des Moines, 177–78; through Adel, 179; through

Anita, 180; travels south side of Platte River, 202–3, 337, 342; Ahmanson as captain in, 227; lose cattle at Buffalo Creek, 292, 339, 341–42; crosses the Platte, 305; at Ash Hollow, 313, 343; statistics on, 338; are outfitted in Florence, Nebraska, 339; trail followed by, 340–43
Willow Bridge Camp, 81
Willow Island Camp, 295
Wilson, Lewis D., 74
Wilson, Meredith, 10
Wilson, Mrs., 272
Wilson family, 76
Winchester, Iowa, 19
Windlass Hill, Nebraska, 310–11
Winter Exodus: through Iowa, 5–6, 10; as first exodus, 23–25; recorded accounts of, 28n
Winter Quarters, Nebraska: as headquarters of Saints' winter encampment, 198, 208, outfits Mormon wagon trains, 199; Mill, 210–11; location and organization of, 212–15; Temple, 216
Winter-Rand House, Burlington, Iowa, 23
Winters, Augusta, 327
Winters, Hyrum, 323
Winters, Oscar, 64n
Winters, Rebecca Burdick, 323–27
Winterset, Iowa, 19, 90
Wiota, Iowa, 180
Wiscotta, Iowa, 179
Wood, Grant, 10, 46, 150
Woodard, Brother, 109
Woodbine, Iowa, 159
Wood River Center, Nebraska, 217, 279–81
Wood River Crossing, Nebraska, 277
Woodruff, Wilford: family, 13, 25, 39; visits Smoots in Ambrosia, 15; records Spring Exodus, 30n; on going through Farmington, 40–41; in Bloomfield, 51; at Mt. Pisgah, 86; on prairie, 96; company, 136, 214; speaks to Saints on Redemption Hill, 138; on mustering of Mormon Battalion, 139; in 1847 Advance Company, 253; on Liberty Pole Camp, 255; on Platte River near Sabbath Camp, 260; receives gift from Thomas Kane, 261; at Fish Camp, 262; on Loup Sabbath Camp, 270; at Ft. Kearny (1850), 284; on staying on north side of Platte, 291; on buffalo, 296; on making soap, 297; on Brady Island Camp, 297; on North Platte Camp, 304; at Ancient Bluffs Ruins, 317, 318; on creating a new road for those to follow, 329; on fishing and misbehavior in camp, 330–32; at Sacred Prayer Camp, 332
Woods, James W., 22
Woolley, Edwin D., 30n
Woolsey, Thomas, 270
"Word and Will of the Lord, The," 212, 247
Wounded Knee Massacre, 300
Wright, Jonathan C., 80
Wyoming, Nebraska: as Mormon wagon train outfitting camp, 199, 219, 233–36; Telescope, 234; important sites of, 236–39; Levee, 239

Y

Yellowstone Expedition, 222
Young, Brigham: leads Camp of Israel, 5–6, 24–25, 56; family, 13; is healed by Joseph Smith, 13; leaves Montrose for mission in 1839, 14; sets up Sugar Creek encampment, 15, 35–36; records Winter Exodus, 28n; on the crossing of the Mississippi, 29–30; moves camp to second Sugar Creek camp, 38; on leaving Missouri, 59; stays at

Locust Creek Camp, 67; at Peter's Bridge Camp, 80; at Willow Bridge Camp, 81; on granite rock near Mt. Pisgah, 85; establishes Mt. Pisgah, 86; recruits for Mormon Battalion, 87, 120, 138; seeks better road through Iowa, 91; leaves Mt. Pisgah, 96; meets with Indian chiefs, 100; reorganizes companies, 101; fishes Mosquito Creek, 115; moves camp from Missouri River, 116; is officially sustained as President of the Church, 126, 140; speaks to Saints on Redemption Hill, 138; hold council meeting near Middle Mormon Ferry landing, 145; blesses Battalion leaders, 145; requisitions work from Wicks sawmill, 149–50; requests permission to travel through Iowa, 166; orders green wood for handcarts, 168–69; home of, in Winter Quarters, 211–12; receives revelation in Winter Quarters, 212; orders building of ferryboat, 229; sends out Miller advance party, 245; in 1847 Advance Company, 253; wife of, in Advance Company, 256; leads 1848 company of pioneers, 257; dedicates Advance Company, 257–58; organizes Advance Company into military order, 260; Express and Carry Company, 264; at Loup Sabbath Camp, 270; at Ft. Kearny Camp, 282–83; on wasting of meat, 290, 308; loses spyglass, 294, 295; requests mechanized odometer, 298; at North Bluff Fork, 304; at Ancient Bluffs Ruins, 318; at Chimney Rock Camp, 320; democracy within company of, 330; reacts strongly to misbehavior in camp, 330–32; at Sacred Prayer Camp, 332–34

Young, Brigham, company: moves to Rolling Prairie Camp, 67–68; at Long Creek Camp, 82; travels to Mt. Pisgah, 84–85; at Twelve-Mile Camp, 97; at Pleasant Valley Camp, 104; at West Nishnabotna River, 113; travels north side of Platte River, 201, 202; location of, in Winter Quarters, 214; at Liberty Pole Camp, 254–55

Young, Brigham, Jr., 302

Young, Clara Decker, 256

Young, Harriet Decker, 256, 320

Young, Joseph W., 235, 239, 287, 342; company, 19, 20, 90, 317

Young, Lorenzo Dow, 53, 256, 320

Young, Lorenzo Sobriski, 256

Young, Phineas, 53n, 333

Young, William G., 172

YX Company, delivers mail, 264

Z

Zahn, Paula, 197

Zanuck, Darryl, 197

Zarahemla, Iowa, 14–15; Stake, 10, 14–15

Zig–Zag, Nebraska, 267

Zimmerman family, 76